First World War
and Army of Occupation
War Diary
France, Belgium and Germany

9 DIVISION
South African Brigade
3 South African Infantry Regiment
1 October 1916 - 31 March 1917

WO95/1783

The Naval & Military Press Ltd
www.nmarchive.com
Published in association with The National Archives

Published by

The Naval & Military Press Ltd

Unit 10 Ridgewood Industrial Park,

Uckfield, East Sussex,

TN22 5QE England

Tel: +44 (0) 1825 749494

www.naval-military-press.com

www.nmarchive.com

This diary has been reprinted in facsimile from the original. Any imperfections are inevitably reproduced and the quality may fall short of modern type and cartographic standards.

Contents

Document type	Place/Title	Date From	Date To
Heading	B E F 9 Div S A Bde 3 S A Infantry Oct 1916		
Operation(al) Order(s)	Ist South African Infantry Brigade. Addendum No. I To Operation Order No. 74	28/10/1916	28/10/1916
Miscellaneous		23/10/1916	23/10/1916
Miscellaneous	1st South African Infantry Brigade.	24/10/1916	24/10/1916
Operation(al) Order(s)	1st S.A. Infantry Brigade. 24th October 1916. Operation Order 74	24/10/1916	24/10/1916
Miscellaneous	1st South African Infantry Brigade. Schedule To Operation Order 71	24/10/1916	24/10/1916
Miscellaneous	1st. S.A. Infantry Brigade. 24th October 1916	24/10/1916	24/10/1916
Miscellaneous	2nd S. African Regt. App 234	26/10/1916	26/10/1916
Miscellaneous	March Table.		
Operation(al) Order(s)	1st S.A. Infantry Brigade H.Q. 27th October 1916. Operation Order No. 73. App 236	27/10/1916	27/10/1916
Operation(al) Order(s)	1st South African Infantry Brigade. Addendum to Operation Order No. 73	27/10/1916	27/10/1916
Miscellaneous	1st South African Infantry Brigade Operation Order No. 73	27/10/1916	27/10/1916
Operation(al) Order(s)	1st South African Infantry Brigade. H.Q. 28th October 1916. Addendum No. 2. to Operation Order 74	28/10/1916	28/10/1916
Operation(al) Order(s)	Move Orders Order No. By Lieut. Col. E.F. Thackeray. C.M.G. Commanding 3rd, S.A.I. (Transvaal Regiment) in the Field 27/10/16 App 237	27/10/1916	27/10/1916
Miscellaneous	A Form. Messages And Signals.		
Miscellaneous	C Form (Duplicate). Messages And Signals.		
Miscellaneous	A Form Messages And Signals.		
Miscellaneous			
Operation(al) Order(s)	H.Q. 1st S.A.I. Brigade. 18th October 1916. Operation Order No. 69. App 226	18/10/1916	18/10/1916
Miscellaneous	Articles to be Carried by the Rear (Carrying) Platoons.		
Miscellaneous	Schedule Accompanying Operation Order No. 69		
Miscellaneous	Move Order, App 227		
Miscellaneous	O.C.D. Coy. App 229	22/10/1916	22/10/1916
Miscellaneous	In the Field App 228	22/10/1916	22/10/1916
Miscellaneous	3rd Regt., App 130	21/10/1916	21/10/1916
Operation(al) Order(s)	1st South African Infantry Brigade H.Q. 23rd October 1916 Operation Order No. 70 App 231	23/10/1916	23/10/1916
Miscellaneous	App 232	23/10/1916	23/10/1916
Miscellaneous	E.T.C. App 216	15/10/1916	15/10/1916
Miscellaneous	C Form (Original). Messages And Signals.		
Miscellaneous	A Form. Messages And Signals App 217		
Miscellaneous	App 218		
Miscellaneous	C Form (Original). Messages And Signals.		
Miscellaneous	C Form Messages And Signals.		
Miscellaneous	App 223	16/10/1916	16/10/1916
Operation(al) Order(s)	1st S.A. Infantry Brigade 15th October 1916 Operation Order 67. App 45	15/10/1916	15/10/1916
Miscellaneous	A Form. Messages And Signals. App 221		
Miscellaneous	App 222		
Miscellaneous			

Map	E. F. Thackeray		
Miscellaneous	O.C. App 224		
Operation(al) Order(s)	H.Q. 1st South African Infantry Brigade 17th October. 1916 Operation Order No. 68 App 225	17/10/1916	17/10/1916
Miscellaneous	C Form (Duplicate). Messages And Signals. App 215 B		
Miscellaneous	App 215 A	14/10/1916	14/10/1916
Miscellaneous			
Miscellaneous	Staff Captain Brigade	02/12/1916	02/12/1916
Miscellaneous	Copy of Priority Telegram to 3rd 3. A. Infantry From S.A. Brigade.	14/10/1916	14/10/1916
Operation(al) Order(s)	Operation Order By Lt. Colonel B.F. Thackeray. C.M.G. Commanding 3rd S.A. Infantry. In the Field 14/10/16	14/10/1916	14/10/1916
Miscellaneous	E.T. 6. Octr. 15.1916	15/10/1916	15/10/1916
Miscellaneous	S.A. Bde. Confidential.		
Miscellaneous	9th Division Confidential.	15/10/1916	15/10/1916
Miscellaneous	1st S.A. African Brigade. No. X. 5/1893 17th October, 1916	17/10/1916	17/10/1916
Miscellaneous	Move Order. By Lieut. Col. E.F. Thackeray. C.M.G. Commanding 3rd S.A. Infantry (Transvaal Regiment) Order No. 17 In The Field 22/10/1916 App 239	22/10/1916	22/10/1916
Miscellaneous	9th Seaforths (Pioneers). 107th Coy. ASC. 1st S.A. Infantry. 2nd S.A. Infantry. 3rd S.A. Infantry. 4th S.A. Infantry. Brigade Headquarters. 28th Machine Gun Coy. (with T/Mortar Hand-carts) 64th Field Coy. R.E. S.A. Field Ambulance.		
Operation(al) Order(s)	1st South African Infantry Brigade. Operation Order No. 74 App 238	28/10/1916	28/10/1916
War Diary	Grand Rullecourt	01/10/1916	04/10/1916
War Diary	Bonnieres	05/10/1916	07/10/1916
War Diary	La Haussoye	08/10/1916	09/10/1916
War Diary	High Wood	10/10/1916	12/10/1916
War Diary	Starfish Line	12/10/1916	13/10/1916
War Diary	Acid Drop	13/10/1916	16/10/1916
War Diary	Starfish Trench	17/10/1916	19/10/1916
War Diary	Bazantin & Grand	20/10/1916	20/10/1916
War Diary	High Wood	21/10/1916	23/10/1916
War Diary	Bazantin & Grand	24/10/1916	24/10/1916
War Diary	Mametz Wood	25/10/1916	26/10/1916
War Diary	Millencourt	27/10/1916	27/10/1916
War Diary	Herrissart	28/10/1916	28/10/1916
War Diary	Wanquetin	29/10/1916	31/10/1916
Operation(al) Order(s)	Move Order Order No. C 8 By Lieut. Col. E.F. Thackeray. C.M.G. Commanding 3rd. South African Infantry. (Transvaal Regiment) In The Field. 4/10/16	04/10/1916	04/10/1916
Operation(al) Order(s)	9th Division Operation Order No. 80	05/10/1916	05/10/1916
Miscellaneous			
Operation(al) Order(s)	1st South African Infantry Brigade. 4th October 1916 Operation Order 61 App 187	04/10/1916	04/10/1916
Miscellaneous			
Operation(al) Order(s)	March Table Operation Order 61		
Operation(al) Order(s)	Move Order By Lieut. Col. E.F. Thackeray C.M.G. Commanding 3rd. South African Infantry. In The Field 4/10/16 App 188	04/10/1916	04/10/1916

Operation(al) Order(s)	Move Order. By Lieut. Colonel E.F. Thackeray. C.M.G. Commanding 3rd. Regiment S.A. Inf. (Transvaal Regiment) Order No. 98 In The Field 26/10/1916	26/10/1916	26/10/1916
Miscellaneous	Priority (Pa O/C By Field RE)	13/10/1916	13/10/1916
Miscellaneous	O/C C Coy.	12/10/1916	12/10/1916
Miscellaneous	A Form. Messages And Signals.	13/10/1916	13/10/1916
Miscellaneous		13/10/1916	13/10/1916
Miscellaneous	C. Coy The Adjutant E M App 202	13/10/1916	13/10/1916
Miscellaneous	Batt SAI, App 201	13/10/1916	13/10/1916
Miscellaneous	OC. C Co App 202	13/10/1916	13/10/1916
Miscellaneous	C Form (Duplicate). Messages And Signals.		
Miscellaneous	C Form (Original). Messages And Signals.		
Miscellaneous			
Operation(al) Order(s)	Operation Order No C 11. App 207	13/10/1916	13/10/1916
Miscellaneous	C Form (Duplicate). Messages And Signals.		
Miscellaneous	Brigade Major App 208	13/10/1916	13/10/1916
Miscellaneous	C Form (Duplicate). Messages And Signals.	13/10/1916	13/10/1916
Miscellaneous	App 210	14/10/1916	14/10/1916
Miscellaneous	The O.C. 3rd S. African Inf. App 211	14/10/1916	14/10/1916
Miscellaneous	C Form (Duplicate). Messages And Signals. App 213	14/10/1916	14/10/1916
Miscellaneous	C Form (Duplicate). Messages And Signals.		
Miscellaneous	Messages And Signals. App 212		
Operation(al) Order(s)	Operation Order. App 214	10/10/1916	10/10/1916
Miscellaneous	C Form (Original). Messages And Signals. App 215		
Miscellaneous	Message And Signals.	12/10/1916	12/10/1916
Miscellaneous	A Form. Messages And Signals.	13/10/1916	13/10/1916
Miscellaneous	Rearguard		
Miscellaneous			
Operation(al) Order(s)	1st South African Infantry Brigade. 5th October 1916 Operation Order No. 62 App 189	05/10/1916	05/10/1916
Miscellaneous	1st S.A.I. Brigade. 9th October 1916	09/10/1916	09/10/1916
Miscellaneous	1st South African Infantry Brigade 6th October 1916	06/10/1916	06/10/1916
Miscellaneous	1st South African Infantry Bde 7th October 1916	07/10/1916	07/10/1916
Operation(al) Order(s)	1st South African Infantry Brigade. 6th October 1916 Operation Order No. 63 App 189	06/10/1916	06/10/1916
Miscellaneous	1st S.A.I. Brigade And Attached Units March Table-Operation Order 63 7th Oct 1916	07/10/1916	07/10/1916
Miscellaneous	Move Order. By Lieut. Col. E.F. Thackeray, C.M.G., Commanding 3rd South African Infantry. In The Field 6/10/16	06/10/1916	06/10/1916
Operation(al) Order(s)	1st S.A. Infantry Brigade 8th October 1916 Operation Order 64 App 193	08/10/1916	08/10/1916
Miscellaneous	1st S.A.I. Brigade. 7th October 1916. Warning Order. App 192	07/10/1916	07/10/1916
Miscellaneous	1st S.A.I. Brigade March Table To Operation Order 64		
Operation(al) Order(s)	1st South African Infantry Brigade H.Qrs. 9th October 1916 Operation Order 65 App 195	09/10/1916	09/10/1916
Miscellaneous	1st S.A. Brigade Table Accompanying Operation Order 65		
Operation(al) Order(s)	1st South African Infantry Brigade 11th October 1916 Operation Order No. 66	11/10/1916	11/10/1916
Map	SAI Bde Accompanying O.O. No		
Miscellaneous	Messages And Signals.		
Miscellaneous	A Form. Messages And Signals.	12/10/1916	12/10/1916
Diagram etc	Sketch Map Accompanying 00 66		

Miscellaneous		12/10/1916	12/10/1916
Miscellaneous	Trench Mortars.		
Miscellaneous	Strong Points And Consolidation.		
Map	Sketch Map SAI Bde Accompanying		
Heading	Folio 155 is An Negative and Has Been Returned to Modern Record Department for Listing		
Miscellaneous	155		
War Diary	Wanguetin	01/11/1916	30/11/1916
Miscellaneous	S.A Infantry Training Programme W/Ending November 18th 1916	18/11/1916	18/11/1916
Miscellaneous			
Miscellaneous	Programme of Training (Sports)		
Heading	3 SA Infy Bn Vol 9 Dec 1916		
War Diary	Wanquetin	01/12/1916	03/12/1916
War Diary	Arras	03/12/1916	03/12/1916
War Diary	Sub Section J III	04/12/1916	14/12/1916
War Diary	Arras	15/12/1916	27/12/1916
War Diary	Sub Section J III	23/12/1916	31/12/1916
Miscellaneous	General Continued		
Miscellaneous			
Operation(al) Order(s)	Order No. 3/122 By 3rd S.A. Infantry.		
Miscellaneous	3rd South African Infantry Warning Order.	21/01/1916	21/01/1916
Miscellaneous	Battalion Headquarters	23/01/1916	23/01/1916
Miscellaneous	3rd South African Infantry Warning Order.	17/01/1916	17/01/1916
Operation(al) Order(s)	Order No. 3. R/124 By 3rd South African Infantry.		
Miscellaneous	Working Party.		
Miscellaneous	Patrol Report O.C. "W" Coy App 257		
Operation(al) Order(s)	Operation Order Coy Bank.	12/12/1916	12/12/1916
Operation(al) Order(s)	Operation Order No 3R/5 App 256	06/12/1916	06/12/1916
Miscellaneous	Patrolling.	05/12/1916	05/12/1916
Miscellaneous	C.C. W. Coy. Bank Patrols.	12/12/1916	12/12/1916
Miscellaneous	C Form (Original). Messages And Signals. App 253		
Miscellaneous	C Form (Original) Messages And Signals. App 254		
Miscellaneous	C Form (Original). Messages And Signals. App 252		
Miscellaneous			
Miscellaneous	O.C. W. Coy Z Coy Bank, Patrols.	13/12/1916	13/12/1916
Miscellaneous	To O.C., W. Coy X Coy Y Coy Z Coy App. 258	12/12/1916	12/12/1916
Miscellaneous	O.C. "B" Coy "C" Coy. Bank, Patrolling. App 255		
Operation(al) Order(s)	June 2/30 BM Operation Order By Bank.	09/12/1916	09/12/1916
Miscellaneous	1st South African Infantry Brigade Operation Order 77. App 256		
Operation(al) Order(s)	Operation Order No. 676 B Lieut-Colonel E.F. Thackeray. C.M.G., D.S.O. Commanding 3rd S.A. Infantry (Transvaal Regiment) App 251	03/12/1916	03/12/1916
Operation(al) Order(s)	1st South African Infantry Brigade 2nd December 1916 Operation Order 76 App 248	02/12/1916	02/12/1916
Operation(al) Order(s)	Operation Order By O.C. Bank App 267	26/12/1916	26/12/1916
Miscellaneous	Head Quarters 1st S.A.I. Brigade. December 1st 1916 App. 24	01/12/1916	01/12/1916
Operation(al) Order(s)	Operation Order. To O.C. "A" Coy. H.Q. Coy. "B" Coy M.O. "C" Coy. Q.M. "D" Coy. T.O. and B. Officer App 263	22/12/1916	22/12/1916
Miscellaneous	Brigade Major South African Brigade. App 264	23/12/1916	23/12/1916
Miscellaneous	C Form (Duplicate). Messages And Signals.		
Miscellaneous	O/C A Coy D Coy B Coy App 266	26/12/1916	26/12/1916
Operation(al) Order(s)	Operation Order. Patrols.	24/12/1919	24/12/1919

Operation(al) Order(s)	Operation Order. Patrol.	23/12/1916	23/12/1916
Miscellaneous	Operation Order To Officer Commanding Company Bank Move App 261	18/12/1916	18/12/1916
Miscellaneous	Brigade Major S.A. Brigade. Prince.	23/12/1916	23/12/1916
Operation(al) Order(s)	Operation Order By Bank	25/12/1916	25/12/1916
Miscellaneous	O/C D Coy		
Miscellaneous	C A Coy D Coy B Coy, Wiring.	27/12/1916	27/12/1916
Miscellaneous	C Form (Duplicate). Messages And Signals. App 247		
Miscellaneous	A Form Messages And Signals App. 250	02/12/1916	02/12/1916
Miscellaneous	C Form (Duplicate). Messages And Signals. App 249	02/12/1916	02/12/1916
Miscellaneous	C Form (Duplicate). Messages And Signals. App 245		
Miscellaneous	C Form (Original). Messages And Signals. App 246	01/12/1916	01/12/1916
Operation(al) Order(s)	Order No. 3R/119 By Lt. Col. E.F. Thackeray C	18/01/1918	18/01/1918
Operation(al) Order(s)	Operation Order O/C C Coy Bank B Coy Bank		
Operation(al) Order(s)	Operation Order.1. App 270	29/12/1916	29/12/1916
Operation(al) Order(s)	Operation Order Patrols App 270	29/12/1916	29/12/1916
Miscellaneous			
Operation(al) Order(s)	Operation Order. Patrols. App 269		
Operation(al) Order(s)	Operation Order By O.C. Bank O.C. A Coy. D Coy. B Coy. Patrols. App 267	26/12/1916	26/12/1916
Operation(al) Order(s)	Operation Order O/C C Coy Bank B Coy	31/12/1916	31/12/1916
Miscellaneous	Operation Order. O.C. A Coy D Coy. B Coy. Patrols. App 268	27/12/1916	27/12/1916
Operation(al) Order(s)	Operation Order O/C "B" Coy "B" Coy Patrols App 270	29/12/1916	29/12/1916
Miscellaneous	C Form (Original). Messages And Signals. App 243		
Miscellaneous	O.C. A Coy D Coy Bank. Patrols Wiring.	14/12/1916	14/12/1916
Miscellaneous		14/12/1916	14/12/1916
Miscellaneous	Acquittance Roll (All Arms).		
Miscellaneous			
Miscellaneous	Acquittance Roll (All Arms)		
Operation(al) Order(s)	1st South African Infantry Brigade Operation Order No 79	21/12/1916	21/12/1916
Miscellaneous	Completion of Relief.	04/01/1918	04/01/1918
Miscellaneous	Completion of Relief.	13/01/1916	13/01/1916
Operation(al) Order(s)	Order No. 3 R/113 By Blush App 475		
Operation(al) Order(s)	Order No. 3 R/115 By Blush App 477		
Operation(al) Order(s)	Order No. 5/R. 117 By Blush	12/01/1918	12/01/1918
Miscellaneous	Sanitation.		
Miscellaneous	Headqrs.	31/01/1918	31/01/1918
Operation(al) Order(s)	Order No. 3 R/124 By Blush	29/01/1916	29/01/1916
Miscellaneous	Instruction No. 1 Reference Order No. 3 R/123 Issued this morning.	27/01/1918	27/01/1918
Operation(al) Order(s)	Order No. 3 R/123 by Blush Map Reference Gauche Wood 1/10,000 Sheet 37 C. 1/40,000		
War Diary	Arras J III Sub. Sec.	01/01/1917	09/01/1917
Miscellaneous	11		
War Diary	Arras J III Sub Section	10/01/1917	16/01/1917
War Diary	Arras	16/01/1917	24/01/1917
War Diary	J III Sub Sec.	24/01/1917	31/01/1917
Miscellaneous	Brigade Major 1st S.A.I. Bgdr	01/01/1917	01/01/1917
Operation(al) Order(s)	Operation Order To O/C A Coy Bank.	01/01/1917	01/01/1917
Operation(al) Order(s)	Third South African Infantry Operation Order No. 3 R/29	01/01/1917	01/01/1917
Operation(al) Order(s)	Operation Order		
Operation(al) Order(s)	Operation Order To O/C A. Coy.	04/01/1917	04/01/1917

Operation(al) Order(s)	Operation Order 3/R 36 Dated 23/1/1917	23/01/1917	23/01/1917
Operation(al) Order(s)	Operation Order by Bank.	03/01/1917	03/01/1917
Miscellaneous	Sheet II		
Miscellaneous	C Form Messages And Signals	04/01/1917	04/01/1917
Miscellaneous	Operation Order To O.C. A Coy.	07/01/1917	07/01/1917
Miscellaneous	Operation Order To A	10/01/1917	10/01/1917
Miscellaneous	Operation Order	13/01/1917	13/01/1917
Miscellaneous			
Miscellaneous	Operation Order By Captain H. Montgomery. Temporarily Commanding 3rd S.A. Infantry In The Field (Transvaal Regiment.) 15/1/17	15/01/1917	15/01/1917
Operation(al) Order(s)	1st South African Infantry Brigade Operation Order No. 8	14/01/1917	14/01/1917
Miscellaneous	Operation Order O C A Coy Bank A Coy Bank.	19/01/1917	19/01/1917
Miscellaneous	Operation Order By Bank.	23/01/1917	23/01/1917
Miscellaneous	War Diary Operation Order	27/01/1917	27/01/1917
Operation(al) Order(s)	1st South African Brigade. Operation Order No. 81	02/01/1917	02/01/1917
Miscellaneous	B Form Messages And Signals	24/01/1917	24/01/1917
Miscellaneous			
Operation(al) Order(s)	Operation Order No. 3 R 38	30/01/1917	30/01/1917
War Diary	J III Arras	01/02/1917	13/02/1917
War Diary	J III Batt Hqrs-(Reserves)	14/02/1917	17/02/1917
War Diary	No I Section Right Sector	18/02/1917	26/02/1917
War Diary	Arras J III	26/02/1917	28/02/1917
War Diary	Arras old J III Sub Section	28/02/1917	28/02/1917
Operation(al) Order(s)	Operation Order. 3 R/45	10/02/1917	10/02/1917
Operation(al) Order(s)	1st South African Infantry Brigade Order No. 86	07/02/1917	07/02/1917
Miscellaneous	Operation Order	08/02/1917	08/02/1917
Miscellaneous	Operation Order	02/02/1916	02/02/1916
Miscellaneous	Operation Order by Bank.	21/02/1917	21/02/1917
Miscellaneous	Operation Order by Bank.	17/02/1917	17/02/1917
Miscellaneous	Countersigns		
Operation(al) Order(s)	1st South African Infantry Brigade Order No. 86	16/02/1917	16/02/1917
Operation(al) Order(s)	1st South African Infantry Brigade Order No. 87	18/02/1917	18/02/1917
Miscellaneous	Operation Order.	10/02/1917	10/02/1917
Operation(al) Order(s)	1st South African Infantry Brigade Operation Order No. 84	22/02/1917	22/02/1917
Miscellaneous	Operation Order By Bank.	24/02/1917	24/02/1917
Miscellaneous	Operation Order By Bank.	17/02/1917	17/02/1917
Miscellaneous			
Miscellaneous	Operation Order by Bank.	26/02/1917	26/02/1917
Miscellaneous	Operation Order Reinforcing		
Miscellaneous	A Form Messages And Signals		
Miscellaneous	Operation Order	05/02/1917	05/02/1917
Miscellaneous			
Operation(al) Order(s)	1st South African Infantry Brigade Order No. 89	24/02/1917	24/02/1917
Miscellaneous	Confidential. 1st S.A.I.	16/02/1917	16/02/1917
Miscellaneous	A Form Messages And Signals.		
Miscellaneous	C Form Messages And Signals	29/03/1917	29/03/1917
War Diary	Reserves Old J III Hqrs Arras	01/03/1917	03/03/1917
War Diary	Etrun Y Huts Penin	04/03/1917	04/03/1917
War Diary	Penin	05/03/1917	12/03/1917
War Diary	Marquay	12/03/1917	21/03/1917
War Diary	Haute Avesnes	21/03/1917	24/03/1917
War Diary	Y Hutments Etrun	24/03/1917	28/03/1917
War Diary	Arras	28/03/1917	30/03/1917

War Diary	Arras Centre Battn	30/03/1917	30/03/1917
War Diary	In Trenches	31/03/1917	31/03/1917
War Diary	Arras Centre Battn	31/03/1917	31/03/1917
Operation(al) Order(s)	1st South African Infantry Brigade Order No. 91	02/03/1917	02/03/1917
Miscellaneous	12		
Miscellaneous	Operation Order By Bank.	02/03/1917	02/03/1917
Operation(al) Order(s)	March Table to accompany S. African Infantry Brigade Order 91 dated 3/3/17	03/03/1917	03/03/1917
Miscellaneous	3rd Regiment.	02/03/1917	02/03/1917
Miscellaneous	3rd Regiment	02/03/1917	02/03/1917
Miscellaneous	1st South African Infantry Brigade.	02/03/1917	02/03/1917
Miscellaneous	Operation Order By Bank.	02/03/1917	02/03/1917
Operation(al) Order(s)	Operation Order 3R/49 By Bank	02/03/1917	02/03/1917
Miscellaneous	Operation Order By Bank.	02/03/1917	02/03/1917
Miscellaneous	C Form. Messages And Signals.	10/03/1917	10/03/1917
Miscellaneous	1st South African Infantry Brigade.	03/03/1917	03/03/1917
Miscellaneous			
Miscellaneous	C Form Messages And Signals	20/03/1917	20/03/1917
Miscellaneous	Trench Operation Infy.	29/03/1917	29/03/1917
Operation(al) Order(s)	1st South African Infantry Brigade Order No. 92	09/03/1917	09/03/1917
Miscellaneous	To Accompany Brigade Order No. 98		
Miscellaneous	C Form Messages And Signals		
Miscellaneous	1st S.A.I. 2nd S.A.I. 3rd S.A.I. 4th S.A.I.	10/03/1917	10/03/1917
Miscellaneous	C Form Messages And Signals.		
Miscellaneous	C Form Messages And Signals		
Operation(al) Order(s)	Addendum No. 1 To Operation Order 92	10/03/1917	10/03/1917
Miscellaneous	Third South African Infantry	20/03/1917	20/03/1917
Miscellaneous	1st S.A. Brigade 3rd S.A. Infy.	10/03/1917	10/03/1917
Miscellaneous	C Form Messages And Signals		
Miscellaneous	1st S.A.I. 2nd S.A.I. 3rd S.A.I. 4th S.A.I. Saltm Battery.	11/03/1917	11/03/1917
Operation(al) Order(s)	3rd South African Infantry Order No. 3 R/50	10/03/1917	10/03/1917
Miscellaneous	1st South African Infantry Brigade.	16/03/1917	16/03/1917
Operation(al) Order(s)	1st South African Infantry Brigade Order No. 93	20/03/1917	20/03/1917
Miscellaneous	1st South African Infantry Brigade. March Table Issued With Brigade Order No. 93, 20/3/1917	20/03/1917	20/03/1917
Miscellaneous	1st South African Infantry Brigade Working Party Table.		
Miscellaneous	To O.C. A Coy. I.O.	11/03/1917	11/03/1917
Miscellaneous	3rd South African Infantry	23/03/1917	23/03/1917
Miscellaneous	O.C. A B C D	23/03/1917	23/03/1917
Operation(al) Order(s)	1st South African Infantry Brigade Order No. 94	22/03/1917	22/03/1917
Miscellaneous			
Miscellaneous	3rd Regiment S.A.I.	11/03/1917	11/03/1917
Operation(al) Order(s)	Order No 60	30/03/1917	30/03/1917
Operation(al) Order(s)	1st South African Infantry Brigade Order No. 97	29/03/1917	29/03/1917
Miscellaneous	Third South African Infantry.	20/03/1917	20/03/1917
Miscellaneous	Third South African Infantry.	28/03/1917	28/03/1917
Miscellaneous	O/C A B C D	27/03/1917	27/03/1917
Miscellaneous	3rd S.O. Infantry	26/03/1917	26/03/1917
Operation(al) Order(s)	1st South African Infantry Brigade Amendment To Brigade Order No. 96	27/03/1917	27/03/1917
Operation(al) Order(s)	1st South African Infantry Brigade Order No. 96	27/03/1917	27/03/1917
Miscellaneous	C Form. Messages And Signals.		

BEF

9 DIV

5 A Bde

3 S A INFANTRY

OCT 1916

11 pm

2

1st SOUTH AFRICAN INFANTRY BRIGADE.

ADDENDUM No.I.TO OPERATION ORDER No.74

The 9th Division have just advised that supplies will not be delivered tonight, but will be delivered at destinations tomorrow.

Blankets and cooking utensils will therefore be carried by Battalions in the Motor Lorries at their disposal.

The 64th Field Co.R.E., Machine Gun Company, Trench Mortar Battery and S. A. Field Ambulance will carry their blankets on the men . Arrangements will be made at WANQUETIN to take over the blanket of the 64th Field Co.R.E. and convey them to ARRAS.

TIME 7.20 pm.
28/10/1916.

J. Mitchell Baker
Major,
Brigade Major,.
1st S.A.Infantry Brigade,.

3

II

Kits etc, to be stacked E of Kitchens near road, under a guard of 1 N.C.O. of 'A' Coy and one man from B. C. D. + H.Q. Coys.

Blankets, Great coats, + Jerkins to be carried by the men

Kits etc of working parties etc to be stacked at Company Dumps under a Sentry.

O.C. Comp^ys will arrange to warn their working parties, and for the return of such parties to the new Quarters

Lines to be inspected by the 2/in Command and M.O. before leaving and a report to be rendered on arrival at New Quarters

Picks + Shovels to be carried by all ranks in proportion laid down i.e 1 pick to 4 shovels

[signature]
Lieut Col
Comm^dg 9 E.Y.

12.45 pm
23/10/16

[initials]

4

1st SOUTH AFRICAN INFANTRY BRIGADE.

24th OCTOBER 1918.

IMMEDIATE.

APP Z3LA 8.5 am

1st Regiment.
2nd Regiment.
3rd Regiment.
4th Regiment.
28th Coy.M.G.Corps.
S.AL.T.M.Battery.

All orders regarding the Brigade being in Reserve to the Division for the next Attack are cancelled - Also all orders re Working parties to be furnished today excepting party of 100 men furnished by the 3rd Regiment, S.A.Infantry at CATERPILLAR WELL.

The Brigade will move today to ALBERT by march route , Units will prepare to move immediately and will report to Brigade Headquarters at once the earliest hour at which they will be ready to march.

Transport will accompany Units.

Mitchell Baker
Major,
Brigade Major.
1st S. A. Infantry Brigade,.

Rd
8.5 am
HLB

1st S.A. Infantry Brigade.
24th October 1916.

5

SECRET AND URGENT.
Map Reference [illegible]
[illegible]

APP 133

OPERATION ORDER 75.

[illegible] 1st S.A.I. Brigade will move today in accordance with the [illegible] schedule.

TRANSPORT. Transport will not accompany units except in the case of [illegible] S.A.I. The Transport lines of the other three battalions [illegible] at present. The O.C. 1st S.A.I. will arrange to split up his transport as necessary between working parties and the remainder of the battalion.

TENTS AND SHELTERS. Tents and shelters are to be handed over [illegible] relieving units, a party being left behind if necessary to hand over and obtain receipts on proper forms.

BOMBS AND TOOLS. All bombs excepting the 64 boxes in charge of [illegible] will be handed over to the nearest Divisional Dump.

Units will retain tools at present in their possession [illegible] exception of the 1st S.A.I. who will only retain those [illegible] in the mobilization table, plus 50 shovels and 25 picks, (see table attached).

BLANKETS. Those units proceeding by train to ALBERT should carry [illegible] blankets on the man to ensure the men having their blankets tonight.

WORK. The 2nd, 3rd and 4th S.A.I. will receive orders for work daily direct from the C.E. III Corps.

300 men of the 1st S.A.I. will be employed on work on the FRICOURT-CONTALMAISON road under "C" Company, 2nd Labour Battalion, and will be camped at X.28.a.5.4. This party will rendezvous for work daily at X.27.B.1.1.

50 men of the 1st S.A.I. will be employed on hut sites under the 281st Company R.E. at X.26.C.8.0. where they will live.

O.C. 1st S.A.I. will send representatives at once to X.28.a.5.4. and X.26.C. 8.0. to arrange to take over as early as possible today.

ORDERLIES. Each battalion will arrange for two orderlies to be in attendance at the Brigade H.Q. at present occupied by Headquarters S.A. Brigade as that is the nearest telegraph office through which messages can be transmitted.

J Mitchell Baker
Major.
Brigade Major.

Issued by orderly at 12.45 p.m.,
As per S.A. Brigade Operation Order distribution list.

1st SOUTH AFRICAN INFANTRY BRIGADE.

SCHEDULE TO OPERATION ORDER 71.

UNIT.	WHERE TO MOVE.	TIME TO MOVE.	REMARKS.
1st S.A.Infantry.	(a) 300 plus Officers & N.C.Os. to X.28.A.54. (b) 50 plus Officers & N.C.Os. to X.26.C.00.	As soon as possible.	Party(b) will take fifty shovels and twenty five picks. Transport to be divided between (a) (b) and (c) as found necessary.
	(c) Battalion less (a) plus (b) to ALBERT.........	To be notified later.	
2nd S.A.Infantry.	Lines of 4th NORTHUMBERLAND FUSILIERS (X.23.B.)	Move to be completed by 1. p.m,.	Transport lines remain where they are.
3rd S.A.Infantry.	Lines of 4th YORKSHIRE REGIMENT (X.23.D.)	-do-	-do-
4th S.A.Infantry.	Lines of 5th YORKSHIRE REGIMENT (X.23.D.)	-do-	-do-
28th M.Gun Company.	ALBERT.	To be notified later.	
S.A.L.T.Mortar Battery.	ALBERT.	To be notified later.	
BRIGADE H/Quarters.	A LBERT.	To be notified later.	

[signature]

Major.
Brigade Major.
1st S. A. Infantry Brigade,.

6

7

IMMEDIATE.

1st S.A.Infantry Brigade.

24th October 1916.

9.45 am.

1st S.A.Infantry
2nd do.
3rd do.
4th do.

With reference to the move the following orders have just been received from Division.

3 Battalions - 2nd, 3rd, and 4th S.A.I. - will move into quarters in MAMETZ WOOD at present occupied by three battalions of the 50th Brigade.

350 men of the 1st S.A.I. with the necessary complement of officers and N.C.O.s will proceed to FRICOURT FARM under command of Major HEAL.

Brigade Headquarters, 1st S.A.I. less 350 men, Machine Gun Company and Trench Mortars will move to ALBERT.

Transport will as previously ordered move with units.

The move into MAMETZ WOOD is to be completed by 1 pm today. Advance parties will report at Brigade Headquarters at 11 a.m., when instructions will be issued to the officers in charge. The men of advance parties will be formed up opposite Brigade Headquarters clear of the road and railway.

[signature]
Major.

Brigade Major.

11. 10. AM.

24/10/16

App 234 8

2nd S.African Regt.
3rd S.African Regt.
4th S.African Regt.
O.C. S.A.Working Party (300 men) working under O. Coy. 2nd Labour Bn.
O.C. S.A.Working Party (50 men) " " 281 A.T.Coy. R.E.
O.C. S.A.Working Party (78 men) " " 214 A.T.Coy. R.E.
1st S.African Bde.
O.Coy. 2nd Labour Battalion.
O.C. 281 A.T.Coy. R.E.
O.C. 214 A.T.Coy. R.E.

No. X.5/1922. 26th October, 1916.

---

1. Working parties furnished by 1st S.African Bde. for the C.E. III Corps, 2nd Labour Battalion, 281 and 214 A.T.Coys. R.E., will return to their Brigade at MILLENCOURT (D.5.a. and b.) on October 27th.

The move of these parties will be carried out in accordance with march table attached.

2. Intervals of 200 yards will be kept between Companies and 100 yards between platoons.

3. Please acknowledge by wire.

[illegible]
Major,
General Staff
9th (Scottish) Division.

Recd at 2-15 pm
26/10/16

[illegible]
Maj

MARCH TABLE.

Date.	Unit	From	To	S.P.	Time to pass	Route.
Octr. 27th.	2nd S.A.Regt.	MAMETZ WOOD	MILLENCOURT	Cemetery X.17.c.0.0.	8.30 am.	CONTALMAISON ALBERT.
	3rd S.A.Regt.	do	do	do	9.0 am.	
	4th S.A.Regt.	do	do	do	9.30 am.	
	S.A.Working Party under 2nd Labour Bn. (100 men).	X.28.a.5.4.	MILLENCOURT	Cross Roads FRICOURT X.3.b.1.4.	8.0 a.m.	BECOURT
	S.A.Working Party under 281 A.T.Coy R.E. (50 men).	X.28.c.0.0.	MILLENCOURT	Billets	8.0 a.m.	BECOURT.
	S.A.Working Party under 214 A.T.Coy R.E.	S.19.d.9.7.	MILLENCOURT	Billets	8.0 a.m.	BECOURT.

SECRET AND URGENT. Recd 4/45 pm.
Map Reference.
LENS 1/100,000.

1st S.A.Infantry Brigade. H.Q.
27th October 1916.

COPY NO. 3 10

OPERATION ORDER NO. 73.

MOVE. The 1st S.A.I.Brigade, 64th Field CO. R.E. 9th Seaforth (Pioneers) and South African Field Ambulance will move on the 28th instant as per attached march table.

A distance of 200 yards will be kept between companies and 100 yards between platoons.

BILLETING PARTIES. Advance billeting parties proceeded today at 2 pm, in accordance with instructions issued separately.

AMBULANCES TO ACCOMPANY BATTALIONS. O.C., S.A.Field Ambulance will detail one ambulance wagon to accompany each battalion on the march. Ambulance wagons will report at Battalion H.Q. half-an-hour before the time battalions march.

INSPECTION OF BILLETS. Os.C. Units will detail an officer (to be accompanied in the Infantry Units by the Medical Officer) to inspect billets which have been occupied by their units. A written report to be signed by that officer, in Infantry Units by the Medical Officer also, will be forwarded to brigade H.Q. as soon as possible.

REPORTING ARRIVAL IN BILLETS. Os. C. Units will report to Brigade H.Q. the arrival of units in billets. The report will ~~say~~ state the number, if any who fell out on the line of march, and give map reference of unit H.Q.

TRANSPORT. Transport will accompany units.

BRIGADE HEADQUARTERS. Brigade Headquarters will be at HERISSART.

J Mitchell Baker
Major.
~~Brigade Major.~~

Issued by orderly at 3.30 pm.
~~as per S.A.Bde distribution list.~~

1st SOUTH AFRICAN INFANTRY BRIGADE.

Addendum to Operation Order No.73

The O/Commanding S.A.Field Ambulance reports that he cannot detail One Ambulance Wagon to accompany each Battalion on the march as ordered by the A.D.M.S. and the following arrangements will therefore be made:-

I Horse Ambulance will follow in rear of 1st S.A.I.				
I	-do-	-do-	-do-	3rd S.A.I.
I	-do-	-do-	-do-	9th SEAFORTHS.

The S.A.Field Ambulance will move in the rear of the whole Column and Motor Ambulances will pick up any men authorise to fall out on line of March and for whom there is no accommodat in the horse Ambulances.

Men unable to march will report at Brigade Headquarters tomorrow morning at eight O'clock and the O/C.S.A.F.Ambulance will send an Officer to Brigade H.Qrs at that hour to ascertain the number of such men and to arrange for their conveyance.

In the Field.
27th October 1916.

J. Mitchell Baker
Major,
Brigade Major,
1st S. A. Infantry Brigade.

1st SOUTH AFRICAN INFANTRY BRIGADE.

OPERATION ORDER No.73.

27th OCTOBER 1916.

DATE.	UNIT.	FROM.	TO.	STARTING POINT.	Time to pass STARTING POINT.	ROUTE.
OCTOBER 28th.	BRIGADE H.Qrs.	MILLENCOURT.	HERISSART.	500 yards EAST of HENENCOURT.	8.30 am.	
	1st Regt. S.A.I.	-do-	-do-	-do-	8.45 am.	HENENCOURT, WARLOY, CONTAY, & HERISSART.
	2nd Regt. S.A.I.	-do-	-do-	-do-	9.30 am.	-do-
	3rd Regt. S.A.I.	-do-	-do-	-do-	10.15 am.	-do-
	4th Regt. S.A.I.	-do-	-do-	-do-	II. am.	-do-
	28th M. G. Coy,..	HENENCOURT WOOD.	-do-	I Mile WEST of HENENCOURT.	8.15 am.	-do-
	S.A.L.T.M.BATTERY.	-do-	-do-	-do-	8.30 am.	-do-
	64th FIELD CO. R.E.	MILLERCOURT.	RUBEMPRE'	500 yards EAST of HENENCOURT.	II.45 am.	-do-
	9th SEAFORTHS (Pioneers).	-do-	-do-	-do-	12.15 pm.	-do-
	S.A.FIELD AMB,.	LAVIEVILLE.	-do-	JUST CLEAR OF LAVIEVILLE.	I.pm.	-do-

****

13

Recd 11 pm

1st South African Infantry Brigade. H.Q.

28th October 1916.

Addendum No. 2. to
Operation Order 74.

Add at end of paragraph 2.

" All units will be in position ready to enbus at 8 a.m.,"

MOVE ORDERS. ORDER NO.

APP 237 14

By Lieut.Col. E.F.THACKERAY.C.M.G.
Commanding 3rd.S.A.I.
(Transvaal Regiment)

IN THE FIELD.
27/10/16.

---

1. MOVE. In accordance with operation order No.73 from South African Infantry Brigade date 27/10/16. the Regiment will move from MILLENCOURT to HERISSART via HENENCOURT,WARLOY,and CONTAY tomorrow the 28th inst.

2. ORDER OF MARCH. The Regiment will parade at 9.50.a.m.and move off by platoons with an interval of 100 yards,and 200 yards between Companies in the following order :-
Headquarters,A,B,C,D Companies.

3. DRESS. As ordered for today,except that jerkins will be worn beneath jackets. Men will carry graetcoats in pack and not blankets. Rifles will not be carried in sand bags but rifle covers will be carried where in possession.Every body in possession of a steel helmets will wear them.

4. BAGGAGE. All kit and baggage will be uploaded on transport by 9.30.a.m. The transport is at North West of camp.
BLANKETS. Blankets to be rolled in bundles of ten and labelled with tin lables and piled on Regimental Dump near Field Kitchens by 9.30.a m. for placing on the motor lorry.

5. TRANSPORT. Transport will accompany units

6. BILLETING PARTY. A billeting party of 1 Offficer and 4 O.R. was sent forward today.

7. CAMP INSPECTION. An inspection of the camp will take place as ordered for today.

6-30 P.m

H Harvey Hemming

MAJOR.

Acting Adjutant.
3rd.Regiment S.A.Inf.
(Transvaal Regiment)

"A" Form.

MESSAGES AND SIGNALS.

No. of Message

Prefix ...... Code ...... m. Office of Origin and Service Instructions.	Words / Charge / Sent At ...... m. To ...... By	This message is on a/c of: ...... Service. (Signature of "Franking Officer.")	Recd. at 15 m. Date ...... From app 198 By app

TO B M C B. Priority.

Sender's Number.	Day of Month.	In reply to Number.	AAA
* S 50	12.10.16		

Capt	MONTGOMERY	reports	his
Coy	taken	over	late	front
line	K.R.	Containing	2	Officers
and	100	men	Q.L.	He
in	Command	at	MILL.	your
...	303	...	pushing	Capt
INGDALES	D.	Coy		into
trench	vacated	by	C	Coy
at	SPRENGERS	B	Coy	remains
in	position	at	FLERS	SWITCH
ENEMY	ceased	shelling	this	line

[signature] Major

Actg Adjt

From E.M.

Place

Time

The above may be forwarded as now corrected. (Z)

Censor. Signature of Addressor or person authorised to telegraph in his name.

* This line should be erased if not required.

35,000. W 14042—M 41. H. W. & V., Ld. 12.15.

(4198) Wt. W14042—M14. 300000 Pads. 12/15. Sir J. C. & S

16

"C" Form (Duplicate).
MESSAGES AND SIGNALS.

Army Form C. 2123.
(In books of 50's in duplicate.)
No. of Message

	Charges to Pay. £ s. d.	Office Stamp.
S.D. MT 26		KK 13-10-16
Service Instructions. Priority CB		

Handed in at Office m. Received 2-1 a.m.

TO KK

Sender's Number	Day of Month	In reply to Number	AAA
BM 321	13th		

Cancel my BM 307 aaa
Reoccupation of post however as
to be effected by 5 am
as ordered in my BM 317

FROM CB
PLACE & TIME 12:40 am

Wt. 432—M 897 500,000 Pads. H.W.V. 5/16. Forms C.2123

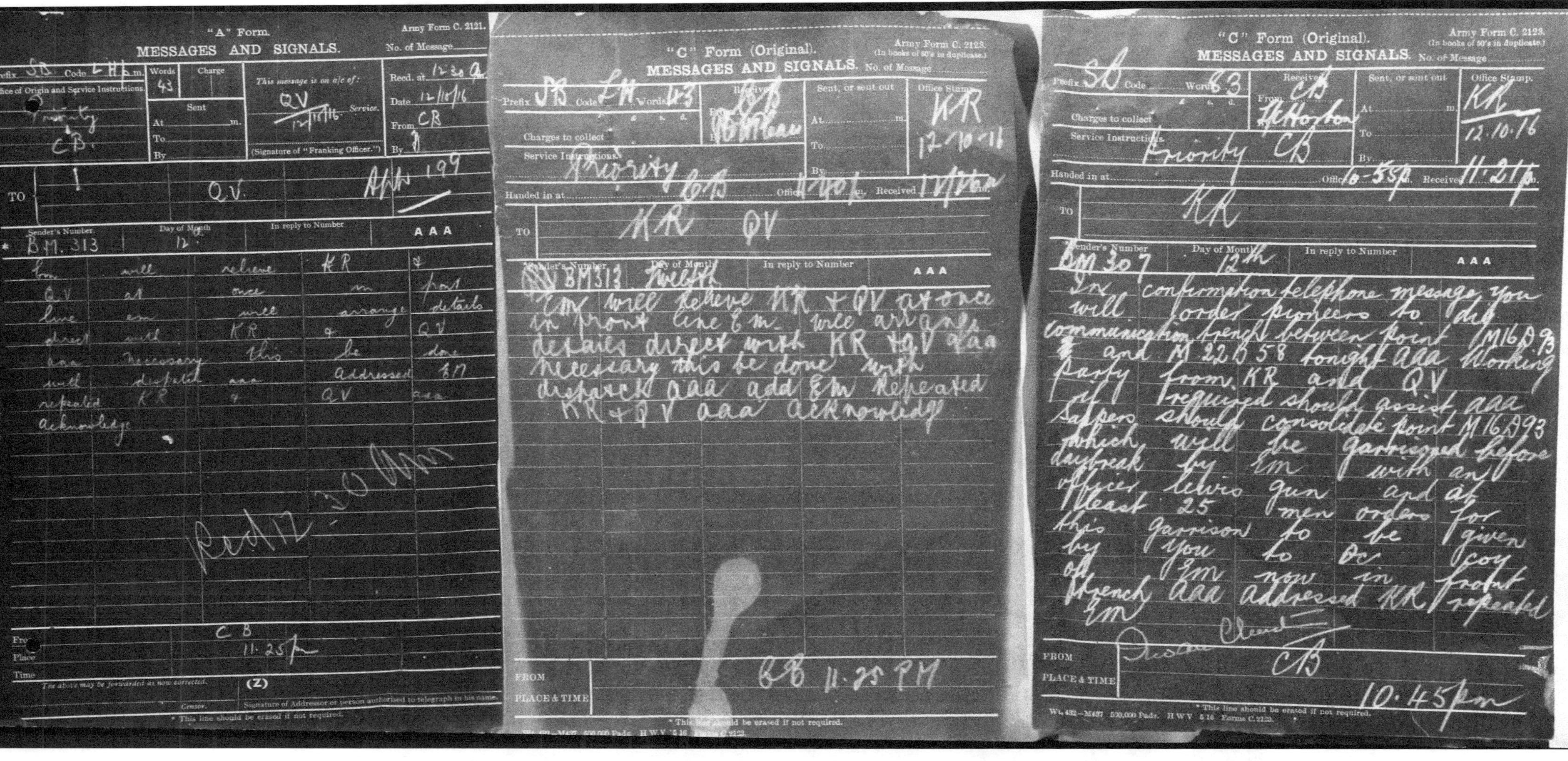

"A" Form. MESSAGES AND SIGNALS. Army Form C. 2121.

Prefix SB Code LHI Words 43 — Office of Origin and Service Instructions: Priority CB — This message is on a/c of: QV Service. 12/10/16 — Recd. at 12.30 a — Date 12/10/16 — From CB — By J

TO: 1 QV. AHW 199

Sender's Number: B.M. 313 Day of Month: 12 In reply to Number: AAA

Em will relieve KR & QV at once in front line Em will arrange details direct with KR & QV aaa necessary this be done with dispatch aaa Addressed EM repeated KR & QV aaa acknowledge

Recd 12.30 am

From CB Place Time 11.25 pm

"C" Form (Original). MESSAGES AND SIGNALS. Army Form C. 2123.

Prefix SB Code EM Words 43 — Charges to collect — Service Instructions: Priority CB — Handed in at — Office 11.40 p — Received 11.55 p.m. — Office Stamp: KR 12-10-16

TO: KR QV

Sender's Number: BM313 Day of Month: twelfth In reply to Number: AAA

Em will relieve KR & QV at once in front line Em will arrange details direct with KR & QV aaa necessary this be done with dispatch aaa add Em Repeated KR & QV aaa acknowledge

FROM PLACE & TIME: CB 11.25 PM

"C" Form (Original). MESSAGES AND SIGNALS. Army Form C. 2123.

Prefix SB Code Words 83 — Received From CB — Charges to collect — Service Instructions: Priority CB — Handed in at — Office 6-55 p — Received 11.21 p.m. — Office Stamp: KR 12.10.16

TO: KR

Sender's Number: BM 307 Day of Month: 12th In reply to Number: AAA

In confirmation telephone message you will order pioneers to dig communication trench between point M16D93 and M22B58 tonight aaa Working party from KR and QV if required should assist aaa Sappers should consolidate point M16D93 which will be garrisoned before daybreak by Em with an officer Lewis gun and at least 25 men orders for this garrison to be given by you to OC coy of Em now in front trench aaa addressed KR repeated Em

FROM PLACE & TIME: CB 10.45 pm

III

D Coy 2 Guides from Strongpoint for
1 platoon 1st S.A.I (D Coy)
A Coy will detail 2 Guides
to lead A Coy 1st S.A.I as above
detailed.
C Coy 3rd S.A.I to detail 2 Guides for
C Coy 1st S.A.I.
B Coy 3rd S.A.I 2 Guides to B Coy
1st S.A.I
M.O 3rd S.A.I 2 Guides to M.O 1st S.A.I
Head Qrs 3rd S.A.I to H Qrs 1st S.A.I
All spare water-tins to be carried
and care to be exercised not
to leave behind tools &c.
O.C. Coys to report in writing to
the Adjutant immediately on completion
of relief showing any change in
tactical situation. Reports to be
rendered 2 AM + 2 PM.

H. [illegible] Major
A/Adjt
E.M.

19

MACHINE GUNS. The guns at present in the support trench and those in M.22.D. and 28.A and B., will from ZERO onwards during the attack fire on enemy's trenches and roads north of a line drawn East and West through M.17.central but will not shoot on any ground West of M.11 and 17. The BAPAUME main road should be traversed.

Immediately the objective is gained, the O.C., Machine Gun Coy will move four machine guns into the captured trench. One of these guns will be placed in the strong point at trench junction M.17.c.4.4. and another at approximately M.17.C.1.8.

Positions for the other two will be selected by the Machine Gun officer in charge in consultation with the Infantry officer in Command on the spot.

Once the Machine Gun officer has decided on a position for a Machine gun, it is NOT to be changed except under the orders of the Brigade or the Battalion Commander.

STOKES MORTARS. The O.C., S.A.L.T.M.Battery will make all arrangements for the 2 minutes barrage from ZERO being carried out by his battery and for an adequate supply of ammunition being forward with the mortars.

He will, immediately the barrage ceases, have his mortars ready to fire at extreme range over the objective to deal with any counter attack from the north.

ENGINEERS AND PIONEERS. One section of 64th Field Co. R.E. and half a company of 9th Seaforths (Pioneers) are attached to the Brigade for the operations.

The Engineers will assist the Infantry in making the strong point at M.17.C.4.4. and the block at M.16.C.1.8.

The Pioneers will cut a communication trench from approximately M.17.C.7.1. to M.17.C.7.6.

The Officers in command of the Engineers and Pioneers will report to the O.C., 1st S.A.I. at his headquarters at M.22.D.3.2. at least two hours before ZERO.

COMMUNICATIONS. A main Divisional receiving station has been established M.29.D.4.4. which is visible from the whole front to be attacked.

Arrangements as ordered by the O.C., Signal Section will be made for visual communication to be established with this station from the captured line.

Where staples supporting telephone lines in trenches are found detached they should be replaced. All ranks are required to assist in this way in the maintenance of communications.

LIGHTS. Red flares will be shown by the advanced Infantry to show their positions to the contact aeroplanes which will fly over the fr as soon as light permits.

If progress up the SWITCH TRENCH is held up by our own barrage a single red light should be sent up as a signal to the artillery to lift gradually. If the signal has to be repeated, there should be at least half-a-minute interval between signals.

FIGHTING OUTFIT. The normal fighting outfit for each man will be as per appendix "D" of Instructions for training issued by 9th Division, excepting that the pack may be substituted for the haversac the S.A.A. carried on the man is reduced to 120 rounds and every man will carry two bombs. Every thing in excess of the normal outfit will be dumped by battalions at a spot near their H.Q. and left in charge of a gu All men will carry the Infantry entrenching tool and all men excepting specialists, i.e., snipers, Lewis gunners, Machine Gunners, etc., will carry a pick or a shovel in the proportion of six shovels to one pick.

Page 3.

MATERIAL TO BE CARRIED.-
Carrying platoons will carry the material etc., setforth in the Annexed Schddule.

REPORTS. Situation reports will be sent in as frequently as possible.

DUMP. The Brigade advanced Dump is at M.28.d.5.4 .
Ammunition, Bombs and Stores will be sent forward by the Brigade carriers on receipt of a request for same - The bearer of the request acting as guide.

MEDICAL ARRANGEMENTS.
The line of evacuation for wounded is from collecting posts at EAUCOURT L' ABBAYE by railway to WEST of HIGH WOOD thence by Ambulance to advanced Dressing Station at BAZENTIN LE PETIT .
Walking wounded will be directed along this route.

PRISONERS.
The Collecting station is at BAZENTIN LE PETIT S.8.d.4.5.
Escorts which should be in proportion of 15% to 20% will proceed as far as this collecting station only and then return to their Battalions - Prisoners will not be searched by Units except for arms.

ASSISTANCE BY BRIGADE ON LEFT.
The 46th Brigade are assisting with Machine gun fire on Enemy trenches ; The BUTTE de WARLENCOURT , and on known and suspected enemy Machine gun positions but will not fire on any ground SOUTH of a line EAST and WEST through M.17 CENTRAL .
Their STOKES MORTARS will also be in action ready to deal with any hostile Machine guns about M.10.d.

BATTALION HEADQUARTERS.
The Headquarters of the 1st S.A.I,.will be at M.22.d.2.3

BRIGADE HEADQUARTERS.
Brigade H.Qrs will be at S.15.b.3.5.

ALL RANKS ARE REMINDED THAT IN ADDITION TO GAINING THEIR OWN OBJECTIVE IT IS THEIR DUTY TO ASSIST THEIR NEIGHBOURS TO GAIN THEIRS.

J Mitchell Baker
Major,
Brigade Major.

Issued by Orderly at 2.30 p.m. as per S.A.Brigade distribution list.

H.Q. 1st S.A.I.Brigade.
18th October 1916.

App 226

SECRET & URGENT.
Map reference.
ALBERT 1/40,000.

Copy No........ 21

OPERATION ORDER NO. 69.

The 1st S.A.I.Brigade will be relieved in the line on the 19th and the night of the 19th/20th October, by the 27th Infantry Brigade in accordance with the attached schedule.

Advanced parties to take over the camping areas from the 6th K.O.S.Bs and the 11th Royal Scots will be sent by the 4th and 2nd S.A.I., respectively to report to the H.Q. of the 27th Infantry Brigade at S.30.a.6 8. at 8 am on the 19th. Similarly advanced parties of the 6th K.O.S.Bs and 11th Royal Scots will report at 8 am on the 19th at the H.Q. of the 4th S.A.I. and 1st S.A.I. Brigade to take over camping sites from the 4th and 2nd S.A.I. respectively. The O.C. 2nd S.A.I. will send a guide to Brigade H.Q. (S.A.) to meet the advance party of the 11th Royal Scots.

On relief the 3rd S.A.I. will proceed to BAZENTIN LE GRAND and take over camping area vacated by the 11th Royal Scots and the 1st S.A.I. on relief will proceed to the camping area in HIGH WOOD vacated by the 6th K.O.S.Bs. The Os.C. 1st and 3rd S.A.I. will send advance parties to take over these camping sites at 4 pm on the 19th.

The 2nd and 4th S.A.I. will take with them all picks and shovels in their possession.
The 1st and 3rd S.A.I. will hand over to their relieving battalions all picks, shovels, bombs and ammunition.

Completion of relief to be reported to Brigade Headquarters by the message "NATAL".

Brigade Headquarters will remain at BAZENTIN LE GRAND.

ACKNOWLEDGE.

J Mitchell Baker
Major.
Brigade Major.

Issued by orderly at 9.15 pm
as per S.A.Brigade distribution
list.

Recd 9.10 pm

22

ARTICLES TO BE CARRIED BY THE REAR (CARRYING) PLATOONS.

	Each Section.	Total per Platoon.	Total per Battalion.
Sandbags	100.	400.	1600.
Rolls French Wire.	2.	8.	32.
Rifle Grenade No.23	50.	200.	800.
Very Pistols.	I.	4.	16.
Very Lights, Pkts.	I.	4.	16.

ZERO WILL BE 3.40 a.m. on 18th inst. - Divisional time will be given over phone to Officer Commanding 1st Regt.S.A.I. at 9.30 p.m. tonight.

Os/C. Machine Gun Coy and Trench Mortar Battery will send a representative either to Brigade Headquarters or to those of 1st S.A.Infantry to set watches.

J Mitchell Baker
Major,
Brigade Major.
1sr S.A.I.Brigade,....

23

SCHEDULE ACCOMPANYING OPERATION ORDER NO. 69.

UNIT BEING RELIEVED.	UNIT RELIEVING	Hour of relief	Hour and place at which guides will meet relieving units.	REMARKS.
2nd S.A.I.	== 11th Royal Scots.	11 a,m, 19/10/16.	--------	
4th S.A.I.	6th K.O.S.Bs	11.15 a.m., 19/10/16.	--------	
1st S.A.I.	6th K.O.S.Bs	About 6 pm.,	5 pm 19/10/16 at Headquarters 6th K.O.S.Bs, HIGH WOOD.	17 guides will be sent. One for each platoon, one for Headquarters.
3rd S.A.I.	11th Royal Scots	About 6-30pm	5-30 pm 19/10/16 at H.Q. of 11th Royal Scots BAZENTIN LE GRAND. (Near Bde H.Q.)	-do-
28th M.G.Coy	27th M.G.Coy	About noon 19/10/16	11.30 am H.Q. 4th S.A.I.	
S.A. L.T.M.Battery	27th Bde L.T.M.Battery	11 am. 19/10/16.	10 am S.A.Bde H.Q.	The S.A.Brigade Trench Mortars will be left in the line.

Move Order APP No 1 C 2/3. 7 24

(1) by Lt. Col. E F Thackeray C.M.G

Move In the field 19/10/16

In accordance with operation Order No 69 1st SAI Brigade the Regt will be relieved in the Support Lines by the 11th Royal Scots.

(2) Relief commencing about 6.30 pm today. The 3rd regiment will take over camping area vacated by 11th R Scots at BAZENTIN L GRAND.

BILLETTING PARTIES & Guides OC Coys will each detail for a billetting party of 1 Sr NCO & 1 man per platoon - Head Qrs 1 man for each HQ detail to report to 2/Lt EGAN at Regimental HQ at 1.30 pm precisely to ~~take over~~ proceed to take over new camping area - O.C. Coys (including HQs) will each ~~[illegible]~~ detail 2 guides ~~at Regtl HQ~~ to report to Lt EGAN at HQ at the same time as billetting parties - OC "A" Coy will detail 2 additional guides who are acquainted with the ~~[illegible]~~ PROVE trench line - Lt EGAN after instructing these guides in the best route from STARFISH and other Coy LINES to BAZENTIN L'GRAND will furnish them with written instructions & personally hand them over to the HQ at the 11th Royal Scots at BAZENTIN L'GRAND (No SAI Bde. HQrs)

OC. Billetting party after taking over Regtl area will take measures

II

to send his Billeting guides well back along the road to meet the Regiment –

Order of Relief. A Coy. Head Qrs C + 'B' Coy. but each unit to move off independantly as soon as its relief arrives –

Tools + Ammunition Coys will hand over to the relieving units all picks + shovels, bombs, and ammunition flares + surplus VERY lights but will take with them sand-bags

Great Coats all great coats to be rolled in bundles of 10 with tin tickets and piled at COUGH DROP DUMP by 5 p.m. – O.C. HQ details will furnish a guard

Reports on arrival at new camping area O.C. Coys will report in writing to the Adjt when their Coys are complete.

10.10. AM.

Recd. 4.15 pm

[signature]
Major
a/Adjutant
E.M.

From	Code	Words	Charge		
Office of Origin and Service Instructions	Sent		This ... Service.	Date	
	At ... m.			From	
	To				
	By		(Signature of "Franking Officer.")	By	

TO Major Young O.C. Details 8A7

Sender's Number.	Day of Month.	In reply to Number.	
S116.	19/10/16.		AAA

The Regiment has received orders to relieve 11th Royal Scots at Bazentin L Grand – Kindly give necessary instructions for Rations + water to be there tonight after 7 PM.

Also please have transport sent up to COUGH DROP DUMP as soon after dark as possible for the purpose of removing approximately 150 Great coats. New Regtl HQrs after about 7.30 pm will be HQrs 11th Royal Scots (nr Brigade Head Quarters –

[signature]
Major
a/Adjt

From E.M.

Place Telephone Communication will be continued

Time from Brigade to here until the Regiment moves.

The above may be forwarded as now corrected. (Z)

Censor. Signature of Addressor or person authorised to telegraph in his name.

* This line should be erased if not required.

M509. H. W. & V., Ld. 6/16.

25

App 229

22 Octr/16

From O.C. D. Coy
To Adjt.

APP 229

In accordance with your instructions I reported to the O.C. 1st Regt on the afternoon of the 17th who directed me to occupy the support trench running S.E. from the Mill by 3.15 am the following morning making the Mill my H Qrs. I left PRUE TRENCH at midnight & was in position by 3 a.m. It was raining hard during this period. I reported to the O.C. 1st Regt, who instructed me to move my Company to the FRONT LINE (PEARSE'S TRENCH). I was informed that two Companies of the 1st Regt. had a footing in the German trench running N.E. from nose of switch but the exact position was not known & I was to send out a patrol to obtain information and to push a platoon from PEARSE TRENCH over the open into the GERMAN TRENCH. I sent out Lt. Lee and a small patrol & at the same time reported that in my opinion it was useless to attempt to push anyone across the open in daylight, but that it could be done after dark and that I was waiting for further definite instructions.

Lt. Lee returned with his patrol at 2 p.m & reported that he could obtain no information from any of the men of the 1st Regt who had returned during the day as to where the Coys were. He had scouted out a little himself but could find out nothing. In the meantime I had seen the C.S.M. of C. Coy 1st Regt, who informed me where he had last seen A Coy of the 1st Regt. Col. Dawson then sent for me and handed me the attached written instructions to attack the Switch TRENCH at M 17 C. 4.5 at 5.42 p.m. from the South in conjunction with D Coy 1st Regt who would attack from the ~~[illegible]~~ PIMPLE. I received instructions at 4.26 p.m. and left Btn HQrs at 4.35. Owing to the very bad state of the Com. TRENCH I

did not reach my H Qrs till after 5 p.m. I sent for my officers & N.C.Os. As they did not arrive after 15 minutes I went down the trench myself & found it congested with troops. I did not arrive at PEARSE'S POINT till 5.37 which left me no time to give any instructions.
I would not take out my Coy without giving my officers & N.C.Os any idea of what they were going to do, so I gathered together one Platoon which was in PEARSE'S SAP & 2 Lewis Gun teams. I gave them the idea & took them out myself at 5.43 p.m. deciding I would give MAJOR ORMISTON what assistance I could from the SOUTH in the attack.
We skirmished across to the GERMAN TRENCH apparently without being observed, though there was heavy enemy shell fire at the time on this open ground. I arrived at the Trench at a point about M17 c 6.5 and proceeded about 200 yards up the trench to find the other two Coys of the 1st but could find no trace of them. I came back & blocked the trench leaving a Lewis Gun team there & proceeded down the trench in the direction of the NOSE of the switch. I had 17 men with me & the other Lewis Gun. It was then about 6 p.m. & I had heard no sounds of an attack from the other end except a few bombs & a little M.G. fire. I felt that I was not strong enough to attack myself, so waited there for about an hour. I could not decide whether it were best to remain in the trench & send for the remainder of the Coy, but by this time I had come to the conclusion that the trench was a trap, so I retired my men back to PEARSE'S SAP & reported to Col. Dawson with a view to finding out what had happened to the other attack.
Col Dawson then sent me written instructions to re-occupy the trench with the whole of my Coy & informed me that Capt Ross would attack the point during the night with 120 men. If the attack was a success I was to stay the following day, if a failure I was to be relieved before daylight. I returned to my Coy in PEARSE'S TRENCH & found it very congested. Various men of the 1st Regt had been returning during the day & settled down in the trench which is very narrow. I was obliged to take off the valises from the men's backs to get them through. I eventually re-occupied the trench at midnight & reported by runner to Col. Dawson. I went down the trench with Sgt Wall followed by a party of bombers & a Lewis Gun.
I arrived at about the same place as before, when we encountered a party of Germans, coming towards us up the Trench about 10 feet away. I shot the first man with my revolver & several bombs were thrown at us, which though they fell quite near did no damage. We replied with bombs & drove them back. I pushed forward after them when I received a message from Lt. Lee that two strong parties of the enemy were coming round on each flank to surround us. I at once blocked the trench at

that point & placed a Lewis gun there & extended my men across the trench about 75 yards each side & formed a semi circle facing the Germans. There were three M.G.s firing at us from well concealed positions & a very heavy rifle fire. The whole body behaved very well in this attack & opened a good steady rifle fire on the Germans who by this time were getting too close for him to use his M.G.s.

We also bombed him successfully from this point & compelled him to retire. I was much outnumbered & was waiting for Capt. Ross to attack. The ground was again heavily shelled & I withdrew most of my men into the trench & waited. We had only three casualties & the Germans must have suffered from our fire & bombs. It then began to rain heavily & the rifles became very muddy. At 4 am. I received a message from Capt. Ross that I could withdraw my men from the trench.

I saw the Scottish coming down the trench from the same place where I had entered it & as it was still dark I told my men to creep over the parapet & leave the trench open for the Scottish.

I then went to look for Capt. Ross. I had got about half way down my Company when we were suddenly attacked by the Germans at the same point as before.

The Germans were using the Flamenwerfer & bombs, & his flanks were covered by his M.Guns.

The first jet caught the Lewis Gun & two of the team.

There was a slight panic at this time. I stopped the men in front of me & doubled them out to the same formation I had adopted before.

We had to retire some little way as it took some time to assure the men there was nothing to fear from the fire which was certainly very demoralizing. There was heavy M.G. fire on us at this time too. Our rifles would not work after the magazine was empty.

The remainder of my Company had by this time come into the Scottish & the G. bay & in the dim light the Germans must have thought we were concentrating reinforcements, for he stopped his attack, branched off to the left & began a further attack on the Regt. on my right.

I got very little assistance from the Vickers gun – possibly because the guns were too muddy.

I tried to get the men to charge with the bayonet, but they were too exhausted, this being their second night out on duty.

I had no casualties amongst the men who stayed with me as far as I know. I then saw the Scottish occupying the trench – the fighting there had ceased.

I withdrew my men who had no more bombs & whose rifles were useless to PEARSE'S SAP.

I left 2nd Lt. Lee to bring in the remainder who had by this time come into touch with the Regt on my right, who had I understand given what assistance they could with their bombs.

I had seven casualties altogether whilst out of our trenches & lost one Lewis Gun.

Lt. Lee gave me every assistance in this attack being very cool and prompt. There are also one or two names I should like to place before you, that you may submit to the Commdg Offr for their excellent behaviour under very trying circumstances.

I counted over 70 Germans in this bombing attack

(Sgd) Geo. H. Langdale
Capt.
O.C. B. Coy.

P.S. I feel that I was right in withdrawing my men the first time. If the Germans had attacked that party we should undoubtedly have been scuppered.

(intd) G.H.L.
Capt.

To ADJT

APP 228

EM

In the field
22. 10. 16.

At about 12.10 pm on the 19th inst I received urgent written orders from [illegible] to reinforce the firing line with my Company & an offr & 20 O.R. of [illegible] Coy, & to report at once for orders to O.C. T.E. I gave the necessary move orders to my Coy, & after fixing a point at which I would join them later, reported to O.C. T.E. at 12.25 pm.

My instructions were verbal, & to this effect: – I was to proceed with my party to a sap leading N from PEARCE'S TRENCH, & under certain conditions occupy the Enemy Trench about 50 x N of this sap & if necessary, [illegible] down Trench W to a point about 100 x E of the nose of Switch, & to establish connection with the 26th Brigade on my right, who were occupying a portion of this Enemy Trench.

En route to the sap, I received further written orders from OC T E which did not materially alter my [illegible] verbal orders, except in that I was to push into Enemy Trench at once.

(2)

The march thro' the Trenches to the Sap was a most difficult one, & thoroughly exhausted & [illegible] out my party, as the trenches were in most places [illegible] deep in sticking mud, very narrow & for the greater part of the way congested with other troops, & I often at various points had to move out of trenches overland.

(at 2.30 pm) I eventually arrived at the Sap with 2 offrs & about 70 men, & after leaving orders for the remainder of my party to follow, as they arrived, I gave orders to 2/Lt Van Ryneveld to lead ✗ the Sap & push over to Enemy Trench, & I & 2/Lt Egan accompanied this party, 2/Lt Van Ryneveld leading.

In accordance with my orders, 2/Lt Van Ryneveld pushed W along Enemy Trench, & eventually arrived at a point about 200 x E of nose of Switch, capturing 5 of the enemy en route, & shooting one, & then came & reported to me that he could get no further because of our artillery fire which was very severe.

Whilst awaiting the remainder of my party, I & 2/Lt Egan was busy sniping at the enemy who were retiring from the Trench I had occupied & those [illegible]

(3)

[illegible] yards beyond this Trench; & despite
[illegible] of fire from [illegible]
[illegible], they made very good practice.
When the artillery barrage had lifted, I
ordered 2/Lt Cook with a party 20 OR to
push to within 100x of the [illegible] of Switch,
& when he had succeeded in doing this, to
[illegible], & hold out if attacked
from either his front or left, & to report
to me, & I would reinforce his party.
In the meantime I had sent to 2/Lt Hallewell
to reinforce my party from the left I had
left him, & placed him to the right of my
Trench with his party of about 30 OR
to get into touch with the 76th Brigade who
were on my right. I then told off 2/Lt Estcel &
[illegible] to guard an enemy communication trench
[illegible] leading N from the right centre of my
position, & myself took command of a
party of 2 Offrs & about 17 OR, with two
machine guns to hold the left centre of my
position, directly opposite an enemy T
[illegible] about 100x N, & where the enemy
were showing signs of activity.
My instructions to all parties was to hold
the Trench until relieved by another unit.
Just after dark, the enemy began sniping,
& at intervals between 6 pm & 8 pm turned
[illegible] machine guns on my position, one

(4)

one of my machine guns replying.
Enemy patrols approached my position at
various points, but were bombed off, two
prisoners, one of which I believe was an
officer being captured.
My relief came about
12.40 am, under Lt Kerr of the KOSB, &
I left the Trench with my party about 1.30 am
& under an arrangement with Lt Kerr, I
left 2/Lt Hallewell's party, who were on my
extreme right to be relieved later, as
soon as more bombs could be obtained,
& his stragglers arrived.
I handed over all my bombs & a machine
gun to Lt Kerr.
I attach herewith a MAP given me by
OC [illegible] T E & all written orders I had
received.
I wish to point out that altho' our artillery
made splendid practice in front of my position,
that in the ~~[illegible]~~, many shells fell into
my Trench, one of which killed 4 men &
wounded two others, & buried the machine
gun. I attach a rough sketch of my position.

I have the honour to be
Sir
Your obedient Servant
[illegible] Lt.
OC B. Coy

31

S/C IV/40

Bde Adv Qrs
21/10/16.

32

APP 130

3rd Regt

In continuation of previous orders your Regiment will move today to the camping site at HIGH WOOD now occupied by 1st Regt S.A.I.

The move to be completed by 4pm and report to be sent to this office which will then be established at new Bde Qrs X30 a 5.8.

Acknowledge please.

12/20pm

[signature] Pepper Capt. S/C
for Bde Major

App 231 33

SECRET & URGENT.
Map Reference.
ALBERT 1/40,000.

1st South African Infantry Brigade H.Q.
23rd October 1916.

COPY NO...3.....

OPERATION ORDER NO. 70.

The following moves will take place today:-

1st S.A.Infantry : From BAZENTIN LE GRAND to Mametz to the quarters vacated by the 7th Seaforths To be clear of BAZENTIN LE GRAND by 12 noon.

3rd S.A.Infantry : From HIGH WOOD to BAZENTIN LE GRAND, to the quarters vacated by the 10th Argyll & Sutherland Highlanders. NOT to leave HIGH WOOD till 4 pm.

The 1st S.A.I. will send an advance party to the camping site of the 7th Seaforths to take over quarters at 9.30 am.

The 3rd S.A.I. will send an advance party to the camping site of the 10th A & S. High'rs to take over quarters at 2 pm.

The quarters vacated by the 1st and 3rd S.A.Infantry will be at the disposal of the 27th Infantry Brigade.

Acknowledge.

Acknowledged

J Mitchell Baker
Major.
Brigade Major

Issued by orderly at 9 am 23/10/16.
As per S.A.Brigade distribution list.

Recd 11 am

34

Move Order APP 232
by Lieut Col. E.F. Thackeray CMG
(Secret & Urgent.) Commanding 3rd S.A.I

Map reference Albert 1/40.000

In the Field 23/10/16

In accordance with Brigade Operation Order No 70 the 3rd S.A.I will move from HIGH WOOD to BAZENTIN LE GRAND to the quarters vacated by the 10th Argyll & Sutherland Highrs not to leave HIGH WOOD till 4 P.M.

An advanced party of 1 Officer 1 Sgt. 1 Corpl. & 8 men from each Coy & H.Q Coy will take over the quarters of the 10th A&S Highlanders at 2 PM.

The Officer in charge of each party will send back two guides for each Coy & H.Q Coy. All details Officers servants, Cooks, Q.Mrs Staffs O.R. Staff will move off to reach new quarters not earlier than 2 pm.

If Kitchens still near new site they will be taken over at once

All ranks will move fully equipped. attention is drawn to orders regarding the carrying of 4 Bombs, 2 Sand-bags, 2 Smoke Helmets, and all rifles to be encased in Sand-bags.

BAGGAGE. Officers baggage, spare O. Room

APP 216

E.T. 6 35
Octr 15th 1916

Brigade Major
1st S.A.I. Bgde

App 216

Re your order B.M. 257. 14.10.16 and the operation carried out in accordance with them I beg to report

This order was ~~given~~ delivered to me while General Lukin was giving me instructions at 3.20 p.m 14.10.16 and was read over to me by him. I then at once sent for Company Comdrs to meet me at 4.30 p.m, but owing to heavy shelling two were delayed and did not reach me till 5 p.m

I at once issued verbal orders and went through the whole plan in detail and confirmed these orders in writing. Copy attached marked A.

I instructed Company Comdrs to see into all details and to form up all ready to move and to phone me when all details were complete. The R.E. Officers arrived while they were with me, and all the various

working parties & tasks were explained
An officer of 1st S.A.I also arrived
together with Capt Lane who conducted
him up to the front where he had
to work. This meeting of C.Cs took
till 7 p.m including a conference
of C.Cs after I had issued orders
Captn Springer reported all ready
to move at 11.50 and moved off
at once with B Co followed by
a working party of 50 men of A Coy
under Lt Goodwin. Company Comdrs
A, C & E reported all quiet at 12.5 a.m
Lt. Harris reported arrival at point
out 16.d.7.4 at 1.35 p.m and
that Lt. Mallett had pushed East
wards the Mound 93.
Captain Springer rang up at
.30 a.m reporting that he was
wounded and I ordered Capt
Lane to take command of the
operations.
Lt. Harris reported at 1.45 am
that he was moving East and
that Lieut. Goodwin and working
party had joined up in rear
at 7.35 P.M/ Captn Montgomery
reported that neither he or Capt

Lane were yet in communication
with anyone
From 3.15 a.m. to 3.20 a very heavy
barrage was put up on our
front line
At 3.40 Capt. Lane reported that
Lieut Goodwin was digging in
towards road
At 4.10 am Lieut Harris message
of 2.15 am reached me that objective
not yet reached, the bearer had
been wounded
At 5 am received report from Lt
Harris dated 4.20 am that
objective was held by Lt Medlicott
25 R.C.O. men & 1 L. gun & that
Lt Mallet and 20 men hold
extreme Eastern end of enemy trench
Lts Estill and Harris situated in
another part of trench (with approx
20 men) They were very heavily
bombed in taking trench, and
Lt Mallet was wounded severely.
At 6.20 am Capt Lane reported
Lt. Goodwin and party had
returned
Lt. Goodwin reported to me that
they had not been able to dig
much owing to ~~heavy~~ heavy

and close fire and that after
consultation with officers left
in B Co who were of opinion
that they could hold out till
tonight he brought his party
back at dawn, as to remain
would have greatly congested
such trenches as there were
Capt. Lane reported 5.30 that
Lt Harris & Estill with remainder
of B Co holding trench to East of
Mound 93 and was instructed to
send over to them 13 men as a
reinforcement with picks and bombs.
I reported the situation to the BM at
5.40 am & at that time Lt Cruddas
(covering party) was reported
dug in along the front of PIERRE
TRENCH in small parties along a
front of 80 yards
I ordered A Co to occupy left
point of line and C Co to hold
Pierre Trench and B Co in support
I attach a map showing position
at present as far as is known & in
reply to your B.M.380 recd. 6.35 am
am sending this report.
The only reasons I can give for
the time taken in reaching the

36

objective are that it takes very considerable time to organise a whole Battn for such an expedition and it took a long time to carry the move out through the trenches under fire and hampered as they were by numerous wounded and working parties, and also the necessity of great care in moving forward to the attack in the open in the face of heavy artillery, M.G. and rifle fire.

Further the regiment is considerably exhausted by continuous movement, want of sleep, hard work, lack of cooked warm food under a continual heavy bombardment since 8 am 12th inst, which unfits them for further attack & sustained effort required to hold on and consolidate, and as B. Co. and a large proportion of C. Co. are isolated they would not be available for forward movement and attack, and I recommend that fresh troops may carry out any such operations.

(Sgd) E F Thackeray
Lt Col
Comndg 3 S.A.I.

7.40 a.m.
15.10.16.

Wired 7.30 am 15.10.16 No. S.75
Wired No S.75 B.M. 7 am 15/10/16 [illegible]

"C" Form (Original).
MESSAGES AND SIGNALS.

Army Form C. 2123.
(In books of 50's in duplicate.)
No. of Message

Code ... Words ... £ s. d.
Charges to collect
Service Instructions. PRIORITY EM

Received: From ... By ...
Sent, or sent out: At ... m. To ... By ...
Office Stamp.

Handed in at ... Office ... m. Received ... m.

TO

Sender's Number	Day of Month	In reply to Number	AAA

consider men not fit for any long attack or to hold out at the end of week

[illegible]

F. A. [illegible]

From EM

A Form
MESSAGES AND SIGNALS.

Army Form C. 2121
No. of Message

Prefix SB Code CKA m. Words 30 Charge.
Office of Origin and Service Instructions.
PRIORITY
CB

Sent: At ... m. To ... By ...

This message is on a/c of: ... Service.
(Signature of "Franking Officer.")

Recd. at ... m.
Date 15.10.16
From CB
By [illegible]

TO EM

Sender's Number.	Day of Month.	In reply to Number.	AAA
* BM 383	15.10.16		

Your explanation as called for in BM 380 received aaa Can you give rough estimate your casualties last nights operation aaa wire same priority

38

From CB
Place
Time 7.45 am

The above may be forwarded as now corrected. (Z)

Censor. Signature of Addressor or person authorised to telegraph in his name.

* This line should be erased if not required.

(8.0. 1019). Wt. W 5148/M 701. 50,000 Pads. 8/16. McC. & Co. Ltd. London.

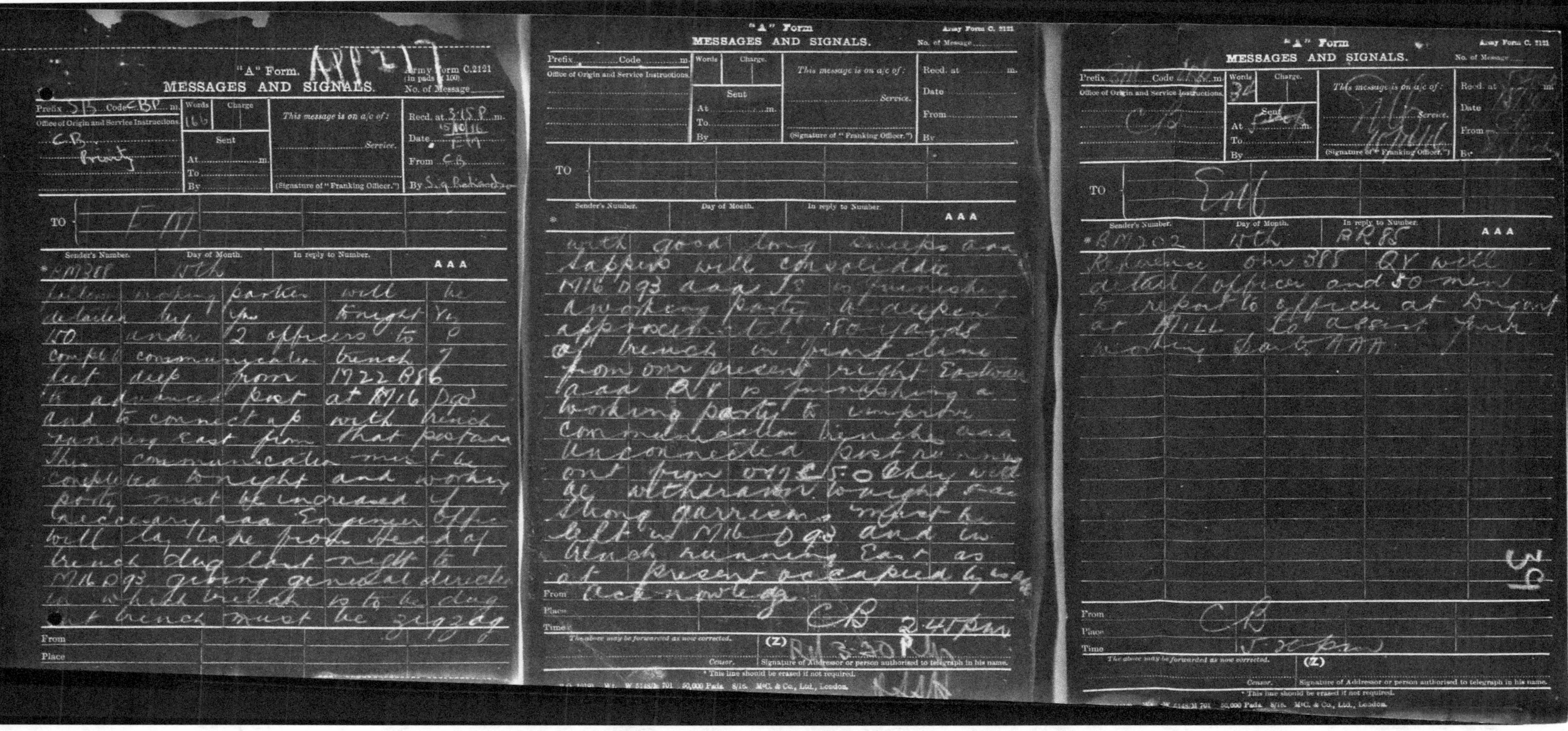

"A" Form. APP 217
MESSAGES AND SIGNALS.
Army Form C.2121 (in pads of 100)
No. of Message

Prefix SB Code EBP m. Words 166 Charge
Office of Origin and Service Instructions. C.B. Priority
Sent At m. To By
This message is on a/c of: Service. (Signature of "Franking Officer.")
Recd. at 3.15 P m. Date 15/10/16 From C.B. By Sig. Richardson

TO E M

Sender's Number.	Day of Month.	In reply to Number.	AAA
BM388	15th		

Following working parties will be detailed by you tonight Y.. 150 under 2 officers to complete communication trench 7 feet deep from 1722 B86 to advanced post at M16 D93 and to connect up with trench running East from that post aaa This communication must be completed tonight and working party must be increased if necessary aaa Engineer Officer will lay tape from Head of trench dug last night to M16 D93 giving general direction in which trench is to be dug but trench must be zigzag

From
Place

"A" Form
MESSAGES AND SIGNALS.
Army Form C. 2121
No. of Message

Prefix Code m. Words Charge
Office of Origin and Service Instructions.
Sent At m. To By
This message is on a/c of: Service. (Signature of "Franking Officer.")
Recd. at m. Date From By

TO

Sender's Number.	Day of Month.	In reply to Number.	AAA

with good long sweeps aaa Sappers will consolidate M16 D93 aaa [illegible] is furnishing a working party to deepen approximately 180 yards of trench in front line from our present right Eastward aaa QY is furnishing a working party to improve communication trenches aaa Unconnected post running out from 0172 C5.0 they will be withdrawn tonight [illegible] Strong garrisons must be left in M16 D93 and in trench running East as at present occupied by us [illegible] acknowledge

From
Place
Time
CB 2.45 pm

The above may be forwarded as now corrected. (Z) Rd 3.30 P
Censor. Signature of Addressor or person authorised to telegraph in his name.
* This line should be erased if not required.

"A" Form
MESSAGES AND SIGNALS.
Army Form C. 2121
No. of Message

Prefix SM Code m. Words 32 Charge
Office of Origin and Service Instructions. CB
Sent At m. To By
This message is on a/c of: Service. (Signature of "Franking Officer.")
Recd. at m. Date From By

TO EM

Sender's Number.	Day of Month.	In reply to Number.	AAA
BM202	15th	RR85	

Reference our 388 QY will detail 1 officer and 50 men to report to officer at Dugout at MILL to assist your working party AAA

From CB
Place
Time [illegible] pm

The above may be forwarded as now corrected. (Z)
Censor. Signature of Addressor or person authorised to telegraph in his name.
* This line should be erased if not required.

39

Operation Order No. C 12
by Lieut. Col. E. J. [illegible] C.M.G.
Commanding E. M. In the Field 17/11/16 APP 2 18

RELIEF. A Coy will relieve B Coy in the STRONG POINT M11 d 9.3. and the Trench running EAST therefrom by 7.30 tonight.

D Coy will relieve "A" Coy in the front line by 6.15 pm tonight, this includes the strong POINT on the WARLENCOURT ROAD

B Coy will take up the line at present held by D Coy in the supports. The two Coy Lewis Guns of A Coy relieving the Lewis Guns of "B" Coy in MOUND 93. O.C. "D" Coy will attach one of his Lewis Guns & team to "A" Coy for this operation to report to O.C. "A" Coy at 6.30 tonight for the relief of the Regtl. Lewis Gun team now in Trench East of MOUND 93 which will return to Headquarters.

Reports to be sent by telephone and confirmed by RUNNER on completion of reliefs (O.C. "A" Coy by RUNNER.

I **WORKING PARTIES** O.C. "C" Coy will detail one Officer & 30 other ranks & O.C. "D" Coy 1 Officer & 50 O.Rs as a working party to complete communication trench across (7) feet deep from M2.?.b 8.6 (the end of WEST Communication

II

Trench) to MOUND 93 Engineer Officer will lay tape from head of trench dug last night, to MOUND 93 to show general direction. Trench must be zig zag with good long sweeps.

SAPPERS will consolidate MOUND 93.

O.C. "A" Coy will use every available man without unduly weakening his garrison in order to cut communication trench from Mound 93 to late enemy trench running EAST. It is vital important that this should be completed tonight.

GENERAL O.C. "C" Coy will evacuate unconnected post running out from his right strong post to M17.c.5.0. but not the strong point itself.

O.C. "A" Coy will ensure taking a good supply of bombs, sandbags, lights, water & rations. Special lights & directions for O.C. "A" Coy delivered herewith.

Working Parties continued H.Q. 5 A I to furnishing a working party to improve communication trenches.

Please acknowledge receipt on envelope.

H. [illegible] Major
Adjt [illegible] Cond. Bn.

E.J.

4.58 pm.

Operation Order No. C. 12
By Lieut. Col. E. J. THACKERAY C.M.G.
Commanding E. M. In the Field 17/11/16

RELIEF. [illegible] M.11 d 9.3 and the [illegible] 7.30 tonight.

[illegible] WARLENCOURT Road.

[illegible] D [illegible]

II **WORKING PARTIES.** [illegible] will detail [illegible] 30 [illegible] 50 [illegible]

30 F

[illegible] communication [illegible] Pound 92. [illegible] Coy [illegible] Pound 92 [illegible] must be zigzag [illegible]

[illegible] Pound 92 [illegible] every available man [illegible]

GENERAL [illegible]

O.C. [illegible] Coy [illegible]

WORKING PARTIES [illegible]

[illegible]

4.40 P.M. H. [illegible] Henning

[illegible] Adjutant
[illegible]

Castle Hill
15.10.16.

O.C.
A. Coy.

In the event of Enemy attacking Pound 92 or adjoining trenches and a Barrage is desired 3 green lights must be sent up. Barrage will then be placed across the Valley in front of your position running East of Road in 17c just far enough to cross Enemy Trench running diagonally through 17c.

A supply of Green lights has been sent up with Operation Orders

H. [illegible] Henning
Major

A. [illegible]
3rd [illegible]

5. P.M.

[illegible]

O.C. [illegible] Coy

[illegible] 15.10.16.

[illegible] D [illegible]

[illegible] Operation Orders [illegible] III [illegible] by D. Coy in [illegible]

[illegible]

H. [illegible] Henning.

[illegible]
[illegible] Adjutant

41

"C" Form (Original).
MESSAGES AND SIGNALS.

Army Form C. 2123.
(In books of 50's in duplicate.)

No. of Message ....

Prefix ...... Code ...... Words ...... £ s. d.	Received	Sent, or sent out	Office Stamp.
Charges to collect	From	At ...... m.	
Service Instructions.	By	To	
		By	

Handed in at ...... Office ...... m. Received ...... m.

TO 2

*Sender's Number	Day of Month	In reply to Number	AAA

trench will move into firing line and their place will then be taken by company of support battalion AAA Remainder of brigade will stand fast and await orders AAA All machine guns with field of fire north of M17 and 18 central will open fire on ground north of that line and east of MARTINPUICH – WARLENCOURT road AAA STOKES GUNS in position to put up barrage in front of our line will do so AAA

FROM

PLACE & TIME

Over

"C" Form (Original).
MESSAGES AND SIGNALS.

Army Form C. 2123.
(In books of 50's in duplicate.)

No. of Message ....

Prefix ...... Code ...... Words ...... £ s. d.	Received	Sent, or sent out	Office Stamp.
Charges to collect	From	At ...... m.	
Service Instructions.	By	To	
		By	

Handed in at ...... Office ...... m. Received ...... m.

TO 3

*Sender's Number	Day of Month	In reply to Number	AAA

Acknowledge AAA Addressed all units

M.G.O.

Return this [illegible]

H A [illegible]
Maj

acknowledged
[illegible]
O/c
Machine Gun Corps

FROM CB

PLACE & TIME 7.15 pm

"C" Form (In books of 50's in duplicate)

MESSAGES AND SIGNALS. No. of Message

Prefix SM Code GDAAJ Words 168

Received From CB By

Sent or sent out At m. To By

Office Stamp APP 219 EM 15/10/16

Charges to collect

Service Instructions.

Handed in at CB Office m. Received 7.40p m.

TO EM 43

*Sender's Number	Day of Month	In reply to Number	AAA
BM 399	15th		

in event of enemy attacking Divisional front Battalion in front line will man the fire trench with all available men less one Company which will remain in support line running S E of MILL approximately M 23 A middle AAA Support battalion will move Company in FLERS SWITCH into communication trench running up to MILL AAA On arrival of that Company in communication trench Company of front line battalion in support

FROM

PLACE & TIME

4 copies

Over

* This line should be erased if not required.

Wt. 432—M437 500,000 Pads. H W V 5 16 Forms C.2123.

E.T. 10.
Oct. 16th 1916.

APP 223

Brigade Major
1st S.A.I. Brigade

The attack and capture of Mound 93 and portion of enemy trench at M.16.d.9.3. by "B" Coy 3rd S.A.I. under Capt. Sprenger on the night of October 14th–15th 1916 I beg to report.

Acting on your order No. B.M. 166 13/10 Lieut Mallett with a party of Regtl. Bombers reconnoitered the Mound 93 on the night of Oct. 13/14th.

This reconnaissance was delayed in starting owing to the urgency of work that had to be carried out in front line.

He proceeded NORTH from our front line trench M.22-b-6-6 along the valley just East of Road to a point about 400 yards NORTH. Then turned EAST and a little SOUTH and came upon Mound 93 about 160 yards EAST of road. He surprised an enemy sniper or sentry and captured his rifle on

on the mound and reconnoitered the mound and surroundings.

He returned as it was getting light at dawn, and reported: The Mound was about 60 feet by 25 by 12 high. contains two large dugouts – a gun emplacement and 2 gun emplacements some enemy gun ammunition but no signs of any British occupation. The enemy trenches were within a few yards and were occupied.

These trenches appear to run N. by S. and there appear to be several trench possibly some enemy, EAST.

C Coy 3rd S.A.I. were to have come & held the point on this night but owing to daylight the attack had to be postponed.

On your order B.M. 257. 14/10/16 B Coy under Capt Sprenger was detailed to carry and hold Mound 93 and as much enemy trench as possible.

Lieut Mallett led the assault with two fighting sections of Regimental and "B" Coy bombers and a Lewis Gun who proceeded as he had done on his reconnaissance, the previous night, starting at 11-55 pm 14th.

Again all the operation was hampered by the urgency of the work at the front line trench.

"B" Coy (was supported by 50 men of "A" Coy 3rd S.A.I.) followed Lieut Mallett with a party of 25 men and a Lewis Gun under Lieut Medlicott who had orders to seize, consolidate and hold Mound 93. Captain Sprenger and Lieut Estill with the balance of the Company and Lieut Harris, Lewis Gun Officer and his detachment and carriers with orders to reinforce the leading parties and consolidate the enemys trenches when captured. Lieut Mallett crept up and rushed the mound which was at once occupied by Lieut Medlicott and his party. Lieut Mallett bombed the enemy out of a trench running NORTH for some 60 yards, but was held up and driven back by a very heavy Machine Gun fire and bombs and motars on the Mound.

Lieut Mallett was at this period severely wounded. Another party at the same time and drove the enemy out of that portion of this trench running SOUTH from the mound which was then held by Lieut Estill & Lt Harris who blocked the trench

44

Copy No. 3

1st S.A.Infantry Brigade

15th October 1916.

App 45

220

OPERATION ORDER 67.

The 1st S.A.I. will relieve the 3rd S.A.I. in the line tomorrow night (16th) after the moon rises. Time of the relief to be arranged between Commanding Officers.

Troops will move by platoons at 200 yards distance.

Completion of relief to be reported to Brigade Headquarters by message "ALBERT"

On relief the 3rd S.A.I. will occupy the line now held by the 1st S.A.I.

Please acknowledge.

[signature]
Major.
Brigade Major.

Issued by orderly as per S.A.Bde distribution list. at 6.30 am 16/X/16.

"A" Form.
MESSAGES AND SIGNALS.

Army Form C.2121
(in pads of 100).
No. of Message

Prefix ... Code ... m.	Words	Charge	This message is on a/c of:	Recd. at ... m.
Office of Origin and Service Instructions.	Sent		... Service.	Date
	At ... m.			From
	To			
	By		(Signature of "Franking Officer.")	By

TO CB Priority 46

Sender's Number.	Day of Month.	In reply to Number.	AAA
* 590	16/10/16		

ork done M 2.2 b. 7.8 joined with
OUND average 5 to 6 feet
OUND joined to enemy's trench
rage 4 to 5 feet
emy trench almost joined PEARSE
ench at ~~[illegible]~~ 23 a 1½. 8½
~~[illegible]~~ This may be
ompleted by some other
eport follow shortly. Mound
nsolidated and two maxims
ounted. Enemy trench consolidated
+ with two Lewis Guns one
wis gun in Mound.

From EM
Place
Time 8.30 [illegible]

[signature] Major
a/adjt

The above may be forwarded as now corrected. (Z)

Censor. ...ddressor or person authorised to telegraph in his name.

* This line sho... ...required.

750,000. W 2186—M509. H. W. & V., Ld. 6/16.

MESSAGES AND SIGNALS

Code .... m. / Origin and Service Instructions	Words	Charge	This message is on a/c of:	Recd. at .... m.
	Sent		Service.	Date
	At .... m.		APP 222	From
	To			
	By		(Signature of "Franking Officer.")	By

To { C.B 47

Sender's Number.	Day of Month.	In reply to Number.	AAA
S 91	16/10/16		

A Coy in Mound and
[e]nemy trench B Coy
[w]ithdrawn to support trenches
[illegible] as parties withdrawn,
[l]ine from THOMAS POST to
[illegible] Brigade re-occupied

To S.O.S sent up on
[t]his sector by [illegible] [illegible]
[re]port and plan of mound
+ trench following shortly
[illegible] my application for aerial
photograph

[signature]
Major
a/ Adjt.

From E.M 9 am E.M
Place
Time

The above may be forwarded as now corrected. (Z)
Censor. Signature of Addressor or person authorised to telegraph in his name.

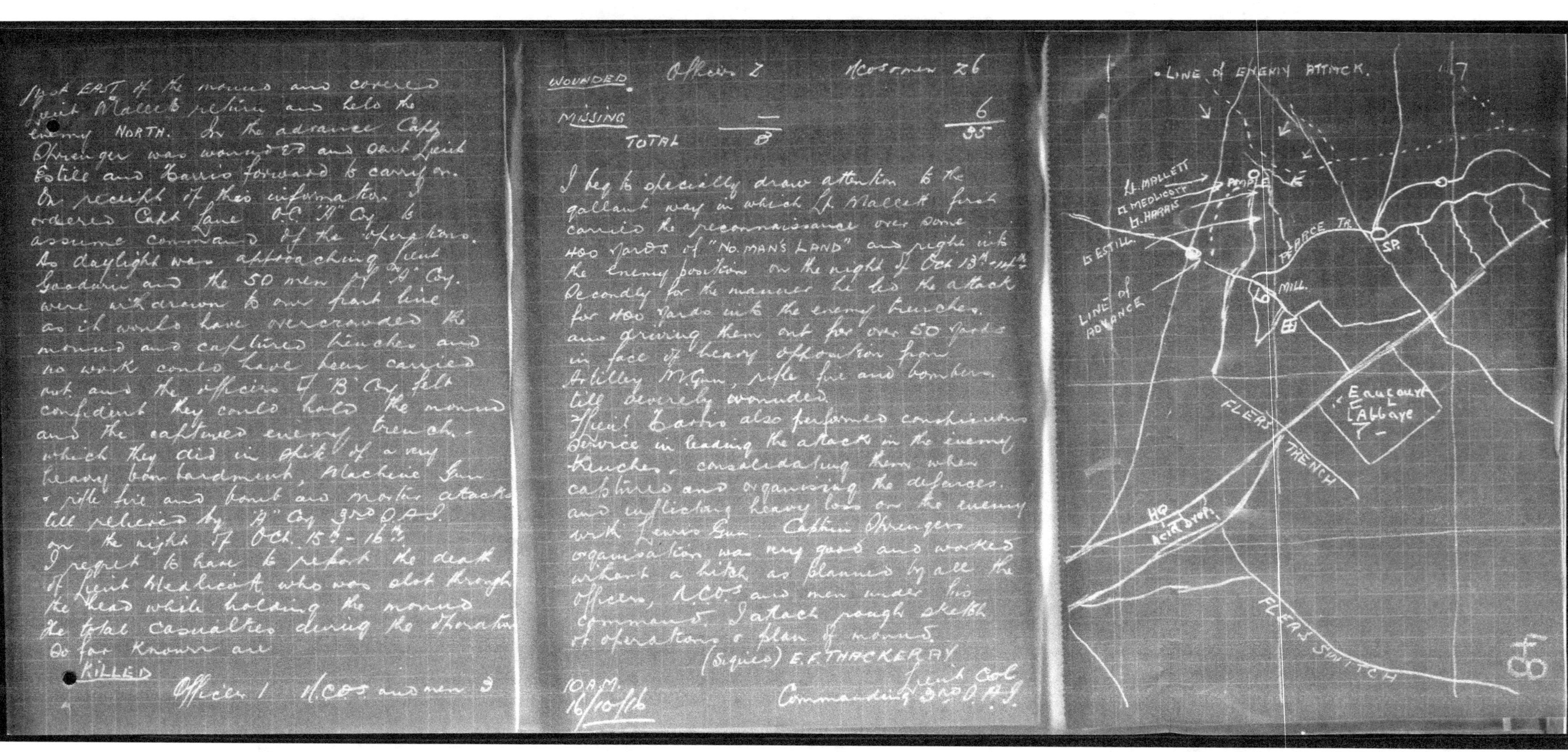

Spot EAST of the mound and covered Lieut Mallett's return and held the enemy NORTH. In the advance Capt Ohrenger was wounded and 2nd Lieut Estill and Harris forward to carry on. On receipt of this information I ordered Capt Lane O.C. "A" Coy to assume command of the operations. As daylight was approaching Lieut Goodwin and the 50 men of "A" Coy. were withdrawn to our front line as it would have overcrowded the mound and captured trenches and no work could have been carried out, and the officers of "B" Coy felt confident they could hold the mound and the captured enemy trench - which they did in spite of a very heavy bombardment, Machine Gun & rifle fire and bomb and mortar attacks till relieved by "A" Coy 3rd O.A.S. on the night of Oct. 15th-16th.

I regret to have to report the death of Lieut Medlicott who was shot through the head while holding the mound. The total casualties during the operation so far known are

	Officers	N.C.O.s and men
KILLED	1	9
WOUNDED	2	26
MISSING	—	6
TOTAL	3	35

I beg to specially draw attention to the gallant way in which Lt. Mallett first carried the reconnaissance over some 400 yards of "NO MAN'S LAND" and right into the enemy position on the night of Oct 13th-14th. Secondly for the manner he led the attack for 400 yards into the enemy trenches and driving them out for over 50 yards in face of heavy opposition from Artillery M.Gun, rifle fire and bombers till severely wounded.

2nd Lieut Harris also performed conspicuous service in leading the attack in the enemy trenches, consolidating them when captured and organising the defences and inflicting heavy loss on the enemy with Lewis Gun. Captain Ohrenger's organisation was very good and worked without a hitch as planned by all the officers, N.C.O.s and men under his command. I attach rough sketch of operations & plan of mound.

(Signed) E.F. THACKERAY
Lieut Col
Commanding 3rd O.A.S.

10 A.M.
16/10/16

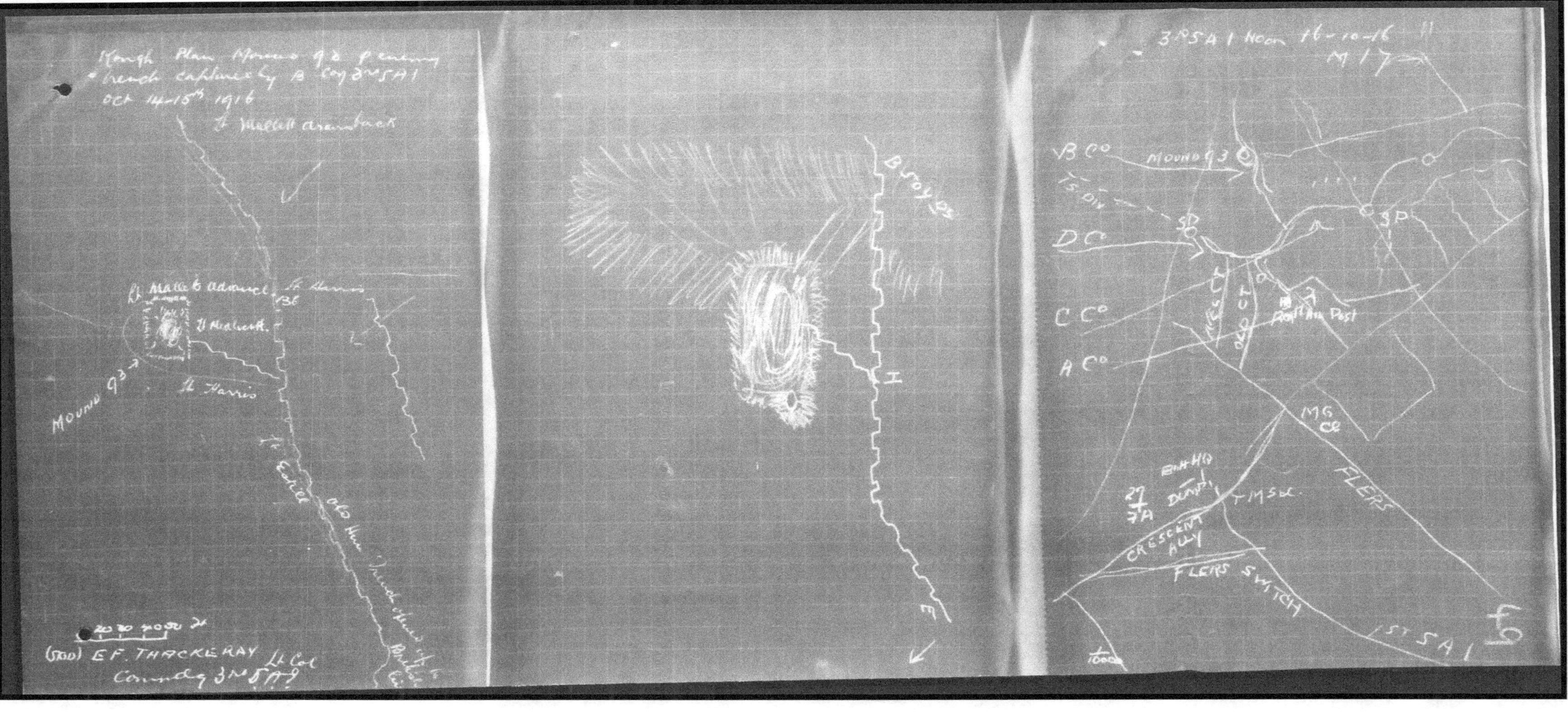
Rough Plan Mound 93 & enemy trench captured by B Coy 3rd SAI
Oct 14–15th 1916
Mound 93
Lt Harris
(Sgd) E.F. THACKERAY Lt Col
Commdg 3rd SAI
B
H
E
3rd SAI Noon 16-10-16
M 17
B Co
Mound 93
D Co
C Co
A Co
SP
MG Co
FLERS
Bn HQ
Dump
27
7A
TMSC
CRESCENT ALLY
FLERS SWITCH
1st SAI
49

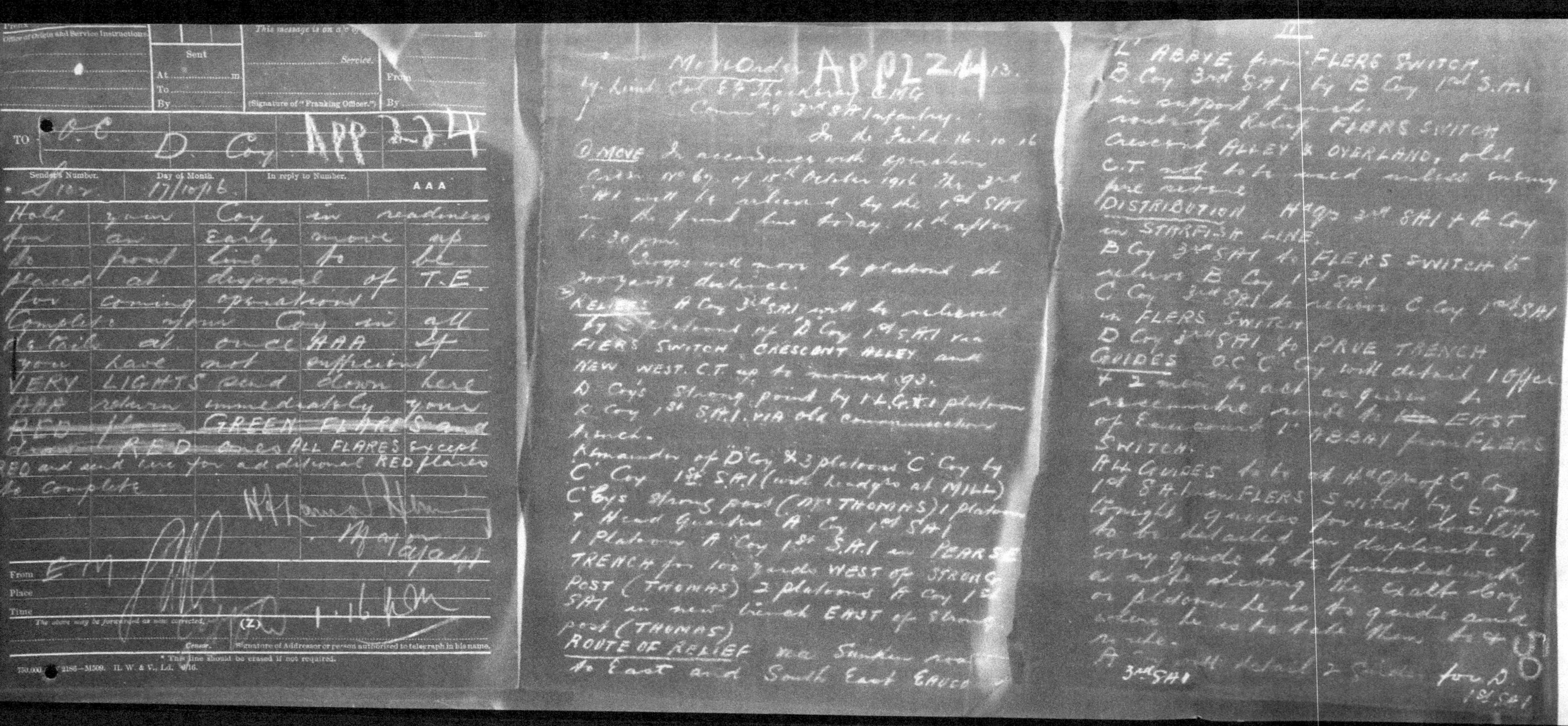

Office of Origin and Service Instructions | Sent At ... m. To ... By ... | This message is on a/c of: ... Service. (Signature of "Franking Officer.") | From ... By ...

TO O.C. D. Coy APP 224

Sender's Number.	Day of Month.	In reply to Number.	AAA
S107.	17/10/16.		

Hold your Coy in readiness for an Early move up to front line to be placed at disposal of T.E. for coming operations. Complete your Coy in all details at once AAA If you have not sufficient VERY LIGHTS send down here AAA return immediately your ~~RED flares~~ GREEN FLARES and ~~[illegible]~~ RED ones ALL FLARES except RED and send [illegible] for additional RED flares to complete.

[signature] Major [illegible] Adjt

From E.M.
Place
Time 1.16 [illegible]

The above may be forwarded as now corrected. (Z) Censor. Signature of Addressor or person authorised to telegraph in his name.
* This line should be erased if not required.
750,000. W 2186—M509. H. W. & V., Ld. 9/16.

Move Orders APP 224 13.
by Lieut. Col. E.F. Thackeray C.M.G.
Comm^dg 3rd S.A. Infantry.
In the Field 16.10.16

1) MOVE In accordance with Operation Order No 69 of 15th October 1916 the 3rd S.A.I. will be relieved by the 1st S.A.I. in the front line today 16th after 6.30 pm.
Troops will move by platoons at 200 yards distance.

2) RELIEF: A Coy 3rd S.A.I. will be relieved by [illegible] platoons of "D" Coy 1st S.A.I. via FLERS SWITCH, CRESCENT ALLEY and NEW WEST C.T. up to ~~[illegible]~~ 93.
D Coy's Strong point by 1 L.G. & 1 platoon K Coy 1st S.A.I. via old communication trench.
Remainder of "D" Coy & 3 platoons "C" Coy by "C" Coy 1st S.A.I. (with headq^rs at MILL)
C Coy's strong post (at THOMAS) 1 platoon & Head Quarters "A" Coy 1st S.A.I.
1 Platoon "A" Coy 1st S.A.I. in PEARSE TRENCH for 100 yards WEST of STRONG POST (THOMAS) 2 platoons A Coy 1st S.A.I. in new trench EAST of strong post (THOMAS)
ROUTE OF RELIEF via Sunken road to East and South East EAUCOURT

II

L'ABBAYE from FLERS SWITCH.
B Coy 3rd S.A.I. by B Coy 1st S.A.I. in support trench.
Route of Relief FLERS SWITCH Crescent ALLEY & OVERLAND, old C.T. not to be used unless enemy fire necessitate.
DISTRIBUTION H^d Q^rs 3rd S.A.I. & A Coy in STARFISH LINE.
B Coy 3rd S.A.I. to FLERS SWITCH to relieve B Coy 1st S.A.I.
C Coy 3rd S.A.I. to relieve C Coy 1st S.A.I. in FLERS SWITCH
D Coy 3rd S.A.I. to PRUE TRENCH
GUIDES O.C. "C" Coy will detail 1 Officer & 2 men to act as guides to reconnoitre route to ~~[illegible]~~ EAST of Eaucourt L'ABBAYE from FLERS SWITCH.
All Guides to be at H^d Q^rs of C Coy 1st S.A.I. in FLERS SWITCH by 6 pm tonight. Guides for each locality to be detailed in duplicate. Every guide to be furnished with a note showing the exact Coy or platoon he is to guide and where he is to take them to & [illegible].
A [illegible] will detail 2 Guides for D. 1st S.A.I.
3rd S.A.I.

8

H.Q., 1st South African Infantry Brigade.
17th October 1916.

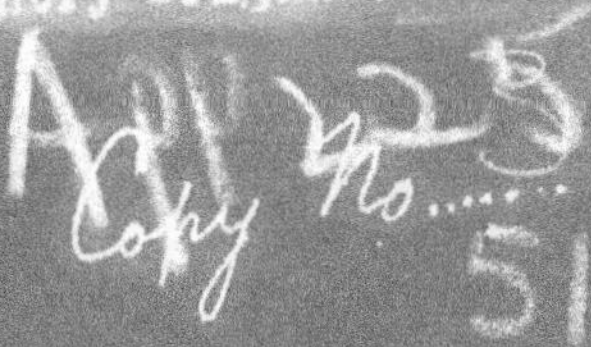

SECRET. URGENT.
Map Reference.
Sketch Map attached.

OPERATION ORDER NO 68.

The 9th Division will attack the enemy's position in M.17.C and D on 18th October 1916.

The hour of ZERO will be notified later.

The 1st S.A.I.Brigade will be on the left of the Divisional front with the 26th Brigade on the right.

The 46th Infantry Brigade is holding the line on the left of the 9th Division.

BRIGADE BOUNDARY. The boundary between the 26th Infantry Brigade and the 1st S.A.I.Brigade is a North and South line through M.17.C.9.9. at which point there is a single tree which forms a directing mark as shown on sketch map attached.

OBJECTIVE. The Brigade;s objective will be the enemy's trenches in M.17.C.

ASSAULTING TROOPS AND FORMATION OF ATTACK. The assault will be carried out by the 1st S.A.I. with three companies in line, each on a platoon frontage with the fourth company in support and one company of the 3rd S.A.I. in reserve

ASSEMBLY. The 1st S.A.I. will be assembled in the front trenches 20 minutes before ZERO. The company of the 3rd S.A.I. in reserve will be assembled in the support trench 20 minutes before ZERO.

CARRIERS. There will be one platoon of carriers to each company. Carrying platoons will be assembled 20 minutes before ZERO in the communication trench running up to point M.16.D.9.3. They will advance and join their companies as soon as the objective has been gained.

BARRAGE. The attack will be preceded by an artillery barrage on the enemy's line from ZERO to ZERO plus one minute. The barrage will be intensified by a Stokes mortar barrage which will be maintained on the enemy's trench till ZERO plus 2 minutes.

A smoke barrage will be arranged so as to blind the BUTTE de WARLENCOURT and the valley between the BUTTE and Le SARS north of the line joining M.17.central and M.16.central.

THE ATTACK. The assaulting troops will be formed up in NO MAN'S LAND in three waves by ZERO. When the barrage opens the leading wave will creep up as close as possible under it, assaulting the enemy's line as soon as the barrage lifts.

A special party will be detailed to fight up the SWITCH TRENCH on the left of the Brigade's objective, and to clear it of the enemy as far as approximately M.17.C.1.8., where it will be blocked and held.

STRONG POINTS AND CONSOLIDATION. On gaining the objective a strong point will be established at trench junction M.17.C.4.4. The enemy's line will be consolidated immediately it is captured, covering patrols being pushed forward at once.

Recd 6.15 AM

"C" Form (Duplicate). Army Form C. 2123.
(In books of 50's in duplicate.)

MESSAGES AND SIGNALS. No. of Message ....

58 FEBRN 52 | Charges to Pay. £ s. d. | Office Stamp. EM 15/10/16

Service Instructions. PRIORITY CB

Handed in at CB Office 6.22a m. Received 6.22a m.

TO EM

Sender's Number	Day of Month	In reply to Number	AAA
BM 350	15TH		

Forward explanation as to why orders received by you yesterday afternoon before 4pm regarding [illegible] of [illegible] 93 [illegible] as soon as [illegible] after dark [illegible] not carried out till 4.15pm aaa Explanation to be sent [illegible] by [illegible] to reach here by 8 am

FROM CB

PLACE & TIME

"C" Form (Original). Army Form C. 2123.
(In books of 50's in duplicate.)

MESSAGES AND SIGNALS. No. of Message 576

Prefix ...... Code ...... Words ...... £ s. d. | Received From ...... By ...... | Sent, or sent out At ...... m. To ...... By ...... | Office Stamp.

Charges to collect

Service Instructions.

Handed in at ...... Office ...... m. Received ...... m.

TO EM

Sender's Number	Day of Month	In reply to Number	AAA

Reference your BMO 20 beg to point out following points for information G.O.C. 13 Bty [illegible] in enemy's trench at Mound 93 eastwards [illegible] in no man's land [illegible] towards front Reserve Trench [illegible] regiments in front [illegible] our sector all men considerably exhausted owing continuous movement and want of sleep heavy work and exposure continuous [illegible] lack of any warm comfort food and shortage of water since 8.30 am 15th inst

FROM

PLACE & TIME

52

To O.C. 3rd S.A.I. — Secret — B.M. 20

APP 21-A

The G.O.C. wishes you to make your arrangements to carry out the assault on the enemy's trench which was the 1st objective at the last attack — portion shown on attached sketch.

It is possible this assault may have to be made in the early hours of the 16th inst.

As the assault will be made in the dark and as our trenches are now considerably nearer the objective the G.O.C. considers that your Battalion — approximately 350 strong — should be sufficient to carry and hold the objective.

He therefore proposes to carry it out with your Bn; holding the 1st S.A.I. in reserve in the trenches.

If you wish to discuss matters with the G.O.C. please ring up and the G.O.C. will fix a time and place to meet you. Please ack.

[signature] Major
B.M. 4th Inf Bde

14. 10. 16
8 pm

Recd 9.30 PM
[initials]

53

strong point on the WARLANCOURT ROAD.
O.C. 'C' Company will take over the whole of "PEARSE" Trench to the right of our line.
O.C. D. Company will extend to his left and join up with A Coy at the head of the Western communication trench & will hold his Coy in readiness to repel a counter attack on our front line.
<u>REPORTS.</u> O.Cs A.B.C.D Companies will meet at the MILL before commencement of operations, when O.C. D Company will report to Headquarters by 'phone when all ~~[illegible]~~ are ready. O.C. 'A' Coy will then take up his Headquarters at the head of the Western Communication trench. O.C. B Coy will proceed with his Company to carry out the assault and will report to Headquarters every ½ hour. Further orderly & Runners from Headquarters & each from C. D Companies will be attached to B. Coy.
<u>GENERAL</u> O.C. B. Coy will take steps to ensure ~~[illegible]~~ sufficient bombs, Very lights, flares and ammunition & [illegible] for his assaulting party. In the event of it proving impossible to capture any portion of the enemy's main trench and there not being time to complete the trench between the enemy's strong point and M.17.c.[illegible].0

O.C. C. Company will ensure that the working party & his covering party will construct a series of strong points along the side of the trench under supervision of the R.E. Officer attached to the company, which he will garrison there until an suitable opportunity occurs to complete the construction of the trench. He will get 1 Lewis Gun out in an suitable place in each of these strong points & see that all of them are supplied with WATER, RATIONS & BOMBS.
<u>FLARES</u> Attention is called to the necessity for showing flares to contact aeroplanes when necessary by all units holding front line positions.

[illegible signature]

10.25 PM.

55

Confidential

Staff Captain
S.A. Brigade

War Diary

War Diary for Regiment under my command forwarded herewith with necessary appendices attached

B L Young Major
for Lt Col
Commdg 3rd S.A.I.

In the Field
7/1/16.

COPY OF PRIORITY TELEGRAM TO 3RD S.A.INFANTRY FROM S.A.BRIGADE.

B.M. 357. 14.10.16.

Division order following to be done tonight AAA M.16.d.9.3. is to be occupied this evening after dark and joined up with our line at M.17.c.5.0. and with road at approximately road junction M.16.d.7.4. where Battalion on your left will join up AAA Communication trench will be dug from M.22.b.7.7. to new line as above AAA R.E. section will improve trenches in right of our section AAA Pionneers will dig communication trench as above AAA Working party of 200 of which you will furnish 50 and T.E. 150 will dig new front trench as above AAA Arrange for your 50 under an officer to dig portion to ~~eastxxx~~ west of M.16.d.9.3. and for T.Es party which will be under two officers to dig portion to east AAA Party to capture and occupy M.16.d.9.3. should proceed as soon as it is dark together with covering party for working party AAA R.E. officer will arrange for tape to mark off line AAA T.E.s party will report at your H.Q. at 6 pm. AAA Q.V. is furnishing working party of 150 to deepen and improve the communication trenches up to present front line AAA Acknowledge.

(sd) J.Mitchell Baker, Major.

Brigade Major.

2.45 pm.

trench/

between the enemy's STRONG POINT and M.17.c.5.0..
O.C. "C" Company will ensure that the working party and his covering party will construct a series of strong posts along the site of the trench under supervision of the R.E.officer, attached for the purpose, which he will garrison and hold until a suitable opportunity occurs to complete the constructionx of the trench.
He will put one Lewis gun at a suitable place in one of these STRONG POINTs and will see that all of them are supplied with water, rations and BOMBS.
FLARES. Attention is called to the necessity of exposing flares to "Contact aeroplanes" when necessary, by all units holding front line positions.
Please acknowledge.

(sd) H.S.L.aman HEMMING,Major.
Acting Adjutant
E.M. (3rd S.A.I.)

10.25 pm.

57

No.11.

OPERATION ORDER
by Lt. Colonel E.F.Thackeray, C.M.G.
Commanding 3rd S.A.Infantry.

In the Field 14/10/16.

In accordance with B.M. telegraphic instructions No.257 of 14th instant, the 9th Division orders this regiment to take andconsolidate the "strong point" at M.16.d.9.3. and dig a trench between it and the right of this regiment at M.17.c.5.0 and with road junction at M.17.d.7.4. and also cut communication trench between the left sector held by B Coy and the STRONG POINT to be captured.

ASSAULT. The assault will be carried out by B Coy.
The O.C. BCoy will detail Lieut. MALLETT and the Regimental bombers and the Regimental Lewis Guns and four carriers to take the STRONG POINT.
Lieut. MALLETT will have a second party under him of Corporal HUGHES and B CoyBombers, and a fighting section of ten other ranks.
Lieut. MALLETT will seize the STRONG POINT and endeavour to push up the enemy's trench which runs towards the North East. He will detail Corporal HUGHES and his party to bomb up and capture that part of the enemy's trench, which runs N.NW from the STRONG POINT.
Lieut. MEDLICOTT with the Coy Lewis Gunners and twenty other ranks, will move in support of Lt. MALLETT's party, and when the STRONG POINT has been captured will immediately consolidate it.
Lieut. ESTILL with his machine gun and garrison of the STRONG POINT at the left of B Coy's line will be relieved by a light party detailed by O.C. "A" Company and will be at the disposal O.C. "B" Coy.

WORKING PARTIES. O.C., "A" Company will detail Lieut. GOODWIN and 50 other ranks with Lewis Gun to cut a trench between the enemy's STRONG POINT when captured and the road junction at M.16.d.7.4.
The following working parties are detailed by Brigade Headquarters 150 men from the 1st S.A.I. to cut a trench between the Enemy's STRONG POINT at M.16.d.9.3. and the right of our line at M.17.c.5.0.
(O.C. "C" Coy will detail a covering party for this working party) also a working party of 150 men from the 4th S.A.I. to deepen and improve a communication trench to the present front line; also a company of pioneers to dig a communication trench fromM.22.b.7.7. to the enemy's STRONG POINT when captured.

RELIEFS. O.C., "A" Coy will take over the sector at present held by "B" Coy from the head of the Western communication trench to the STRONG POINT on the WARLENCOURT ROAD.
O.C., "C" Company will take over the whole of PEARSE trench to the right of our line
O.C. "D" Company will extend to his left and join up with "A" Coy at the head of the Western communication trench and will hold his company in readiness to repel a counter-attack, or support the FRONT LINE

REPORTS. O.sC. A.B.C. and D companies will meet at the MILL before commencement of operations, when O.C. " B" will report to Headquarters by phone when all is ready. O.C. "A" Coy will then take up his Headquarters at the head of theWestern communication trench. O.C."B" company will proceed with his company to carry out the assault, and will report to Headquarters every half-hour. For this purpose eight runners from Headquarters and two each from C and D companies will be attached to B company.

GENERAL. O.C., "B" Coy will take steps to issue sufficient bombs, sandbags, VERY light Flares and ammunition and tools for his assaulting party. In the event of it proving impossible to capture any portion of the enemy's/main trench and there not being time to complete the trench

E.T. 6. Octr.15.1916. 59

Brigade Major

Re your order B.M. 257 14/10/16. and the operation carried out in accordance with them, I beg to report

Thisorder was delivered to me while General Lukin was giving me instructions at 3.30 pm 14/10/16 and was read over to me by him I then at once sent for Company Commanders to meet me at 4.30 pm, but owing to heavy shelling two were delayed and did not reach me till 5 pm.

I at once issued verbal orders and went through the whole plan in detail - and confirmed these orders in writing - copy attached marked "A".

I instructed Company Commanders to see into all details and to form up all ready to move andto phone me when all details were complete. The R.E. officer arrived while they were with me and all the various working parties and tasks were explained. An officer of the 1st S.A.I. also arrived and met Captain Lain who conducted him up to the front where he hadto work. This meeting of Coy Commanders took till 7 pm including a conference of C.Cs after I had issued orders.

Captain Sprenger reported all ready to move at 11.50 and moved off at once with B company followed by a working party of 50 men of A coy under Lieutenant Goodwin. Company Commanders A.C.D reported all quiet at 12.5 am. Lieut. Harris reported arrival at point about 16.d.7.4 at 1.35 am and that Lieut. Mallett had pushed east towards the mound 9.3.

Captain Sprenger rang up at 1.30 am reporting that he was wounded and I ordered Captain Lain to take Command of the operation .

Lt. Harris reported at 1.45 am that he was moving last and that Lieut Goodwin and working party had joined up in rear. At 2.55 pm Captain Montgomery reported that neither he nor Captain Lain were yet in communication with anyone.

From 3.15 am to 3.20 a very heavy barrage was put up on our front line.

At 3. 40 Captain Lain reported that Lieut. Goodwin was digging in towards road.

At 4.10 am Lieut. Harris' message of 2.15 am reached me that objective not yet reached - The bearer had been wounded.

At 5 am received report from Lt Harris dated 4.20 am that objective was held by Lt. Medlicott, 25 N.C.Os and men and 1 Lewis Gun, and that Lt. Mallett and 20 men hold extreme ~~xxxxxx~~ eastern end of enemy trench.

Lt Estill and Harris situated in another part of trench (with approximately 20 men). They were very heavily bombed in taking trench. and Lt. Mallett was wounded severely. At 5.20 am Captain Lain reported Lt. Goodwin and party had returned.

Lt. Goodwin reported to me on phone that they had not been able to dig much owing to hurry and close fire and that after consultation with officers left in B.Coy who were of opinion that they could hold on till tonight he brought his party back at dawn, as to remain would have greatly congested trenches as they were.

Captain LANE reported 5.20 that Lts. Harris, Estill with remainder of B Coy holding trench to east of mound 9.3. and was instructed to send over to them 12 men as a re-inforcement with picks and bombs. I reported the situation to the BM. at 5.40 am. and at that time Lt. Cruddas covering party was reported dug-in along the front of PIERCE trench in small parties along a front of 80 yards.

I ordered A company to occupy left front of line and C Coy to hold PIERCE trench and D coy in support.

I attach a map shewing position at present as far as is known and in reply to your B.M. 380 timed 6.35 am., am sending this report

P.T.O.

The only reason I can give for the time taking in reaching the objective is, that it takes a very considerable time to organize a whole battalion for such an operation and it took a long time to carry the move out through the trenches under fire and hampered as they were by numerous wounded and working parties and also the necessity of great care in moving forward to the attack in the open in face of heavy artillery, Machine Gun and rifle fire.

Further the regiment is considerably exhausted by continuous movement, want of sleep, hard work, lack of cooked warm food, and under a continued heavy bombardment since 8 am 12th instant, which unfits them for further attack and sustained effort required to hold on and consolidate. And as B Coy and a large proportion of C Coy are isolated, they would not be available for forward movement and attack, and recommend that fresh troops may carry out any such operations.

Wired No. S. S.7.5 at 7.30 am 15/10/16.
Wired No. S.75 at 7 am in reply to BM. 15/10/16.

(sd) E.F.Thackeray Lt.Col.
Cmmdg.3rd S.A.I.

7.40 am. 15/10/16.

S A Bde.

Confidential

61

The G.O.C. agrees with you that it should have been possible, while it was certainly desirable, to carry out this minor operation at an earlier hour.

It is most important that ~~the~~ the C.O. should explain his plan clearly to his subordinates and that they should be given time to do likewise, but there appears to the G.O.C. to be no adequate reason for these preliminaries taking so long a time as 8 hours. Half that time should have sufficed.

The G.O.C. is further of opinion that the language used by the O.C. 3rd S.A.I. in the last para of his minute of 15/10 is exaggerated. He is well aware of the calls he has to make on the courage and endurance of all ranks, but it is for this very reason that he looks to Commanding officers to prevent their officers and men thinking for a moment ~~that~~ they are being asked to do anything more than their due share. If, indeed, this seems to the C.O. to be the case, he should make his men realize ~~that~~ this in itself is an honour to the regiment.

The G.O.C. knows well ~~that~~ it was in this fine spirit ~~that~~ Lt Col. Thackeray kept his men together during the 18th – 19th July in Delville Wood.

63

Confidential

R.M. 11/10

9th Division

Attached please find (1) Copy of my orders in connection with an operation to be carried out by the 3rd S.A. Infty on the night of the 14th-15th inst.

(2) Report of the O.C. 3rd S.A. Infty.

I have informed the O.C. 3rd S.A.I. that I consider there was unnecessary delay in carrying out the orders referred to.

My object in issuing instructions that the M.15. Sap was to be captured and occupied as soon as it was dark was in order that the necessary work on the communication trench could be completed during the night.

Orders were received at 3rd S.A.I. Hd Qrs at 3-30 pm. Troops moved to the attack at 11-50 pm.

In the field
15/10/16

H. T. Lukin B.G.
1st S.A.I. Bde

CONFIDENTIAL.

64

1st S.African Brigade.

No. X.5/1893. 17th October, 1916.

Reference 1st S African Bde No. B.M. 11/10 of 15/10/16

The G.O.C. agrees with you that it should have been possible, while it was certainly desirable, to carry out this minor operation at an earlier hour.

It is most important that the C.O. should explain his plan clearly to his subordinates and that they should be given time to do likewise, but there appears to the G.O.C. to be no adequate reason for these preliminaries taking so long a time as 8 hours. Half that time should have sufficed.

The G.O.C. is further of opinion that the language used by the O.C. 3rd S.African Infantry in the last para of his minute dated 15/10 is exaggerated. He is well aware of the calls he has to make on the courage and endurance of all ranks, but it is for this very reason that he looks to Commanding Officers to prevent their officers and men thinking for a moment that they are being asked to do anything more than their due share. If, indeed, this seems to the C.O. to be the case, he should make his men realize that this in itself is an honour to the regiment.

The G.O.C. knows well that it was in this fine spirit that Lieut.Col. Thackeray kept his men together during the 18th and 19th July in DELVILLE WOOD.

R Stewart
Lieutenant Colonel,
General Staff,
9th (Scottish) Division.

APP 289

MOVE ORDER. ORDER NO. 17

By Lieut.Col E.F.THACKERAY.C.M.G.
Commanding 3rd S.A.Infantry
(Transvaal Regiment)

IN THE FIELD.
29/10/1916.

---

1. MOVE. In accordance with Brigade Operation Order Number 74, received 11.p.m. last night, the Regiment will parade in full marching order at 7.30.a.m.and enbus at 8.a.m.at a point midway on the road between HERISSART and PUCHEVILLERS, to proceed to WANQUENTIN

2. ORDER OF MARCH. The order of moving off will be as follows :-
Headquarters,B,A,C,D.
Headquarters,B and A Companies will parade in the road running past the Quartermasters Store with head of column in road running past Headquarters.
C and D Companies will parade in that order in front of Headquarters ready to follow on as the column passes.

3. BAGGAGE. Blankets and cooking utensils will be carried on the motor lorries. All officers kits and Company baggage to be uploaded on the Regimental Transport in the Transport Lines by 5.45.a.m.tomorrow the 29th inst.
Blankets to be uploaded on the lorry.
Great coats and rations to be carried on the person,also Lewis Guns and 16 magazines per gun.

4. TRANSPORT. Cookers will proceed with the Regimental Transport at 8.a.m.Dixies will be carried in the busses.
It is improbable that we shall join the Regimental Transport again until the afternoon of the 30th,so arrangements must be made accordingly.

5. GENERAL. Company Commanders will make allarrangements to have an early breakfast.
I hear unofficially that the Regiment will move about 9.a.m. by busses to the new area at WANQUENTIN.
No.man is to wear a great coat on the march.

Issued
7.30am
H.

H. Harman Fleming
MAJOR.
Acting Adjutant.
3rd Regiment S.A.Infantry.
(Transvaal Regiment)

O/O. No. 74. contd.

TRANSPORT.

11 pm

66

9th SEAFORTHS (PIONEERS).
107th Coy. ASC.
1st S. A. Infantry.
2nd S. A. Infantry.
3rd S. A. Infantry.
4th S. A. Infantry.
BRIGADE HEADQUARTERS.
28th MACHINE GUN COY. (with T/Mortar hand-carts)
64th FIELD COY. R.E.
S.A. FIELD AMBULANCE.

Starting point for transport will be the CROSS ROADS at N. W. edge of RUBEMPRE on the RUBEMPRE-LE-VAL-DE-MAISON ROAD.

The 9th Seaforths transport to pass starting point at 6.30 am; transport of other units to follow in order stated above in close succession - All transport to be clear of starting point by 7.30 am.

The transport of the 9th Seaforths will join the 27th Infantry Brigade group at NEUVILETTE.

7. SICK. Units will arrange for men unable to march to the enbussing point being conveyed there by motor lorry either prior to Supplies (or blankets) being conveyed there or at the same time if there is sufficient room. At WANQUETIN the S.A.F. Ambulance will take over and dispose of men who are unable to march who belong to Units proceeding beyond that place.

8. BILLETS. Units will be billetted in the new area as under - subject to any change which may be found to be necessary after Billets are examined :-

1st S.A. Infantry	DUISANS.
2nd S.A. Infantry	AGNES LES DUISANS.
3rd S.A. Infantry	WANQUETIN.
4th S.A. Infantry	ARRAS.
64th Field Coy. R.E.	ARRAS.
28th Machine Gun Coy.	WANQUETIN.
S.A. L.T.M. Battery.	WANQUETIN.
S.A. Field Ambulance.	WANQUETIN.

9. Each O/C. Unit will detail an Officer to report to the Brigade Major at 8 am. at the road junction where the head of the Column of buses will rest.

The O/C. S.A. Field Ambulance will send his Interpreter to report to the Brigade Major at the same time and place.

10. BRIGADE HEADQUARTERS. Brigade H.Qrs. will be at LATTRE St. QUENTIN.

11. REPORTING UNITS IN BILLETS. O.s.C. Units will report to Brigade Headquarters arrival of their Units in billets.

J Mitchell Baker
Major.
Brigade Major.
1st S.A. Infantry Brigade.

Issued by orderly at 7.15 pm.
as per S.A. BRIGADE distribution list.

1st SOUTH AFRICAN INFANTRY BRIGADE.

28th OCTOBER 1916.

SECRET AND URGENT
Map Reference.
LENS 1/100,000.

COPY No...3....

67

APPx 238

OPERATION ORDER NO. 74.

1. MOVE The 1st S.A.I.Brigade, 64th Field Co. R.E. and S.A.Field Ambulance will move tomorrow by road and bus to the WANQUENTIN area.
The 9th Seaforth (Pioneers) will move to the FLERS area under orders issued to them by 9th Division.

2. BUSES. Head of Column of buses will rest facing North at the right angle road junction 1 mile NORTH WEST of HERISSART.
Units will form up in the following order on the right of the RUBEMPRE - PUCHEVILLERS ROAD, clear of the road, in mass or other close formation suitable to the ground - the 4th S.A.Infantry with its head at the right angle road junction above mentioned. The 64th FIELD Coy.R.E. just to the NORTH of the road junction.

64th Field Coy. R.E.
4th S. A. Infantry.
3rd S. A. Infantry.
2nd S. A. Infantry.
1st S. A. Infantry.
Brigade Headquarters.
28th Coy.Machine Gun Corps.
S.A.L.T.M.Battery.
S.A.Field Ambulance.

} 400 yards distance between the heads of Battalions and between the head of the rear battalion and Brigade H.Qrs. - Between the heads of Units other than battalions 200 yards.

3. MACHINE & LEWIS GUNS - Lewis guns and 16 drums per gun will be taken in the buses with the men, the carts travelling as light as possible.
Vickers guns will travel in their limbers. A proportion of the personnel will accompany Vickers gun limbers and Lewis gun carts.

4. SUPPLIES. Supplies for Consumption on October 30th (less forage and rations for the Transport personnel) will be drawn tonight and will be carried in the same buses as the men - the supplies being distributed over several buses.
These supplies will be conveyed to the buses by the Motor Lorries placed at the disposal of Units. Motor lorries after delivering the supplies at the road side will return to carry the blankets etc., of units and thereafter proceed to unit destination.
Lorries conveying supplies as above must be clear of the RUBEMPRE - PUCHEVILLERS road by 8 am.
If supplies are not delivered tonight blankets instead of supplies will be carried on the buses and supplies and cooking utensils will then be carried on the motor lorries. The arrangements for conveying blankets to the buses will be the same as those setforth above for conveying supplies there.
SUPPLY RAILHEAD on October 29th will be at FREVENT.

5. TRANSPORT BILLETTING PARTY. Each O/C.Unit except 9th SEAFORTHS will detail a billetting representative (mounted on a horse or bicycle) to report to the O/C.107th Coy.A.S.C.at the starting point at 6.15 am tomorrow. These billetting representatives are for the transport and are quite apart from the billetting representatives proceeding to the WANQUENTIN area tonight.

6. TRANSPORT. All Vehicles and animals of the above units will proceed by road tomorrow to DOULLENS and will march under orders of the O/C. 9th DIVISIONAL TRAIN.
Transport will move in the following order :-

Instructions regarding War Diaries and Intelligence Summaries are contained in F. S. Regs., Part II. and the Staff Manual respectively. Title Pages will be prepared in manuscript.

WAR DIARY or INTELLIGENCE SUMMARY

(Erase heading not required.)

Army Form C. 2118

3rd S.A.

41

Place	Date 1916	Hour	Summary of Events and Information	Remarks and references to Appendices
GRAND RULLECOURT	1 Oct		In accordance IX Division No X5/1826 dd 21/9/16, the Regiment went into training. Good training grounds were found at the Brigade Training Area near the CHATEAU at the Headquarters of the Regiment. Weather in the forenoon good, in the afternooon raining hampered training.	App 186
"	2 "		Training at Brigade Area. Company Commanders taken on Staff Ride by O.C. In accordance with Div. Orders all Gas Helmets handed in for redipping.	
"	3 "		Weather rainy. Training under Company arrangements. Authority received from G.O.C. 1st. S.A.I. BRIGADE to promote 11 other ranks to Commissioned Ranks to make up vacancies caused by casualties.	
"	4 "	12.15 pm.	Weather very rainy. Training under Company arrangements, but much hampered by wind & rain. Operation Order No. 61 1st. S.A.I. BGDE received at 12.15 pm. with instructions for Regiment to proceed to BONNIERES tomorrow, thus cutting short all training. During the recent fighting in Delville Wood & the vicinity the Regiment was almost completely destroyed, losing 33 officers & nearly 900 other ranks. These casualties have since been made good by Drafts of Officers & other ranks from the DEPOT at BORDON. Owing to duty in the trenches, constant demands for large working parties & about 20% of the Regiment being attached for work with Tunnelling Companies, Engineers & for other Regimental Duties, Officers have not had the opportunity of having their Companies under their own hands, nor have the men had the opportunity of making themselves acquainted with their officers. Regimental Move Order No. C. 8 issued at 4.30 pm	" 187 " 188

1875 Wt. W593/826 1,000,000 4/15 J.B.C. & A. A.D.S.S./Forms/C. 2118.

Army Form C. 2118

WAR DIARY
or
INTELLIGENCE SUMMARY
(Erase heading not required.)

Instructions regarding War Diaries and Intelligence Summaries are contained in F. S. Regs., Part II. and the Staff Manual respectively. Title Pages will be prepared in manuscript.

42.

Place	Date	Hour	Summary of Events and Information	Remarks and references to Appendices
BONNIERES	5 OCT		The Regiment marched out of GRAND RULLECOURT at 9.30 a.m. Strength 28 officers & 757 other ranks & proceeded by road to BONNIERES, taking over Billets by 2 p.m. No men fell out on the line of march. Distance about 12 miles. Owing to heavy rains during the night roads in bad condition for marching. In accordance with permission given by G.O.C. 1st. S.A.I. BRIGADE the Regiment hired 5 waggons from the local inhabitants for the conveyance of the men's overcoats, haversacks, surplus ammunition, etc, in order that the men may arrive in the firing line as lightly fatigued as possible. This was done out of Regimental Funds, the average cost of each waggon being 30 francs a day. In accordance with Regimental Orders men were marched carrying contents of haversacks in the packs. During the march the G.O.C. 9th DIVISION inspected the Regiment & complimented the O.C. on their fine appearance.	
			Regiment was issued with coloured shoulder patches to be sewn on beneath shoulder straps on outside of arm. Red for "A" Coy, Yellow for "B", Blue for "C" & Green for "D" no distinguishing marks for Headquarters. This is in accordance with scheme of Company Colours adopted throughout 9th Division for purposes of speedy recognisition in Battle.	
BONNIERES.	6 Oct.		Weather fine. 8.45 p.m. Operation Order No 63 relating to Regiment to proceed by Motor Busses and march route from BONNIERES to LA HAUSSOYE passing the starting point at 7-20 a.m. on 7 Oct. Regimental Move Order No C10 issued.	App 190. " 191
BONNIERES.	7 Oct.		Weather rainy & very muddy. Regiment proceeded by route march to ARBRES and embarked on 25 motor Busses. Owing to embarkation arrangements having been handed over to French Transport Authorities and taken out of hands of Regts. Officers very considerable inconvenience ensued. Regiments of the Bde were mixed up. Officers separated from their men etc. The journey was made via DOULLENS and AMIENS to a point about 3 miles from CONTAY whence Regiment proceeded by march route to LA HAUSSOYE about 2½ miles. Transport proceeded by road. Tremendous congestion of motor traffic on road caused considerable delay.	app 192
		11-50 am.	Warning Order No BM.17 received at 11.50 pm. to proceed by march route & train to	
LA HAUSSOYE.	8 Oct.	9-30 am	Operation Order No 64 received relating to Regiment. Weather rainy roads very bad wind strong. Main road MAMETZ WOOD. via AMIENS-ALBERT road. & tactical railway at Vivier hill E16 B7.0. Transport left at D12 d 9.9 March about 10 miles. Transport proceeded via ALBERT & MAMETZ WOOD. Regiment arrived at FRICOURT Railhead at 4 pm.	

Army Form C. 2118

WAR DIARY
or
INTELLIGENCE SUMMARY
(Erase heading not required.)

Instructions regarding War Diaries and Intelligence Summaries are contained in F. S. Regs., Part II. and the Staff Manual respectively. Title Pages will be prepared in manuscript.

Place	Date	Hour	Summary of Events and Information	Remarks and references to Appendices
	Oct 9th		Proceeded by road & look at position along SOUTH EAST Border of MAMETZ WOOD. B.M.O. I received at 8-45 am. calling conference of Regimental Commanders at Brigade Headquarters at 9-30 am.	app 193
		11am	2nd in command & Company Commanders proceeded by road to reconnoitre the ground to be taken over by Regiment at HIGH WOOD. Operation Order No. 65 received at 10 am. modified by verbal instructions received by O.C. Regiment. moved off under the Adjutant from MAMETZ WOOD at 3 pm. by platoons at 200 yards interval. The leading platoon arrived at HIGH WOOD by 4 pm. Regiment disposed along S.N. Border of HIGH WOOD to left. A.B. Headquarters C & D Companies acting as Reserve to 26 Brigade & relieving the 142nd Brigade. S.A. Bde disposed: 2nd Regt. firing line 4th Regiment supports 3rd Regiment Reserve 1st Regt Brigade Reserve with 26th Brigade. 9th Division on the Right & 27th Brigade in Divisional Reserve. 26th Brigade started to arrive into position about 9 pm. Weather fine but roads very muddy. Traffic very congested. Heavy & continuous shelling in progress all round but not on Regiment.	app 194 app 195
HIGH WOOD	Oct 10th		Weather fine. Enemy started shelling Northern portion of HIGH WOOD with H.E. Shells at 7-30 am. & ceased at 11-30 am. Regimental Area found to be much strewn with debris of Battle & large numbers of partially buried men. Work proceeding on Salvage & burial. Very scanty dug out accomodation. Being improved. A working party of 4 officers & 104 Other Ranks furnished for 5-30 pm for work on road to front line under of R.E. Three tasks were finished in 3 hours. Party returned back without casualties. Another working party of 1 officer & 104 O.R. furnished at 6-30 pm. for work under R.E. deepening & widening communication trench to front line. Party of 1 officer & 10 O.R. called for to bring wounded from Headquarters 2nd S.A. Infantry in front line near Eau Court l'Abbaye. Portion of the party engaged in removing wounded of the London Regiment from NO MANS LAND. Weather fine. Heavy and continuous shelling all day but not on Regimental Area after noon. A draft of 10 other Ranks arrived at 1st Line Transport. The following Officers and other ranks were left at 1st Line Transport at MAMETZ WOOD on 9th Oct. Major B Young — 2nd in Command Lieut R.H. Ellis — Assistant Adjutant Capt W.H. Carding — Quartermaster 2/Lt A.S. Money — Transport Officer Lt G. Elliot — B Coy " G. Mallett — D " 2/Lt G.C. Strickland — A " " C.M. Egan — C " and 100 Other Ranks. From the completion of the move from LA HAUSSOYE to MAMETZ WOOD the S.A. Bde. as part of the 9th Division was removed from the XVII Corps & transferred to the III Corps of the 4th Army.	

70

Instructions regarding War Diaries and Intelligence Summaries are contained in F. S. Regs., Part II. and the Staff Manual respectively. Title Pages will be prepared in manuscript.

WAR DIARY
or
INTELLIGENCE SUMMARY
(Erase heading not required.)

Army Form C. 2118

Place	Date 1916	Hour	Summary of Events and Information	Remarks and references to Appendices
High Wood	Oct 11	5.30 AM pm 3.15 3.35	"Carrying wounded". Party reported back at 5.30 AM. Casualties 2 OR wounded weather cold + rainy. Note from BHQ received at 10 AM that our artillery would make a CHINESE BOMBARDMENT of the enemy's lines between 1.20 & 1.40 pm and 3.15 + 3.35 pm but that no attack would follow + we were to make observations where the enemy's barrage was put also that due precautions were taken to keep the men under cover. The first CHINESE BOMBARDMENT did not take place. The second bombardment was followed by retaliation by the enemy on the West of HIGH WOOD with high explosive shells. At this time we had a salvage party working on Battle debris to the West of HIGH WOOD which suffered casualties 6 killed + 5 wounded from this bombardment.	
HIGH WOOD.	Oct. 12	8. AM	The G.O.C. 1st S.A.I Brigade visited Regimental Hd Qrs on his way from the front line at 8 am today and gave the O.C. verbal instructions modifying Operation Order No 66 d/d 11.10.16 which was received at 8.15. am that the Regiment should start dribbling forward at once.	app. 196.
			The Regiment received orders to take over the line held by the 4th S.A.I and to act as support to the attack to be made at 2.5 pm. today by the 9th DIVISION with the S.A.I BRIGADE and the 26th BRIGADE in the assaulting line. The regiment started to dribble forward in ones + twos at 100 yards interval from HIGH WOOD	
		9.45 A.M.	to FLERS SWITCH, PRUE TRENCH + STARFISH LINE at 9.45 am a distance to FLERS SWITCH of about 3.500 yards	
			The original instruction vide Operation Order No 66 had been that the 3rd S.A.I should move forward at ~~Regiment~~ 10 minutes after ZERO (2.5 pm) but as this would have entailed very considerable casualties the "Dribbling method" was adopted with a large amount of success.	
			This operation was carried out with the loss of 2/Lieut PHILLIPS and 6 O. Ranks wounded. The O.C. and H.Qrs of the regiment left	
		1.20 pm	HIGH WOOD at 1.20 pm and reached H.Qrs STARFISH LINE at 1.40 pm when the regiment was reported to B.H.Q. as present in the new position the position then being	71

Instructions regarding War Diaries and Intelligence Summaries are contained in F. S. Regs., Part II. and the Staff Manual respectively. Title Pages will be prepared in manuscript.

WAR DIARY
or
INTELLIGENCE SUMMARY
(Erase heading not required.)

Army Form C. 2118

Place	Date 1916	Hour	Summary of Events and Information	Remarks and references to Appendices
STARFISH LINE	Oct 12	1.40 pm	B Coy FLERS SWITCH C Coy Do Do & FLERS SUPPORT D Coy PRUE TRENCH HQrs & A Coy STARFISH LINE. The latter was found in a very damaged condition from shell fire with a large amount of battle debris scattered about. Apparently very little attempt had been made to keep the trench in repair. All hands were put to work immediately constructing such shelters as possible in view of the possibility of an enemy bombardment.	
	Oct 12.	2.5 pm	Punctually at ZERO (2.5 pm) our artillery opened an intense bombardment. The enemy made a vigorous reply on our front line, no shells coming this way. Our bombardment slackened	
		3.0 pm	at 3 pm and at 3.20 was reduced to the normal activity.	
		4.5 pm	Orders from B. HQrs were received by telephone to send one company forward. In accordance with this order, C Coy was sent forward to hold the Front Line trench originally held by the Scottish. About 9 pm the enemy began to shell STARFISH	
		9 pm	LINE. No Casualties.	
		10 pm	Hear indirectly C Coy taken over front line trench. In accordance with BM 303. D Coy under Capt. LANGDALE pushed forward from PRUE to FLERS SWITCH SUPPORT TRENCH Grave delay in all messages coming by telephone from Bde HQrs and to Front Line owing to wires being cut by shell fire.	app 198
STARFISH LINE	Oct 13	12.30 A.M.	Wire received from Bde HQrs d/d 11.25 pm 12th inst ordering regiment forward to relieve 2nd and 4th S.A.I at once in the Front Line. All Coys ordered by phone to be ready for move. A Coy pushed forward to PRUE. O.C. and Head Qrs went forward to front line to arrange details of relief with O.C.s 2nd and 4th S.A.I.	app 199.
		2.0 A.M.	On arrival there at 2 AM considerable confusion was found to prevail owing to the fact that the assault carried out by the 2nd & 4th S.A.I and the 26th Brigade	

72

1875 Wt. W593/826 1,000,000 4/15 J.B.C. & A. A.D.S.S./Forms/C. 2118.

Army Form C. 2118

WAR DIARY
or
INTELLIGENCE SUMMARY
(Erase heading not required.)

Instructions regarding War Diaries and Intelligence Summaries are contained in F. S. Regs., Part II. and the Staff Manual respectively. Title Pages will be prepared in manuscript.

Place	Date	Hour	Summary of Events and Information	Remarks and references to Appendices
			had been repulsed with severe loss and the regiments concerned having	
ACID DROP.	Oct 13	7.0 A.M.	lost nearly all their Officers and been disorganised.	
		2.10	Wire received from Bde Major (app 204) at 2.10 am. ordering O.C. to use working party of pioneers and another from the 2nd & 4th S.A.I to dig communication trench between STRONG POINT M16.d.9.3. and M17 c.5.8. and consolidate strong point. Endeavours were made to find pioneers without success, no men of the 2nd S.A.I could be found and the condition of communication trenches negated the possibility of obtaining the working party from the 4th S.A.I	app 204
		2.10 A.M.	Wire from Brigade through 2nd S.A.I ordering O.C. 'C' Coy 3rd S.A.I to send out patrol to occupy Strong Point at M16 d 9 3. which was evacuated by 2nd S.A.I yesterday morning and to establish another Strong Point on the left of our line connecting up with 15th Division - Garrisons of strong points to take Lewis Guns, rations, and water, and to send frequent situation reports.	app 205
		5.30 A.M.	Officers Patrol Reports from 2/Lts VAN RYNEVELD & THOMAS 3rd S.A.I and 2/Lieut GREEN 2nd S.A.I attached hereto (app 200). They were dispatched to ascertain whether the 1st objective of the Brigade Assault had been carried and on the result of their reconnaissance, which was in the negative, the following wire from Brigade Major was received at 5.30 AM saying as it is now definitely established that the object of attack was not attained no isolated posts in the front line need be held - It was now however too late to withdraw the men Great difficulty was experienced in obtaining reliable guides from the 2nd S.A.I (owing to their great losses) to guide the Companys of 3rd S.A.I to their positions in the front line, and owing to this cause and congested state of communication trenches due to large numbers of wounded coming down, and to the activity of the Enemy's artillery, flowing in fire and communication trenches the relief was not completed until 6 A.M. well after dawn. During the night message received from Brigade that contact aeroplane would fly over front line at dawn and that boys in front line to show flares	app 200

1875 Wt. W593/826 1,000,000 4/15 J.B.C. & A. A.D.S.S./Forms/C. 2118

Army Form C. 2118

WAR DIARY
or
INTELLIGENCE SUMMARY
(Erase heading not required.)

Instructions regarding War Diaries and Intelligence Summaries are contained in F. S. Regs., Part II. and the Staff Manual respectively. Title Pages will be prepared in manuscript.

Place	Date	Hour	Summary of Events and Information	Remarks and references to Appendices
ACID DROP	Oct. 13.	~~7.10 a.m.~~	in order to shew their positions in the front line, but owing to the uncertainty of the position of the remnants of the attacking force of the previous day who were dug in in unascertained points in NO MANS LAND, flares could not be shown as they might have given deceptive impression of the line we actually held.	
		7.10 a.m.	Runner from 2/Lt PEARSE 2nd S.A.I. reporting this Officer's position critical that he was dug in with about 70 other ranks, (many of whom wounded) and exposed to artillery, machine gun and rifle fire. The O.C. instructed O.C. B Coy to endeavour to open visual communication with him and inform him that it was impossible to relieve him until after dark. Position remained very obscure until about 10 A.M. when the following appeared to be the situation. C Coy in Front line from MILL to EASTWARD position of EASTERN flank uncertain. B Coy in Front Line from MILL WESTWARD to WARLENCOURT ROAD with its left flank resting on Strong point on the road. The Garrison of Strong point 2/Lt Van Ryneveld 20 o. Ranks and 1 Lewis Gun. This post had been garrisoned in accordance with orders received at 7.10 a.m. see appendix 205. It had been guided by an officer of the 2nd Regt. D Coy in support line FLERS TRENCH to South West of EAUCOURT L'ABBAYE. A Coy on the left of D to within about 200 yards of the WARLENCOURT ROAD. Regimental H.Qrs in old German dug-out in sunken road M.23.1 called ACID DROP. During morning O.C. B Coy sent a patrol under Lt MALLETT to open communication with unit on his left this unit (8th Seaforth Hqrs) 44th B.de 15 Divn. It was then discovered	app 201

74

Army Form C. 2118

Instructions regarding War Diaries and Intelligence Summaries are contained in F. S. Regs., Part II. and the Staff Manual respectively. Title Pages will be prepared in manuscript.

WAR DIARY
or
INTELLIGENCE SUMMARY
(Erase heading not required.)

Place	Date	Hour	Summary of Events and Information	Remarks and references to Appendices
ACID. DROP.	1916. Octr 13.		that Lt Van Ryneveld's post was not at M16. d 9.3 but on the left of B Coy, and separated from it by 40 yards of old destroyed trench raked by artillery and Machine Gun fire	
		11 AM	Report from O.C. "C" Coy stating visual communication with 2/Lieut PEARSE impossible but that 2/Lt Cruddas had crossed NO MANS LAND to Lieut PEARSE and ascertained his position and the position of Lt Donaldson 4th SAI who was occupying part of destroyed trench running N.E from near the MILL. Lieut Donaldson sent runner to O.C. during morning stating he had 25 men (4th SAI) under him and asking to be relieved. O.C. 3rd SAI sent orders to O.C. "B" Coy to extricate Lt Donaldson after dark and occupy portion of trench held by him and also to O.C. D Coy to relieve Lt PEARSE after dark and both Coys to dig a trench joining up these two positions to make a new front line trench. Casualties to noon 2 Officers Wounded (Lt Phillips 2/Lt Yeomans) 7 O.R. wounded 1 missing. Enemy artillery Machine Guns & Snipers very active	
		7.15. pm	Report from Lt Van Ryneveld that his strong post much damaged by shell fire & several casualties	
		7.35 p.m.	Wire received from 9th Divn through SAI Bde; ordering Regiment to reconnoitre Strong Point M.16 d 9.3 and if found to be held by enemy to take it (app 206). O.C. B & C Coys report relief of	app 206
		9. 0. p.m.	2/Lt Donaldson & 2/Lt Pearse complete - Orders sent to O.C. "B" Coy to relieve 2/Lt Van Ryneveld of the post held by him in order to extend B Coy to the left of our position. Large working parties from other Regiments sent up to assist in deepening communication trenches, and to dig new trench from right of our line to Strong Point M16 d 9.3	

1875 Wt. W593/826 1,000,000 4/15 J.B.C. & A. A.D.S.S./Forms/C. 2118.

Army Form C. 2118

WAR DIARY
or
INTELLIGENCE SUMMARY

(Erase heading not required.)

Instructions regarding War Diaries and Intelligence Summaries are contained in F. S. Regs., Part II. and the Staff Manual respectively. Title Pages will be prepared in manuscript.

Place	Date	Hour	Summary of Events and Information	Remarks and references to Appendices
ACID DROP	13/10/16		when required. O.C. 'C' Coy (Capt Montgomery) was ordered to send out reconnaissance to strong point M16. d9.3. under command of Lt Mallett with 16 regtl bombers and to be ready to support him with his whole Company and Lewis Gunners and the two Regtl Lewis Gunners. O.C. B Coy ordered to co-operate with C Coy in covering the attack should it be necessary. O.C. D Coy ordered to move up front line trench in support of 'B' Coy. These orders were confirmed by O.O. No C11 issued at 10.15 p.m. (app. 207). At 11 pm. O.C. made representations to B.H.Qrs that the attack if necessary would probably develop into a considerable affair as the enemy was holding these trenches in force and requested the support of artillery & of the 1st SAI should it be necessary. (app 208) Large supplies of bombs ammunition Very Lights etc were sent up front line trenches to be at disposal of O.C. 'C' Coy	app 207 app 208
		11.40 P.M	Wire received from Brigade (app 209) to the effect that working parties to continue work while reconnaissance in progress but to be withdrawn under cover should attack be necessary, the presence of these working parties in the trenches, and condition of trenches owing to enemy activity made all movement extremely difficult and greatly delayed operations.	app 209.
ACID DROP	14/10/16	1.30 A.M.	Report from O.C. A Coy that enemy bombarded his section of trench (FLERS TRENCH) and much damaged it - Report from	
		1.35 A.M.	O.C. D Coy his trench much damaged by enemy bombardment.	
		3.0 A.M.	Situation report to Brigade copy app. 210 reporting enemy activity and that patrol sent out to reconnoitre M16 d9.3. not returned	app. 210
		—	A Coy continuing work on new communication trench between FLERS TRENCH and B Coys. trench in front line	

Army Form C. 2118

WAR DIARY
or
INTELLIGENCE SUMMARY

(Erase heading not required.)

Instructions regarding War Diaries and Intelligence Summaries are contained in F. S. Regs., Part II and the Staff Manual respectively. Title Pages will be prepared in manuscript.

Place	Date	Hour	Summary of Events and Information	Remarks and references to Appendices
ACID DROP.	14/10/16.		and also new fire trench from the MILL Eastward through the position held by Lt. Donaldson and Pearse, it was not deemed advisable to start reconnaissance of the Strong point M.6. d. 9. 3. hereafter called "THE PIMPLE" until for the 15th A.M. - Lieut. Mallett reached the Pimple at 5.4. A.M. under some sniping fire, and surprised one or more Enemy snipers in it who made off. Report of Lt. Mallett (app 211) received at 6.15. A.M. he reports 2 deep dug-outs in Pimple 1 Field Gun emplacement and 2 Machine gun emplacements, but no sign of the trench having been previously occupied by British troops, although plenty signs of recent German occupation. This point was supposed to have been occupied by 3rd Regt for several days, and it was this error which led to so much confusion in orders yesterday. Lt. Mallett verbally reported that the PIMPLE was close up against the German main line trenches, and it was nearly day-light when he finished his reconnaissance. He considered it inadvisable to attempt occupation with the force at his disposal - O.C. called on by wire from Bde Hqrs to explain reason for delay in making reconnaissance, copy of written report attached hereto (app 212). Considerable difficulty experienced in obtaining water and all water and rations have to brought up by carrying parties from HIGH WOOD. over 3.000 yards in the rear. This morning only 30 tins were brought up instead of 110 impossible to light fires owing to enemy artillery - men cannot obtain warm food or tea - Enemy Gun located at Butte at Warlencourt M17 A3.6. and on this information two of our 6" Batteries bombarded the point -	App 211 app. 212
		3pm.	Two of our 4.5 Batteries shelled the PIMPLE and neighbouring	

1875 Wt. W593/826 1,000,000 4/15 J.B.C.&A. A.D.S.S./Forms/C. 2118.

77

Instructions regarding War Diaries and Intelligence Summaries are contained in F. S. Regs., Part II. and the Staff Manual respectively. Title Pages will be prepared in manuscript.

WAR DIARY
or
INTELLIGENCE SUMMARY
(Erase heading not required.)

Army Form C. 2118

78

Place	Date	Hour	Summary of Events and Information	Remarks and references to Appendices
			trench held by the enemy	
ACID DROP.		3 pm	Situation report rendered to Bde reporting enemy bombarding FLERS TRENCH Casualties for past 24 Hrs 2 O.R. killed 20. O.R wounded and 2. O.R. missing from patrol	
		3.20 pm	G.O.C. S.A.1 Bde: having gone round front line trenches had conference with the O.C. at ACID DROP. and explained a telegram received at the same time (app 213) from 9th Division. This telegram orders the regiment to occupy the PIMPLE after dark and join it with the left of our front line trench and large working parties from other units and from this Regt. to improve existing trenches and make new ones. These working parties totalled 400 O.R. and a proportion of Officers. Working parties were ordered to continue their work under covering party furnished by this regiment during the operations to capture the PIMPLE.	App. 213
		4.30 P.M	Meeting of Company Commanders called by O.C. but owing to heavy enemy artillery bombardment they were much delayed + were all knocked down by shell explosion. O.C. gave them orders for the conduct of coming operations and confirmed this by Operation Order (app 214) Capt. Spranger O.C. D Coy was placed in immediate command of the operation with Lt. Hallett and regimental bombers + Lt. Harris + regtl. Lewis Gunners. Tgram from Brigade recd. 6.55 pm (app 215) ordering that if new front line trench could not be completed between THE PIMPLE and the road junction at M.23. a.6.8. that strong points were to be formed along its course to be held by small garrisons with Lewis Guns	App. 214 App 215
		11.20 pm.	Phone message from Brigade that contact aeroplanes would fly over front line at 9.30 AM tomorrow + flares to be shown.	

Army Form C. 2118

Instructions regarding War Diaries and Intelligence Summaries are contained in F. S. Regs., Part II. and the Staff Manual respectively. Title Pages will be prepared in manuscript.

WAR DIARY
or
INTELLIGENCE SUMMARY
(Erase heading not required.)

Place	Date	Hour	Summary of Events and Information	Remarks and references to Appendices
	Oct 14		to inadequate new front line garrison. Owing to collapse of trenches under bombardment, to the bringing down of wounded to	
ACID DROP.		11.55	the tremendous congestion caused by large working parties moving up, the movement of Companys to take up new positions to resist a possible counter-attack by the enemy was very slow. The enemy's bombardment was continuous and telephone wires to front line trench to the MILL were cut six or seven times during the night. All Coy Cdrs were ordered to take up their quarters at the MILL until the commencement of the operations in order to facilitate quick communication but in spite of all efforts Capt Springer could not report ready to move off until 11.55 p.m.	
	Oct 15	1.30 a.m.	Capt. Springer reported by phone that he was wounded. Capt. Lane ordered to take over operations	
		1.35 a.m.	Report from 2/Lt Harris ~~saying~~ reporting attacking force had gone forward in three columns & he was moving forward in support with his two Lewis Guns.	
		2.35 a.m.	Capt. Montgomery was not able to get in communication with attacking force	
		4.15 a.m.	Capt Springer reported to Regt HQrs and went to hospital.	
		5.0 a.m.	Report from Lt Harris we have obtained objective with Lt Medlicott and one Lewis Gun as garrison and Lt Mallett and 20 OR and 1 Lewis Gun in portion of Enemys trench adjoining	
		5.0 a.m.	Situation report rendered to Bde to effect heavy bombardment on our front. Operations preceding working parties well digging in	
		5.15	Report of Lt Mallett wounded	

79

Army Form C. 2118

Instructions regarding War Diaries and Intelligence Summaries are contained in F. S. Regs., Part II. and the Staff Manual respectively. Title Pages will be prepared in manuscript.

WAR DIARY
or
INTELLIGENCE SUMMARY
(Erase heading not required.)

Place	Date	Hour	Summary of Events and Information	Remarks and references to Appendices
ACID DROP	Oct. 15	5.20 A.M.	Phone report from Capt. Lane that Lt. Goodwin & working party (50) detailed to cut comm. trench between PIMPLE and GALLENCOURT ROAD to join with 15th Division did not carry out task owing to dawn having broken & his position being open to machine gun and artillery fire. He further that 2/Lt Estill & 2/Lt Harris with the remainder of B Coy were in occupation of enemy trench adjoining PIMPLE	
		5.40 A.M.	Phone order to O.C. A Coy to occupy that portion of front line trench to West of M.11 vacated by B Coy	
		6.40 A.M.	Lt. Cruddas with his covering force to working party reported to be dug in in small posts along enemy front in M.17.c	
		6.35 A.M.	Wire from Brigade asking for explanation of why operations ordered to take place immediately after dark were not started till 11.15 pm.	app. 215 B
		7.55 A.M.	Wire from Brigade asking for rough estimate of casualties for operations.	
		8.35 A.M.	Reply to casualty wire Capt. Sprague wounded Lt. Mallett wounded approximately O.R. 3 killed – 10 wounded	
		8.40 A.M.	written report from OC to Bde. (app 216) giving explanation of delay in operations stating that it takes a considerable time to organise the whole Battn in difficult trenches for such an operation & to move them into suitable positions to resist a possible counter attack, while the trenches were filled with large working parties and hampered with the passage of numerous wounded and under heavy fire, and also the necessity of great caution in moving over open in face of heavy artillery, machine gun & rifle fire. Further that the regiment is considerably exhausted by continuous movement, want of sleep, hard work, lack of cooked warm food under continuous heavy bombardment since 8 A.M. on 12th inst. further that B Coy and considerable portion C Coy were in isolated positions, in view of the fact they would not be available for a forward movement.	app 216

1875 Wt. W593/826 1,000,000 4/15 J.B.C. & A. A.D.S.S./Forms/C. 2118.

Army Form C. 2118

WAR DIARY
or
INTELLIGENCE SUMMARY
(Erase heading not required.)

Instructions regarding War Diaries and Intelligence Summaries are contained in F. S. Regs., Part II. and the Staff Manual respectively. Title Pages will be prepared in manuscript.

Place	Date	Hour	Summary of Events and Information	Remarks and references to Appendices
ACID DROP.	15/10/16	8.40 a.m.	in the early hours of tomorrow morning. In consequence of the above considerations and of recent casualties this Regiment will hardly have available more than 180 men instead of the 350 it was credited with in the appendix order No 215A ~~The following details of the morning's operation have been gradually collected~~	
		3.0 p.m.	Situation report rendered to Bde as follows: Enemy artillery active particularly ~~active~~ at dawn & trenches damaged thereby. Contact aeroplane flew over at 9.40 a.m. - our front line trenches exposed flares to indicate their position	
		3.30 p.m.	Wire from Brigade detailing working party 2 officers 150 O.R. of this Regt to complete commn trench from West of our front line to PIMPLE, and 1st S.A.I and 4th S.A.I furnishing working parties to improve front line trenches & Commn trenches.	
		5.20 p.m.	Representations made to Bde that this regt could not find working party of more than 100 O.R. (app. 217).	app 217.
		5.0 p.m.	Regtl Operation Order C12 issued (app. 218) ordering A Coy to relieve B Coy in PIMPLE and capture portion of enemy trench. D Coy to take over line ~~[illegible]~~ vacated by A Coy. B Coy to come back in support in line vacated by D Coy - C Coy to stand fast. also detailing working parties to dig communication trench to PIMPLE and organise PIMPLE and adjoining trench. Wire received from Bde: indicating that S.O.S signal 3 green Very lights to be used in case of enemy attack on PIMPLE when our barrage fire would be put over Enemy trenches.	app 218.
		7.40 p.m.	(Appendix 219) giving details dispositions on 9th Batt front in case of Enemy attack. Battn in front line to man fire trench all available men less one Coy held in support trench. Battn in support to move one Company to Commn trench running to MILL.	app. 219.
		7.40 p.m.	Lt Harris reported back from PIMPLE and reports 2/Lt Medlicott killed during day.	
		10.p.m.	Report from O.C. B Coy that his Coy had be relieved in PIMPLE by A Coy and that he has taken up his position in support line	

1875 Wt. W593/826 1,000,000 4/15 J.B.C. & A. A.D.S.S./Forms/C. 2118.

Army Form C. 2118

Instructions regarding War Diaries and Intelligence Summaries are contained in F. S. Regs., Part II. and the Staff Manual respectively. Title Pages will be prepared in manuscript.

WAR DIARY
or
INTELLIGENCE SUMMARY
(Erase heading not required.)

Place	Date	Hour	Summary of Events and Information	Remarks and references to Appendices
ACID DROP.	15/10/16	11.35 pm	Orders from Bde to send out L. Gun patrols to prevent enemy putting wire in front of his trenches. Following Officers have come up from 1st Line Transport to replace casualties Lt. Elliott & Lt. Ellis, Lt. Mallett (afterwards killed) 2/Lt. Strickland 2/Lt. Egan.	
	16/10/16	3.0 A.M	Situation report rendered to effect cold rain falling and enemy artillery very active on front line & PIMPLE	
		8. A.M	Report from Lt. Gueddes commdg. L Gun patrols saying he had seen nothing of enemy working parties	
		8.30 A.M	Operation order No 67 by S.A.I Bde (app 220) (dated 15 Octr) to effect 1st S.A.I will relieve 3rd S.A.I in front line today after moon rises, time and details of relief to be arranged by C.O.s.	app 220
		8.30 A.M	(app. 221) work report of trenches dug during night rendered to Bde	app. 221
		9.0 A.M	Situation report rendered (app. 222) stating the dispositions of Coys and that no S.O.S signal had been sent up by us, last night between 8 & 9. pm. and from about 11. to 11.30 our artillery put a very heavy barrage over Enemy positions in reply to some green lights thrown up by the enemy	app. 222
		10. A.M	Full report with maps rendered to Bde by O.C on recent operations app. 223. details of assault on PIMPLE and enemy trench evolved from various reports are as follows. Lt. Mallett led the assault with two fighting sections and Regtl & B Coy bombers and a Lewis Gun following the route of his reconnaissance of the morning of the 14th he was supported by B Coy and 50 men of A Coy all under command of Capt. Sprenger. Lt. Mallett was followed by 2/Lt. Medlicott with 25 men & a Lewis Gun who had orders to re-inforce Lt. Mallett if necessary & consolidate the PIMPLE when captured. Lt. Mallett rushed the PIMPLE which was garrisoned and consolidated by 2/Lt. Medlicott. Lt. Mallett then rushed the enemy's trench running N. and W. from the PIMPLE and bombed the enemy out of a portion of about 60 yards of this trench running N but was eventually driven back by heavy machine gun fire & bombs and was himself severely wounded. Another party of Lt. Mallett's force drove the enemy for some distance westwards along this trench which was then blocked and held by 2/Lts. Estill & Harris who placed L Guns in position and so held the enemy. The Enemy from adjoining trenches showed great activity during the night with trench mortars machine Guns & bombs but did not venture a counter-attack. Early in the operations Capt. Sprenger was knocked down & wounded by a shell & Lt. Estill remained in command	app. 223.

1875 Wt. W593/826 1,000,000 4/15 J.B.C. & A. A.D.S.S./Forms/C. 2118.

82

Army Form C. 2118

Instructions regarding War Diaries and Intelligence Summaries are contained in F. S. Regs., Part II. and the Staff Manual respectively. Title Pages will be prepared in manuscript.

WAR DIARY
or
INTELLIGENCE SUMMARY
(Erase heading not required.)

Place	Date	Hour	Summary of Events and Information	Remarks and references to Appendices
ACID DROP.	16/10/16		of the garrison and the PIMPLE. Soon after dawn a ~~working~~ party of from 300 to 400 of the enemy was seen to be approaching the mound at about 300 yards off, they were in close order when Lt Harris turned a Lewis Gun on them, and killed and wounded a very large number of them and dispersed the remainder. It was not possible to bring in the wounded from the PIMPLE until the garrison was relieved there by A Coy. Our total losses for this operation were 2/Lt Maddicott killed and 3 O.R. — Capt. Spenser & 2/Lt Mallett wounded (2/Lt Mallett afterwards died of wounds) O.R. wounded 26. missing 6. total 3 officers 35. O.R.	
		11.50 a.m.	In reply to a query from B^de the following was reported as garrison of the PIMPLE and captured enemy trench 4 Officers 100. O.R. + 3 Lewis Guns. 3rd S.A.I. 1 Offcr 7 maxims + teams M.G. Corps	
		3.0 p.m.	Reg^tl Operation Order No C 13 issued (app 224) giving details of relief of 3rd S.A.I. by 1st S.A.I which had been arranged in conference by Col Dawson & Lt Col Heathcote. Relief to commence at 6. 30 pm by Comp^ys 3rd S.A.I returning to their old positions in FLERS SWITCH + STARFISH TRENCH in support to front line	app 224.
		4.0 ~~3.30~~ pm	~~[illegible]~~ Orders from B^de for this Reg^t to cut fire steps in front line trenches before relief + to widen new communication trench	
		6.20 pm	Orders sent out to Coys to detail 33 O.R. each under Lt Egan to remain behind for work on Westerly Comm^n trench.	
		6.30 pm	Relief commenced, but owing to presence of large working parties and congestion in Comm^n trenches progress very slow	
		9.0 pm	Rain falling greatly impeding operations enemy artillery very active and great display of coloured lights	
		12 midnight	Relief still proceeding enemy artillery still active rain falling and almost impossible to walk	83

1875 Wt. W593/826 1,000,000 4/15 J.B.C. & A. A.D.S.S./Forms/C. 2118.

Army Form C. 2118

WAR DIARY
or
INTELLIGENCE SUMMARY
(Erase heading not required.)

Instructions regarding War Diaries and Intelligence Summaries are contained in F. S. Regs., Part II. and the Staff Manual respectively. Title Pages will be prepared in manuscript.

Place	Date	Hour	Summary of Events and Information	Remarks and references to Appendices
STARFISH TRENCH	17/10/16	2 AM	Move to new trenches complete. Report from O.C. A Coy that enemy threw large number of Gas shells into no man's land to his Coy was being relieved no casualties.	
		1.16 pm	In accordance with telephonic instructions from Bde A Coy were instructed to hold themselves in readiness for early move back to front line to be placed at disposal of O.C. 1st S.A.I.	
		2.35 pm	Wire sent to Bde. representing the total strength of Officers with Regt now only 19 asking for new Officers to be promoted to comm. rank	
		3.10 p.m.	Situation report by wire to Bde. Enemy putting over occasional Shrapnel & H E shells on to our trenches our artillery very active as usual	
		6.10 p.m.	Operation Order 68 17th Oct. received from Bde. (app. 225) giving detail of operations about to be taken against the enemy	225.
		6.20 p.m.	Report from O.C. D Coy that he is ordered to report to O.C. 1st S.A.I. at the Acid drop at 1. AM tomorrow	
		7.45 p.m	Meeting of Coy Comdrs held and O.C. explains coming operations. Today has been spent in as far as possible re-equipping the Regt and repairing trenches which were in a very dilapidated condition. Dug-outs have been made and dug-boards made.	
		8.0 pm	~~Rain falling~~. Enemy throwing over occasional shells especially on FLERS SWITCH TRENCH. Casualties to noon today wounded 12 O.R. missing 2 O.R. 1 Officer shell shock	
	18/10/16	7. P.M.	Continued work on repair of trenches. Enemy artillery intermittently active during day on FLERS SWITCH and on the night of STARFISH TRENCH. Casualties to 12 noon 1 Offr (Mr Harris wounded) 5. O.R. wounded	
		4.15 pm	~~Rain falling~~ Operation Order No 69 S.A.I. Bde. dated 18th Oct (app. 226) received giving details of relief of 1st S.A.I. Bde by the 27th Bde 9th Division in front line and support trenches on the 19th inst.	226
STARFISH TRENCH	19/10/16.		Reg. move order C.B. issued at 10.10 am giving details of relief of the Reg by the 11th Royal Scots - Regiment proceeded to BAZENTIN LE GRAND relief commencing at 6. 30 pm. Guides for incoming Reg' + for 6th K.O.S.B's proceeding to front line were sent to HIGH WOOD at 6.30 pm.	move order app. 227

84

Army Form C. 2118

Instructions regarding War Diaries and Intelligence Summaries are contained in F. S. Regs., Part II. and the Staff Manual respectively. Title Pages will be prepared in manuscript.

WAR DIARY
or
INTELLIGENCE SUMMARY
(Erase heading not required.)

Place	Date	Hour	Summary of Events and Information	Remarks and references to Appendices
STARFISH TRENCH	19/10/16	4.10 AM	Verbal orders recd from Bde Major 11.10 AM requiring (one) 1 Coy this Regt at least 100 strong to be placed at disposal 1st S.A.I. B Coy under Lt G Elliott re-inforced by 25 men of C Coy under Lt Van Ryneveld were immediately dispatched.	
		3 pm	Enemy putting over occasional shrapnel & H.E shells	
		4.30 pm	advance parties 11th Royal Scots arrived continuous rain all day doing much damage to trenches and making movement difficult	
		6.30 pm	1st Coy of 11th Royal Scots came in and were sent on to FLERS SWITCH	
		10.20 pm	H.Qrs and remaining Coys 11th Royal Scots came in at irregular intervals. O.C & H.Q. 11th Royal Scots arrived at 9.30 pm and O.C & H.Q 3rd SAI moved out at 10.20 pm owing to continuous rain going was very slippery and difficult over country almost every yard of which was ploughed up by shell-holes. The last of the Regiment arrived at BAZENTIN L. GRAND at 12 midnight	
BAZENTIN L GRAND	20/10/16	5 AM	B and D Coy and portion of C Coy attached to B arrived in camp after extraordinary difficulties in comm: trenches owing to rain & mud. Heavy fighting and lack of food, and large numbers of wounded coming down	
		12.20 pm	Information recd from Bde H.Qrs to move to MAMETZ WOOD. The whole of the rest of the day men were dribbling in from front line trenches, the Regt being much exhausted as much rest as possible was taken, taking into consideration that rain was continually falling, the weather cold, the ground a sea of mud and little shelter available	
HIGH WOOD	21/10/16	12.20 AM	Orders recd from Bde that the Regt to be in reserve to Bde in the firing line. Every effort being made to re-equip Regt with a large amount of clothing & equipment lost and destroyed during recent operations. Reports recd from O.C's B.D. Coys on the recent operations carried out by them while attached to 1st SAI (app 228/9) Casualties to 12 noon today 2 Offrs wounded Lt & QM Cunning 2/Lt Williamson and 40 O.R killed wounded & missing. Orders from B.H.Qrs that 3rd SAI will relieve 1st SAI in HIGHWOOD relief to be completed by 4 pm today (app 230) move completed by 4.20 p.m.	app. 228/229 app 230
		4.20 pm	weather rainy & cold	
HIGHWOOD	22/10/16	12 noon	Regt in position at HIGH WOOD, large working parties supplied from work in BAZENTIN L GRAND remainder of Regt employed in cleaning up and improving trench and in salving battle debris. Casualties to 12 noon today 3 O.R wounded	
HIGH WOOD	23/10/16	11 AM	Operation No 70 1st SAI Bde d/d 23rd Oct received ordering Regt to move	231

1875 Wt. W593/826 1,000,000 4/15 J.B.C. & A. A.D.S.S./Forms/C. 2118.

85

Instructions regarding War Diaries and Intelligence Summaries are contained in F. S. Regs., Part II. and the Staff Manual respectively. Title Pages will be prepared in manuscript.

WAR DIARY
or
INTELLIGENCE SUMMARY
(Erase heading not required.)

Place	Date	Hour	Summary of Events and Information	Remarks and references to Appendices
HIGH WOOD	23/10/16		from High Wood to Bazentin & Grand relieved by 4th S. Highlanders not to leave HIGH WOOD until 4 pm.	
		12.45 pm	Regtl Move Order issued (app 232) E	app. 232
		6.30 pm	Move complete and reported to Brigade. weather cold and rainy. Enemy occasionally shelled camping area during day.	
		9.30 pm	Order from G.O.C. 9th Divn informing 9th Divn that in coming operations they would be fighting side by side with 15th Divn for first time during the war and calling on every officer NCO & man to make a special effort to surpass their former records	
BAZENTIN & GRAND	24/10/16	9.5 AM	Instructions recd. from Bde H.Q. would proceed by march route to ALBERT today and asking what time Regt could be ready to move. time stated 12 & informed Bde. Regt ready to move at 1 pm later instructions received that Regt to move to MAMETZ WOOD move complete to MAMETZ WOOD area at 5 pm. rain falling continuously movement very difficult (app 233) [Operation Order No 74 of 24/10/16 1st S.A.I. Bde confirming the move was received at 4.25 pm	app. 232 A 233.
MAMETZ WOOD	25/10/16	9.25 AM	Instructions recd. to supply working party of 400 OR and proportion of officers to be at rendezvous at 6 am today - working parties totalling 260 were all that could be found and dispatched the rendezvous at 11.30 am. weather cold & rainy. Enemy throwing over occasional shells during day but not dropping into camp.	
	26/10/16		Regt called on to furnish working parties of 400 OR. only 320 could be furnished. weather rainy -	
		2.15 pm	(app. 234) Orders recd direct from 9th Divn that Regt is to proceed to MILLENCOURT tomorrow passing starting point at CONTALMAISON at 9 am. Regtl move order (app 235) issued accordingly	app. 234
MILLENCOURT	27/10/16		Move from MAMETZ WOOD through ALBERT to MILLENCOURT a distance of about 10 miles through continuous rain completed by 2 pm.	app. 235
		4.45 pm	Operation Order No 73 1st S.A.I. Bde. 27/10/16 received ordering Regt to move forward by march route to HERRISSART app 236	app. 236
		6.30 pm	app 237. Regtl move order issued. This camp is a new one of huts and accommodation good	app. 237
HERRISSART	28/10/16		Regt moved off from MILLENCOURT at 9.50 AM and reached HERRISSART at 1.45 pm and went into BILLETS raining almost continuously.	
		11 pm	Operation Order No 74 S.A.I. Bde dated 28/10/16 received app 238	238

Army Form C. 2118.

WAR DIARY
or
INTELLIGENCE SUMMARY.
(Erase heading not required.)

Instructions regarding War Diaries and Intelligence Summaries are contained in F. S. Regs., Part II. and the Staff Manual respectively. Title pages will be prepared in manuscript.

Place	Date	Hour	Summary of Events and Information	Remarks and references to Appendices
HERRISSART	28/10/16		Ordering Regt. to move forward tomorrow by bus to WANQUETIN. Regtl. Move. Order No C 17 issued (app 239)	app 239
WANQUETIN	29/10/16	7/30 AM	Regt arrived at [illegible] N bussing point BUCHVILLERS Road at 8 am but did not embus until 10.30 – Regt arrived at WANQUETIN at 3.30 pm raining the whole day. Billeting accommodation very limited whole of 9th Divn moving into this area	
	30/10/16		Day spent in cleaning up and re-organisation of regiment. Total casualties for month. 9 Officers & 154 O.R. weather rainy	
	31/10/16		Re-organisation of Regt. into fighting sections total strength of Regt. with H.Qrs less detached 27 Officers 649 O Ranks	

[illegible signature] Lieut. Col.
Commanding 3rd S.A.I.

87

88

M O V E   O R D E R.

ORDER NO. C 8.

By Lieut.Col.E.F.THACKERAY.C.M.G.
Commanding 3rd.South African Infantry.
(Transvaal Regiment).

In The Field.
4/10/1916.

In accordance with Operation Order No.61.of the 1st.S.A.I. Brigade datedOctober,4th.1916.the Regiment will proceed by road to BONNIERES tomorrow the 5th.inst.

ROUTE.VIA LE COUROY and ESTREE WAMAN,REBRENVETTE to BONNIERES.

MOVEMENT.The Regiment will be ready to move off at 9.30.a.m. in the following order :- Headquarters,C,B,D,A Companies, Transport and Rearguard.Companies will move off direct from theirbillets,joining the line of march at the Northern end of the Transport Lines on the LIENCOURT ROAD.
The leading Company will not enter or pass LIENCOURT-REBRENVETTE-FREVENT ROAD by 10.5.a.m. The Transport to be clear of GRAND RULLECOURT - REBRENVETTE-FREVENT ROAD by 11.30.a.m.

BILLETING PARTIES. Each Company,including Hradquarters will detail one senior N.C.O.and 4 men (Hqrs.1 N.C.O.and 6 men) to parade outside the Regimental Orderly Room at 2.15.p.m. today to proceed forthwith to BONNIERES.

CONTENTS OF HAVERSACKS. The Haversack will contain Cap, Spare Drawers,Socks and Mess-Tin cover.All spare shirts to be rolled up in Great Coat.

AMMUNITION. Only 100 rounds of ammunition will becarried on the person.The remainder will be carried in sacks on Company Transport.

CONTENTS OF PACK.The following articles ONLY will be carried in the pack :- Washing and Shaving Kit,1 pair socks, Cardigan jacket,Waterproof Sheet,Smoking Gear and Rations.

MARCHING IN STATE. Marching In States are to be rendered tom the Adjutant immediately on the Companies arrival in billets,showing any men who fell out on the line of march.

TIME.Time to be obtained at the Regimental Orderly Room at 6.p.m.today.

INFORMATION. The name of our destination is to be made known to all ranks.

INSPECTION OF BILLETS.The 2nd.in Command,and M.O.will inspect the billets of the Regimental Area after the Regiment has moved off and will make a written report in duplicate to be signed by both Officers for the information of the O.C.
The Sanitary Sergt.and Staff will accompany this inspection.

SALVAGE.O.C. Headquarter Company will detail 1 N.C.O.and 2 men to the 2nd.in Command on his billet inspection for the purpose of salvage.

BAGGAGE.All blankets will be rolled in bundles of tenand marked with tin tickets and stacked outside Quartermasters Stores by 7.30.a.m. for converance on lorry. All Great Coats (in which spare shirts should be tied)are to be rolled in bundles of ten and marked with tin tickets.Company Officers and other Company baggage to be stacked outside the Quarter-masters Store by 8.a.m. - Haversacks to be tied together in convenient bundles

2. TRANSPORT

TRANSPORT. In addition to the Regimental transport, local transport has been hired Regimentally at the rate of one per Company and one for Geadquarters, to be at their respective Headquarters by 8.a.m. The Quartermaster and Transport Officer will make all arrangements with this order.

SHOULDER PATCHES. Shoulder Patches are to be drawn immediately and sewn on beneath the shoulder seam, on the outside of the arm. Every endevour is ti be made to have each Company complete in this respect before the Regiment moves tomorrow.

REARGUARD. O.C. "A" Company will detail one Officer, one Sgt. and 20 men to act as rearguard. O.C. Rearguard will be strictly responsible that no straggling is allowed amongst the hired transport. Should there be any break-down, he will furnish the driver with a written pass to the destination and leave one as guard with the waggon.

H. Hammond Fleming

M A J O R.
Acting Adjutant 3rd. Regiment.
South African Infantry.

3rd Rgt

90

S E C R E T.

Copy No 3e.

9th Division Operation Order No. 80.

5.10.18.

1. The 9th Division will be transferred from the First Army (IV Corps) to the Fourth Army (XV Corps).

2. The 9th Division (less Divisional Artillery) will move on October 5th in accordance with march table attached.

3. Brigades will move with not less than five minutes interval between Units.

The traffic on the main ST. POL - DOULLENS Road is to be delayed as little as possible when formations are crossing. Each formation will detail an Officer to regulate the traffic at the point on this road where it crosses.

4. The Supply Sections of the Division Train will move into the BONNIERES area on the morning of October 5th under orders to be issued by O.C., Train.

They will be clear of LIENCOURT-FREVENT Road by 8 a.m.

Roads available -

1. GRAND RULLECOURT - BEAUDRICOURT - BOUQUEMAISON-NEUVILLETTE - BARLY.

2. HOUVIN HOUVIGNEUL - FREVENT - BONNIERES.

3. Any roads between 1 and 2.

Baggage vehicles of the Train will move with Units.

5. Accommodation table for ordinary billetting in the area is attached.

[signature]
Major,
General Staff,
9th (Scottish) Division.

Issued at 4.15 pm.

Copies to:-

No. 1 to 26th Bde.	13 to 9th Signals.
2 to 27th Bde.	14 to A.A. & Q.M.G.
3 to 1st S.A.Bde.	15 to A.D.M.S.
4 to C.R.A.	16 to A.D.V.S.
5 to 50th R.A.Bde.	17 to A.P.M.
6 to 51st R.A.Bde.	18 to Third Army.
7 to 52nd R.A.Bde.	19 to 17th Corps.
8 to Trench Mortars.	20 to 4th Corps.
9 to 9th Div. Colm.	21 to 15th Corps.
10 to C.R.E.	22 War Diary.
11 to 9th Seaforths.	23 File.
12 to 9th Div. Train.	

MARCH TABLE.

Date.	Unit	From	To	Route	Instructions	Remarks.
Octr. 5th.	26th Inf. Bde.	LIENCOURT - ETREE WAMIN - BERLENCOURT - DENIER Area.	Area MEZEROLLES FROHEN GRAND REMAISNIL NOEUX.	(a) LIENCOURT-ETREE WAMIN -BEAUDRICOURT-BOUQUEMAISON -NEUVILETTE-BARLY. (b) HOUVIN HOUVIGNEUL - FREVENT-BONNIERES-NOEUX. (c) All roads between (a) and (b).	1. Not to enter or cross LIENCOURT - FREVENT Road till 8.15 a.m. 2. To be clear of DENIER by 9 a.m. 3. To be clear of GRAND RULLECOURT - REBREUVIETTE - FREVENT Road by 10 a.m. 4. 63rd Fld.Coy. to be south of REBREUVIETTE-BONNIERES Road by 10.15 a.m.	63rd Fld.Coy. & 26th F.Amb. to move under orders to be issued by G.O.C. 26th Inf. Bde.
	63rd Fld. Coy.	HOUVIN HOUVIGNEUL.				
	26th Fld. Amb.	HOUVIN HOUVIGNEUL.				
	1st S.A.Bde.	GRAND RULLECOURT LIGNEREUIL. AMBRINES.	Area BONNIERES	(a) GRAND RULLECOURT - ETREE WAMIN-REBREUVIETTE - BONNIERES. (b) HOUVIN HOUVIGNEUL - FREVENT - BONNIERES. (c) All roads between (a) and (b).	1. Not to enter DENIER till 9.5am. 2. To be clear of DENIER by 10 am. 3. Not to enter ETREE WAMIN till 10.5 am. 4. Not to enter or cross the LIENCOURT-REBREUVIETTE-FREVENT road till 10.5 am. 5. To be clear of GRAND RULLECOURT - REBREUVIETTE-FREVENT road at 11.45 a.m. 6. To be clear of GRAND RULLECOURT by 10.5 a.m.	64th Fld.Coy. & S.African Fld. Amb. to move under orders of G.O.C. 1st S.A.Bde. 64th Fld.Coy. to be billeted at BOFFLES.
	64th F.Coy. S.A.Fld.Amb.	HOUVIN HOUVIGNEUL. GRAND RULLECOURT.	FORTEL. BOFFLES.			

Date.	Unit.	From.	To	Route	Instructions	Remarks.
Octr. 5th.	Mob.Vet. Section.	PENIN.	Area BONNIERES FORTEL. BOFFLES.	FREVENT.	To move from billets at 1.30 p.m. G.O.C. S.A.Bde. to arrange billets in new area	90th Fld.Coy. and 27th Fld.Amb. to move under orders to be issued by G.O.C. 27th I.Bde.
	27th Inf. Brigade.	BEAUFORT MANIN VILLERS SIR SIMON PENIN.	Area NEUVILLETTE	(a) MANIN-BEAUFORT-GRAND RULLECOURT - BEAUDRICOURT - BOUQUEMAISON. (b) HOUVIN HOUVIGNEUL - REBREUVIETTE-ARBRE-MONT LEBLOND-CANTELEUX. (c) All routes between (a) & (b).	1. Not to enter DENIER or LIGNEREUIL till 10.15am. 2. Not to enter or cross the LIENCOURT -REBREUVIETTE -FREVENT Road till 12 noon. 3. To be clear of GRAND RULLECOURT-REBREUVIETTE-FREVENT Road by 1 p.m. 4. To be clear of HOUVIN HOUVIGNEUL by 12.30 p.m. 5. *Not to pass GRAND RULLECOURT till 10.30 am.	*Note. The GRAND RULLECOURT - BEAUDRICOURT - FOUQUEMAISON Road is available for 27th Bde. after 10.30 a.m.
	90th F. Coy. RE.	HOUVIN HOUVIGNEUL.	BARLY.			
	27th F. Amb.	PENIN.				
	9th Seaforths.	AVERDOINGT.	VILLERS l'HOPITAL.	MAGNICOURT-HOUVIN HOUVIGNEUL-FREVENT-BONNIERES.	Not to pass HOUVIN HOUVIGNEUL till 12.30 pm.	S.A.Bde. to arrange that march of 9th Seaforths through BONNIERES not delayed.

1st South African Infantry Brigade.

4th October 1916.

93

Copy No 3

APP187

SECRET. URGENT.
Map Reference
Sheet LENS II
1/100,000

OPERATION ORDER. 61.

I. MOVE. (a) The 9th Division will be transferred from the First Army (I Corps) to the FOURTH ARMY (XV) Corps
(b) The Brigade will move by Units on October 5th as per march table attached.

2. MOVEMENT. The Brigade will move with notless than five minutes interval between units.
The traffic on the St.POL - DOULLENS road is to be delayed as little as possible when units are crossing. Each Unit will detail a mounted officer to regulate the traffic at the point on this road where it crosses.

3. TRANSPORT. All transport including baggage vehicles will move with units.

4. ROUTE. The route to be taken by each unit is shewn on the attached march table.

5. INSPECTION OF BILLETS. Os.C. Units will detail an Officer (to be accompanied in Infantry Units by the Medical Officer) to inspect billets which have been occupied by their Units.
A written report signed by that Officer (In Infantry units by the Medical Officer also) will be forwarded to Brigade Headquarters by 6 p.m. on day of inspection.

6. MARCHING IN STATE. Marching in states to be rendered within one hour of arrival at new billets. On this will be given the number of men, if any, who fell out on the line of march.

7. BILLETING PARTIES. The usual billeting parties will proceed in advance. The Billeting Officers of the Units at BONNIERES will report to Captain STEVENSON at the x Church, BONNIERES at 2 p.m. today.
Units at FORTEL at the x Church, FORTEL at 3 pm today.

x(Church)

8. REPORTS. Os.C. Units will report to Brigade Headquarters at BONNIERES the arrival of their Units in Billets and give the Map Reference of Unit Headquarters.

A L Pepper
Captain,
Actg. Brigade Major, . . .

Copy No. I. 1st Regiment.
2. 2nd Regiment.
3. 3rd Regiment.
4. 4th Regiment.
5. 28th Coy. M.G.Cy.
6. S.A.L.T.M.Battery.
7. 64th Field CoY R.E.
8. Bde Signal Section.
9. 107th Co. A.S.C.
10. S.A.Field Ambulance.
II. 26th Infantry Brigade.
12. 27th Infantry Brigade.
13. 9th Division.
14. Brigadier-General.
15. Brigade Major.
16. Staff Captain.
17. Office.
18. War Diary.
19. Bde Transport Officer.
20. Post Corporal.

Recd 12.15 PM

14/10/16.
9.50 pm. Orders recd from Brigade. G.O.C. orders the Regiment to make arrangements to carry out
assault on Enemy's position which was
first objective in last attack made by
2nd & 4th S.H.I.
The assault possibly to be made
early hours 15th inst — App. 215 A

94

MARCH TABLE   OPERATION ORDER 61.

&&&&&

DATE.	UNIT	FROM	TO	ROUTE	Approximate distanxe in miles.	Hour of Start	INSTRUCTIONS.
5th October 1916.	Bde H.Q. & Signallers	AMBRINES	BONNIERES	via MAGNICOURT sur CANCHE HOUVIN HOUVIGNEUIL-FREVENT BONNIERES.	12	9,15am	
	64th Field Co. R.E.	Houvin-Houvigneuil	BOFFLES	via FREVENT	$8\frac{1}{2}$	8 am	
	1st S.A.I.	GD.RULLECOURT	BONNIERES	via LE CAUROY-EST.WAMIN REBREUVETTE-BONNIERES.	11	9.15 am	Not to enter or cross the LIENCOURT-REBREUVETTE FREVENT Road till 10.5am To be clear of GD RULLE-COURT-REDREUVETTE - FREVENT Rd at 11,15am,
	2nd S.A.I.	LIGNEREUIL	FORTEL	via MAGNICOURTsurCANCHE HOUVIN HOUVIGNEUIL-FREVENT FORTEL.	$13\frac{1}{2}$	8 am	Not to pass thro'DENIER.
	3rd S.A.I.	GD RULLECOURT	BONNIERES	via LE CAUROY-ESTREE WAMIN REBREUVETTE-BONNIERES.	11	9.30 am	Not to enter or cross the LIENCOURT-REBREUVETTE-FREVENT Rd till 10.5 am. To be clear of GD RULLE-COURT-REBREUVETTE-FREVENT Rd at 11.30 am.
	4th S.A.I.	AMBRINES	BONNIERES	via MAGNICOURTsurCANCHE HOUVIN HOUVIGNEUIL-FREVENT BONNIERES	12	9 am	
	S.A.F.A.	GD, RULLECOURT	BONNIERES	via LE CAUROY-EES.WAMIN-REBREUVETTE-BONNIERES	11	9.45am	Not to enter or cross the LIENCOURT-REBREUVETTE-FREVENT Rd till 10,5 am. To be clear of GRAND RULLECOURT-REBREUV-ETTE-FREVENT Rd. at 11,45 am,

To be clear of GD.RULLECOURT by 10.5 am,

95

96

Page 2 of MARCH TABLE to OPERATION ORDER 61.

DATE	UNIT	FROM	TO	ROUTE	Approx. Distance in miles.	Hour of start	INSTRUCTIONS.
5th Octr 1916.	28th M.G.Coy.	MAIZIERES	FORTEL	via MAGNICOURT sur CANCHE - HOUVIN-HOUVIGNEUIL-FREVENT FORTEL.	12	8 am.	
	Trench Mortar Batterry	GUOYenTERNOIS	BOFFLES	via HOUVIN-HOUVIGNEUIL - FREVENT-BOFFLES.	11	8 am	
	Möbile Veterinary Section	PENIN	FORTEL	via FREVENT	13½	1.30 p.m.	To move from billets at 1.30 pm.

Order No. 96
APP 188
97

MOVE ORDER.

IN THE FIELD.
4/10/1918.

By Lieut.Col.E.F.THACKERAY.C.M.G.
Commanding 3rd.South African Infantry.

In accordance with ~~Provisional~~ Operation Order No.84.of the 1st S.A.I. Bde. dated October 4th,1918. the Regiment will proceed by road to BONNIERES tomorrow the 5th.inst.

ROUTE.-Via LE COUROY and ESTREE WAMAN,REBRENVETTE to BONNIERES.

MOVEMENT.- The Regiment will be ready to move off at 9.30.a.m. in the following order :-
Headquarters,C,B,D,A Companies, Transport and Rearguard. Companies will move off direct from their billets, ~~commencing~~ joining the line of march at the Northern end of the Transport Lines on the LIENCOURT ROAD. The leading Company will not enter or pass LIENCOURT - REBRENVETTE - FREVENT ROAD before 10.5.a.m. Transport & Rear Guard to be clear of GRAND RULLECOURT - REBRENVETTE - FREVENT ROAD by 11.30.a.m.

BILLETING PARTIES.- Each Company,including Headquarters, will detail 1 Senior N.C.O.and 4.men (Hdqrs.1 N.C.O. & 10.R.) to parade outside the Regimental Orderly Room at 2.15.p.m. today to proceed forthwith to BONNIERES.

TRANSPORT.- ~~All Blankets will be rolled up in bundles of 10, and marked with tin tickets and stacked outside Qr.Mrs. Stores by 7.30.a.m.and all their Company baggage,including Overcoats, (which should be tied together in convenient bundles) for conveyance in Company wagon. Local transport has been hired Regimentally at the rate of one wagon per Company and one wagon for Headquarters will be readiness to convey this baggage~~

CONTENTS OF HAVERSACK.- The Haversack will contain Cap, Spare Drawers,Socks and Mess-tin Cover.All spare shirts to be rolled up in the Great Coat.

AMMUNITION.- Only 100 rounds of ammunition will be carried on the person. The remainder will be carried in sacks on Company Transport.

CONTENTS OF PACK.- The following articles ONLY to be carried in the pack :- Washing and Shaving Kit,1 pair socks, Cardigan Jacket,Waterproof Sheet,Smoking Gear, and rations

MARCHING IN STATE.- Marching In States are to rendered to the Adjutant immediately on the Companies arrival in billets showing any men who fell out on the line of march.

TIME.- Time to be obtained from the Regimental Orderly Room at 6.p.m. today.

INFORMATION.- The name of our destination to be made known to all ranks.

INSPECTION OF BILLETS.-The 2nd.in Command and M.O.will inspect all billets of the Regimental Area after the Regiment has moved off,and will make a written report in duplicate to be signed by both Officers for the information of the O.C. The Sanitary Sergt.and Staff will accompany this inspection.

SALVAGE.- O.C.Headquarter Company will detail 1 N.C.O.and 4 men to the 2nd in Command on his billet inspection for the purpose of salvage.

War Diary

App 25

MOVE ORDER. ORDER NO.

By Lieut.Colonel E.F.THACKERAY.C.M.G. IN THE FIELD.
Commanding 3rd.Regiment S.A.Inf. 26/10/1916.
(Transvaal Regiment)

98

---

1. MOVE. In accordance with orders received direct from the 9th. Division dated 26/10/16. the Regiment will move from MAMETZ to MILLENCOURT via CONTALMAISON and ALBERT tomorrow the 27th. October, 1916.

2. ORDER OF MARCH. The Regiment will parade at 8.30.a.m. and move off by platoons with an interval of 100 yards and 200 yards between Companies, in the following order :- Headquarters, A, B, C, D, Coys.

3. DRESS. Marching order, greatcoats and W.P.Sheets in packs, jerkins to be worn, skin outside, and over jacket, gloves and steel helmets to be worn, rifles in sandbags.

4. TOOLS. All tools except entrenching implements to be deposited on Division Dump by 8.p.m. tonight.

5. AMMUNITION. Every man to carry 120 rounds of ammunition. Any deficiencies to be made up from spare Lewis Gun ammunition.

6. BAGGAGE. All kits and baggage to be on Regimental Dump by 8.a.m. O.C. Coys. will detail a party of 1 N.C.O and 2 men to upload their baggage on the Transport. These men will parade with their full marching order and will fall in rear of Regimental Transport as baggage guard under a sergeant to be detailed by O.C."D" Coy. This N.C.O. will be responsible that all baggage is correctly loaded up
BLANKETS. Blankets to be rolled in bundles of ten, labelled with tin lables and piled on the Regimental Dump together with other Company baggage.

7. TRANSPORT. Field Kithens, water carts, and mess cart to move at the head of the Transport column. Transport Officer and Quartermaster will make necessary arrangements in conformity with these orders.

8. CAMP INSPECTION. Officers Commanding Companies are responsible that their lines are left clean, latrines, and refuse pits filled in. Each Company will leave 2 orderlies in its lines when moving off, who will not rejoin their Companies until they receive orders to do so from the 2nd in Command.
The 2nd in Command and M.O. together with the Sanitary Sergt. will inspect the Regimental area after the Regiment has moved off and furnish a report to be signed by both officers as to the condition in which they found the camp.

9. GENERAL. Arrangements are to be made for breakfast before leaving to be finished by 7.30.a.m. in order that kitchens may be prepared for dinners.

MAJOR.
Acting Adjutant.
3rd.S.A.Infantry.

99

Priority (per Mc by 4 Hdq) Rd

To C.B 199A

B Coy 9th SEAFORTH PIONEERS started work on TRENCH from S17 C 44 – on Trench occupied by 4th SAI in direction parallel to road running NORTH

Machine gun opened immediately from NORTH WEST – along valley.

VERY LIGHTS fell among working party.

Took 50 men and connected RIGHT of SAI to LEFT of 26th Bde

Remainder worked on existing TRENCH.

CASUALTIES – 2 killed
3 wounded
Machine gun fire

4·am
13·10·16

W. E. [illegible] Capt
O/c B Coy 9 Sea

12 10/16

O/C C Company

On Instructions I proceeded on patrol to find out whether our men are in the First Objective :-
* They have consolidated a position which looks like an old disused German Trench, and not their original Front Line. The ELBOW (Strong Point) is still held by the Germans, we have established a Strong Point within about Fifty yards of them. A C.T. is being dug from this Strong Point to our old Front Line now held by C Coy 4 [illegible].

* I got in touch with Lieut Harries of the 4th Leeds

T [illegible] 2/Lieut.

12 10 16

To O.C. C Coy.

On instructions received I proceeded with [illegible] Evans of the K.R. to reconnoitre the front of our line. We advanced from M.17 c. 8.3 and proceeded about 150 yards north of the trench occupied by our troops. And it was quite apparent that none of our troops where in front

[illegible] were sniped at and [illegible] very heavy shell [illegible] the enemy. Up to the time of writing Corpl Adams one of the party has failed to return.

W.H. [illegible]

The Adjutant

E.M.

Forwarded for your information please. I have sent [illegible] to O.C. K.R.

[illegible] Capt [illegible]

12.55 [illegible] 13/10/16

100

12/7/16 101

O/C C Company.

On Instructions, I proceeded on Patrol to find out whether our men are in the First Objective.

I got in touch with Lt. Harris of the 4th and ascertained that they have consolidated a position which looks like and old disused German Trench and not their original Front Line. The ELBOW (Strong Point) is still held by the Germans, we have established a Strong Point within about Fifty yards of them.

A Communication Trench is being dug from this Strong Point to our old Front Line, now held by C Company 4th Regt.

T. [illegible] 2/Lieut.

13 10/16. 102
3-30 Am

O/C. C Coy

Taken over position Correct-
as ordered.

T Woodhouse
2/Lieut

~~The cap…~~

Forwarded, please.

[illegible]
Capt
O.C. C Coy

13/7/16

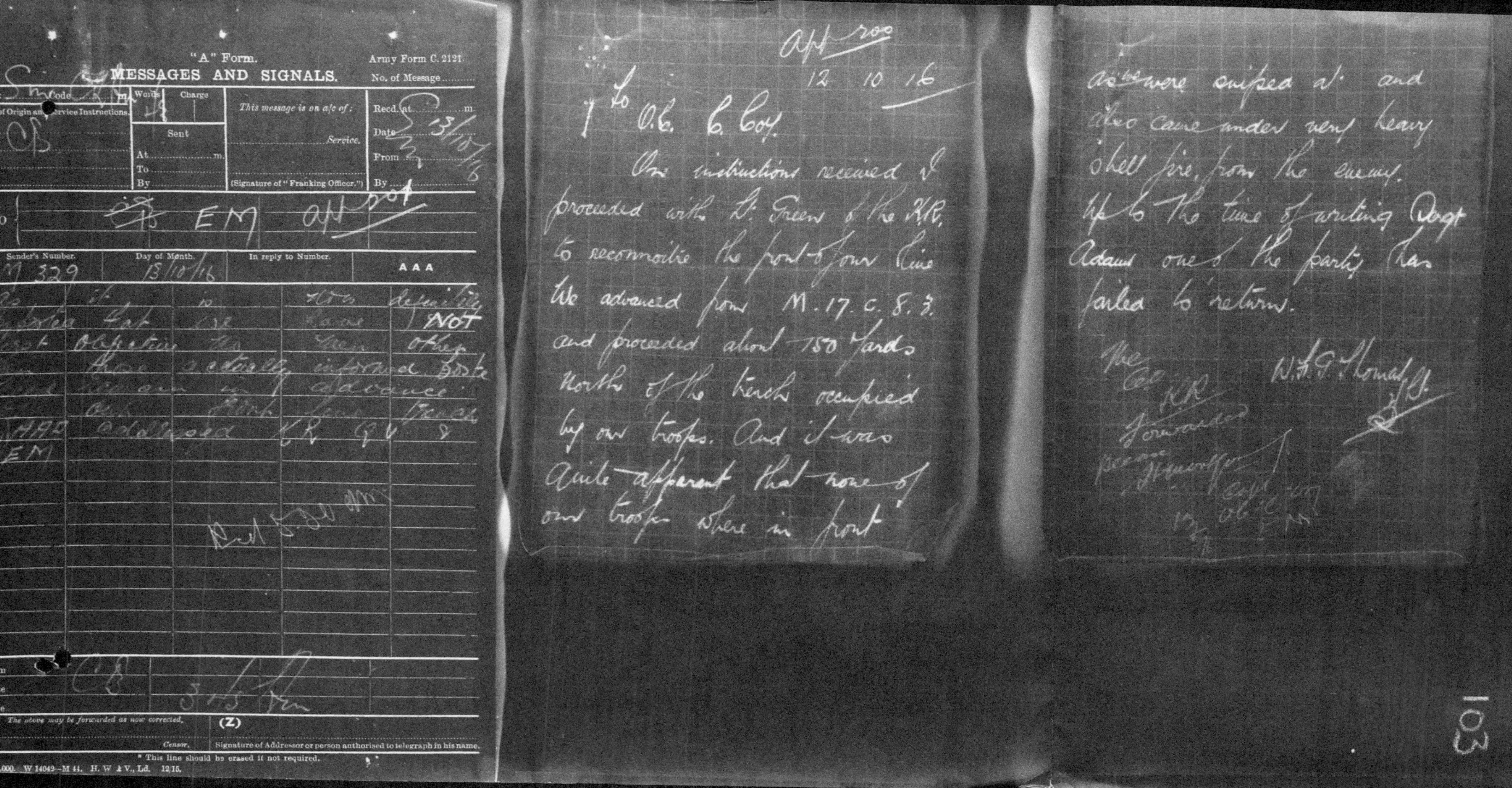

"A" Form.
MESSAGES AND SIGNALS.
Army Form C. 2121.
No. of Message

Prefix SM Code Words 49 Charge
Office of Origin and Service Instructions.
Sent At m. To By
This message is on a/c of: Service.
(Signature of "Franking Officer.")
Recd. at m.
Date 13/10/16
From
By

TO EM

Sender's Number. SM 329
Day of Month. 13/10/16
In reply to Number.
AAA

NOT

AAA
EM

From CB
Place
Time 3.15 pm

The above may be forwarded as now corrected.
(Z)
Censor.
Signature of Addressor or person authorised to telegraph in his name.
* This line should be erased if not required.

W 14049—M 44. H. W. & V., Ld. 12/15.

12 10 16

1 to O.C. C. Coy.

On instructions received I proceeded with Lt. Green of the K.R. to reconnoitre the front of our line. We advanced from M.17.C.8.3. and proceeded about 150 yards North of the trench occupied by our troops. And it was quite apparent that none of our troops where in front as we were sniped at and also came under very heavy shell fire, from the enemy. Up to the time of writing Sergt Adams one of the party has failed to return.

W. A. G. Thomas 2/Lt.

The Co. K.R.
Forwarded

103

No. Date 13.10.16 Time 12.20 p.m. Place In the Trenches

To Place

Adjutant

E.M. 104

Report as to reconnaissance carried out by 2nd Lt Cruddas to get touch with unit on my right was sent to you at about 11.45 p.m. by Pte Arnold, Headquarters Signaller, who was returning to H.Q.

The signal flare Patrol Plan was noted; flares were not put up. I learn that Lt [illegible] of 2nd Regt is in front of my position. I understand that instructions are that flares be put up from front line only. This matter is referred to in my report of Lt Cruddas' re.

2

Instructions re control of flares are complied with. If flares are to be put up from my present position please instruct me.

My trenches do not rest on MILL but join up with B. Coy short of that position.

I attach tracing of trenches from map 1/10,000 and also rough sketch showing position.

Your runner, Pte Blackwell, was sent on to B. Coy with message to Capt Sprenger.

Instructions re Patrol Party noted.

[illegible] 2nd Lt
for Capt
O.C. "C" Coy.

Your second message just received. My sketch not clear till another attempt.

"C" Coy.

Appx 30 2

The Adjutant
E M

In compliance with C.O's instructions attached, I endeavoured to get into communication with Lt. Pearse by report. However Lt. Cruddas interviewed Lt. Pearse and I am submitting report [illegible] same.

H. Montgomery
Capt.
O.C. "C" Coy.

1/7/16

"C" Coy.

The Adjutant
E M

In compliance with your order I endeavoured to get in touch with Regt. on my right. Lieut Cruddas was detailed for the work. He reports that he went down the trench as held by "C" Coy (marked on Sketch) then went along Sunken road west and entered a communication trench running N.E. which was last night held by 4th, but is at present unoccupied, this trench joins up with the position held by Lieut. Pearse, who [illegible] Lieut Pearse informed Lt. Cruddas that he have joined up on his right with the Seaforths who were relieved early this morning by the Lancashire [illegible]. Lt. Pearse is not certain as to name of relieving Regt. but thinks it was the latter Regt. named. The Connection between Lt. Pearse Post & the Regt. on the right is not yet complete. Lt. Cruddas returned by trench marked on sketch as being occupied by "B" [illegible] [illegible] portion unoccupied. The trench is very shallow and under continuous enemy sniping. The 4th occupies a portion of the trench which joins up with "B" Coy.

105

106

2nd Batt SAI

App 20V 13/10/16

We are connected
with a regiment on
our right.
On our left there
is no one the
4 SAI having departed.
Our strength is 60
Please send instructions
what to do

T Pearse Lt.
2 SAI

Recd
9.20 [illegible]

ET. 1.
7.25. A.M.
13-10-16

O.C. "C" Co. 3rd

approx

The bearer PTE ARNOLD 2nd S.A.I. has arrived with a message from LT. PEARSE 2nd S.A.I. who says that he is hung up and dug in at a point 17. C. 4. 4. with some 60 men. He thinks he is connected on his right with some metres of another Brigade probably 26th. He asks for instructions and ARNOLD thinks you could signal him with discs he is on the look out.

Try and signal him that it is impossible to relieve him & for him to come back in daylight. so he must do his best to hang on till dark

vision he will be relieved or
ordered to come back.

In signalling great care
must be taken not to
expose Eastern position.

Let me know results
at once.

P. J. Shaughnessy Lt Col
Comdg 3rd S.A.I.

7.45 AM.

I enclose map.

"C" Form (Duplicate).
(In books of 50's in duplicate.)

MESSAGES AND SIGNALS. No. of Message

OB MV 144 Copies Sucker

Charges to Pay. £ s. d.

Office Stamp. ARMY TELEGRAPHS 13.XI.16 B

Service Instructions. Priority

Handed in at 36 CB Office 12.40 a m. Received 1.50 m.

TO EM APPZ05

Sender's Number	Day of Month	In reply to Number	AAA
BM 317	13th		

Order OC Company EM in front line to immediately send out patrol towards post evacuated by your men this morning at M16D93 aaa That post is to be reoccupied and another post connecting up with 15th Divn established at approximately M16D64 aaa Posts will be officers posts if possible if not less than 20 each with 2 Lewis Gun aaa Posts will dig themselves well in aaa They must take water and rations aaa Officers or NCOs in charge will send written reports to his Hq before daybreak

FROM

PLACE & TIME

Wt. 432—M437 500,000 Pads. H W V 5/16 Forms C.2123.

MESSAGES AND SIGNALS. No. of Message

Charges to Pay. £ s. d.

Office Stamp. ARMY TELEGRAPHS 13.XI.16 B

Service Instructions.

Handed in at Office m. Received m.

TO

Sender's Number	Day of Month	In reply to Number	AAA

reporting his posts in position and giving situation as regards enemy attitude etcetera aaa 15th Divn will establish a post about M16D46 and post to be established at M16D64 should endeavour get into touch with that post reporting whether successful in report aaa Acknowledge aaa Addressed KR repeated EM

Recd 2.10 am. WWH

FROM CB

PLACE & TIME 12.30 am

Wt. 432—M437 500,000 Pads. H W V 5/16 Forms C.2123.

107

"C" Form (Original).

Army Form C. 2123.
(In books of 50's in duplicate)

MESSAGES AND SIGNALS. No. of Message

Prefix SB Code KLAM Words 63

Received From CB By [illegible]

Sent, or sent out At m. To By

Office Stamp. BT 13/10/16

Charges to collect

Service Instructions. Priority

108

Handed in at Office m. Received 12 4 m.

TO EM

APP 204

*Sender's Number BM 307 | Day of Month twelfth | In reply to Number | AAA

In confirmation telephone message you will order pioneers to dig communication trench between point M16D93 and M22B5M8 tonight aaa Working party from KR and QV if required should assist aaa Sappers should consolidate point M16D93 which will be garrisoned before daybreak by EM with an officer Lewis gun and at least 25 men orders for this garrison to be given by you to O.C. Company of EM now in front trench aaa Addressed KR repeated EM

R12 10 am

FROM CB

PLACE & TIME 10.15 PM

* This line should be erased if not required.

Wt. 432—M437 500,000 Pads. H W V 5 16 Forms C.2123.

109

Should the wind be favourable smoke bombs are to be utilized.

Kindly acknowledge receipt.

(SGD) H.S. LAMOND HEMMING.

Major

Acting Adjutant

E.M.

APP 207

Operation Order

Time of Issue 10-15 p.m. 13/10/16 No C 11

In accordance with telegram from T.A. received via C.B. at 9.35 pm. 13/10/16 You will carry out a reconnaissance of strong point at M.16.d.9.3 tonight about midnight. If you find it held by the enemy you will capture it.

Working Parties. Before proceeding on operation to capture this point you will ascertain that Working Parties are withdrawn under cover.

Bombers. 16 Regimental Bombers under Lieut MALLETT will report to you before midnight for use in the enterprise if necessary. You will see that they have a good supply of Mills Grenades with them also instruct them to make full use of Rifle Grenades in covering the attack. 8 of the 16 Regimental Bombers you are to retain with you in reserve.

Lewis Guns. The Regimental Lewis Gun Officer & Lewis Gun team are ordered to you before midnight. You will make use of them & your own available Lewis Guns for the purpose of covering the attack & repelling any counter attack. O.C. B Coy will direct his Lewis Guns to cooperate with you in this matter as far as possible.

General. B Coy will cooperate with C Coy in covering the attack from its trenches. D Coy will move into the trenches occupied by C Coy in support. A Coy will stand to arms at the commencement of the attack and remain under arms until the enterprise is reported complete, for the purpose of repelling a counter attack.

Snipers. You will make full use of your snipers in cooperation with the Bombers in the attack.

Hour of Attack. O.C. C Coy will notify Head Qrs. Commander of Coys of the hour of attack.

Medical. The Regimental M.O. will make necessary arrangements at the 1st Aid Post to deal with casualties.

Runners. All Regimental and Company Runners to be held in readiness for dispatch carrying.

Assault. Fire will not be opened if the place can be carried by the Bayonet.

S.O.S. In the event of a counter attack O.C. C Coy may call for Artillery support by the S.O.S. Signal of 3 Red Very Lights fired in quick succession.

MESSAGES AND SIGNALS. No. of Message

SB Cpm 44 CB

Charges to Pay. £ s. d.

111

Office Stamp. EM 13/10/16

Service Instructions. Priority CB.

Handed in at CB Office 7.15pm. Received 7.35pm.

TO EM APP 20

Sender's Number	Day of Month	In reply to Number	AAA
BM 166	13th		

Following from TA begins CB will reconnoitre strong point M16.D9.3 tonight and if found to be held by the enemy to capture it AAA Please comply and report hour and arrangement made by wire AAA Wire result as soon as possible AAA Acknowledge

FROM CB

PLACE & TIME 7.10pm.

Wt. 432—M437 500,000 Pads. H W V 5/16 Forms C.2123.

APP 208
19/10/16
112

Brigade Major.

In reference to conversation the Brigade Major had with Major Hemming over the telephone at 10.15 p.m. tonight my impression is that this operation may develop into a considerable affair owing to the presence of the enemy in force round the objective.

I therefore beg that arrangements be made for co-operation of Artillery and the immediate support of the 1st Regiment if required.

Owing to curtailment of time for work the advanced trenches must necessarily be of a weak nature.

(SGD) E.F. THACKERAY.
Lt Col
Commdg E.M.

P.S. If trench Mortars were available in the front line their assistance would be valuable
11 p.m.

(SGD) E.F. THACKERAY
Lieut Col
Commdg E.M.

13/10/16. 113

APP 208

Brigade Major

In reference to conversation the Brigade Major had with Major Hemming over the telephone at 10.15 pm tonight my impression is that this operation may develop into a considerable affair owing to the presence of the enemy in force round the objective.

I therefore beg that arrangements be made for co-operation of artillery, and the immediate support of the 1st Regt. if required –

Owing to curtailment of time for work the advanced trenches, must necessarily be of a weak nature.

E. F. Macnaghten Lt. Col.
Commdg EM.

P.S. – If Trench Mortars were available in the front line their assistance would be valuable.

E. F. Macnaghten Lt. Col.
Commdg EM.

11 pm.

"C" Form (Duplicate). Army Form C. 2123. (In books of 50's in duplicate.)

MESSAGES AND SIGNALS. No. of Message ....

	Charges to Pay. £ s. d.	Office Stamp.
Service Instructions.	114	EMG 13/10/16

Handed in at .... Office .... m. Received .... m.

TO ...

Sender's Number	Day of Month	In reply to Number	AAA

On SOS tonight place Barrage on line M16D77 to M17c96 AAA Address EM repeated as TE and ABJ AAA For latter information reconnaissance will not be made till after midnight AAA Acknowledge

FROM CB

PLACE & TIME 10.55pm

Wt. 432—M497 500,000 Pads. H W V 5/16 Forms C.2123.

115

MESSAGES AND SIGNALS. No. of Message....

Prefix .... Code .... m.	Words	Charge	This message is on a/c of:	Recd. at .... m.
Office of Origin and Service Instructions.	Sent		.... Service.	Date
C	At .... m.			From
	To			
	By		(Signature of "Franking Officer.")	By

TO: C.B. — APP Z10

Sender's Number.	Day of Month.	In reply to Number.	AAA
* S 63.	14/10/16.		

Situation Report — WIND S.W. Situation [illegible] still [illegible] [illegible] 6.30 [illegible] [illegible] quiet [illegible] [illegible] RECONNOISSANCE Patrol sent out not yet returned [illegible] [illegible] between 2.30 and [illegible] morning

[illegible signature]

Major
a/adjt. — EM

From: E.M.
Place
Time: 3.0 AM

The above may be forwarded as now corrected. (Z)

Censor. Signature of Addressor or person authorised to telegraph in his name.

* This line should be erased if not required.

225,000. W 14042—M 41. H. W. & V., Ld. 12.15.

MESSAGES AND SIGNALS. No. of Message

8 [illegible] 11/SP 114 CB [illegible]	Charges to Pay. £ s. d.	Office Stamp
Service Instructions. CB Priority	[illegible]	EBM 13/10/16

Handed in at .... Office .... m. Received 11 40

TO: EM — APP Z09

Sender's Number	Day of Month	In reply to Number	AAA
BM 349	13/10		

Reference BM 166 strong point M 16 D 93 is to be reconnoitred before attacking troops move forward AAA Meanwhile working parties are to continue work AAA If and when post is found to be held by enemy dispositions for attack will then be made and working parties withdrawn AAA TE will place a Company at your disposal if required and has been ordered to place himself in communication with you to make necessary arrangements AAA Artillery will [illegible]

FROM
PLACE & TIME

Wt. 432—M437 500,000 Pads. H W V 5/16 Forms C.2123.

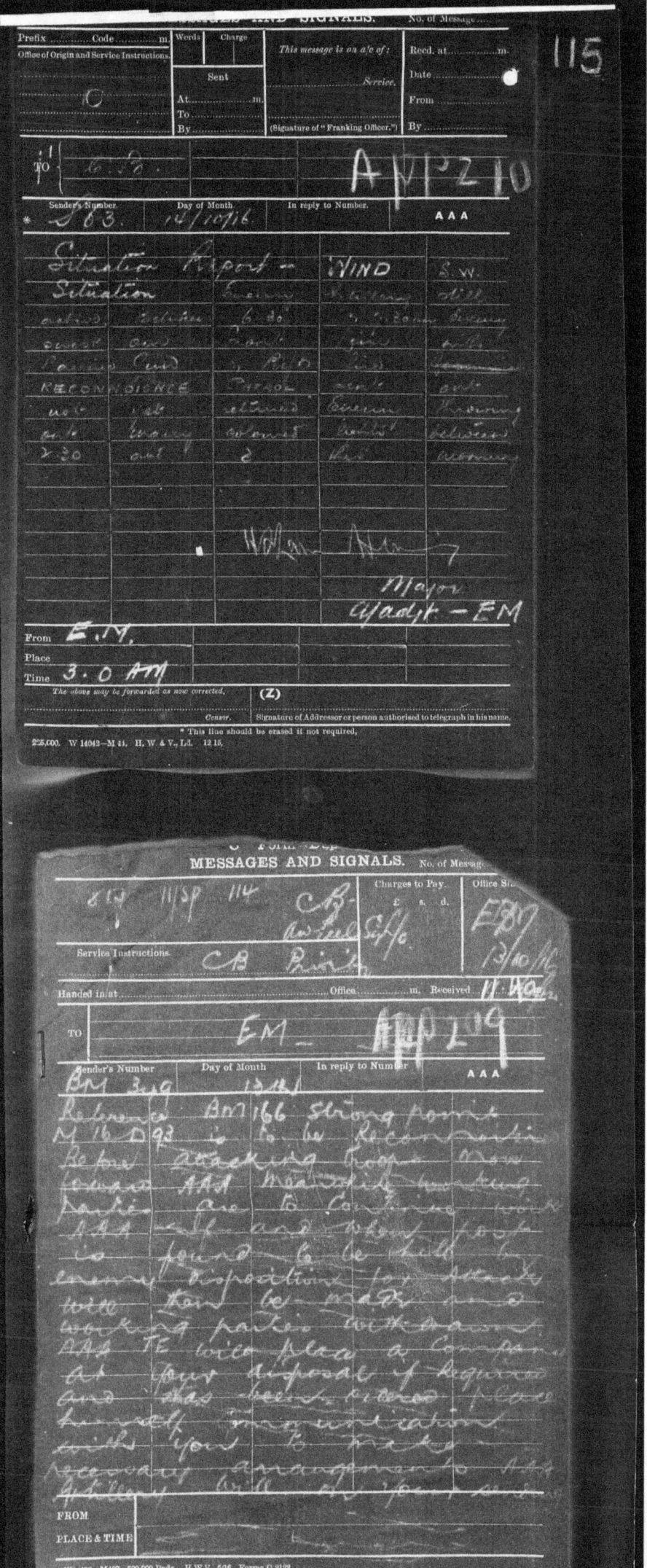

A PP 211 14/10/16

The O. C. 3rd S. African Inf.

As instructed I with 2nd Lt Van Ryneveld and Seven Regimental Bombers proceeded on a reconnaissance patrol to the Strong Point M.16.D.9.3.

Capt Montgomery was in charge of operations and was in rear with a Company of men in the new front line trench.

I left our trench at M 22 B 6.7 at 4.15 am and proceeded north along the road running to WARLENCOURT for about 300 yards and then worked East towards our Objective.

I had no difficulty in reaching the Strong point barring a few Sniping Shot which I thought were fired at us, and reached the point at 5.4 am.

The Strong point has two deep dug out with the entrances

2

facing Westwards.

There is a field gun emplacement in the Centre of the point (well hidden) and I noticed a few live Shells lying about but my impression is that the point had not been used for some considerable time.

We disturbed a Sniper as we approached the point but could not get him we found a German Rifle with four bullets in the magazine one of which was a self-made "Dum-Dum".

We did not have much time to look about us as it had now become daylight but the points I noticed were these.

(1) The Strong point dominated certain portion of the enemy trenches but was, in return dominated by the BUTTE de WARLENCOURT

(2) A machine gun placed on the mound would be able to play on our present trenches from M 22 B 6.6 to about M 16 C 8.0

The mound is 60' long, 25' [illegible]

3

and from [illegible] high [illegible] 5 [illegible] East of the mound which [illegible] [illegible] with the Enemy front line which [illegible] 170 [illegible] mound [illegible] was not a [illegible] of [illegible] British occupation but it is evident that [illegible] and Observers [illegible] utilise the point.

S. [illegible], Lieutenant.

3rd S. A. Infantry

Recd 6.15am

116

"C" Form (Duplicate). MESSAGES AND SIGNALS.

Army Form (In books of 50's in duplicate.)

No. of Message

SB 8IPM 197

Charges to Pay. £ s. d.

Office Stamp. EM 14/10/16

117

Service Instructions. PRIORITY GB

Handed in at Office 2·45 p.m. Received 3·20 p.m.

TO EM

APP 213

Sender's Number	Day of Month	In reply to Number	AAA
BM 257	14TH		

Division order following to be done tonight aaa M16D9.8 is to be occupied this evening after dark and joined up with our line at M17C5.0 and with road at approximately road junction M16D7.6 where battalion on your left will join up aaa communication trench will be dug from M22B7.7 to new line as above aaa R E section will improve trenches in right of our section aaa pioneers will dug communication trench as above aaa working party of 200 of which you will furnish 50 and TE 150

FROM

PLACE & TIME

432—M457 500,000 Pads. H W V 5/16 Forms C.2128.

118

Covering Party by C ✗
Strong points sand bags, dams, guns, water.
Walsh + Ratt bombers + Cpl Hayes + 1 Sgt LG + Coy bombers + fighting coy 10
Lt Wallscott + 20 to hold + 1 Coy LG consolidate strong point 8 etc
Lt Goodwin + 50 + 1 LG + bombs + water + Sandbags

Reports every ½ hour.

Runners 2 from ea coy Hqrs + 2 from C+D Coy all to B.

Very pistols + flares

S. O. S.

Report by phone when ready

Phone Bgde warn gunners

Form (Duplicate).

Army Form C. 2123.
(In books of 50's in duplicate.)

MESSAGES AND SIGNALS.

No. of Message..................

	Charges to Pay. £ s. d.	Office Stamp.
	(2)	119

Service Instructions.

Handed in at............................Office..............m. Received..............m.

TO

Sender's Number	Day of Month	In reply to Number	AAA

will dig new front trench
as above aaa arrange for
your 50 under an officer
to dig portion to west of
M16D9.3 and for the party which
will be under 2 officers to dig
portion to east aaa party
to capture and occupy
M16D9.3 should proceed as
soon as it is dark together
with remaining party for working
party and RE officer will arrange
for tape to mark off line aaa
this party will report at your
hq at 6pm aaa QV is furnishing
working party of 150 to deepen
and improve the comm[illegible] [illegible]

FROM

PLACE & TIME

Wt. 432—M437 500,000 Pads. H W V 5/16 Forms C.2123.

MESSAGES AND SIGNALS. (In books of 50's in duplicate.) No. of Message

Service Instructions.	Charges to Pay. £ s. d.	Office Stamp.
(2)		

Handed in at .... Office .... m. Received .... m.

TO

Sender's Number	Day of Month	In reply to Number	AAA
8			

~~trenches up to present front line aaa acknowledge~~

FROM CB

PLACE & TIME 2.45pm

Wt. 432—M437 500,000 Pads. H W V 5/16 Forms C.2122.

Oct 14th 1916

APP. 212

Brigade Major
1st O.A.S. Bde.

APP 212

In accordance with your B.M. 186 13/10/16 instructions to reconnoitre usual strong point Capt Montgomery O.C. C Coy 3rd O.A.S. was verbally instructed to carry out the order at about 7-45 pm when the message was received.
In view of the possibility of the situation developing I phoned you re Artillery support & the support of the 1st O.A.S. if necessary. I pointed out that the operations would ~~[illegible]~~ clash with & prevent the carrying out of urgent orders in ~~[illegible]~~ and occupying the line held by Lt. PIERCE 2nd SAS & Lt DONALDSON 4th SAS & on your instructions that the patrol must proceed 'seize the point' written orders were sent to Capt Montgomery to that effect to let the work go on to midnight and when all working parties were clear to seize the point. The urgent work of the trenches could not be completed till (midnight) 3 am when the patrol when went forward & seized the point, as ordered.

I send Mallett's report attached.
As it was by then dawn I rang you up & received the order that Lt Mallett had not returned and received your wire that no attack was to take place.
Lt Mallett returned shortly afterwards. He found the point within 5 yards of the western end of the enemy trench which looked new & unoccupied. The point is some 60 by 25 yds & 12 ft high and on a level with trench but is commanded by the BUTTE. There are two deep dugouts in it & also a concealed gun emplacement & 2 M.G. emplacements. He surprised an enemy sniper & captured his rifle. The point has been destroyed by our gun fire & is some 300 yds in front of our line. I have pointed it out to ~~many~~ any R.A. officers who have reported to me. There were no signs of previous British occupation.
All Coys & Lewis gunners stood by ready for cooperation if necessary.
C Coy moved up into fire trench & D Coy moved into the line vacated by C Coy.
Commanding

(SIGNED) E.F. THACKERAY
Commanding 3rd O.A.S.

120

strong point on the WARLANCOURT ROAD.
O.C. "C" Company will take over the whole of "PEARSE" Trench to the right of our line.
O.C. D. Company will extend to his left and join up with A Coy at the head of the Western communication trench & will hold his Coy in readiness to repel a counter attack on our front line.
REPORTS. O.Cs A.B.C. & D Companies will meet at the MILL before commencement of operations, when O.C. B Company will report to Headquarters by 'phone when all [illegible] are ready. O.C. "A" Coy will then take up his Headquarters at the head of the Western Communication trench. O.C. B Coy will proceed with his Company to carry out the assault & will report to Headquarters every ½ hour. For this purpose 8 Runners from Headquarters & 2 each from C & D Companies will be attached to B. Coy.
GENERAL O.C. B. Coy will take steps to ensure sufficient bombs, sandbags, Very Lights, flares and ammunition & tools for his assaulting party. In the event of it proving impossible to capture any portion of the enemy's main trench and there not being time to complete the trench between the enemy's strong point and M.17 c. 3.0

O.C. C. Company will ensure that the working party & his covering party will construct [illegible] points of strong points along the site of the trench under supervision of the R.E. Officer attached for the purpose, which he will garrison & hold until a suitable opportunity occurs to complete the construction of the trench. He will put 1 Lewis Gun at a suitable place in each of these strong points & see that all of them are supplied with WATER, RATIONS & BOMBS.
FLARES Attention is called to the necessity for showing flares to contact aeroplanes when necessary by all units holding front line positions.

H. [illegible] MAJOR
Acting Adjt. EM

10-25 PM. Please acknowledge

121

Operation Order

By Lieut Colonel E.F. THACKERAY, C.M.G.
Commanding E.M. in the Field
14.10.16 –

In accordance with B.M. Telegraphic instructions No. [illegible] of the 14th inst, the 9th Division orders this Regiment to take and consolidate the Strong Point at M.16 d 9.3 and dig a trench between ~~[illegible]~~ & and the right of this Regiment at M.17 c.5.0 and with road junction at M.16 d.9.4 and also dig a communication trench between the left centre held by D. Company and the strong point to be captured.

ASSAULT. The assault will be carried out by B. Company. The O.C. B. Company will detail Lieut. Mallett and the Regimental Bombers and the Regimental Lewis Guns [illegible] to take the strong point. Lieut Mallett will have a second party under him of Cpl HUGHES. B. Company Bombers and a FIGHTING SECTION of 10 other Ranks. LIEUT MALLETT will seize the Strong Point and endeavour to push up the ENEMY'S TRENCH which runs towards the North EAST. He will detail Cpl HUGHES & his party to bomb up and [illegible] that part of the ENEMY'S TRENCH which runs North North West from the Strong Point. LIEUT. MEDLICOTT with the Company

Lewis Gunners and 1/20 Other Ranks will move in support of Lieut MALLETT'S party and when the Strong Point has been captured will immediately consolidate it. LIEUT. ESSELL with his Machine Guns and garrison of the Strong Point at the left of B. Coy's line will be relieved by a light party detailed by O.C. A. Coy & will be at the disposal of O.C. B. Coy in support.

WORKING PARTIES. O.C. A Coy will detail LIEUT GOODWIN and 30 Other Ranks with Machine Guns to cut a trench between the enemy's Strong Point when captured and the road junction at M.16 d 7.4. The following Working Parties are detailed by Brigade Headquarters:- 150 men from the 4th S.A.I. to cut a trench between the enemy's strong point at M.16 d.9.2 and the right of our line at M.17 c.2.0. (O.C. C. Company will detail a covering party for this working party) also a Working Party of 150 men from the 4th S.A.I. to deepen and improve a communication trench to the present front line; also a Company of Pioneers to dig a communication trench from M.21 b 7.7 to the enemy's strong point when captured.

RELIEFS. O.C. A Coy will take over the line at present held by B. Coy from the of the western communication trench

"C" Form (Original).
MESSAGES AND SIGNALS.

Army Form C. 2123.
(In books of 50's in duplicate.)

Prefix SB	Code 11[illegible]	Words 55	Received From CB By Sighm[illegible]	Sent, or sent out At To By	Office Stamp. APP 215

Charges to collect

Service Instructions. Priority

Handed in at CB Office m. Received 6.[illegible] m.

TO EM

Sender's Number	Day of Month	In reply to Number	AAA
BM 367	14		

If continuous trench cannot be dug tonight - certain points must be dug sufficiently deep to permit small garrisons of 1 NCO and 6 men with Lewis gun being established therein AAA If continuous trench dug it is to be held lightly with small garrison and Lewis guns AAA Acknowledge

FROM CB
PLACE & TIME 6.40pm
Phone

Operation Order. APP 214 No. ....
By Lieut Colonel E.A. THACKERAY, C.M.G.
Commanding E.M. in the Field
14.10.16.

In accordance with B.M. Telegraphic instructions No. 257 of the 14th inst, the 9th Division orders this Regiment to take and consolidate the Strong Point at M.16 d 9.3 and dig a trench between [illegible] it and the right of this Regiment at M.17 c.5.0 and with road junction at M.16 d.7.4 and also cut a communication trench between the left sector held by D. Company and the strong point to be captured.

ASSAULT. The assault will be carried out by B. Company. The O.C. B Company will detail Lieut Mallett and the Regimental Bombers and the Regimental Lewis Guns [illegible] commence to take the strong point. Lieut Mallett will have a second party under Lieut [illegible] HUGHES - B. Company Bombers and a FIGHTING SECTION of 10 Other Ranks. LIEUT MALLETT will seize the strong point and endeavour to push up the ENEMY'S TRENCH which runs towards the North [illegible]. He will detail Lieut HUGHES [illegible] party to bomb up and capture that part of the ENEMY'S TRENCH which runs North North West from the Strong Point. LIEUT MEDLICOTT with the Bombers

and Gunners and [illegible] Other Ranks will move in support of Lieut MALLETT'S party and when the Strong Point has been captured will immediately consolidate it. LIEUT ESTILL with two Machine Guns and garrison of the Strong Point at the left of B. Coy's line will be relieved by a light party detailed by O.C. A. Coy and will be at the disposal of O.C. B. Coy in support. O.C. A Coy will detail

WORKING PARTIES. LIEUT GOODWIN and 50 Other Ranks with Machine Guns to cut a trench between the enemy's Strong Point when captured and the [illegible] junction at M.16 d 7.4. The following Working Parties are detailed by Brigade Headquarters:- 150 men from the 4th S.A.I. to cut a trench between the enemy's strong point at M.16 d.9.3 and the right of our line at M.17 c.5.0. (O.C. C. Company will detail a covering party to this Working Party) also a Working Party of 150 men from the 4th S.A.I. to deepen and improve a communication trench to the present front line; also a Company of Pioneers to dig a communication trench from M.2[illegible] [illegible] 7.7 to the enemy's strong point when captured.

RELIEFS. O.C. A Coy will take over the sector at present held by D. Coy from the head of the Scottish communication trench to the

MESSAGES AND SIGNALS. No. of Message ....

Prefix .... Code .... m. Office of Origin and Service Instructions.	Words	Charge	This message is on a/c of: .... Service. (Signature of "Franking Officer.")	Recd. at ....
	Sent At .... m. To .... By			Date .... 125 From .... By ....

TO O.C. K.K.

Sender's Number.	Day of Month.	In reply to Number.	AAA
* C.O. 86	13/10/16.		

My C Company coming forward now to take over your original front line trench please provide guides & telephone wire if possible to connect up with Flers Switch Trench

[illegible]
Lieut Colonel

From E.M. [illegible] Bn
Place [illegible]
Time

The above may be forwarded as now corrected. (Z)

Censor. Signature of Addressor or person authorised to telegraph in his name.

* This line should be erased if not required.

225,000. W 14042–M 41. H. W. & V., Ld. 12.15.

"A" Form.

MESSAGES AND SIGNALS.

Army Form C. 2121.

No. of Message ....

Prefix .... Code .... m. | Words | Charge

Office of Origin and Service Instructions.

Sent — At .... m. To .... By ....

This message is on a/c of: .... Service. (Signature of "Franking Officer.")

Recd. at .... m. Date .... From ... 126 By ....

TO: Brigade Major C.B.

Sender's Number: O.C. | Day of Month: 17/10/16 | In reply to Number. | AAA

Have sent C Company now to hold front line Will report when complete.

Lieut Colonel

From: E M

Place

Time

* The above may be forwarded as now corrected. (Z)

Censor. Signature of Addressor or person authorised to telegraph in his name.

* This line should be erased if not required.

225,000. W 14042—M 41. H. W. & V., Ld. 12.15.

"A" Form.

MESSAGES AND SIGNALS.

Army Form C. 2121.

No. of Message ....

Prefix .... Code .... m. | Words | Charge

Office of Origin and Service Instructions.

Sent — At .... m. To .... By ....

This message is on a/c of: .... Service. (Signature of "Franking Officer.")

Recd. at .... m. Date .... From .... By ....

TO: O.C. A Coy.

Sender's Number: O.C. | Day of Month: 17/10/16 | In reply to Number. | AAA

C. Coy. has been ordered to hold front line [illegible] held by K.R. Hqrs. & other Coys remain [illegible] report

Lieut Colonel

From: E.M.

Place: [illegible]

Time

* The above may be forwarded as now corrected. (Z)

Censor. Signature of Addressor or person authorised to telegraph in his name.

* This line should be erased if not required.

225,000. W 14042—M 41. H. W. & V., Ld. 12.15.

127

REARGUARD - O.C. "A"Coy. will detail 1 Sgt. 1Corpl. and 12 men to act as rearguard and bring in all stragglers. The Rearguard will move behind the Transport.

MARCH DISIPLINE.- O.C.s are strictly responsible for keeping correct intervals and the March Disipline of their Units. An interval of 5 minutes will be maintained between ~~Companies~~ Regiments. When the Regimemt is halting no Company or Transport is to halt within 50 yards of a cross road.

LEWIS GUNS.- Companies will be accompanied by their Lewis Guns.

STRETCHER BEARERS.- All Stretcher Bearers will move with their respective Companies.

N. Lamont Fleming

MAJOR.
Acting Adjutant.
3rd.S.A.I.

Masters Stores by 7.30.a.m.for conveyance on lorry.
All Great Coats (in which spare shirts should be tied) are to be rolled in bundles of ten and marked with tin tickets.Company Officers and otherCompany baggage to be stacked outside Company Headquarters by 8.a.m. 128

TRANSPORT.- In addition to the Regimental Transport,local Transport has been hired Regimentally and will distributed at the rate of one wagon per Company and one for Headquarters. to be at respective Headquarters by 8.a.m. Quartermaster and Transport Officer will make all arrangements in accordance with these orders.

SHOULDER PATCHES.-Shoulder Patches are to be drawn immediately and sewn on,beneath the shoulder seam,on the outside of the arm.Every endevour is to be made to have each Company complete in this respect before the Regiment moves tomorrow.

App 19
129

VERY URGENT.

1st S.A.I.Brigade.
9th October 1916.

Officer Commanding,
1st S.A.Infantry
2nd do.
3rd do.
4th do.
S.A.L.T.M.Battery.
28th M.G.Coy.

B.M.O. 1.

The G.O.C. will see Battalion Commanders at Brigade Headquarters at 9 am today. Os.C. Machine Guns and Trench Mortars should also report to Bde. H.Q. at that hour. Os. C. Units will thereafter proceed to the H.Q. of the 142nd In: Brigade at BAZENTIN LE GRANT S.15.b.3.5. Coy. Commanders with two N.C.O.s per company should meet them there at 10.30 am.

Recd 8.45 am

Magr.
Brigade Major.

COPY NO.....3.....

130

App 189

Recd 8 P.m

ET URGENT.
reference.
t LENS 11.
00,000.

1st South African Infantry Brigade.
5th October 1916.

OPERATION ORDER NO.62.

MARCH. The transport of the 1st S.A.I.Brigade, 64th Field Co. R.E. S.A.Field Ambulance (less Motor Ambulance) Mobile Veterinary section and 107th Co., A.S.C. will proceed by march route from the BONNIERES area to TALMAS on 6th October, via NOUVILLETTE and DOULLENS.

All riding horses, Lewis-gun carts and Trench Mortar carts will accompany the Transport.

ORDER OF MARCH. The order of march will be,-

(1) 4th S.A.I. (2) 107th Co. A.S.C.
(3) 1st S.A.I. (4) 3rd S.A.I.
(5) B.H.Q. & Signallers (6) S.A.Field Ambulance.
(7) 2nd S.A.I. (8) 28th M.G.Coy (with T.M.Carts)
(9) Mobile Veterinary Sect. (10) 64th Field Co. R.E.

All transport (less 4th S.A.I.) will be formed up in the above order on the BONNIERES-FORTEL-BOFFLES road-facing east- ready to move at 7.15 am- each unit's transport closing well up on that preceding it.

The transport of the 4th S.A.I. will be formed up ready to move at the hour mentioned on the BEAUVOIR-CANTELEUX road facing south east.

All cross roads and junctions will be left clear.

. STARTING POINT. The starting point will be the cross roads at the eastern end of BONNIERES.

The transport of the 107th Co. A.S.C. will pass the starting point at 7.15 am.

. O.C. COLUMN. The column will march under the orders of the O.C., 107th Co., A.S.C.

. T.M.BATTERY CARTS. The hand-carts of the Trench Mortar Battery will be hitched on to the G.S.limbers of the 28th M.G.Coy ~~xxxx~~ Arrangements for this will be made between the O.C.,M.G.Coy and L.T.M. Battery.

. LEWIS GUNS. Lewis guns and 16 drums per gun will be retained by battalions the Lewis gun carts should travel as lightly as possible. A proportion of the personnel will accompany Lewid gin and Trench Mort carts. This proportion must be the minimum compatible with the carts being properly handled and looked after during the march.

. BILLETING REPRESENTATIVES. A billeting representative from each unit, mounted on a bicycle,(who should have strength of personnel and animals accompanying transport) will report to the O.C.,107th Coy A.S.C. atbthe starting point at 7 am.

Smith Baker
Major.
Brigade Major.

Copy Nos 1 to 4 to 1st to 4th Regts.		Copy no.11 to	26th Infantry Bde.
5	28th M.G.Coy	12	27th do.
6	S.A.L.T.M.Battery	13	9th Division.
7xx	64th Field Co.R.E.	14	Brig General.
8	Bde Signal Section.	15	Brigade Major.
9	107th Co. A.S.C.	16	Staff Captain.
10	S.A.Field Ambulance	17.	Bde. Transport Officer.

131

1st South African Infantry Brigade.

6th October 1916.

Recd 1/10/15 pm

Officer Commanding
1st S.A.Infantry
2nd do.
3rd do.
4th do.

No civilian transport hired by units is to proceed beyond TALMAS. Loads carried on these vehicles should be dumped at TALMAS and guards left in charge. This baggage will be collected later by lorries. Civilian transport to be dismissed and sent back to their homes.

Please cause the acknowledgement to this memo to be handed to the Staff Captain at 8 am tomorrow, by the officer mentioned in para 8 of Operation Order 63 of today's date.

A.D. Pepper

Captain.
Staff Captain.

SECRET & URGENT

1st South African Infantry Bde.

7th October1916.

Officer Commanding,
1st S.A.Infantry
2nd do.
3rd do.
4th do.
S.A.L.T.M.Battery
28th M.G.Coy.
64th Field Co. R.E,
107th Co. A.S.C.
S.A.Field Ambulance.

The Brigade will be ready to move tomorrow at 9 am. Further orders will be issued tomorrow morning as soon as received from Division.

[signature]
Major.

Brigade Major.

B.M. 10

O.C. [illegible]

Units will march tomorrow in full marching order unless otherwise ordered in the morning.

No details have yet been received from the Division

[signature]
Major

10.40 pm
7.10.16

[initials]

Recd 11-15 pm

132

Copy No. 3

1st South African Infantry Brigade.

6th October 1916.

App 189

133

SECRET URGENT.

Map Reference
Sheet LENS 11.
1/100,000.

Recd 8.45 pm

OPERATION ORDER NO.63.

The 1st S.A.I.Brigade and attached units will proceed tomorrow by march route and buses to the 3rd Corps Area.

(2) Buses hold 25 each - The drivers are French.

(3) Units will march two deep to the point of embarkation as per attached march table.

(4) The head of the column- Brigade Headquarters- will halt at the road junction at ARBRES about one mile to the north of BOUQUEMAISON and units in rear will close up.

(5) The column will form up as clear as possible on the right side of the road facing FREVENT - two deep - and told off in twentyfive

(6) Buses will be allotted as follows:-

Brigade Headquarters	4.
1st S.A.I.	33
2nd S.A.I.	31
3rd S.A.I.	30
4th S.A.I.	33
Machine Gun Coy.	13 (including 1 for Machine guns)
T.M.Battery	6 (including 1 for Mortars)
64th Field Co. R.E.	6
S.A.Field Amb.	7
Total	163.

(7) The above figures allow for one bus for each unit H.Q. office and 2 men. Other officers will be distributed throughout the unit convoy.

(8) An officer from each unit will report to the Staff Captain at MAISON LEBLOND at 8 am tomorrow to take over the buses for their unit

(9) The O.C., 1st S.A.I. will detail his Interpreter to report at Brigade Headquarters to Lieutenant McLean at 6.25 tomorrow morning.

(10) Lieutenant McLean - attached Brigade Headquarters-Staff- will report to a Divisional Staff Officer at DOULLENS Citadel -East entrance gate - on DOULLENS-AMIENS road at 7.15 am tomorrow morning.

(11) The O.C. S.A.Field Ambulance will detail a motor ambulance at 6.30 xx tomorrow morning to convey Lieut. McLean and Interpreter to DOULLENS. This ambulance will return to its unit direct from DOULLENS.

(12) Lieutenant King - attached Brigade Headquarter Staff - will will travel in the last bus.

(13) When the column is formed up on the road between MAISON LEBLOND and ARBRES, preparatory to embarking, Battalion Signallers will be on the lookout for signal messages being passed along the line.

(14) Os.C.Units will send a signal message to the Brigade Major at the head of the column as soon as their units are embarked. Units without signallers will send a message through the nearest signallers.

J Mitchell Baker
Major.
Brigade Major.

Issued by orderly at 7.30 pm. 6/10/16.

Copies		Copy No.	
1 to 4	to 1st to 4th S.A.I.	11	to 26th Infantry Brigade
5	28th M.G.Coy	12	27th do.
6	S.A.L.T.M.Battery	13	9th Division.
7.	64th Field Co. R.E.	14	Brig. General.
8.	Bde. Signal Section.	15.	Brigade Major.
9.	107th Co. A.S.C.	16.	Staff Captain.
10.	S.A.Field Ambulance	17.	Bde. Post Corporal.

1ST S.A.I. BRIGADE AND ATTACHED UNITS MARCH TABLE - OPERATION ORDER 63 - 7TH OCT. 1916.

UNIT	Time at which to pass starting point.	Starting point	ROUTE.
Bde. H.Q. & Signallers	7 am	Five roads junction North East of BEAUVOIR.	Cross roads about 500 yards North West of MAISON LEBLOND - MAISON LEBLOND.
S.A. Field Amb.	7.5 am		
4th S.A.I.	7.10 am		
3rd S.A.I.	7.20 am		
1st S.A.I.	7.30 am		
2nd S.A.I.	7.40 am		
Machine Gun Co.	7.50 am		
T.M. Battery	7.55 am		
64th Field Co. R.E.	8 am		

134

No. C.10. App 190

135

MOVE ORDER.

By Lieut.Col. E.F.THACKERAY, C.M.G., Commanding 3rd. South African Infantry.

IN THE FIELD 6/10/16

---

1. MOVE. In accordance with Operation Order No.6e, 1st.S.A.I. Brigade, the Regiment will proceed by march route and busses to the 3rd. Corp Area.

2. ROUTE. The Regiment will proceed via the "Starting Point" at the 5 Roads Junction Noth. East. of BEAUVOIR (1½ miles east of BONNIERES), thence to ARDRES.

3. TRANSPORT. 30 Busses are allotted to the Regiment. The leading Buss is detailed for Head Quarter Officers. Company Officers will be distributed with their Companies. Busses hold 25 each.
Lieut. Phillips and 2 men will report to the Staff Captain at MAISON LEBLOND at 8 a.m. tomorrow to take over the Busses for the Unit.

4. PARADE. The Regiment will parade along the road running from Head Quarters Mess to C. Company Billets, head of the column opposite C. Company Billets by 6.30 a.m. Order of Parade Head Quarters, D., A., B., C.

5. SIGNALLERS. The Signalling Officer will detail Signallers to be on the look-out for signals from the head of the Column.

Officers commanding Companies will make the necessary arrangements to provide the men with breakfast before starting.

6. BILLET INSPECTION. The Second in Command and the Medical Officer will inspect the Billets in the Regimental Area and render the usual certificate. O.Cs. Companies, including Head Quarters, will detail 1 N.C.O. and 3 men to remain behind in their Billets until this Inspection is completed.

(sgd.) H.S.LAMOND HEMMING,
Major,
Acting Adjutant,3rd.S.A.I.

No. C.10.

MOVE ORDER.

By Lieut.Col. E.F.THACKERAY, C.M.G., Commanding 3rd. South African Infantry.

IN THE FIELD 6/10/18

136

---

1. MOVE. In accordance with Operation Order No.66. 1st.S.A.I. Brigade, the Regiment will proceed by march route and busses to the 3rd. Corp Area.

2. ROUTE. The Regiment will proceed via the "Starting Point" at the 5 Roads Junction Noth. East. of BEAUVOIR (1½ miles east of BONNIERES), thence to ARDRES.

3. TRANSPORT. 30 Busses are alletted to the Regiment. The leading Buss is detailed for Head Quarter Officers. Company Officers will be distributed with their Companies. Busses hold 25 each.
Lieut. Phillips and 2 men will report to the Staff Captain at MAISON LEBLOND at 8 a.m. tomorrow to take over the Busses for the Unit.

4. PARADE. The Regiment will parade along the road running from Head Quarters Mess to C. Company Billets, head of the column opposite C. Company Billets by 8.30 a.m.
Order of Parade Head Quarters, D., A., B., C.

5. SIGNALLERS. The Signalling Officer will detail Signallers to be on the look-out for signals from the head of the Column.

Officers commanding Companies will make the necessary arrangements to provide the men with breakfast before starting.

6. BILLET INSPECTION. The Second in Command and the Medical Officer will inspect the Billets in the Regimental Area and render the usual certificate. O.Cs. Companies, including Head Quarters, will detail 1 N.C.O. and 3 men to remain behind in their Billets until this Inspection is completed.

(sgd.) H.S.LAMOND HEMMING,
Major,
Acting Adjutant,3rd.S.A.I.

No. C.10.

137

MOVE ORDER.

By Lieut.Col. E.F.THACKERAY, C.M.G., Commanding 3rd. South African Infantry.

IN THE FIELD 6/10/16

---

1. **MOVE**. In accordance with Operation Order No.66, 1st.S.A.I. Brigade, the Regiment will proceed by march route and busses to the 3rd. Corp Area.

2. **ROUTE**. The Regiment will proceed via the "Starting Point" at the 5 Roads Junction Noth. East. of BEAUVOIR (1[illegible] miles east of BONNIERES), thence to ARDRES.

3. **TRANSPORT**. 30 Busses are allotted to the Regiment. The leading Buss is detailed for Head Quarter Officers. Company Officers will be distributed with their Companies. Busses hold 25 each.
Lieut. Phillips and [illegible] men will report to the Staff Captain at MAISON LEBLOND at 8 a.m. tomorrow to take over the Busses for the Unit.

4. **PARADE**. The Regiment will parade along the road running from Head Quarters Mess to C. Company Billets, head of the column opposite C. Company Billets by 5.30 a.m.
Order of Parade Head quarters, D., A., B., C.

5. **SIGNALLERS**. The Signalling Officer will detail Signallers to be on the look-out for signals from the head of the Column.

Officers commanding Companies will make the necessary arrangements to provide the men with breakfast before starting.

6. **BILLET INSPECTION**. The Second in Command and the Medical Officer will inspect the Billets in the Regimental Area and render the usual certificate. O.Cs. Companies, including Head Quarters, will detail 1 N.C.O. and 3 men to remain behind in their Billets until this Inspection is completed.

(sgd.) H.S.LAMOND HEMMING,
Major,
Acting Adjutant, 3rd.S.A.I.

No.C.10.

138

MOVE ORDER.

By Lieut.Col. E.F.THACKERAY, C.M.G. Commanding 3rd.South African Infantry

IN THE FIELD 6/10/16.

---

1. MOVE. In accordance with Operation Order No.65, 1st.S.A.I. Brigade, the Regiment will proceed by march route and busses to the 3rd. Corps Area. X

2. ROUTE. The Regiment will proceed via the "Starting Point" at the 5 Roads Junction North East of BEAUVOIR (1½ miles East of BONNIERES), thence to ARDRES.

3. TRANSPORT. 30 busses are allotted to the Regiment. The leading bus is detailed for Head Quarter Officers. Company Officers will be distributed with their Companies. Busses hold 25 each.
Lieut. Phillips and 2 men will report to the Staff Captain at MAISON LEBLOND at 8 a.m. tomorrow to take over the busses for the Unit.

4. PARADE. The Regiment will parade along the road running from Head Quarters Mess to C. Company Billets, head of the Column opposite C. Company Billets by 6.30 a.m. Order of Parade Head Quarters, D., A., B., C.

5. SIGNALLERS. The Signalling Officer will detail Signallers to be on the look-out for signals from the head of the Column.

Officers commanding Companies will make the necessary arrangements to provide the men with breakfast before starting.

6. BILLET INSPECTION. The Second in Command and the Medical Officer will inspect the Billets in the Regimental Area and render the usual ~~statement~~ certificate. O.Cs. Companies including Head Quarters will detail 1 N.C.O. and 3 men to remain behind in their Billets until this inspection is completed. X

H.W. Lamont Henry
Major,
Acting Adjutant, 3rd.S.A.I.

App 193

139

COPY NO. 3

1st S.A.Infantry Brigade.

8th October 1916.

SECRET & URGENT.
Map Reference.
AMIENS 17. 1/100,0 0.
& ALBERT (Combined sheet)
57d.S.E., 57 c S.W.
62d N.E., 62c,N.W. 1/40,000.

OPERATION ORDER 64.

1. RELIEF. The 9th Division is relieving the 47th Division in the right sector of the Third Corps front.

2. MARCH. The 1st S.A.I.Brigade and 64th Field Co. R.E. will march today in accordance with the attached table to MAMETZ WOOD to relieve 141st Infantry Brigade.
On completion of the relief the Brigade will become reserve Brigade to the 47th Division.

3. TRANSPORT. Transport will move by road via ALBERT-BECOURT-LOZENGE WOOD under the orders of the Brigade Transport Officer.
Units transport to be formed up by 10.30 am in the order of march of units with head of column at cross roads on main AMIENS ALBERT road 1 mile N.E. of LAHOUSSOYE and to march in rear of the 3rd S.A.I. till that unit strikes off main road.
Units will arrange to have their transport met and guided to destination.
O.C. Infantry Units will each send four officers and O.C. 64th Field Co. R.E. 28th M.G.Coy and S.A.L.T.M.Battery one officer each to Brigade H.Q. to report there this morning at 9.30. These officers will be taken by motor lorry to reconnoitre the area to be taken over by the Brigade.

4. MOVEMENT. Whilst in the Third Corps Area troops will move with the following intervals (a) 200 yards between Battalions and other units (b) 100 yards between platoons, companies and sections of regimental transport.
The following rules must be strictly observed in the front area.
(a) East of a line North and South through ALBERT troops must not move by daylight in larger bodies than platoons at 200 yards ~~xxxxxxxx~~ distance.
(b) East of a line North and South through BECOURT vehicles are not to proceed at a faster pace than a walk.

Arrival at destonation will be immediately reported to Brigade H.Q. together with an accurate reference of Unit H.Q.

Issued by Orderly at 8.30 am.

J Mitchell Baker
Major.
Brigade Major.

Copies 1 to 4 to 1st to 4th S.A.I.
5 to M G.Coy.
6 S.A.L.T.M.Battery
7 64th Field Co. R.E.
8 Bde. Signal Section
9 107th Coy. A.S.C.
10 S.A.Field Amb

Copy No. 11 to 26th Infantry Bri[gade]
12 27th do.
13 9th Division
14 Brigadier Genl.
15 Brigade Major.
16. Staff Captain.
17. Brigade Transport Of[ficer]
18. Post Corporal.

Recd 9.30 am

SECRET.

1st S.A.I.Brigade.
7th October 1916.

App 192

Officer Commanding,
1st S.A.Infantry
2nd do.
3rd do.
4th do.
S.A.L.T.M.Battery
28th M.G.Coy.

B.M. 12.

140

WARNING ORDER.

The Brigade will probably move tomorrow.

The G.O.C. wishes C.Os. to issue such orders as will ensure the rank and file wearing their packs in a uniform manner.

Only the regulation kit is to be carried.

[signature]
Major.
Brigade Major.

f01

141

1ST S.A.I.BRIGADE MARCH TABLE TO OPERATION ORDER 64.

UNIT.	STARTING POINT	Hour of march	ROUTE	REMARKS.
1st S.A.I.	Cross roads on main AMIENS-ALBERT road one mile N.E. of LAHOUSSOYE.	9.15 a.m.	Main AMIENS ALBERT road to road junction E.7.c.1.8. Thence via DERNANCOURT to railhead at VIVIER HILL E.16.b.7.0. thence by train to X.29.c. thence march to MAMETZ WOOD.	To arrive at Railway staton by 1.30 p.m.
3rd S.A.I.	-do-	9.45 am	-do-	To arrive Railway station by 2 pm.
Bde H.Q.	On BEHENCOURT-FRANVILLERS road - 1 mile east of BEHENCOURT.	10 am.	-do-	To arrive Railway station by 2.45 pm.
2nd S.A.I.	-do-	10.15 am	-do-	To arrive Railway station by 3 pm.
4th S.A.I.	-do-	, 10.45 am	-do-	To arrive Rly station by 3.30 pm.
28th M.G.Coy	do.	11.15 am	-do-	To arrive Rly station by 4 pm.
L.T.M.Battery	do.	11.20 am	-do-	-do-
64th Field Co. R.E.	do.	11.25 am	-do-	-do-

NOTE:- The Railway by which troops will travel is a tactical railway carrying troops with their kit only. Machine Guns will go in limbers with transport.

SECRET & URGENT
Map Reference
1/40,000 ALBERT
(Combined Sheet)

App 19 142

Copy No...........

1st South African Infantry
Brigade H.Qrs.
9th October 1916.

OPERATION ORDER 65.

The 1st S.A.I.Brigade will relieve the 142nd Infantry Bde. in the left half of the 47th Divisional front on 9th October. Relief will be carried out in accordance with the attached table.

Battalion Commanders with their Company Commanders and such other officers as they may desire to take will report today at H.Qrs.of the 142nd Brigade at Bazentin Le Grand S.15.b.3.5.at 10.30.a.m. where guides will be furnished to show them the areas to be taken over by their Battalions , with the exception of the area to be taken over-by theixx battalionxx in the line - that Battalion will take over the line as held by the 142nd Brigade when relieved by the 1st S.A.I.Brigade.

The 1st and 3rd S.A.I. will move into their new areas by daylight under Regimental arrangements. The 2nd S.A.I. will mo into HIGH WOOD by daylight moving forward therefrom after dark. The 4th S.A.I.will move to BAZENTIN LE GRAND by daylight moving forward therefrom at 5.p.m.

O.C.Machine Guns will detail 4 Machine Guns to accompany the 2nd S.A.I.and 4 to accompany the 4th S.A.I.- These guns to report to the Os.C.Units to which they are being attached by 11.a.m. today.

The Brigade Transport lines will be at X.30.a.Central.

When relief is complete Brigade H.Q.will be established at S.15.b.3.5.

Os.C.Units will report relief complete (by code word CAPE where telephone exists) and will give Map Reference of their H.Q

J Mitchell Baker
Major.
Brigade Major.
1st S. A. I. Brigade,.

Issued through Signals at ...10 am...to...............
as per 1st S.A.I. Distribution List.

Rec 10 AM
NAH

143

1ST S.A.I. BRIGADE TABLE ACCOMPANYING OPERATION ORDER 65.

UNIT RELIEVING	UNIT BEING RELIEVED	AREA TO BE OCCUPIED	PLACE & HOUR AT WHICH GUIDES WILL MEET UNITS.	REMARKS.
2nd S.A.I.	21st & ~~23rd~~ 22nd London Regiments.	Front line as held by 142nd Brigade.	5 pm. at S.3.b.8.2.	The 21st & 22nd London Regts will be in the lin ~~xx~~ and guides from both will be furnished. Ø.
4th S.A.I.	24th London Regt.	support trenches	5 pm at S.9.d.9.0.	Unit will assemble at BAZENTIN LE GRAND during day under regimental arrangements.
3rd S.A.I.	23rd London Regt.	HIGH WOOD		Guides will be furnished to Coy. Commanders at 10.30 and Battn. will take over area under regimental arrangements during day.
1st S.A.I.	---------	HILL trench and BAZENTIN LE GRAND		-do-
28th M.G.Coy) S.A.L.T.M.Battery.)	corresponding unit of 142nd Brigade.	same as occupied by corresponding units of 142nd Brigade.		

Ø Unit will assemble in HIGH WOOD during day under regimental arrangements.

144

Copy No.......

1ST SOUTH AFRICAN INFANTRY BRIGADE.

Sketch map attached. 11th October 1916.

OPERATION ORDER NO. 66.

The 9th Division will attack the enemy's position on the high ground between M.17.d.9.9. and the LE SARS - BAPAUME road on the 12th October at ZERO.

ZERO will be notified later.

The 1st S.A.I.Brigade will be on the left of the Divisional front with the 26th Brigade on the right. The 44th Infantry Brigade is being in the line on the left of the 9th Division.

BRIGADE BOUNDARY. The boundary between the 26th Brigade and this Brigade runs between M.23.A.6.8. and M.17.B.2.7.

OBJECTIVES. The Brigade will have two objectives.
(1) Enemy trench in M.17.C. and
(2) Enemy trench from M.17.B.2.7. to the LE SARS - BAPAUME road, including the BUTTE de WARLENCOURT.

ASSAULTING TROOPS. The assault will be carried out on a one battalion front in column of companies (each company less one platoon - carriers).

ASSEMBLY. The battalions to carry out the assault will be assembled in the front trenches 20 minutes before ZERO.

The 3rd S.A.I. will move forward into the trenches at present occupied by the 4th S.A.I. 10 minutes after ZERO, provided the enemy barrage permits of their doing so.

The 1st S.A.I. will be ready to move into the trenches in HIGH WOOD at present occupied by the 3rd S.A.I. immediately that regiment moves forward.

BASE. Provided the creeping barrage permits the base from which the Brigade will "jump off" will be a line between the Post at present occupied by the 2nd S.A.I. at M.16.D.8.3. to the right of our present front line at M.23.A.8.8.

CARRIERS. There will be one platoon carriers to each company of the assaulting battalions. Carrying platoons will follow in rear of the 4th Regiment in column of half-companies. There will thus be, eight waves of fighting troops followed by four waves of carriers.

BARRAGES There will be two barrages - one a standing barrage, the other a creeping barrage.

The standing barrage will open on the first objective and thereafter lift to the second objective.

The creeping barrage will commence 200 yards in advance of our front line and after three minutes will lift 50/a minute until it is about 200 yards beyond the first objective. From there it will again creep forward at 0 plus 23 minutes at the same rate until it reaches about 200 yards beyond our first objective.

THE ATTACK. The 2nd S.A.I. will go over the parapet at ZERO and form up in four waves on the BASE provided the barrage permits. It will be followed by the 4th S.A.I.

The first wave will creep up as close as possible to the barrage and succeeding waves will follow at 50 yards distance between waves.

The leading wave will move forward with the creeping barrage the other waves conforming.- care being taken that the distance of 50 yards between waves is maintained.

It is essential that the assaulting infantry shall keep as close up as possible to our own barrage.

The first three waves will advance over the first objective, the fourth wave remaining in that objective, until 0 plus 23 when the creeping barrage again proceeds by lifts of 50 yards.

The fifth and following waves will lie down (provided they have not to re-inforce) until the leading waves again move forward, when all excepting the eight wave will advance over the first objective which will be cleared and held by the eighth wave.

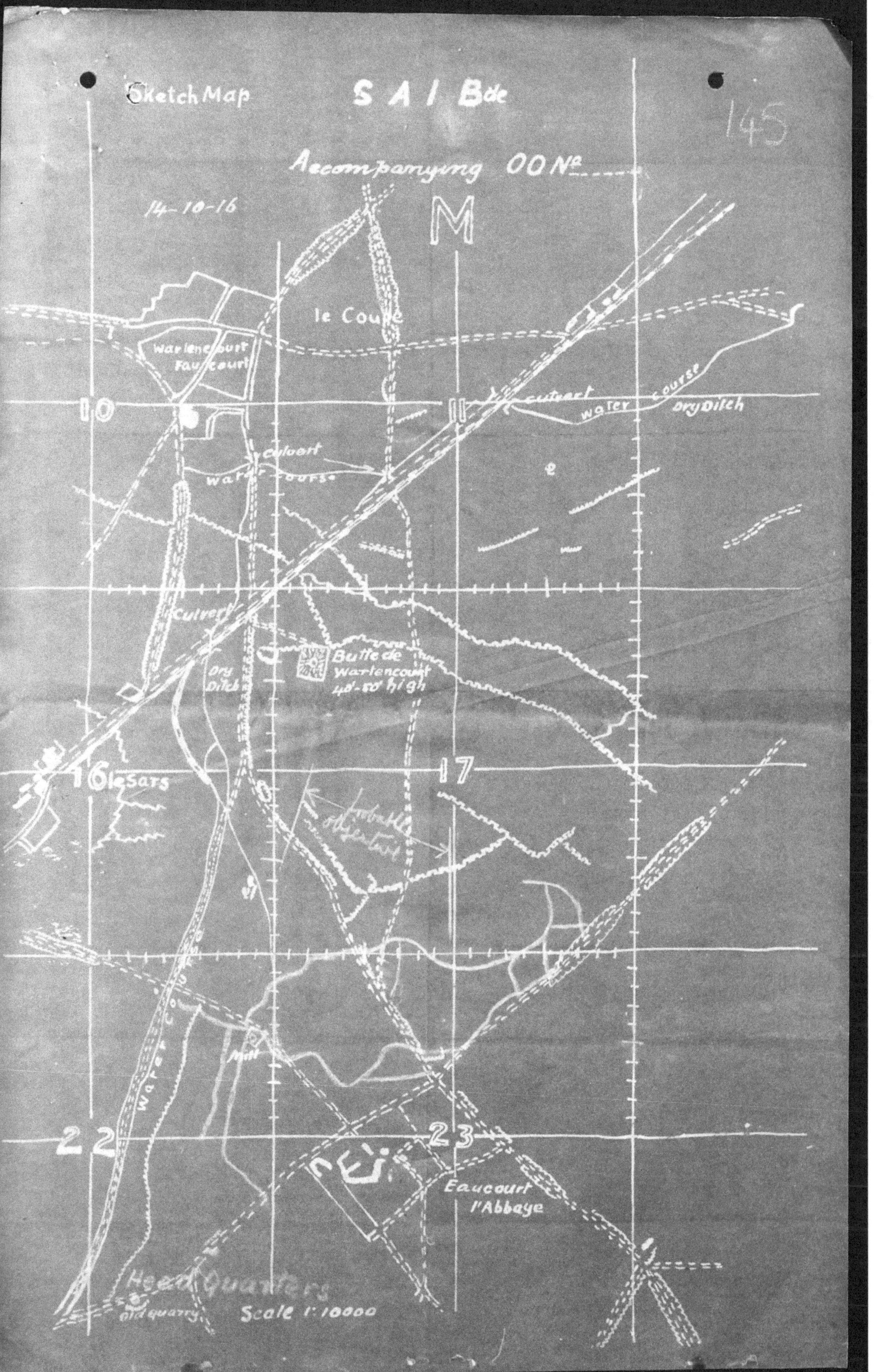

Sketch Map

S A I Bde

145

Accompanying OO No ----

14-10-16

M

le Coupe

Warlencourt Faucourt

10

11

culvert

water course

Dry Ditch

Culvert

water course

Culvert

Butte de Warlencourt 40'-50' high

Dry Ditch

16 le Sars

17

Water Course

Mill

22

23

Eaucourt l'Abbaye

Head Quarters

old quarry

Scale 1:10000

"......" Form.

Army Form C. 2121.

MESSAGES AND SIGNALS.

No. of Message ....

Prefix .... Code .... m. | Words | Charge

Office of Origin and Service Instructions.

Sent

At .... m.

To ....

By ....

This message is on a/c of:

.... Service.

(Signature of "Franking Officer.")

Recd. at 1.46

Date

From

By

Mh 197

TO O.C.
C. Company.

Sender's Number.	Day of Month.	In reply to Number.	AAA
* O.S.	17/10/16		

You are to move out your company to take over line held originally by K. R. Rifles and by fire on completion of move of co. front by Gunners. Hqrs & other Coys remain as before

[illegible]

Lieut Colonel

From E.M.

Place

Time J. 15pm

The above may be forwarded as now corrected.

(Z)

Censor. Signature of Addressor or person authorised to telegraph in his name.

* This line should be erased if not required.

...(1. H. W. & V., Ld. 12/15.

147

"A" Form.
MESSAGES AND SIGNALS.

Army Form C. 2121.
No. of Message..........

Code ... m. | Words 29 | Charge
Office of Origin and Service Instructions.
C B
Priority

Sent
At..........m.
To..........
By..........

This message is on a/c of:
..........Service.
(Signature of "Franking Officer.")

Recd. at 9.30 am
Date EM 12/10/16
From CB
By ...

TO EM

Sender's Number.	Day of Month.	In reply to Number.	AAA
BM267	12th		

In confirmation of verbal instructions send forward your regiment in driblets at your discretion to occupy ~~[illegible]~~ trenches as immediately they are evacuated

From CB
Time 9.20am

The above may be forwarded as now corrected. (Z)

Sketch Map Accompanying O.O.66

148

M

Ditch

SP

SP

Butte de Warlencourt

16

17

le Sars

Mill

Flers Support

Flers Trench

22

23

Eaucourt l'Abbaye

Rutherford Alley

Flers

Switch

Flers Support

Flers Switch

M

Scale 1:10,000

28

29

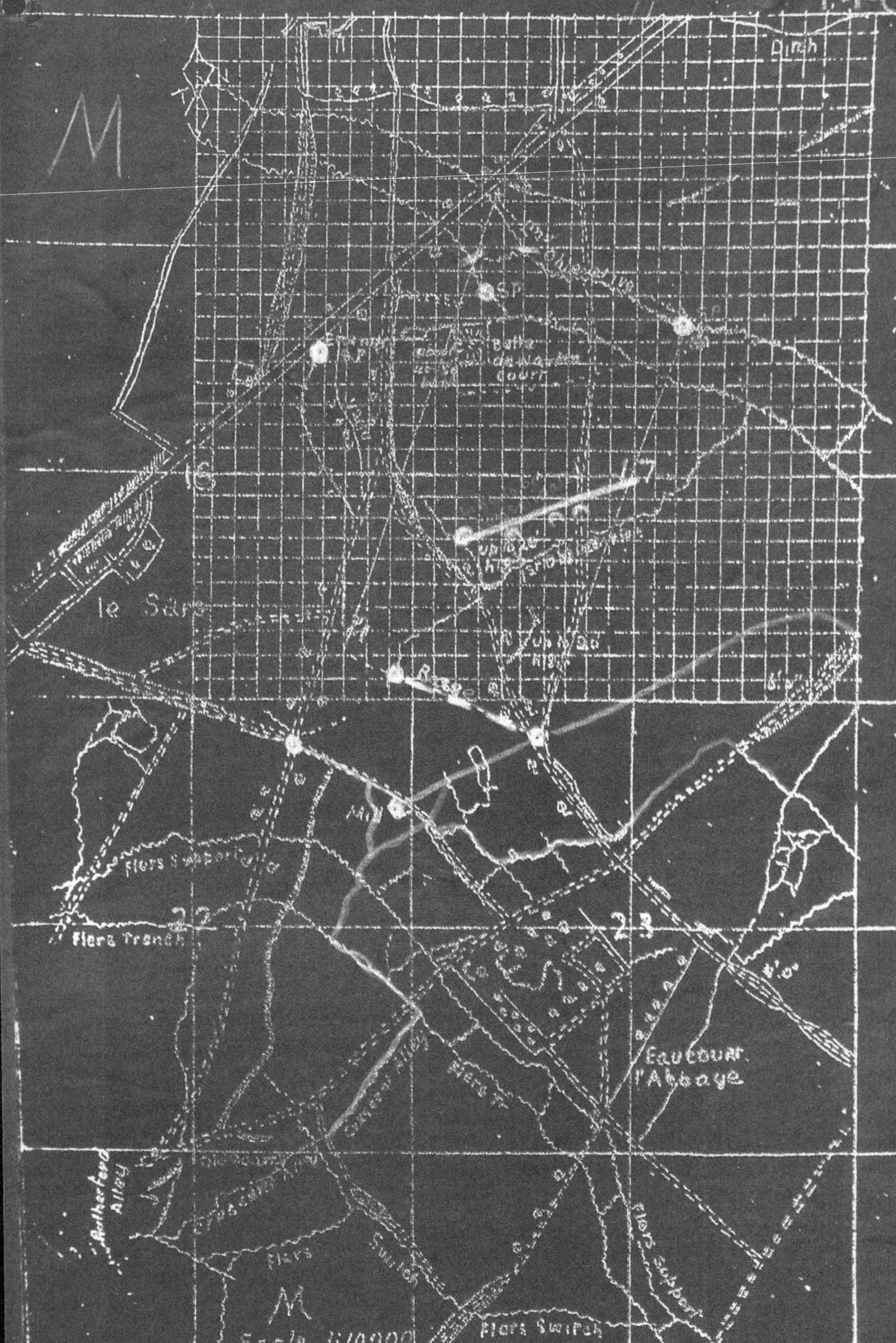

Simultaneously with our attack the 44th Brigade on our left will attack enemy's strong point in the valley at approximately M.16.B.6.3.

The 15th Division is arranging for a smoke screen to be maintained on the enemy's position between LE SARS and WARLENCOURT from ZERO to O plus 45.

The BUTTE will be kept under smoke by them until our leading infantry are approaching it about O plus 28.

All ranks are reminded that in ad ition to gaining their own objective it is their duty to assist their neighbours to gain theirs.

J Mitchell Baker
Major.
Brigade Major.

12.10.16

Issued by orderly at 6.30 am/as per S.A.Bde distribution list.

ARTICLES TO BE CARRIED BY THE REAR (CARRYING) PLATOONS.

	Each Section.	Total per platoon	Total per battalion.
Sandbags	100	400	1600
Rolls French wire	2	8	32
Rifle grenade No.23	50	200	800
Very pistols	1	4	16
Very lights, pkts.	1	4	16

TRENCH MORTARS. The O.C., L.T.M.Battery will hold four stokes mortars in readiness to proceed from their present position in the trenches to the line to be consolidated in M.17.C immediately the final objective is gained. The Officer in charge of these guns will report at the H.Q. of the 2nd S.A.I. half an hour before ZERO.

The O.C., L.T.M.Battery will report at Brigade Headquarters one hour before ZERO.

The O.C., L.T.M.Battery will detail 10 men to report to the O.C., 2nd S.A.I. two hours before ZERO, each of these men will have two stokes' bombs prepared for use to assist in destroying dug-outs or other works in the BUTTE de WARLENCOURT.

PIONEERS "B" Company, 9th Seaforth Pioneers is attached to the Brigade for the operations. It will assemble at the S.W. side of high wood half an hour before ZERO and will proceed in advance of the 3rd S.A.I. to the trenches at present occupied by the 4th S.A.I., and from thence to the front line trenches which it will be ready to leave immediately the final objective is gained.

It will dig communication trenches up to the Brigade's final object[illegible]

The O.C. "B" Company (9th Seaforth Highrs, will report at the H.Q. of the 2nd SMAMI. half an hour before ZERO, and will proceed with the O.C. 64th Field Co, R.E. The latter officer will site the communic[illegible] trenches to be dug by the pioneers

SIGNAL COMMUNICATIONS. Visual signal stations will be established.

Ample service of runners to be arranged by [illegible] Battalions.

Os. C.Units will keep Brigade H.Q. fully posted regarding the progress of the battle.

The importance of prompt and accurate reports cannot be over estimated.

The Brigade has to report the situation to the Division every hour and battalion commanders will send in reports at least as frequently

MEDICAL ARRANGEMENTS. The line of evacuation for wounded is from collec[illegible] [illegible] post at EAUCOURT L' ABBAYE by railway to west of High Wood, thence by ambulance to advanced dressing station at BAZENTIN LE PETIT.

Walking wounded will be directed along this route

FIGHTING OUTFIT. The normal fighting outfit for each man will be as per appendix "B" of Instructions for training issued by 9th Division, excepting that the pack may be substituted for the haversack, the S.A.A. carried on the man is reduced to 120 rounds and every man will carry two bombs.

Every thing in excess of the normal outfit will be dumped by battal[illegible] at a spot near their H.Q. and left in charge of a guard,

All men will [illegible] the infantry entrenching tool andall men except-

speciallists, 1,0, sippers, Lewis Gunners Machine Gunners etc, will carry a pick or a shovel in yho proportion of six shovels to one pick.

MATERIAL TO BE CARRIED Carrying platoons will cary the material etc., set forth in the attached shhedule.

CONTACT AEROPLANE A contact aeroplane will fly over the trenches at 1 hour after ZERO and the advanced infantry will light [illegible] yellow flares in reply to aeroplane signal.

CONNECTING POST. The 4th S.A.I. will gain touch with the 44th Brigade on their left by establishing a post in the neighbourhood of road junction M.16.B.9.0.

ZERO HOUR. A representative from each unit will report at Brigade H.Q tomorrow, 12th instant, at 10 am when ZERO hour will be notified and watches set.

BRIGADE H.Q. Brigade H.Q. will be at S.15.B.3.5.

Brigade Dump is at M 28 D 8 4

STRONG POINTS AND CONSOLIDATION. On attaining the second objective strong points will be established on the forward slopes at approximately M.17.A.3.8. and M.17.B.2.6. to be made and held by the 2nd S.A.I. Each strong point will be under the command of an officer.

Lewis guns will be placed immediately in both of these strong points being replaced by Vickers guns as soon as the positions are consolidated.

Machine guns in the strong point on the right will be placed so as to cover the west face of the spur running N.W. from M.17.B.5.7.

Stops will be placed to prevent the enemy counter-attacking up his trench on the N.W. face of the BUTTE spur.

Advanced posts of not more than sixmen in each will be thrown forward by the second S.A.I. in front of the final objective.

The position of these advanced posts will be sited by an officer who will remain in command of them until they are withdrawn.

The officers in command of the strong points will inform the Officer in charge of advanced posts when they consider the strong points sufficiently consolidated to justify the withdrawal of the posts. These posts will then be withdrawn.

The final objective will be held by means of machine guns and Lewis guns and as thinly as possible as regards garrison.

The main consolidation will be just south of the crest of the BUTTE spur so as to avoid direct land observation on the enemy's part from the LOOPART WOOD high ground.

The line to be consolidated runs approximately from M.17.central to M.17.C.3.7.

A strong point will be made at the latter point.

The 4th S.A.I. will dig this main consolidated trench.

Emplacements for Stokes' guns will be prepared in the line to be consolidated, If it is possible to "Stokes mortar" the BUTTE de WARLENCOURT from there. If it is not possible to do so from the line of consolidation as sited, Trench mortar emplacements will be made in front of that line to enable this being done

ROYAL ENGINEERS: The 64th Field Co, R.E. (less two sections) is attached to the Brigade for the operations. It will construct the T.M. emplacements with such assistance from infantry working parties as may be necessary.

Two N.C.O.s and six sappers will report to the O.C. 2nd S.AI at his H.Q. at M.22.D.5.8. two hours before ZERO. These N.C.Os and sappers will advise infantry working parties regarding construction and consolidation of the strong points on the right and left of our final objective and at M.17.C.3.7.

O.C. 64th Field Co. R.E. will report at the H.Q. 2nd S.A.I. half an hour before ZERO. He will proceed forward with a section of his company to the line to be consolidated immediately the final objective is gained.

The second section of the Field Co will remain in reserve under the orders of the O.C. 64th Field Co, R.E.

MACHINE GUNS. The O.C. Machine Gun Company will detail the following guns to move forward immediately the final objective has been gained, viz., (A) a section of guns to proceed to the final objective - two to be placed in the strong points forward of the BUTTE de WARLENCOURT and two in the strong point at M. 17.B.2.6.

(B) two guns to proceed to strong point M.17. C.3.7.

the Officers in charge of these guns will report to the O.C., 2nd S.A.I. at his H.Q. half an hour before ZERO.

The four guns at present in the FLERS Switch will from ZERO onwards during the attack water the valley in M.11.C.D.

The remaining guns will be held in Brigade reserve.

The O.C., 28th M.G.Coy will report at Brigade H.Q. one hour before ZERO,

Unless under exceptional circumstances once a machine gun has been placed by an officer of the machine gun company it will not be moved except under the orders of a battalion Commander or the Brigade.

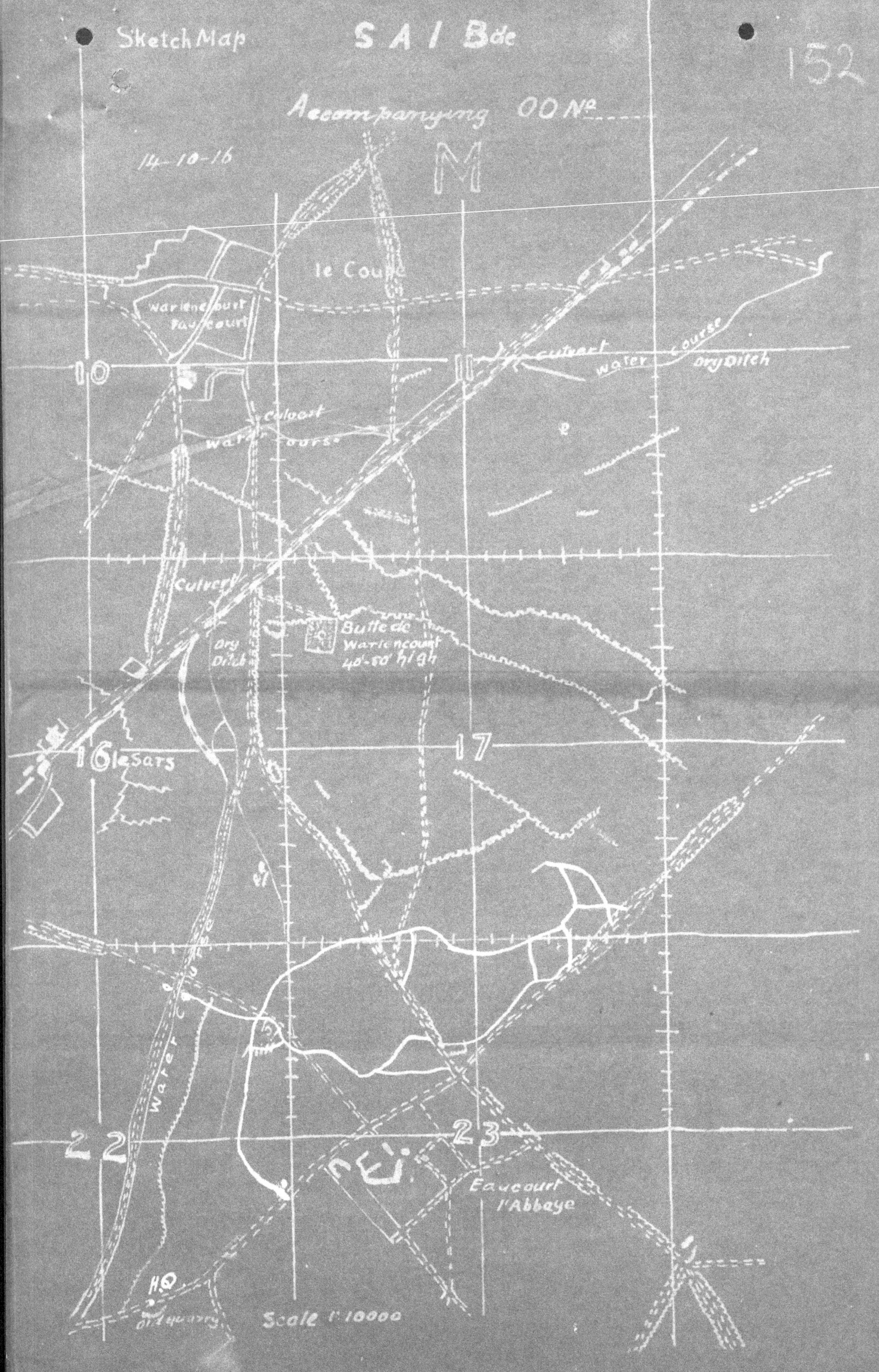

Sketch Map

S A I Bde

152

Accompanying OO No ----

14-10-16

M

le Coupe

Warlencourt Faucourt

10

Culvert

Water Course

Dry Ditch

Culvert

Water Course

Culvert

Butte de Warlencourt 40'-50' high

Dry Ditch

16 le Sars

17

Water Course

22

23

Eaucourt l'Abbaye

H.Q.

Old Quarry

Scale 1:10000

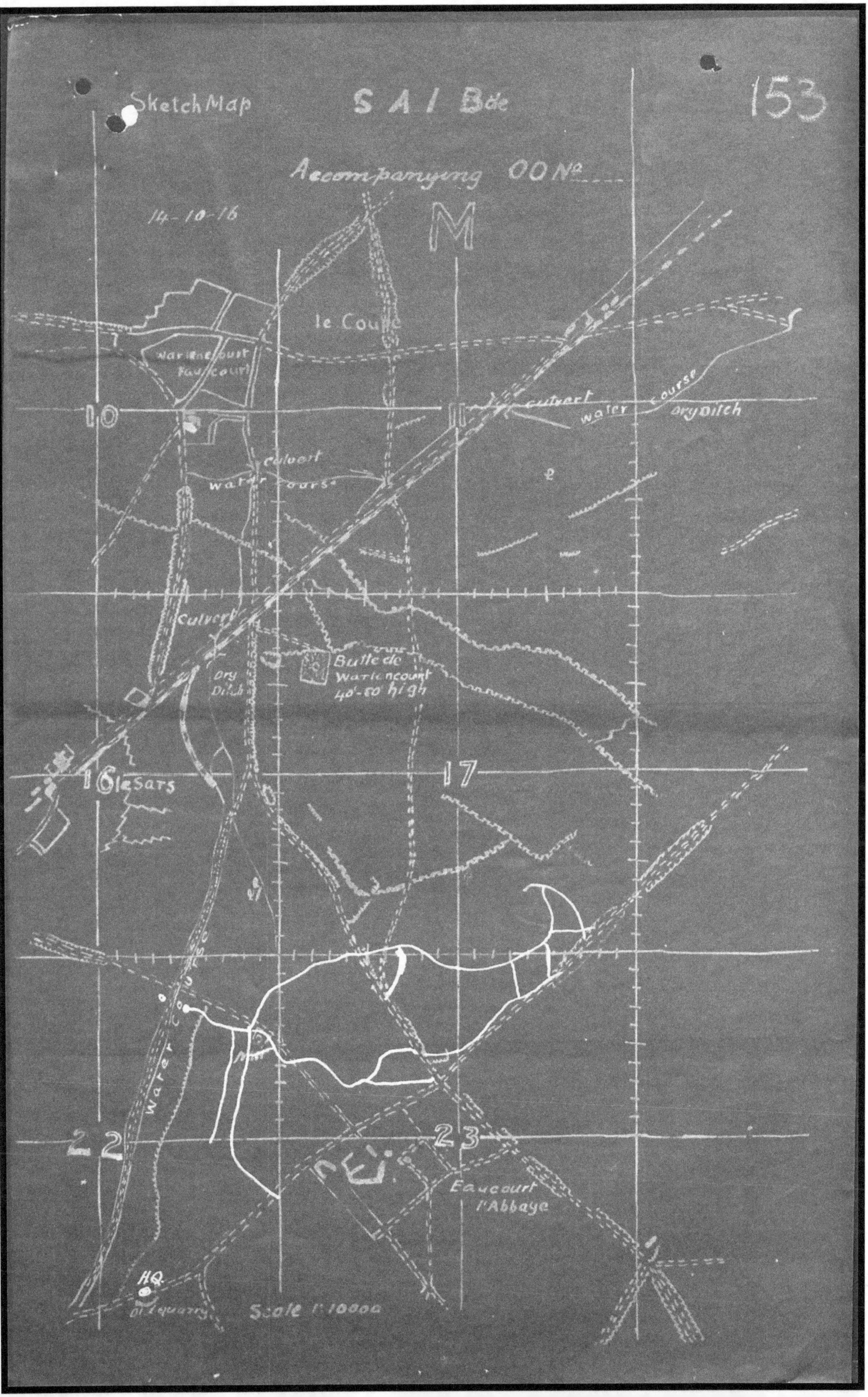

153

Sketch Map

S A I Bde

Accompanying OO No.........

14-10-16

M

le Coulle

Warlencourt
Faucourt

10

culvert

water course

Dry Ditch

culvert

water course

2

Culvert

Butte de
Warlencourt
40'-50' high

Dry
Ditch

16

le Sars

17

Water course

22

23

Eaucourt
l'Abbaye

HQ

Old quarry

Scale 1:10000

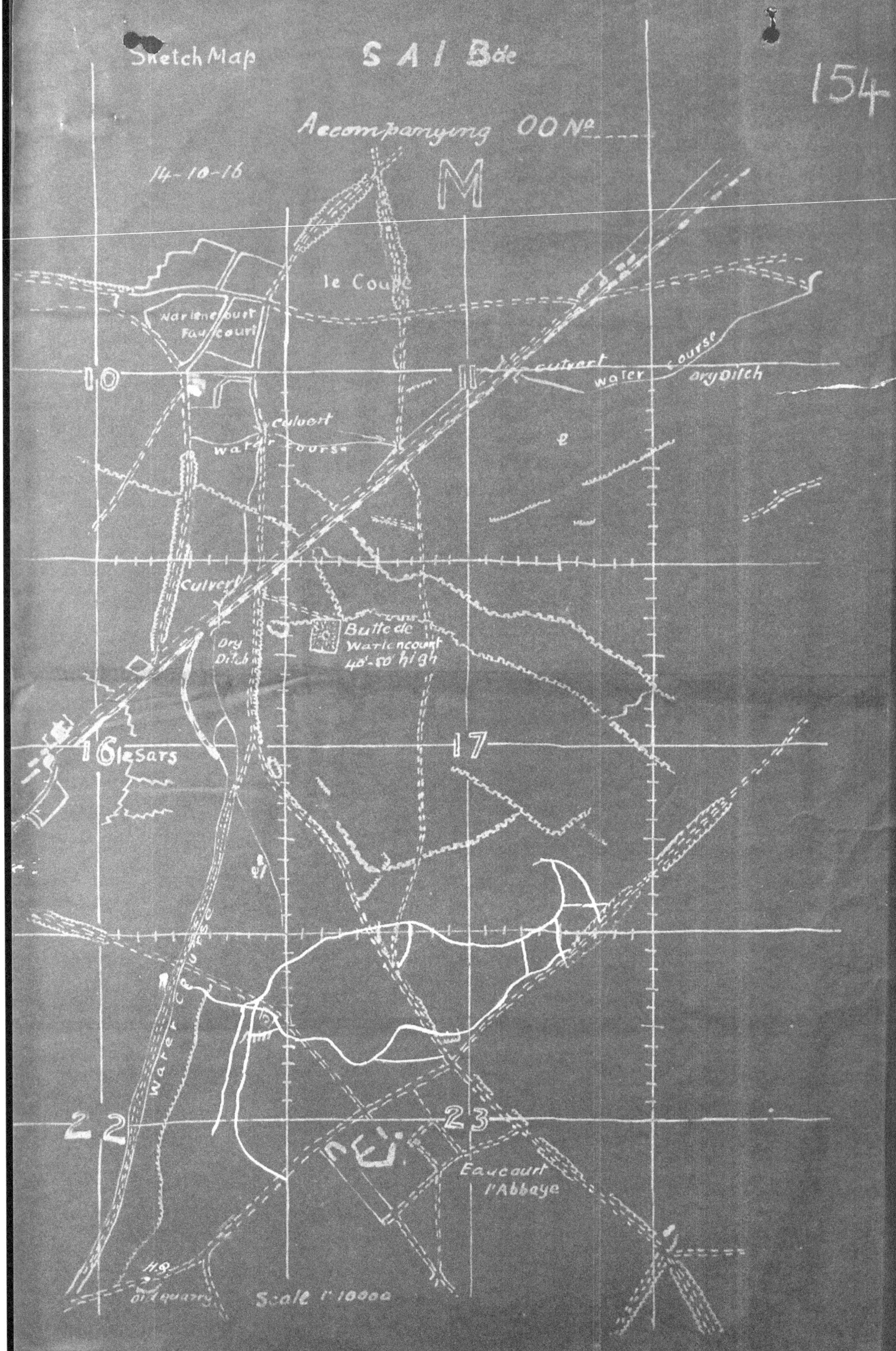

Sketch Map S A I Bde

154

Accompanying OO No ......

14-10-16

M

le Coupe

Warlencourt Faucourt

10

culvert

water course

dry ditch

culvert

water course

Culvert

Butte de Warlencourt 40'-50' high

Dry Ditch

16 le Sars

17

Water course

22

23

Eaucourt l'Abbaye

H.Q.

Old quarry

Scale 1:10000

155

FOLIO 155 IS AN

NEGATIVE

AND HAS BEEN RETURNED TO

MODERN RECORD DEPARTMENT

FOR LISTING.

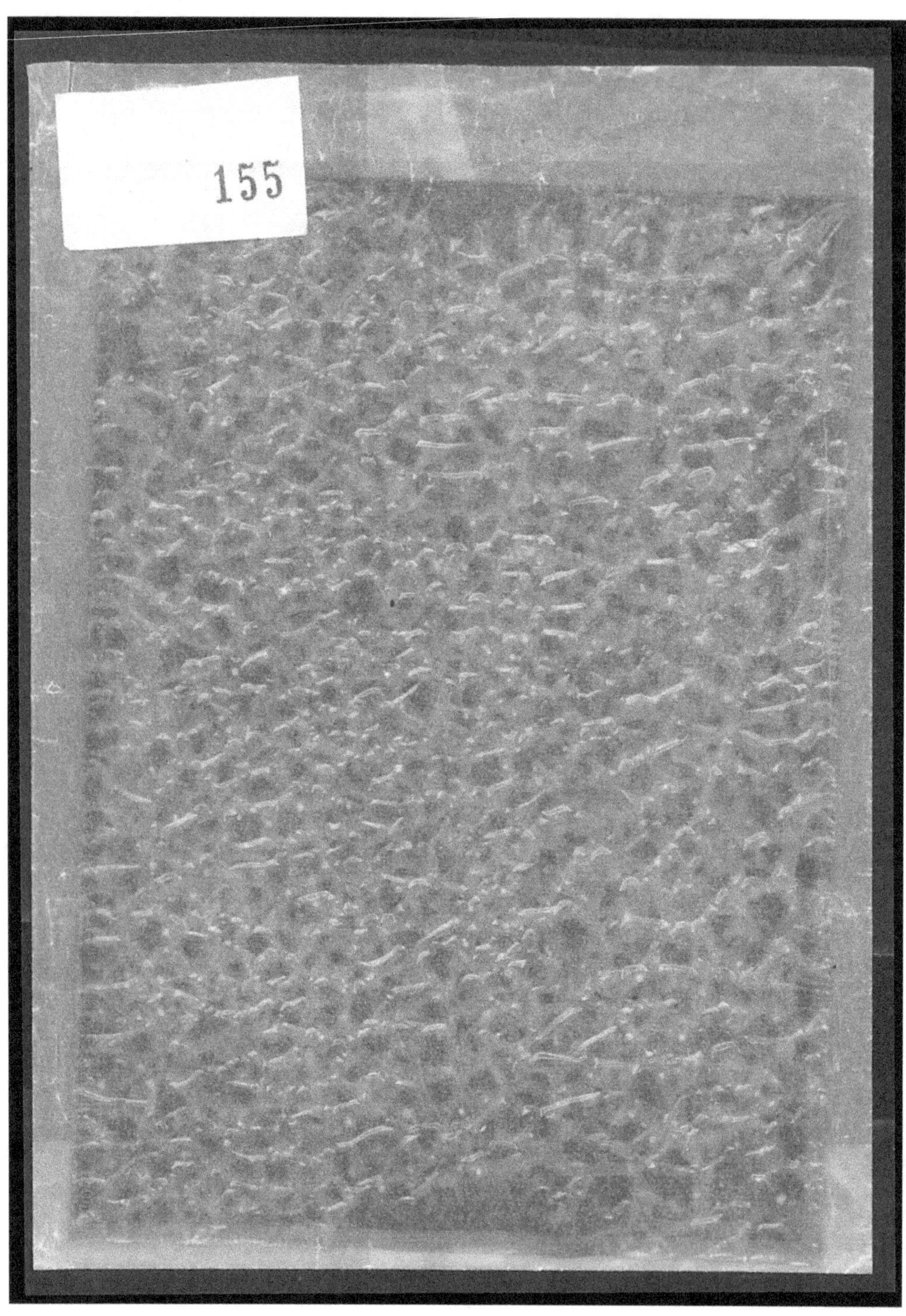
155

Instructions regarding War Diaries and Intelligence Summaries are contained in F. S. Regs., Part II. and the Staff Manual respectively. Title Pages will be prepared in manuscript.

WAR DIARY
or
INTELLIGENCE SUMMARY
(Erase heading not required.)

Army Form C. 2118

Place	Date	Hour	Summary of Events and Information	Remarks and references to Appendices
Wanquetin	1/11/16		Training under Company Arrangements with a view to re-organisation of Regiment & re equipping. Considerable amount of Trench fever has made its appearance amongst Officers & men, due to recent severe Conditions in Trenches. Total strength of Regt in France 30 Officers 721 other ranks. Total with H.Q. 27 offrs 649 o ranks.	
	2/11/16		Training under Coy arrangements. cases of trench fever still increasing	
	3/11/16		Regt. being called on to furnish various working parties for sweeping roads etc.	
	4/11/16		Regt. furnished increased number of working parties as above.	
	5/11/16		Regt. furnishing working parties	
	6/11/16		Regt. furnishing working parties	
	7/11/16		Supplying large number of working parties for road sweeping & Billet repairing at various villages in the vicinity. 17 Officers & about 100 O. Ranks have been affected by trench fever.	
	8/11/16		Every available man not on Regtl employ employed on working parties road sweeping etc thus bringing all	

1875 Wt. W593/826 1,000,000 4/15 J.B.C. & A. A.D.S.S./Forms/C. 2118.

156

WAR DIARY
or
INTELLIGENCE SUMMARY
(Erase heading not required.)

Instructions regarding War Diaries and Intelligence Summaries are contained in F. S. Regs., Part II. and the Staff Manual respectively. Title Pages will be prepared in manuscript.

157

Place	Date	Hour	Summary of Events and Information	Remarks and references to Appendices
Wanquetin	8/11/16		training to a standstill	
"	9/11/16		All ranks available, working on roads repairing billets etc in villages in the vicinity	
"	10/11/16		All available men on working parties consequently training at a standstill	
"	11/11/16		All available men on working parties, totalling about 7 officers & 540 O ranks	
"	12/11/16		About 80 H.Q. details out on Route March all remainder of Regt on working parties. C.O. & portion of Coy. Officers attend lecture on new small box respirator which is about to be issued.	
"	13/11/16		Route March by few H.Q. Details remainder of Regt working parties	
"	14/11/16		Whole Regt employed on working parties	
"	15/11/16		Whole Regt employed on working parties.	
"	16/11/16		Whole Regt employed on working parties. Notification recd from B.H.Q. (T.5). that Brigade would probably be moving shortly to new area for training	
"	17/11/16		Whole Regt employed on working parties.	
"	18/11/16		Whole Regt employed on working parties outbreak of trench fever almost completely eradicated.	

1875 Wt. W593/826 1,000,000 4/15 J.B.C. & A. A.D.S.S./Forms/C. 2118.

Instructions regarding War Diaries and Intelligence Summaries are contained in F. S. Regs., Part II. and the Staff Manual respectively. Title Pages will be prepared in manuscript.

WAR DIARY
or
INTELLIGENCE SUMMARY
(Erase heading not required.)

Army Form C. 2118

Place	Date	Hour	Summary of Events and Information	Remarks and references to Appendices
Wanquetin	20/11/16		Whole Regt. employed on working parties notification from Bde: that Regt. would go into training on 21st inst. C.O. requests BHQ by wire to have all working parties cancelled which was done.	
"	21/11/16		Training all available men under Coy arrangements but owing to fact that most of the Officers including Commanding Officer 2nd in Command and Adjutant were away on Court Martial duty it was impossible to carefully supervise the training.	
"	22/11/16		Regtl. training under Compy. arrangements much impeded by all senior officers being absent on Court Martial duty. Copy of training programme attached hereto	App. 240
"	23/11/16		Every available Officer & man engaged at training	
	24/11/16		Every available Officer & man engaged at training new box respirator being issued as quickly as possible as supplies are drawn from Ordnance. Training ceases daily at 1 p.m. and remaining hours of daylight occupied in various sports organised with a view to every man taking part in them, in accordance with circular letter T/1 received on 20/11/16 from Q.A. BHQ	
	25/11/16		Every available Officer & man on training	

158

1875 Wt. W593/826 1,000,000 4/15 J.B.C. & A. A.D.S.S./Forms/C. 2118.

Army Form C. 2118.

Instructions regarding War Diaries and Intelligence Summaries are contained in F. S. Regs., Part II. and the Staff Manual respectively. Title pages will be prepared in manuscript.

WAR DIARY
or
INTELLIGENCE SUMMARY.
(Erase heading not required.)

3 S A Infy Bde
Vol 8

Place	Date	Hour	Summary of Events and Information	Remarks and references to Appendices
Wanquetin	26/11/16		Sunday Church Parade. Training & Sports programme for W/End Dec. 2nd attached hereto. During the week the whole Regiment passed through Lachrymatory Gas for the purpose of testing new Small box respirator which now has been issued to all ranks.	App. 241
	27/11/16		All ranks at training in accordance with programme	
	28/11/16		All ranks at training in accordance with programme	
	29/11/16		All ranks training as per programme.	
	30/11/16		Training being carried out by all ranks as per programme. total available for training daily about 22 Officers and 440 OR. total strength of Regiment this day with H.Qrs 23 Offrs and 630 O.Ranks. total strength of Regt in France 36 Officers and 754 other ranks.	

B. Young Major
for ....Lt. Col.
Commanding 3rd S. A. Infantry,
(Transvaal Regt.)

159

1577 Wt. W10791/1773 500,000 1/15 D. D. & L. A.D.S.S./Forms/C. 2118.

3rd S.A. Infantry Training Programme W/Ending November 18th 1916

Date	Coy	7 to 7.30 AM	9 to 10 A.M.	10 to 11 A.M.	11 to 12 Noon	12 to 1 P.M.
1916 Nov 20	A	Physical Training	Bombing	Lewis Guns	Intensive Digging	Bayonet Fighting
	B		Lewis Guns	Intensive Digging	Bayonet Fighting	Bombing
	C		Intensive Digging	Bayonet Fighting	Bombing	Lewis Guns
	D		Bayonet Fighting	Bombing	Lewis Guns	Intensive Digging
Nov 21	A	Physical Training	Bombing	Lewis Guns	Gas Helmet Drill & Lectures	Bayonet Fighting
	B		Lewis Guns	Gas Helmet Drill & Lectures	Bayonet Fighting	Bombing
	C		Gas Helmet Drill and Lectures	Bayonet Fighting	Bombing	Lewis Guns
	D		Bayonet Fighting	Bombing	Lewis Guns	Gas Helmet Drill & Lectures
Nov 22	A	Physical Training	Intensive Digging	Bayonet Fg in Gas Helmets	Bombing	Lewis Guns
	B		Bayonet Fg in Gas Helmets	Bombing	Lewis Guns	Intensive Digging
	C		Bombing	Lewis Guns	Intensive Digging	Bayonet Fighting in Gas Helmets
	D		Lewis Guns	Intensive Digging	Bayonet Fighting in Gas Helmets	Bombing
Nov 23	A	Physical Training	Musketry	Bombing	Intensive Digging	Bayonet Fighting
	B		Bombing	Intensive Digging	Bayonet Fighting	Musketry
	C		Intensive Digging	Bayonet Fighting	Musketry	Bombing
	D		Bayonet Fighting	Musketry	Bombing	Intensive Digging
Nov 24	A	Physical Training	Bayonet Fighting	Gas Helmet Drill & Lectures	Bombing	Musketry
	B		Gas Helmet Drill & Lectures	Bombing	Musketry	Bayonet Fighting
	C		Bombing	Musketry	Bayonet Fighting	Gas Helmet Drill & Lectures
	D		Musketry	Bayonet Fighting	Gas Helmet Drill & Lectures	Bombing
Nov 25	A	Physical Training	Trench Warfare by Fighting Sections	Lewis Guns	Intensive Digging by Fighting Sections	Bayonet Fg & Musketry
	B		Lewis Guns	Intensive Digging by Fighting Sections	Bayonet Fg & Musketry	Trench Warfare by Fighting Sections
	C		Intensive Digging by Fighting Sections	Bayonet Fg & Musketry	Trench Warfare by Fighting Sections	Lewis Guns
	D		Bayonet Fighting & Musketry	Trench Warfare by Fighting Sections	Lewis Guns	Intensive Digging by Fighting Sections

Remarks

All training to be carried out with a view to efficiency of fighting sections and [illegible]. Two nights in the week to be devoted to training of fighting sections and men in accordance with 6th Corps circular.

AFTERNOON LECTURES TO OFFICERS

AFTN. LECTURES to N.C.O.s on [illegible] training [illegible] of Command [illegible].

EVENING LECTURES to N.C.O.s [illegible] Economy, Box Respirator, [illegible]

TUESDAY Practical field exercises for Coy Commanders under A.C. 3rd S.A.I.

WEDNESDAY & THURSDAY Practical exercises for platoon commanders & N.C.O.s under Coy Commanders.

FRIDAY, Tactical exercises for officers under C.O. and 2nd in Command.

REGIMENTAL LEWIS GUNNERS attached to Coys for training on Tuesday & Friday [illegible] at Lewis Gun Station under Lewis Gun Officer

SIGNALLERS under Signalling Officer for Station work and Signalling

REGIMENTAL BOMBERS attached to Coys for instructional purposes

SNIPERS (Coy & Regimental) under Sniping Officer daily for special instruction

Night work —

Band Training Ground K27C
Rifle Range K27C99

app. 2+0[?]

6
8

Date	Coy	[illegible]	9 to 10 a m	10 to 11 a m	11 to 12 a m	12 a.m to 1 p.m
Nov 27	A	PHYSICAL TRAINING	Bombing	Bayonet fighting and ARMS DRILL	Intensive digging Trench Construction	Lewis Guns Musketry
	B		Lewis Guns; Musketry	Bombing	Bayonet fighting ARMS DRILL	Intensive digging Trench Construction
	C		Intensive digging + Trench Constn	Lewis Guns + Musketry	Bombing	Bayonet fighting ARMS DRILL
	D		Bayonet fighting and ARMS DRILL	Intensive digging + Trench Construction	Lewis Guns Musketry	Bombing
Nov 28	A		Bombing Close order drill	Intensive digging Trench Construction	Small Box Resp.r Drill ARMS DRILL	Lewis Guns Musketry
	B		Lewis Guns + Musketry	Bombing Close order drill	Intensive digging Trench Construction	Small Box Resp.r Drill ARMS DRILL
	C		Small Box Resp.r Drill + ARMS DRILL	Lewis Guns + Musketry	Bombing Close order drill	Intensive digging Trench Construction
	D		Intensive digging Trench Construction	Small Box Resp.r Drill ARMS DRILL	Lewis Guns Musketry	Bombing Close order drill
Nov 29	A		Bayonet fighting Musketry	Intensive digging Trench Construction	Lewis Guns ARMS DRILL	Bombing Box Respirator Drill
	B		Bombing Box Respirator	Bayonet fighting Musketry	Intensive digging Trench Construction	Lewis Guns ARMS DRILL
	C		Lewis Guns ARMS DRILL	Bombing Box Respirator Drill	Bayonet fighting Musketry	Intensive digging Trench Construction
	D		Intensive digging Trench Constn	Lewis Guns ARMS DRILL	Bombing Box Respirator Drill	Bayonet fighting Musketry
Nov 30	A		Musketry Bayonet fighting	ARMS DRILL Close order drill	Intensive digging Trench Construction	Bombing Box Respirator Drill
	B		Bombing Box Respirator Drill	Musketry Bayonet fighting	ARMS DRILL Close order drill	Intensive digging Trench Construction
	C		Intensive digging Trench Construction	Bombing Box Respirator Drill	Musketry Bayonet fighting	ARMS DRILL Close order drill
	D		ARMS DRILL Close order drill	Intensive digging Trench Construction	Bombing Box Respirator Drill	Musketry Bayonet fighting
Dec 1st	A		Lewis Guns Musketry	Trench warfare (fighting sections)	Close order drill Bayonet fighting	Trench warfare Bombing. ARMS DRILL
	B		Trench warfare Bombing ARMS DRILL	Lewis Guns Musketry	Trench warfare (fighting sections)	Close order drill Bayonet fighting
	C		Close order drill Bayonet fighting	Trench warfare Bombing. ARMS DRILL	Lewis Guns Musketry	Trench warfare (fighting sections)
	D		Trench warfare (fighting sections)	Close order drill Bayonet fighting	Trench warfare Bombing. ARMS DRILL	Lewis Guns Musketry
Dec 2nd	A		Lewis Guns ARMS DRILL	Close order drill (Company)	Bombing (fighting section competition)	Bayonet fighting Musketry
	B		Bayonet fighting Musketry	Lewis Guns ARMS DRILL	Close order drill (Company)	Bombing fighting section competition
	C		Bombing (fighting section competition)	Bayonet fighting Musketry	Lewis Guns ARMS DRILL	Close order drill Company
	D		Close order drill (Company)	Bombing (fighting section competition)	Bayonet fighting Musketry	Lewis Guns ARMS DRILL

Note. Map Training Ground area Sheet 51C K 27 C
Rifle Range K 27 C 9.9
LIVE BOMBING PIT 51C S E [illegible]

NOTES ON TRAINING

Thursday and Friday:- Practical Schemes for Officers under C.O. Map. 30-31. 35 + 36. 2 till 4 p.m.

Monday and Tuesday. 11 to 1 p.m. Simple Tactical Exercises for N.C.O.s. [illegible]

Tuesday and Saturday 6 to 8 p.m. Night training and simple Coy Tactical Scheme Map K 26/27

LECTURES 5.30 to 6 p.m. Monday Wednesday and Friday for N.C.O.s by Coy Officers and R.S.M.

TUESDAY THURSDAY and SATURDAY for OFFICERS, by Adjutant and OC Map reading, Interior Economy Discipline, Regulations, Box Respirator and Gas appliances

NOTE

Regimental Lewis Gunners, Signallers and Bombers training with their Coys.

Band training daily under M.O as stretcher bearers (for 1 hour daily) and 2 hours daily with their respective Coys

Snipers under Sniping Officer

Signallers for Station and Signalling work under Signalling Sergeant.

App 241

161

162

PROGRAMME OF TRAINING.

(SPORTS).

Novr. 27. (1) 2.30 p.m. Practice for six miles Road Race, at least 25% of duty men each Company to turn out. Dress optional, but service boots to be worn.

(2) 3 to 4 p.m. Inter Platoon Tug of War- eliminating pulls.

Novr. 28. (3) 2.30 p.m. Tug of War "A" Coy. vs. "B" Co.

(4) 2.45 p.m. Rugby Match 2nd. Regt vs. 3rd Regiment.

(5) 2 30 p.m.-4 p.m. Inter Platoon Bombing- eliminating trials.

(6) 2.30 p.m.-4 p.m. "A" Company Fighting Section Relay Race (4 miles).

Novr. 29. (7) 2.30 p.m. Tug of War. "C" Coy. vs. "D" Co.

(8) 2.30 p.m. Soccer Match 3rd Regt. S.A.I. vs. 21st Kite Balloon Section.

(9) 2.30 p.m. to 4 p.m. Boxing and Wrestling Preliminary trials.

(10) 2.30 p.m. to 4 p.m. "B" COY. Fighting Section Relay Race (4 miles).

(11) Evening Smoking Concert.

Novr. 30. (12) 2.30 p.m. to 4 p.m. Inter Platoon Bombing Contest. Teams of ten.

(13) 2.30 p.m. to 4 p.m. "D" Coy. Fighting Section Relay Race (4 miles).

Decr. 1 (14) 2.30 p.m. to 4 p.m. Practice 6 Miles Road Race. At least 25% of duty men in each Coy. to turn out. Dress optional, but service boots to be worn.

(15) 2.30 p.m. to 4 p.m. Inter Company bombing. Teams of ten.

(16) Soccer Match. 2nd XI 2nd Regt. vs. 2nd XI 3rd Regiment.

Decr. 2. (17) 2.30 p.m. to 4 p.m. Finals Relay Race Two best Fighting Sections each Company to compete.

(18) 2.30 p.m. to 4 p.m. Finals Boxing and Wrestling.

(19) Finals Tug of War.

(20) Evening Smoking Concert.

Boxing and wrestling practice every evening except Wednesday and Saturday in Room above Regimental Orderly Room.

(sgd) B. YOUNG
Major,
for Lieutenant Colonel,
Commanding 3rd Regiment, S.A. Infantry.

3 SA Infy Bn
Vol 9

Dec 1916

1

3RD S. A. INF. (TRANSVAAL RGT.)

WAR DIARY

Vol

PLACE	DATE	HOUR	SUMMARY OF EVENTS & INFORMATION	Remarks and references to Appendices
WANQUETIN	1/12/16	8.25 AM	Warning telegram received from Brigade Headquarters (BM 927) to effect that Brigade moves into line tomorrow, consequently all training stopped and arrangements made for move	App 243
		11-35 AM	Memo received from B.H.Q to effect that all units move to ARRAS on 3/12/16. 1st SAI to march. All other units to be conveyed by bus. Operation order to be issued later. Coy Commanders warned accordingly.	App 244 " 245
		9-45 pm	Wire received from B.H.Q (BM 945) to effect C.O. & Coy Commanders will be taken to line tomorrow, if transport is available	App 246
	2/12/16	8.15 AM	Wire received from B.H.Q to effect that bus will call for C.O. & other Officers to convey them to Front Line.	App 247
		9 AM	C.O. & Coy Commanders proceeded to Front Line as instructed	
		9.30 pm (Noon)	Operation Order No 76 received from BHQ together with Schedule 'B'	App 248
		10.25 pm	Telegram from B.H.Q (BM 921) instructing that relief of J11 by 2nd SAI will be effected before relief of J111 by 3rd SAI. These Battalions will after delivery move forward to relieve 105th Brigade.	App 249
		11 pm	Preliminary move orders issued in accordance with B.O.O. No 76. Instructions issued for advance party to proceed to FRONT LINE to facilitate taking over section and to furnish guides etc. Transport to remain as at present until further orders.	App 250
	3/12/16	9 am	Further instructions issued in connection with move to ARRAS	App 251
		11/55 am	Received instructions from BHQ (S/C 283) transport to be clear by 4 pm 14/12/16, and to move independently. T.O instructed accordingly. Draft of 16 OR arrived	App 252

164

2

In lieu of
Army Form C 2118

WAR DIARY

PLACE	DATE	HOUR	SUMMARY OF EVENTS AND INFORMATION	REMARKS AND REFERENCES TO APPENDICES
WANQUETIN	3/12/16	3 pm	Recd wire B.H.Q (BM 462) to effect the Regt can move to CANDLE FACTORY at any time but must follow 4th S.A.I. and not move up NOVEMBER and OCTOBER AVENUES until relief of 15th Sherwoods completed.	App 253
ARRAS	"	11 pm	Move completed and Brigade informed. Regt took over S/Section J111 from 15th Cheshires. Marching In Strength 17 Officers 545 O.R. Relief effected without any casualties.	App 254
Sub Section J111.	4/12/16		Situation fairly quiet. Enemy T.M. occasionally active Casualties during day 1 OR Killed 2 wounded. Night patrols sent out to ascertain condition of our wire and enemys wire in "NO MANS LAND". Working party of 36 men supplied for work under the RE	App 255
"	5/12/16		Situation generally quiet except for periodical T.M activity. 2 Night patrols sent out to ascertain condition of our wire and that of the enemy in NO MANS LAND. Wiring party also detailed. Water Supply broken in front line and all water for there had to be carried in petrol tins. Supplied working party of 36 men for R.E.	App 255A
"	6/12/16		Enemy TM more active. 1 OR slightly wounded to duty. Operation Order No 77 dd 6/12/16 received from Brigade HQrs to effect that 4th S.A.I relieve 2nd SAI on 7/12/16. Draft of 4 OR arrived from Base. Usual patrols sent out to examine wire and wiring parties detailed.	App 256
		3-30pm	Inter Coy relief took place as follows:- C Coy from front line to Support A Coy from Support to Front Line. D Coy front Line to Support Line D Coy from Support Line to front line.	

165

~~162~~

~~164~~

IN LIEU OF
ARMY FORM C 2118.

166

~~164~~

WAR DIARY

PLACE ARRAS	DATE	HOUR	SUMMARY OF EVENTS AND INFORMATION	REMARKS AND REFERENCES TO APPENDICES
Sub Section J III	7/12/16		Quiet. Occasional enemy T.M. Shells in Front Support line. Usual night patrols sent out also wiring parties. 1 OR wounded by stray bullet. Sub Section J III visited by Brig Gen S A Bde. Working party of 36 men detailed for R.E. Weather fairly good.	
	8/12/16		Situation normal. All available men employed in repairing trenches, as a result of damage by enemy T.M. Night patrols & wiring parties sent out. For purpose of defence of J III Sub Section Major Young is appointed to command Right Half & Major Hemming Left Half of Line.	
	9/12/16		Occasional shelling by enemy artillery & T.M. Following Inter Coy relief took place: C Coy from Support line to Front line; B Coy from Support to Front line. A Coy from Front line to Support Line; D Coy from Front to Support Line. Usual night patrols and wiring parties detailed. Sub Section J III visited by Brigadier General between 11 a.m. and 1 p.m. Strength in trenches [illegible] 543 OR	~~App 257~~ App 257A
	10/12/16		Situation normal. Usual Patrols and wiring parties sent out. Casualties during the day 1 O.R. killed. 1 O.R. wounded. Weather conditions fairly good. Working party of 24 men supplied to R.E. All available men working on improvement of trenches.	~~App 257a~~
	11/12/16		Situation unchanged. Enemy aircraft more active. One brought down west of our section. Working party of 24 men supplied to R.E. Usual patrols and wiring parties sent out. Weather raining. Casualties 2 OR wounded.	

IN LIEU OF
ARMY FORM C 2118

WAR DIARY

PLACE	DATE	HOUR	SUMMARY OF EVENTS AND INFORMATION	REMARKS AND REFERENCES TO APPENDICES
ARRAS	12/12/16		Situation generally quiet. Repairs to front & Support Line Trenches damaged by enemy T.M. Shells. Usual [illegible] patrols and wiring parties detailed. Inter Company relief [illegible] as follows: A Coy from Support to front line, B Coy from Support to front line, C Coy from front to Support line, D Coy from front to Support line. [illegible] 1 O.R. arrived from Base.	[illegible] 58
	13/12/16		Enemy Artillery and Trench Mortars fairly active. Our guns retaliated. Casualties 1 O.R. wounded. Operation Order No 78 received from Brigade Head Quarters notifying Relief on 15.12.16. Patrols and working parties as usual. Draft of 10 O.R. arrived from Base. Weather fine.	[illegible]
	14/12/16		Situation unchanged. Enemy T.M. fairly active doing some damage to our front Trench. 3 O.R. wounded. Usual patrols and wiring parties sent out as usual. Working party of 36 men supplied to R.E. Draft of 54 O.R. arrived from Base. [illegible] [illegible] of [illegible] work. [illegible] 57 [illegible]	[illegible] 260
ARRAS	15/12/16		Enemy's attitude generally quiet. In accordance with B.O.O. No 78 the Regiment was relieved by 4th S.A.I., Relief completed by 5 pm. Headquarters at HOTEL UNIVERS. D Coy & A Coy at CONVENT ARRAS. C Coy occupied redoubts in RESERVE with 2 platoons in NICHOLLS REDOUBT. B Coy [illegible] CANDIE FACTORY with 1 platoon in BISKY REDOUBT.	

In lieu of
ARMY FORM C 2118

5

WAR DIARY

PLACE	DATE	HOUR	SUMMARY OF EVENTS AND INFORMATION	REMARKS AND REFERENCES TO APPENDICES
ARRAS	16/12/16		Supplied working parties totalling 178 all ranks (3 Officers in charge), also Bde Hqrs guard	
	17/12/16		Detailed same working parties. Had the use of town baths whereby certain number of men had a bath and change of clothing. Capt Vivian reported for duty and took over command of A Coy	
	18/12/16		Inter Coy relief affected as follows B & C Coys to CONVENT, ARRAS being relieved by A & D Coys respectively. Relief completed by 4pm Draft of 6 OR arrived.	App 261
	19/12/16		Situation unchanged. Working parties of 3 Officers + 175 men supplied. Major Henning left for Hospital to eventually have his right hand amputated.	
	20/12/16		Situation unchanged. Same working parties detailed Strength of Regiment 34 Officers 810 OR of which 15 Officers and 253 OR are detached on various duties	

168

IN LIEU OF
ARMY FORM C 2118

WAR DIARY

PLACE	DATE	HOUR	SUMMARY OF EVENTS AND INFORMATION	REMARKS AND REFERENCES TO APPENDICES
ARRAS	21/12/16		Situation unchanged. Supplied various working parties. Received Bde O.O No 79 to effect that 1st SAI would relieve 3rd SAI	App 262
	22/12/16		Issued O Order No 3R/16. Supplied same working parties of 3 Officers & 175 OR for work under RE. Utilised town baths.	App 263
Sub Section J III	23/12/16		In terms of B.O.O No 79, started to effect relief of 4th Regt in Sub Section J III at 9 AM. Relief completed by 2 pm. Situation on taking over quiet. Trenches generally in a bad state owing to heavy rainfall. Party of 2 Officers & 62 OR ordered to proceed to WANQUETIN to undergo special training for raid. Night patrols sent out into NO MANS LAND to ascertain condition of wire and wiring parties also detailed. Candidates for Commissions in the Regt & Imperial Cadet Course seen by Brigadier General.	App 264
	24/12/16		Situation generally quiet. Occasional T.M activity. Detailed working party of 24 men for R.E. Issued instructions re Night Patrols & wiring parties. Weather cloudy but fine.	App. 265

169

7b

WAR DIARY

IN LIEU OF
ARMY FORM C 2118

PLACE	DATE	HOUR	SUMMARY OF EVENTS AND INFORMATION	REMARKS AND REFERENCES TO APPENDICES.
SubSection J III	25/12/16		Situation generally quiet. Working party of 20 + 4 men supplied to RE. Night Patrols sent out to examine wire also wiring parties. All available men occupied in improving condition of trenches.	App 266
	26/12/16		Situation unchanged. Usual Night Patrols ordered also wiring parties. Following Inter Coy relief effected. B Coy Front Line to Support. C Coy from Left F. LINE to Reserve, with 2 Platoons BOSKY REDOUBT 2 Platoons NICHOLLS REDOUBT. A Coy from Redoubt Line to Left Front Line. D Coy from Support Line to Right Front Line. Working parties of 24 men supplied to RE. All available men occupied on trenches	App 267
	27/12/16		Situation quiet. Usual Night patrols sent out to ascertain condition of wire. Wiring parties also detailed. Working party of 24 men supplied to RE	App 268
	28/12/16		Situation Normal. Daily routine for patrols, wiring and working parties as on 27/12/16 carried out.	App 269

170

8

WAR DIARY

PLACE	DATE	HOUR	SUMMARY OF EVENTS AND INFORMATION	REMARKS AND REFERENCES TO APPENDICES
Subsection J111	29/12/16		Situation unchanged. Rainy. Inter Coy relief effected as follows: A Coy from Front Line to Support, D Coy from Front to Reserve C Coy from Reserve to Left Front Line, B Coy from Support to Right Front Line. Patrols + wiring parties as usual also working parties for R.E. Urgent representations to Brigade for the appointment of officers necessary to complete establishment. Received Bde. O.O. No 80 re relief of 4th SAI by 1st SAI.	App 270
	30/12/16		Situation generally quiet except for periodical TM activity. Heavy rain fall during night causing considerable damage to trenches. All NCOs + men employed on their repair. Received notice from Brigade of appointment of Sergts HILL, STILL and THORPE to Commissioned rank.	App 271
	31/12/16		GOC 9th Div + Bg Gen S.A Bde visited lines. Night Patrols + wiring parties sent out. Working party of 24 men detailed for work with R.E. Received notification from Bde of appointment of RQMS DAVIS, CSM PORTEOUS and L/C HOUSEHAM to Commissioned rank. Total casualties during month Killed 2. OR DofW 2 OR, Wounded 1 off 14 OR. Strength at date In Trenches 18 Officers 465 OR Detached on Courses + various duties 17 Officers + 321 OR (including 2 off 63 OR Manning at WANQUETIN)	App 272

E. F. Thackeray
Lt Colonel
Commanding 3rd S.A.I.

171

Instructions regarding War Diaries and Intelligence Summaries are contained in F. S. Regs., Part II. and the Staff Manual respectively. Title pages will be prepared in manuscript.

WAR DIARY
or
INTELLIGENCE SUMMARY.
(Erase heading not required.)

Army Form C. 2118.

Place	Date	Hour	Summary of Events and Information	Remarks and references to Appendices
ACHIET LE PETIT	GENERAL		CONTINUED – but training as a whole has been severely handicapped and retarded owing to large demands for working parties while in back areas, coupled with the fact that continual changes and shuffling has taken place with platoon commanders, making it impossible for them to become	
STRENGTH	O	OR.	acquainted with the N.C.O's and men under their immediate	
WITH UNIT	37	887	command, and thereby impairing organisation etc.	
DETACHED	10	110	This has been brought about by large demands being	
TOTAL STRENGTH	47	997	made for officers to attend various classes of instruction and consequently depleting the establishment. This to a certain extent has now been regulated, and the reinforcements	
CASUALTIES	KILLED.		have considerably improved during training, and are of	
No 10318 4 Cpl CASTLE C.H			a fairly good class of soldier. Concerts, Sports and	
WOUNDED			amusements have been arranged in conjunction with	
16. PTE FRANKENSTEIN D.A.			training with satisfactory and beneficial results. A very	
13935, WILCOX T.P.			large percentage of drafts consisted of men other than from Transvaal	172

[signature] Lt, Col.
Commanding 3rd. S. A. Infantry,
(Transvaal Regt.)

2353 Wt. W2544/1454 700,000 5/15 D. D. & L. A.D.S.S./Forms/C. 2118.

8 continued. WATER.
there.
Q.M. to arrange for Pack Mule Transport to carry up 80 gallons of water in tins to the QUARRY for the use of "A" Company, and Quarry Personnel, and the same amount to the STATION approx. R.25.c.6.1. for the use of "C" and "D" Companies.

9. RATION DUMPS. - The following will be Company Forward Ration dumps :-

"A" Company QUARRY
"B" " and Battalion Hqrs. YORK LANE.
"C" and "D" Companies approx. R.25.c.6.1

10. RATIONS FOR TO-MORROW. - These will be brought up and distributed this afternoon in present positions.

11. R. A. P. - This will be in the QUARRY.

12. SIGNALLING EQUIPMENT. - All signalling equipment will be taken into the line on moving out.

13. TRENCH STORES. - All trench stores, defence schemes, orders for working parties will be handed over, and receipts forwarded to (9.am.) French Battalion Headquarters by 9.a.m. 28th instant. This applies to both Stores taken over and Handed over.

14. SIGNAL COMMUNICATION. - Attention is drawn to Standing Orders regarding use of telephones forward of Brigade Hqrs., and Company Commanders are reminded that to-day is a "Silent Day", and all messages must be sent by Runner except in case of emergency.

15. SANITATION. - Trenches and Shelters must be left scrupulously clean, and a certificate to this effect will be submitted with Trench Store Cards.

16. COMPLETION OF RELIEF will be reported to Battalion Headquarters in the Forward Area by Code Word "P A R T Y".

17. BATTALION HEADQUARTERS will close at Dead Man's Corner at 8.30.p.m and will open at Battalion Headquarters in the Line on arrival.

Capt. & Adjutant.
BLUSH.

Issued at 8.a.m. 27/1/18.

Copy No. 1/4 to "A/D" Coys.
5 " Q.M.
6. " N.ISTER
7 " Headqrs.
8 " Adjutant.
9 " War Diary.

SECRET. 10
Copy No.....

R/
ORDER NO.3/133
by 3rd S. A. Infantry.

SECRET.

485

174

Map reference.
Sheet 57 C 1/40,000
" 62 C 1/40,000
Gouzeaucourt Wood 1/10,000

1. The 1st S.A.I.Brigade will relieve the 26th Infantry Brigade in the LEFT BRIGADE SECTOR on the nights of 23rd/24th and 24th/25th January 1918.

2. Reliefs will be effected in the following order :-
(a) Night 23rd/24th January, the 2nd S.A.I. will relieve 5th Cameron Highlanders in LEFT SUB-SECTION.
3rd S.A.I. will relieve 8th BLACK WATCH in SUPPORT POSITION.
28th Machine Gun Company will relieve 26th Machine Gun Coy.
(b) Night 24th/25th January, the 4th S.A.I. will relieve 7th SEAFORTH Highlanders in RIGHT SUB-SECTION.
1st S.A.I. will relieve 10th Argyle & S.Highlanders in BRIGADE RESERVE, W.2.c.
S.A.L.T.M.Battery will relieve 26th L.T.M.Battery.

3. The 3rd S.A.I. will relieve Companies of the 8th BLACK WATCH in positions as reconnoitred by Company Commanders to-day, and on relief the disposition of the Battalion will be :-
"C" Company on the RIGHT, with Co. Hqrs at Q.35.b.3.7.
"B" " in CENTRE " " " " Q.29.b.3.3.
"D" " on the LEFT.
"A" " in FOX SUPPORT.
Battalion Headquarters at Dead Man's Corner, Q.33.a.7.3.
Regimental Aid Post, QUEEN'S CROSS.

4. ADVANCE PARTIES.
Advance Parties will proceed from this Camp ~~XXXXXXXXXXXXXX~~ to-morrow to take over trench stores, composed as follows :-
Each Company, one officer, and one N.C.O. per platoon, and a Company Runner. Headquarters, L.G.O., R.S.M., and Sergt. Cook, Sergt Signaller, one Runner. Haversack rations will be carried.
These advance parties, together with the men who went up to-day, will act as guides for their Companies.

5. PARADE.
The Battalion will parade at 2.p.m. on the Battalion Parade Ground. DRESS, Full Marching Order, greatcoats will be worn. One blanket in pack. After inspection the Battalion will move off by Companies at 200 yards interval and will entrain at AX.5.d.20.d3.7. at 3.p.m. and will detrain at AX 127.W.3.b.2.2. near TREE DUMP at 5.p.m. Lewis Guns will be carried, and 16 magazines per gun.
After detraining Companies will move off to the relief of BLACK WATCH in the following order :-
"B", "A", ~~"D"~~, "C" D Headquarters. An interval of fifty yards between platoons and 200 yards between Companies will be observed.
All men proceeding to the Detail Camp will parade in rear of the Battalion on the Parade Ground, and will proceed by train as far as SOREL LE GRAND, where they will detrain, and will be marched to Detail Camp under Senior N.C.O.
In the absence of other orders, the Dug-Out Platoon will
E. parade in rear of the Battalion.

6. LEWIS GUNS
All boxes and magazines, other than those being carried, will be dumped by Companies on Bank alongside road running West of the Huts ready for loading at 1.30.p.m. One man per team to be left in charge.

7. BLANKETS, KITS AND BOXES, NOT GOING INTO LINE.
One blanket per man will be rolled in bundles of ten, and, together with officers kits and all boxes not required in the line will be dumped by Companies at above point, ready for loading at 1.30.p.m.

File War Diary

SECRET.

3RD SOUTH AFRICAN INFANTRY.

21. 1. 18. 176

4 84

W A R N I N G   O R D E R.

This Battalion will relieve the 8th BLACK WATCH on night of 23rd/24th instants.

The Battalion will probably entrain on light railway and detrain at TYKE DUMP about 5.p.m. on 23rd instant.

Companies will relieve the same lettered Companies of BLACK WATCH.

Company Commanders will reconnoitre their positions to be taken over, to-morrow starting under Company arrangements before 9.a.m. Each Company Commander will take with him one N.C.O. per platoon and one Company Runner.

2/Lieut A.K.PARROTT will proceed as Intelligence Officer, and will act as such until further notice. Bombing Sergeant and two Headquarter Runners will proceed with 2/Lieut. A.K.PARROTT.

Reconnoitring Parties will report to Support Battalion Headquarters (8th BLACK WATCH) of Left Brigade at Q.23.c.8.3 (Dead Man's Corner), and from there they will ascertain positions of their respective Companies.

Haversack rations will be carried.

The journey to above point will probably take 2 hours marching.

Parties can proceed by light railway with working party entraining at 7.30.a.m. if Company Commanders so wish, this train will take them to TYKE DUMP.

All particulars re. positions to be taken over, water points, ration dumps, etc., should be obtained.

Advance Parties to take over Trench Stores will proceed on morning of 23rd instant.

S B Stokes

Capt. & Adjutant.
3rd. S. A. Infy.

O.C. "A" Company.
" "B" "
" "C" "
" "D" "
I. O.
Q. M.

16. **BATTALION HEADQUARTERS** will close at YORK CAMP at 2.p.m. 23rd instant, and will open at SUPPORT BATTALION HEADQUARTERS, Dead Man's Corner, Q.23.a.7.2. on arrival about 5.30.p.m.

17. **BRIGADE HEADQUARTERS** will close at MOIS LAINS at 3.p.m. on 24th instant, and will re-open on same day and same time at Q.34.a.3.9.

Capt. & Adjutant.
3rd S. A. Infantry.

Issued at 7.a.m. 23/1/18.

Copies to	1/4	"A-D" Coys.
	5	Headquarters.
	6	Q.M.
	7	8th BLACK WATCH
	8	Adjutant.
	9	War Diary.

SECRET. 177482

3RD SOUTH AFRICAN INFANTRY.

17TH JANUARY 1918.

~~MOVING~~ Warning ORDER.

1. The Battalion will move by march route to MOISLAINS to-morrow, 18th instant.

2. Reveille will be at 6.a.m. Breakfast at 6.45.a.m. Sick Parade 7.15.a.m.

3. Company Officers Kits, Mess Boxes, and furniture, together with all mattrasses, stoves, beds, etc. will be stacked on respective Company ration dumps ready for loading at 8.30.a.m.

One blanket per man will be rolled in bundles of ten, and stacked in the same place at this time. C.Q.M.S. and four men per Company will be left in charge, and will be responsible for loading. Each Company will load up on first load their blankets, officers kits, mess boxes, furniture, beds etc. should be loaded on second load.

4. Headquarters officers kits, furniture, Canteen Stores, Pioneer's Stores, Packs of the Band, will be dumped in the Square ready for loading at 8.30.a.m. One blanket per man of Headquarters personnel will be rolled in bundles of ten, and stacked same time and place. Cpl PILKINGTON and four men from Headquarters to be left in charge, and will be responsible for loading.

5. Headquarters Officers Mess.
Mess Cart will call at Headquarters at 8.30.a.m. for Headquarter Mess Boxes.

6. Medical Stores.
Maltese Cart will call at Medical Inspection Room for medical stores at 8.30.a.m. One ~~Motor~~ Ambulance will call same time and place, and will be at the disposal of the M.O. for conveyance of sick marked by him.

7. Orderly Room Boxes.
Regimental Orderly Room boxes will be stacked outside Regimental Orderly Room, together with signalling equipment, ready for loading at 8.30.a.m.

8. LEWIS Guns.
Lewis Guns, Magazines and boxes will be stacked at respective Company Dumps ready for loading at 8.30.a.m. One man per team to be left in charge. The limbers will proceed with their respective Companies.

9. Field Kitchens.
All dixies etc. to be ready on Field Kitchens at 8.30.a.m. These will proceed with their respective Companies.

10. G.S.Wagons.
Seven G.S.Wagons from Brigade and 2 G.S.Wagons from S.A.F.A. will report here at 8.30.a.m. Q.M. to arrange for their distribution and for Regimental Transport to report as detailed above.

11. Parade.
Companies will parade under Company arrangements and will move off in the following order :-
Headquarters, "A", "B", "C", and "D". 5 Minutes interval will be observed between each Company. Headquarters will move off at 9.a.m. and will pass Starting Point, which is the Archway leading on to the METZ Road, at that hour.

12.

7. Continued.

Two men per Company who are proceeding to Detail Camp will be left in charge, under C.Q.M.S.

Headquarters Officers Kits and all boxes not wanted in the
8. Line will be dumped in Sunken Road on duckboards between officers huts and Company Lines ready for loading at 1.30.p.m. Two men to remain in charge.

8. KITS, FOOD CONTAINERS, ETC.GOING INTO THE LINE.

Company Officers trench kits and mess boxes and Gum boots will be loaded on respective Lewis Gun Limbers. Headquarters officers field kits, Orderly Room boxes, Mess boxes, etc. will be dumped at a separate spot in Sunken Road on duckboards, ready for loading at 1.30.p.m.

Canteen Stores will also be stacked at this spot.

9. FIELD KITCHENS, COOKING UTENSILS, ETC.

"A" and "D" Company Field Kitchens will be required in the Line. "B" and "C" Company dixies will be ready for loading at Company Kitchens at 1.30.p.m. Each Company and Headquarters will be allotted an equal number of Food Containers, which will go up with cooking utensils.

10. WATER.

Two water carts will be required in the Line. One at Battalion Headquarters, the other at "D" Company ration dump. These will supply Headquarters, "B", and "C" Companies (Battalion Headquarters/Cart) "A" and "D" ("D" Company cart).

11. TRANSPORT.

Q.M. to arrange for all necessary transport. Transport will proceed under orders of Q.M., and will dump kits, Lewis Guns, etc, at Ration Dumps as follows :-

"A" Company — Queen's Cross.
"B" " & Hqrs. — Dead Man's Corner.
"C" " — Coy. Hqrs. Q.30.a.7.6.
"D" " — Q.24.d.9.7. (near Queen's Cross)

No movement forward of THE DUMP will take place before 5.p.m.

All transport will be located at W.14.a. from 25th instant.

12. TRENCH STORES, FURNITURE, ETC.

All furniture, stoves, beds, mattrasses, and material will be handed over to Advance Parties of 8th BLACK WATCH, and receipts in duplicate will be forwarded to Regimental Orderly Room by 11.a.m. 23rd instant.

All maps, air photos, defence schemes, work programmes, orders for working parties to be found, trench stores, gum boots, will be taken over by Advance Parties of this Battalion, and receipts in duplicate forwarded to Battalion Headquarters by 11.a.m. 24th instant.

13. SANITATION.

This Camp must be left scrupulously clean. Company Commanders must detail special parties to thoroughly sweep out Company Huts, collect all material inside, clean up in the vacinity of their huts and lines. A certificate that huts and lines have been left in a clean and sanitary condition must be rendered to the Orderly Room before Battalion Parade.

14. MARCHING OUT STATES.

These will be collected by R.S.M. on Battalion Parade, and must show the exact distribution of the Company.

15. COMPLETION OF RELIEF will be reported to Battalion Headquarters, Dead Man's Corner, by Code Word "B A B".

16.

CO[illegible] NO. . 8 . .

ORDER NO. 3.R/124 a
by 3rd South African Infantry.

SECRET. 179

War Diary

Map references.
GAUCHE WOOD 1/20,000.
57.C.&62.C. 1/40,000
AMIENS 17 1/100,000

1. The 9th Division will be relieved in its present Sector by 39th Division, and will be withdrawn into G.H.Q. Reserve in the BRAY Area.

2. The 1st South African Infantry Brigade will be relieved by 118th Infantry Brigade in the Line on the night 31st Jan/1st Feb. 1918.

3. The 3rd S.A.I. will be relieved by the 4th/5th BLACK WATCH on night of 31st Jan/1st Feb. 1918 in the Front Line Right Sub-Sector.
This relief will be carried out as follows :-
"A" Coy. BLACK WATCH will relieve "B" Coy. 3rd S.A.I. in RIGHT FRONT LINE.
"C" " " " " " "C" " do. LEFT FRONT LINE.
"D" " " " " " "D" " " as COUNTER ATTACK COMPANY.
"B" " " " " " "A" " " as GARRISON COMPANY.
The relief is expected to commence at 6.30.p.m., but order of Companies marching in is not known.

4. GUIDES. -
Each Company will detail five reliable N.C.O's to act as guides (one per platoon and one per Company Head Quarters). Battalion Headquarters will detail three guides. All guides to report to Lieut. C.C.TARBOTON at Battalion Headquarters at 5.p.m.
As the relieving Unit has four platoons per Company, it will be necessary for Company Commanders to ascertain from the Advance BLACK WATCH Officer in which part of the Line the fourth platoon will be placed, and the guide for this platoon must be selected accordingly. Company Commanders will ensure that their guides are thoroughly acquainted with the best routes to respective posts.
Every precaution must be taken to guard against enemy observation of movement of guides in daylight.

5. TRENCH STORES. -
All trench stores, gum boots, defence schemes, aeroplane photos, maps, all documents relating to Sector and food containers will be handed over to relieving unit, and receipts in duplicate handed in to Battalion Headquarters as Companies move out.

6. On completion of each Company relief, the Company concerned will move out by platoons at 200 yards interval, and will proceed via. FINS-GOUZEAUCOURT Road to DECAUVILLE Station AX 125 (Map ref. W.3.d.9.3.) where 2/Lieut C.C.TARBOTON will be on the Main Road to direct Companies to entraining point. Here all ranks will be provided with hot tea or soup, and "B" and "C" Companies will be issued with one blanket per man, and rations will be issued for following day.
No time must be lost in the issue of above, as the train will leave at 11.p.m.
Entraining Officer. 2/Lieut. C.C.TARBOTON.

7. COOKING UTENSILS. -
The last meal in the Line must be served as soon after 5.p.m. as possible, and cooking utensils must be stacked ready for loading by 5.45.p.m. at following points :-
Headqrs, "A" and "B" Coys. - Ration Dump, [illegible] LANE.
"C" and "D" Coys. - " " STATION.
One limber will call at the STATION for these, and thence to Battalion Headquarters. Company Cooks must proceed in charge.
Canteen Stores must be carried to Battalion Headquarters Ration Dump and loaded on this limber. O.C. "B" Coy. to arrange necessary Carrying Party.

8. WATER CARTS. -
Teams will be sent for these as soon as it is dark.

9. ORDERLY ROOM BOXES, PIONEER'S TOOLS, AND HEADQRS. OFFICERS' MESS BOXES. -
One limber and officers' mess cart will load up these at 6.p.m. at Battalion Headquarters.

HQRS.

Urgent

L. 78.
31. 1. 18.

O.C. "A", "B", "C" and "D" Coys.

War Diary

180

490

SECRET.

WORKING PARTY.

1. In accordance with 1st S.A.I.Brigade instructions W.P.27, dated 31/1/18, this Regiment will provide a working party of 5 officers and 220 O.R. for work in 7th Corps Area.

2. "A" and "C" Coys. together with 50 O.R. of "D" Coy and the Dug-Out platoon are detailed for this work. This party will form a detachment under the command of O.C. "C" Coy. and the following officers in addition will be detailed to proceed :-

Lieut. W.SCALLAN.
2/Lt. E.MIDDLETON.
" G.E.STURGEON.
" A.E.SCOTT.

3. On relief to-night "A" and "C" Coys, Dug Out Platoon and the party of 50.O.R. from "D" Coy under 2/Lieut. E.MIDDLETON, will proceed by march route to FINS, where they will be billetted for the night, and on arrival there the detachment will receive its orders from Capt. B.H.L. DOUGHERTY, Commanding.

4. O.C's "A" and "C" Coys. will instruct their Lewis Gun Limbers to proceed direct to FINS.

5. Orders have been issued for one water cart and one Field Kitchen, together with blankets and rations for the detachment, to be delivered at FINS to-night. Another field kitchen will be placed at disposal of O.C. Detachment later.

6. Only the officers mentioned above will proceed with the detachment. Any other officers of Coys. will entrain as per order issued this morning.

7. Copy of Brigade instructions W.P.27 herewith to O.C. Detachment who will carry out all orders accordingly.

8. Billeting Party. Each Company will detail one N.C.O. to proceed at once to FINS and to report there to 2/Lieut. G.STURGEON to arrange for billets. No point can be given, but these N.C.O's must make enquiries as to where the detachment will be billetted.

9. Company Commanders will render Daily States as usual to Battalion Headquarters to-night, but no further states need be rendered.

10. Company Commanders will note that this detachment will not halt at entraining point, but will proceed straight to FINS. Orders must be issued accordingly.

acknowledge

S.H. Stokes

Capt. & Adjutant.
3rd S.A.Infantry.

NOTE. Please note that any men detailed for courses, next for leave, waiting F.G.C.M., witnesses, or O.T.C.Course to be sent on this detachment. These men should entrain with Battalion.

5 p.m.

PATROL REPORT

O.C.

"W" Coy.

At 2.a.m. on thr 9th inst.Corpl.HENDRY,Pre BAKER and myself were sent out on patrol into "No Mans Land" to inspect the enemy's wire entanglements.

We left the head of Sap 99 and worked our way down a portion of an old trench. We then struck across "No Man's Land"in the open until we got to the enemy's wire.

We followed the wire along to the left for about 100 yards. We spotted a German working party about 12 yards away. In trying to avoid them we ran into a German Sap. The head of this Sap extends right underneath their wire towards our lines and it slopes away to the level. Corpl.HENDRY was leading and found himself right on the Sap without being aware of it. We could see three German heads above the parapet. Corpl.HENDRY was about 2 yards away from them. He then took a bomb and after withdrawing the pin and releasing the lever,held the bomb for a couple of seconds before flinging it into the Germans. Then a German bomb was flung between us and Corpl. HENDRY was wounded. We then found our way back to our lines and entered our trenches by way of Sap 100 at about 2.45.a.m. We discovered the German wire to be very strong.

(Sd) P.A.Van Zyl.
L/c.

3rd Regiment.

The head of the German Sap is about 80 yards N.E. of the head of Sap 100. In my opinion the three Germans were all either killed or wounded,as the bomb flung by Corpl HENDRY fell right among them.

(Sd) P.A.Van Zyl.
L/c.

3rd Regiment S.A.Inf.

5178 Corpl.HENDRY.N.T. left Sap 99 at 2.a.m for the purpose of examining the enemy wire from a point due EAST of Sap 99 towards the Three Sisters. They worked along the wire for some considerable distance,and then suddenly came across an enemy Sap,the head of which extends underneath the enemy wire,towards the outside of it. Corpl.HENDRY found himself staring at 3 Germans at about 2 yards distance. He released the lever of a Mills Grenade,held the bomb in his hand for a couple of seconds,and then flung it among the Germans. At the same time a German bomb exploded near our patrol,which wounded Corpl.HENDRY in the face and shoulder. The other two members of the patrol managed to get Corpl.HENDRY back to our line,and they entered Sap 100 at 2.45.a.m. L/c Van Zyl,one of the patrol,whose report I attach,is of the opinion,that Corpl.HENDRY'S coolness and presence of mind saved the patrol from being all killed or at any rate from being seriously damaged. L/c Van Zyl is positive too,that the three Germans were either killed or wounded,as the bomb flung by Corpl. HENDRY fell right in their midst.

(Sd) P.H.ELLIS.
Capt.
O.C. "W" Coy.

Copy

APP 25 8

Operation Order
by B.W.K.

3R/10

182

12.12.16.

To O.C., W Coy
X "
Y "
Z "

RELIEF

The undermentioned Relief will be effected tonight 12.12.16. under arrangements to be made between Company Commanders.

The SUPPORT LINE relieving the FRONT LINE to commence 4.30 p.m.

I. MOVE A "W" Coy from Support to FRONT LINE
B "Z" " do. do.
C "Y" " do. FRONT to SUPPORT LINE
D "X" do. – do. –

II. Carrying Company Carriers of 1 N.C.O. Parties and 12 men will be relieved after Rations have been carried to FRONT LINE.

A.W.H. McDONALD
Capt. & Adj.
B.W.K.

Issued
4 p.m.

Operation order No 3R/5 183

6.12.16

App 256

To O/C A. W Coy
B X "
C Y "
D Z "

The undermentioned Relief will be effected tonight under arrangements between Company Commanders. The Support Line taking over the front line Trenches as per verbal instructions issued.

I. MOVES. "Y" Coy. from Front Line to Support
W " from Support to Front Line to relieve "Y" Coy.
"X Coy. from Front Line to Support Line
Z " from Support Line to Front Line to relieve X Coy.

II CARRYING PARTIES. The Permanent carrying parties of the Companies in Support must be relieved as soon as possible after Rations have been taken to the LINE tonight.

Issued 9/30 P.M.

A. W. H. McDonald
Capt
BANK.

S E C R E T. 3.R./ 3. 255 A

O.C. 5/12/1916. 184

"B" Coy.
"C" Coy. B A N K.

P A T R O L L I N G.

Copy of Brigade Instruction 0/14/6 read :-

All units in the Front Line will carry out patrols nightly. Company Commanders holding the Front Line will each send out a patrol every night, an Officer being detailed to accompany the patrol on alternate nights only. X Company patrol being under an N.C.O.

Y Company will send out an officers patrol to-night and and X Company tomorrow night, and so on in rotation.

Patrols will be given a definite object to achieve and written instructions, and O.C.s companies will be responsible that units on their right and left are advised of the patrols going out and when they return.

Patrols must not go out tonight before 11.30.P.M. Unit on right of sub-sector has notified his patrol will leaveat 1.A.M.

The patrols tonight will be instructed to patrol "No Mans Land" and should be cautioned against dis-used trenches and deep shell holes. They should report if possible on enemy's wire.

Any unusual incidents must be reported at once, but Company Commanders full report submitted with Intelligence Report each day by 10.A.M.

7.P.M. (Sd) A.W.H. McDonald.
Capt & Adjutant.
5/12/1916. B A N K.

Secret

Copy.

App. 258
3R/12

O.C. W Coy, BANK
Z

12.12.16.

PATROLS

Companies holding RIGHT and LEFT half SUB Sections of FRONT LINE will send out each a patrol into "NO MANS LAND". They will report upon the ground & if possible the enemy's wire.

Patrols are to go out before 2.30 a.m. BROOK are sending out a listening post only.

Notification to flanks must be carefully considered.

A.W.H. McDONALD
Capt &
BANK. Adjt.

"C" Form (Original). 186 Army Form C. 2123

MESSAGES AND SIGNALS. No. of Message..............

Prefix........... Code........... Words..........	Received	Sent, or sent out	Office Stamp.
£ s. d. Charges to collect	From...................... By..........................	At ap ....m. To........................ By......................	252
Service Instructions.			

Handed in at...Office................m. Received..................m.

TO O.C. 3rd S.A.Inf.

*Sender's Number	Day of Month	In reply to Number	AAA
B M 452	3rd		

3rd	S.A.I.	can	move	to
the	CANDLE	FACTORY	at	any
time	but	they	must	follow
4th	S.A.Inf	A A A	They	will
not	move	up	NOVEMBER	and
OCTOBER	AVENUES	until	relief	of
15th	Sherwoods	in	Redoubt	line
is	completed	A A A	Sherwoods	will
leave	a	guide	at	western
end	of	above	avenues	to
let	you	know	when	Sherwoods
are	clear	A A A	Guides	will
meet	3rd	S A I	at G 27	a 9 2½.
at	the	DAINVILLE	entrance	to
the	town	A A A		

FROM SUNSHINE

PLACE & TIME 3.P.M.

* This line should be erased if not required.

W 12250/4108. 37,500 Pads. 11/15. McC. & Co., Ltd. Forms C 2123.

"C" Form (Original).

MESSAGES AND SIGNALS. 187 No. of Message ....

Army Form C. 2123

Prefix .... Code .... Words	Received	Sent, or sent out	Office Stamp.
£ s. d. Charges to collect	From .... By	At .... m.	App 254
Service Instructions.		To .... By	

Handed in at .... Office .... m. Received .... m.

TO CHASE

*Sender's Number	Day of Month	In reply to Number	AAA
SS/35	3/11/14		

GEORGE

FROM BANK

PLACE & TIME 11 pm

* This line should be erased if not required.

W 12250/1108. 37,500 Pads. 11/15. McC. & Co., Ltd. Forms C 2123.

"C" Form (Original). 188 Army Form C. 2123

MESSAGES AND SIGNALS. No. of Message ....

Prefix .... Code .... Words	Received	Sent, or sent out	Office Stamp.
£ s. d.	From	At .... m.	
Charges to collect	By	To	
Service Instructions. Copy		By	

App 252

Handed in at .... Office .... m. Received .... m.

TO 3rd Regt SAI & 4th Regt SAI

*Sender's Number	Day of Month	In reply to Number	AAA
S/C 783	3rd		

Transport line aaa Brigade HQrs and 15th Cheshires K11 A 8.7 aaa 16th Ches and 105 MGC L7.3.5.1 aaa 14th Glos and 15 Sher L8 C66 aaa All units will be clear by 12 Noon 4th except 16 Cheshires who will not go out for some days aaa Transport of SA Bde will leave independently as above Tomorrow 1st Regt Transport standing fast meanwhile aaa Acknowledge.

FROM SA INF Brigade

PLACE & TIME

* This line should be erased if not required.

W 12250/1108. 37,500 Pads. 11/15. McC. & Co., Ltd. Forms C 2123.

I beg to draw attention to the action of Corpl. HENDRY.

This N.C.O. did good service in EGYPT and was wounded in Delville Wood and only returned a few days ago. He has been recommended for a Commission for some months now, and I trust this second wound will no longer delay his promotion.

(Signed) E.F.T.

Lt-Col.

APP 259

Secret

Sent [illegible] p.m.

3R/13 190

13/12/16

O.C., W. Coy
Z Coy, BANK

PATROLS

Coy. Commanders holding RIGHT and LEFT half SUB SECTION of FRONT LINE will send out each a patrol into "NO MANS LAND". They will report upon the ground and if possible the enemy's wire.

Patrol not to go out before 10 a.m.

BROCK will be wiring from 5 p.m. to 9 p.m. between CLARENCE and CUTHBERT and will also patrol between 4 p.m. and 9 p.m. in front of their own Sector.

R.W.H. McDONALD
Capt.
BANK. Adjt.

Secret. Copy APP. 258.

13/12/16.

To O.C., W. Coy
X "
Y "
Z "

Relief. Company Commanders to arrange that the Relief is carried out by at least 1 N.C.O. and 2 men from each Platoon moving over the top from SUPPORT to FRONT LINE.

The above to be always carried out when a Relief is effected.

A.W.H. McDONALD
Captn. &
Adjt.
BANK.

app 255

3 R /2.

192

O.C. "B" Coy.
"C" Coy. B A N K.

P A T R O L L I N G.

Instructions have been received that all units in the Front Line will carry out patrols nightly.

The Officers Commanding Y and X Coys. will send out each a patrol in front of their own sector tonight 4/12/1916., and will furnish a report to the Intelligence Officer on the condition of our wire & etc.

Patrols will be given a definite object to achieve and written instructions.

You must notify Units on your Right and Left that the patrol is going out, and when they return.

The Company Commanders written report of the work carried out by each patrol will be attached to the Intelligence report, and forwarded to Brigade Headquarters at 12 noon daily.

An officer must go out.

Please acknowledge.

(Sd) A.W.H.McDonald.
Capt & Adjutant.

B A N K.

P.S. When there is anything special to report as a result of the PATROL, this will be telegraphed in the morning situation telegram 4.A.M.

(Sd) A.W.H.McDonald.
Capt & Adjutant.

B A N K.

App 259/A

Time 2/30 Am.

No 3R/6
9.12.16

193

Operation Order
by BANK

To O/C W Coy
X "
Y "
Z "

The undermentioned Relief will be effected tonight under arrangement to be made between Company Commanders, the Support Line relieving the Front Line.

I Moves. Y Coy from Support to Front Line
X " " " to Front Line
W " from Front to Support Line
Z " " " to to "

II Carrying PARTIES. Company Carrying parties will be relieved tonight and arrangements re Rations at CANDLE FACTORY made

A.W.H.M. [illegible]
BANK Adt

Copy App 256 194

1st SOUTH AFRICAN INFANTRY BRIGADE. Copy No 3.

OPERATION ORDER 77.

Map Reference
51 B N.W.
3.1/10000.

1. RELIEFS . The 4th South African Infantry will relieve the 2nd South African Infantry tomorrow the 7th inst. in Sub-section J.2,. The 2nd South African Infantry will become the Battalion of the Brigade in Reserve, woth half of the Battalion in support trenches and half of the Battalion in ARRAS.

2. MOVEMENT AND TIME OF RELIEF. Details of Relief will be arranged between Battalion Commanders.
The regulations re Movement in ARRAS must be strictly adhered to.

3. WORKING PARTIES ETC. Standing Working parties, police, trench wardens, etc., found at present by the Reserve Battalion will be taken over by the 2nd South African Infantry, and those found by the Centre Battalion will be taken over by the 4th South African Infantry.

4. LOG BOOKS, MAPS, etc. Log Books, Maps, etc., will be handed over to the relieving Battalions.

5. TRENCH STRORES.
Trench Stores will be taken over and duplicate receipts therefor forwarded to Brigade Headquarters as usual.

6. COMPLETION OF RELIEF. Completion of Relief will be reported to Brigade Headquarters by code word "MARY".

(Sd) J. MITCHELL BAKER.
Major.
Brigade Major.
1st S.A. Infantry Brigade.

Issued through signals in accordance with List filed at Brigade Headquarters at 6.30.p.m.

S E C R E T. 3 R/1.

SECOND PART. 195

Appx 551

OPERATION ORDER No.676.
By Lieut-Colonel E.F.Thackeray, C.M.G., D.S.O.
Commanding 3rd S.A.Infantry.
(Transvaal Regiment) 3/1?/1916.

9 AM.

1. MOVE. In furtherance of Operation Order B.H.Q.No.76 and my C.76, the Battalion will rendezvous at WANQUETIN at point K.32.C.6.8. at 2.30.p.m. facing EAST and will enbus.

2. DRESS. Full Marching Order. Great Coats to be worn.

3. BLANKETS. No blankets will be taken into the trenches, but will be rolled up in bundles of ten (10) and handed in to the Quartermaster, (1st Line Transport)

4. RATIONS. Company Quartermaster Sergeants to be given full instructions that they will be held entirely responsible for the handing over of Company Rations to their Company in the Line. Rations up to, and including the 4th inst. will be carried by all ranks.

5. LOG BOOKS, MAPS ETC. Log Books, Maps, etc., will be taken over and receipts given.

6. TRENCH STORES. Trench Stores will be carefully taken over and Company Commanders will ensure that the completed Yellow Trench Store Card is rendered in duplicate to Battalion Headquarters by noon on the 4th inst.

7. TRANSPORT. The Transport Officer will detail one G.S. limbered wagon per Company, also Officers Mess cart and one G.S. limbered wagon for Headquarters Details, for conveyance of Officers Kit, Orderly Room requirements, and necessary stores. Transport to be packed and ready to move out at 3.30.p.m. Regimental Transport will remain in the Lines at present occupied until further ~~notice.~~ orders.

8. BAGGAGE AND STORES. All baggage and stores to be stored at Quarter Master's Stores and must ne handed over at 2.30.p.m Company Commanders to make their own arrangements with Transport Officer re loading stores for Line, which must be ready to move off at 3.30.p.m. Company Quartermaster Sergts. with one man per Company to proceed with G.S. Limbered wagon.

9. DETAILS. Companies will detail one man each to be left with Company Cookers who must not be Company Cook. Also one man per Company as Storeman to take charge of Company blankets, stores, etc. These men should be unfit for the trenches.

10. MOVE. Companies will enbus in the following order :- "Z", "Y", "X", "W". and Headquarters.

11. CLEANLINESS OF BILLETS. Billets to be cleaned up ready for handing over before parade. Two men per Company to be left in billets to clean finally, and to remain in billets until they have been inspected by the Medical Officer.

(Sgd) A.W.H.McDONALD.
Capt. & Adjutant.

3rd S.A.Infantry.
(Transvaal Regiment)

apx 2178

196

1st SOUTH AFRICAN INFANTRY BRIGADE.

2nd DECEMBER, 1918.

MAP REFERENCE.
51c N.E.
51b N.W.

OPERATION ORDER 76.

S E C R E T   A N D   U R G E N T.

1. MOVE. The 1st South African Infantry Brigade will move to ARRAS 3rd December, to relieve the 105th Brigade in the Line, in accordance with Schedule "A" attached.
O.C.s Units will ensure that their Units, less advance parties, being at the places where their busses will start from in sufficient time to enable enbussing being commenced immediately the buses arrive.

2. MOVEMENT. The 1st South African Infantry will proceed by MARCH ROUTE - Head of Battalion to leave DUISANS at 9.a.m.- and move by parties not larger than Platoons at intervals of 250 yards. All othet Units will proceed by bus as per Schedule "B" attached.

3. ADVANCE PARTIES. Each Battalion excepting the 1st South African Infantry will send forward an advance party not exceeding 25 consisting of one officer and one N.C.O. per Company, Lewis Gunners, Snipers, and Runners.
One lorry per Battalion is alloted for advance parties vide Schedule "B".
The O.C.28th M.G.Company will send as many Machine Gunners as can be accomodated in the 5 lorries being provided for his advance party, (vide Schedule "B") allowing for the Machine Guns which will also be carried in these lorries.
The O.C.Light Trench Mortar Barrery will arrange to have his Trench Mortars and as many of the Battery personnel as can be accomodated with the mortars in two lorries, at the BRIQUETTERIES, K.28.d.6.2. - by 8.45.am. where they will be picked up by the lorries - vide Schedule "B".

4. LOG BOOKS, MAPS, etc. Log Books, Maps, etc., will be taken over by Battalions.

5. TRENCH STORES. Trench Stores will be carefully taken over, and the duplicate receipts forwarded to Brigad Headquarters.

6. BLANKETS. Blankets will NOT be taken into the trenches by the Units in the Front Line but will be left with the 1st Line Transport. The 1st, 2nd and 3rd South African Infantry and Machine Guns Section for the Front Line, will therefore, leave their blankets at their Transport Lines in charge of their Quartermadters. The blankets of Units not going into the Front Line, will be taken with the men on the busses.

7. MEDICAL ARRANGEMENTS. 28th. Field Ambulance will carry out duties of Main Dressing Station for all Brigades in the Line, including sick as well as wounded, scabies and eye cases. South African Field Ambulance will be responsible for collection of all wounded and sick from the line, and their passage through the advanced Dressing Station to the Main dressing Station. This Units will provide four bearers for each of the seven Regimental Aid Posts in the Line.

8. TRANSPORT. No Regimental Transport will pass EAST of L.2.c. or of WARLUS before 4.15.p.m. Regimental Transport will remain in the Lines at present occupied until further orders.

9. COMPLETION OF RELIEFS. Completion of Relief will be reported to Brigade Headquarters by Code Word GEORGE.

P.T.O.

196A

10. BRIGADE HEADQUARTERS. Brigade Headquarters will be in ARRAS at G.22.c.8.7. from 2.p.m. on 3rd inst.

(Sgd) J.MITCHELL BAKER.

Major.

Brigade Major.

1st South African Infantry Brigade....

OPERATION ORDER. 3R/90. 197

B. O.C.

B A N K. 26/12/1916. app 26

O.C. A Coy.
B "
C "
D "
H.Q.
L.G.O.

1. RELIEFS The following relief will take place today under arrangement between Company Commanders.
"B" Coy Front Line to Support.
"C" Coy Left Front Line to Reserve.
2 platoons to BOSKY REDOUBT and 2 platoons to NICHOLLS REDOUBT.
"A" Coy from Redoubt Line to Left Front Line.
"D" Coy from Support Line to Right Front Line.

2. TRENCH STROES. Trench Store Cards to be handed over, the Company Commanders initialling the card which should be clearly marked with the sub-sub-section. The cards will not be taken out of the sub-sub-section.

3. BLANKETS. "A" Coy will return all blankets to CANDLE FACTORY properly rolled in bundles and labelled, and handed over for storage and receipt obtained from R.S.M. "C" Coy will draw y their blankets.

4. DUTIES. Working parties, carrying parties, messorderlies, will detailed as previously and detail handed over by Companies to each other, also special guards in NICHOLLS REDOUBT.

Issued 2.30.p.m. (sd) A.W.H.McDonald.
Capt & Adjutant.

B A N K.

Appx 24 a.

198

HEADQUARTERS,
1st S.A.I.Brigade.
December 1st 1916.

O.C. 1st Regiment S.A.I.
O.C. 2nd Regiment S.A.I.
O.C. 3rd -do-
O.C. 4th -do-
O.C. 28th M.G.Coy.
O.C. T.M.Battery.
O.C. Signal Section.
Office.

All Units will move to ARRAS on the 3rd inst. The 1st South African Infantry will march. All other Units will be conveyed by bus.

Operation Orders will be issued as soon as possible.

Please acknowledge.

ack

(Sd) W.S.Stevenson.
Captain.
for Brigade Major.
South African Infantry Brigade.

OPERATION ORDER. 3/R 16.
22/12/1916.

199 App 263

To O.C. "A" Coy. H.Q. Coy.
"B" COY. M.O.
"C" Coy. Q.M.
"D" Coy. T.O. and B. Officer.

In furtherance of Operation Order Brigade H.Q.No.79 dated 21st instant, the following relief will take place on the 23rd inst The <u>3rd South African Infantry</u> will relieve <u>4th South African Infantry</u> in sub Section J.III.

1. <u>MOVE.</u> The relief will be carried out by day.
The Battalion will occupy the sub Section J III as follows:-

<u>Front Line</u>	2 Companies.
<u>Support Line.</u>	1 Company.
Reserve (in redoubts)	1 Company

"D" Company will hold SUPPORT LINE and will move off from CANDLE FACTORY at 12 noon, less one Platoon, and other Platoon in BOSKY REDOUBT.
The 2 leading Platoons to relieve <u>left</u> SUPPORT of 4th S.A.I. first, and will move into position via OCTOBER AVENUE.
"B" Company will follow the 2 Platoons of D Company, and will be at CANDLE FACTORY, and move off at 12.10 p.m., via OCTOBER AVENUE And CANNON STREET, and relieve the RIGHT FRONT LINE.
"D" Company, remaining 1 Platoon at St.NICHOLAS to follow "B" Coy, and move into RIGHT SUPPORT.
The platoon in BOSKY REDOUBT to be relieved by "A" Coy. so as to move into <u>Right</u> SUPPORT by 12 noon.
"C" Company to follow, moving off from CANDLE FACTORY at 12.40 p.m., via OCTOBER AVENUE and CANNON STREET, and will take over LEFT FRONT LINE.
An interval between all Platoons must be observed.
"A" Company must be in RESERVE with
2 Platoons and Headquarters in NICHOLAS REDOUBT
2 Platoons in BOSKY REDOUBT.
O.C. "A" Company to arrange the relief of "D" Company Platoon, now occupying BOSKY REDOUBT before 12 noon.
Arrangements are being made for the relief of FORESTIER REDOUBT with 1st S.A.Infantry.

2. <u>TAKING OVER</u>. Company Commanders to arrange to send an Officer totake over their LINE, during the morning.
Trench Stores including Cookhouse and utensils to be carefully taken over, and all articles checked, also LOG Books and detail of work. The duplicate copies of Trench Store Cards to be sent to Orderly Room as soon as relief is completed.
The condition of the trenches is to be at once reported upon, and certificate rendered with Trench Store Cards.
The O.C.Headquarter Details will arrange to effect the relief of the undermentioned, commencing at 9 a.m., these men to move to Trench Line in small parties.
1. Lewis Gunners. Snipers and Observers.
Observation Guard Headquarters. Police.
The R.S.M. to take over CANDLE FACTORY and Headquarters Stores.

3. <u>TRENCH WARDENS.</u> The 4 men detailed for November Avenue and 4 men for OCTOBER TRAMWAY to take over duties at once. H.Q.Coy. to detail 1 man as Trench Warden for SEPTEMBER AVENUE.

4. <u>SANITATION</u>. Companies will send forward their Sanitary Staff, to take over during the morning.

5. <u>TELEPHONES</u>. On no account is any Telephone in the sub Section to be used except for Test Calls every 15 minutes, and Artillery Tests, also S.O.S. by order of Company Commanders.

6. <u>WORKING PARTIES : WORK</u>. Company Commanders to take over WORK SHEET, and submit by 7 p.m. daily the proposed work for the following day, shewing task and the number of men to be employed as per instructions B.H.Qrs. O/18 supplied you.

7. <u>BLANKETS</u>. As per previous instructions Companies in the FRONT and SUPPORT LINE, will return all blankets to Coy.Store &

App 2 to ~~W.D.~~ 1/133

23-12-16

Brigade Major
South African Brigade

200

PRINCE

9/40 pm

[signature] Lt Col
Comndt - BANK

"C" Form (Duplicate). Army Form C. 2123.

MESSAGES AND SIGNALS. No. of Message ....

	Charges to Pay. £ s. d.	Office Stamp.
Service Instructions.	201	247

Handed in at .... Office .... m. Received .... m.

TO

Sender's Number	Day of Month	In reply to Number	AAA

stated	from	right	to	left
4th	S A I	in	support	A A A
O.C.	2nd	S A I	will	see
that	bus	proceeds	as	above
to	pick	up	officers	other
units	A A A	O.C.	signal	section
will	take	also	telegraphists	
with	him	A A A	Bus	will
return	at	once	to	be
divided	on	arrival	at	105
Bde	A A A	acknowledge.		

(Sd) J. MITCHELL BAKER.

Major.

Bde Major.

FROM S.A.BDE.

PLACE & TIME 7.15.A.M.

W 12250/4108. 37,500 Pads. 11/15. McC. & Co., Ltd. Forms C 2123.

Diary File MD 162
26-12-16

To O/C A Coy
D "
B "

App 266

WIRING

The O/C Support Coy will detail to report tonight to O/C R and L. Front Line Companies the undermentioned N.C.Os and men for wiring in front of Front Line, to work between the hours of 8 and 12 MN.

Right Front Line Coy. 1 NCO & 5 men – 6
Left " " " 1 NCO & 5 men 6

Total 12

The amount of wiring and locality to be furnished with intelligence report tomorrow 27th/

Issued 4.10 pm

[illegible]
Capt
Adj
Bn I

OPERATION ORDER. 3R/18.
24/12/1916.

app 265

O.C.
"B" Coy.
C "
BANK.

203

P A T R O L S.

Right and Left Front Line Companies sub-section J III will send out each a party into "NO mans Land," tonight between the hours of 1 a.m. and 3.a.m.

They mus patrol the area in front of their own sub-sub-section and report upon enemy wire. The patrols to go out and great care exercised in notifying units on the flanks, of time of departure and probably return. Strength of Patrols as follows :-

B Coy 1 Officer and 2 men.
C Coy 1 N.C.O. and 2 men.

The patrol of "JUMP" leave from 89 in front of their own lines. Wiring in J III as per special instructions.

Issued 3.P.M. Sgd A.W.H.McDonald.
Capt & Adjutant

BANK.

app 264

204

OPERATION ORDER. 3R/17
23/12/1916.

O.C.

C Coy. BANK.

PATROL.

You will send out tonight an Officers patrol to report upon the enemy's wire at point G.6.c.50,00. which has been firedon today by 2" trench mortars in accordance with Y35 TMB and Divisional Artillery Operation Order No 62 of 23/12/1916.

Patrol of 1 officer and 2 men to furnish accurate report on this wire. Please notify your flanks when patrol goes out and returns.

6.5.P.M. Sgd A.W.H.McDonald.
Capt & Adjutant.
BANK.

NOTE. Patrol of "JUMP" 1 Officer and 2 men from about 93 at 11 p.m. Return between 12 and 12.30.a.m. between CUTHBERT AND CLARENCE.

OPERATION ORDER. OR/15. 205

18/12/1916.

To Officer Commanding

____________Company, B A N K.

app 261

M O V E.

1. MOVE. The following Relief will be carried out to-morrow the 19th instant, during the day, under arrangements between Company Commanders.

An Officer or Company Sergeant Major to go up beforehand to take over all duties, all Trench Stores etc. and forward cards to Battn. Headquarters at once.

"[illegible]" Company moves to Convent, Arras

"[illegible]" Company moves to Convent, ARRAS.

"A" Company relieves "B" Company, Redhouse, with one Platoon in BOSKY REDOUBT.

"D" Company relieves "C" Company, with two Platoons NICHOLS REDOUBT, also Company Headquarters. Two Platoons Forestier Redoubt.

The relief to be affected before 4 p.m.

WORKING PARTIES. The Officers Commanding "A" and "D" Companies to arrange that working parties detailed for to-morrow morning 19/12/16 must go forward to their work in full marching order, and will effect relief after such work, and not return to their billets.

Rations are to be arranged for by Companies, for these working parties, and a Field Kitchen at CANDLE FACTORY utilised if required.

A. W. H. McDonald

Captain & Adjutant,

B A N K.

M/183.

23/12/1916.

App 264 206

Brigade Major.
S.A. Brigade.

P R I N C E.

3.40.p.m.

Sgd. E.F. Thackeray.
Lt.Col.
Commanding BANK.

Operation Order 207 3R/19
by BANK 25/12/16

O/C ~~B~~ Coy Sign & return
~~C~~ " pr
~~D~~ " DR 6th Corps.

WIRING

The O/C Support Company will detail to report tonight at 8 pm for WIRING in FRONT LINE under instructions to be issued by Company Commanders B and C Companies the following NCOs and men.

Right FRONT LINE ~~Sub~~ Section. 1 NCO. 5 men 6
LEFT FRONT " " Section. 1 NCO 5 " 6
To work from 8pm till 12 MN. 12.
The above for special wiring of gaps in each Sub Sub Section

Issued 4/45 pm
25/12/16

A. McDonald
BANK Adj

OC D Coy

208

11th W. Reg
7/12/16

O C
A Coy
D "
B "

WIRING

The O/C Support Coy will detail to report tonight to O/C R and L Front Line Companies, the undermentioned NCOs & men for wiring in front line to work between the hours of 8 and 12 MN.

Right Front Line Coy	1 NCO & 5 men	=	6
Left " " "	1 do 5 do	=	6
	Total		12

The amount of wiring and locality to be furnished with Intelligence report tomorrow, also number of coils used.

A. W. H. McDonald
Capt & Adjt
8 A. H. R.

5-35 pm

"C" Form (Duplicate).
Army Form C. 2123.

MESSAGES AND SIGNALS.

No. of Message ....

	Charges to Pay.	Office Stamp.
	£ s. d. 209	
Service Instructions.		

Handed in at .... Office .... m. Received .... m.

TO O.C. 3rd S.A.I.

Sender's Number	Day of Month	In reply to Number	AAA
B M 905	2nd		

Bus	will	call	for	C.O.
and	company	commanders	2nd	S A I
and	O.C.	L T M By	and	O C
Signal	section	at	8 A.M.	A A A
It	will	then	proceed	to
WANQUETIN	and	DUISANS	and	pick
up	C.O.s	and	Company	commanders
of	4th	and	3rd	S A I
and	1st	S A I	A A A	O.C.
L T M B	will	proceed	to	HQ
1st	S A I	and	join	Bus
there	A A A	Officers	will	go
H Q	105	Bde	at	PLASE
st	CROIX	ARRAS	G 22 c 8 7	where
guides	will	meet	them	A A A
1st	2nd	and	3rd	S A I
will be	in	front	line	in order

FROM

PLACE & TIME

W 12250/4108. 37,500 Pads. 11/15. McC. & Co., Ltd. Forms C 2123.

Copy

"A" Form.
MESSAGES AND SIGNALS.

Army Form C.2121
(in pads of 100).
No. of Message

Prefix ...... Code ...... m. | Words | Charge
Office of Origin and Service Instructions.

Sent
At ...... m.
To
By

This message is on a/c of: Secret Service.
(Signature of "Franking Officer.")

Recd. at ...... m. 250
Date
From 210
By

TO Operation Order PART 1
By Lieut Col E.T. Thackeray CMG DSO
Commdg 3rd S A I

Sender's Number. | Day of Month. | In reply to Number. | AAA

In the Field 3/12/16
11 pm

To TRANSPORT Officer
QuarterMaster

Move Regimental Transport will remain in the lines at present occupied until further orders

Sgd J.P. Lukin Lieut
for Actg Lt Col
3/12/16 Comm of 3rd S A I

From
Place
Time

The above may be forwarded as now corrected. (Z)
Censor. Signature of Addressor or person authorised to telegraph in his name.

* This line should be erased if not required.

750,000. W 2186 –M599. H. W. & V., Ld. 6/16.

"C" Form (Duplicate). Army Form C. 2123.

MESSAGES AND SIGNALS. No. of Message ....

SM IDP 56 FH
Sig. G. Lewis

Charges to Pay. £ s. d. 211

Office Stamp. SAC. 2/1X/16

Service Instructions.

Handed in at .... Office 9.30 m. Received 9.25 m.

TO 3rd S A I

Sender's Number	Day of Month	In reply to Number	AAA
BM 921	2nd		

Reference Operation Order 76 Schedule A Relief of J 11 by 2nd S A I will be effected before Relief of J III by 3rd S A I aaa. These Battalions will after debussing move forward to relieve 105 Brigade Unit on Orders representation that Brigade aaa. Address Sunshine and 2nd and 3rd S A I.

Recd 2Dec

FROM CHASE

PLACE & TIME

W 12250/4108. 37,500 Pads. 11/15. McC. & Co., Ltd. Forms C 2123.

"C" Form (Duplicate). 212 Army Form C. 2123.

MESSAGES AND SIGNALS. No. of Message ....

Service Instructions.

Charges to Pay. £ s. d.

App.

Office Stamp.

245

Handed in at .... Office .... m. Received .... m.

TO BRIGADE MAJOR.
S. A. BRIGADE.

Sender's Number	Day of Month	In reply to Number	AAA
SC/22.	1st.		

Wire and preliminary instructions re move of todays date received.

(Sd) W.F. Lukyn.
2/Lieut.

FROM 3rd Regiment.

PLACE & TIME WANQUETIN. 11.35.A.M.

W 12250/4108. 37,500 Pads. 11/15. McC. & Co., Ltd. Forms C 2123.

"C" Form (Original).
MESSAGES AND SIGNALS.

Army Form C. 2123

No. of Message 244

Prefix .... Code .... Words ....

Charges to collect £ s. d.

Service Instructions.
S Z A

Received From .... By ....

Sent, or sent out At 213 m. To .... By ....

Office Stamp. 1/22/16 SAG

Handed in at .... Office .... m. Received .... m.

TO O.C. 3rd S.A.I. and O.C. 4th S.A.I.

*Sender's Number	Day of Month	In reply to Number	AAA
B M 945.	1st		

C.O.s and infantry company commanders will be taken to line tomorrow morning if transport is available and will be ready to proceed on the shortest notice AAA addressed all units.

FROM S A Bde.

PLACE & TIME 9.45.P.M.

* This line should be erased if not required.

W 12250/1108. 37,500 Pads. 11/15. McC. & Co., Ltd. Forms C 2123.

Order No 3 R/119 Secret
by Lt. Col.
E.T. Thackeray Cmg DSO
Commanding 3rd S.A.I.

214 482

map ref
57c 1/40000
62c 1/40000

18/11/18

Cite warning

(1) In accordance with 1st S A I Brigade Order No 155 dated 17/11/18 the Battalion will move this morning by march route to MOISLAINS via NURLU.

(2) Move will be as per Warning Order issued.

Issued at 7.30 am

[illegible]
Capt & adj
3rd S.A. Infy.

A.
B.
C.
D.
Hqrs.

Copy

App 271.

Operation Order.

Secret
O/C C Coy BANK.
B Coy "

Patrols

O/Cs Right and Left FRONT LINE Coys SUB-SECTION J.111. will each send out a patrol into "NO MANS LAND" tonight 30/31st. not leaving their own FRONT LINE before 1-30 AM. They will report upon our own and enemy wire.

Strength of Patrol R. FRONT. Coy 1 Offr. 2 men
" " " L " " 1 NCO 12 men

"JUMP" Patrol leaves from the Right of their own sub-section about 2 am. The patrol signal tonight will be one long and two short blasts on a whistle or with the mouth. Units on flanks to be notified of time of departure and probable time of return of patrols. A report on attempted repair of the enemy's wire and condition of the gaps is required.

Issued 2-45 pm.

(Sd) A.W. H MDonald
Capt & Adjt
BANK

Diary

Operation Order I 3R/24

29.12.16

Secret

216

O/C "A" Coy BANK

"B" "

"C" "

"D" "

L.G.O. "

(1) Relief. The following Relief will take place today under arrangements to be made between Company Commanders.

As per instructions previously issued, a number of men must be detailed to Relieve Over the Top and a Certificate to this effect added to your notification of Relief Carried out.

'A' Company from FRONT LINE to Support LINE.

'D' " from – do – to Reserve "

'C' " from Reserve to Left Front "

'B' " " Support to Right Ft Line.

II TRENCH STORES. Trench Store Cards to be handed over, and initialled by the Company Commander taking over.

Operation ORDER 3R/25

Secret 29.12.16 217

O/C. "B" Coy

App 270

PATROLS

Right and Left Front Line Coys Sub Section J III. will each send out a PATROL into "NO MANS LAND" tonight 29/30th not leaving their own FRONT LINE before 1 AM. These patrols to report upon our and the enemy's wire – Strength of PATROLS –
Right Front Coy. 1 N.C.O and 2 men

Left Front Coy 1 Officer + 2 men.
"Thump" PATROL leaves 2 O/C from SAP 95. working Right between CLARENCE and CUTHBERT.
Right PATROL of BANK to inspect gully in wire in front of CLAUDE CRATER.
The Senior Coy Cor to arrange verbal signal word. – Units on flank to be notified of patrol movements and time.

Issued 3/15 pm.

A.W. H. M'Donald Capt Adjt
BANK

TRENCH Stores : These Store Cards are not to be removed from their Sub Sub Section. No Copies are required at Battalion O Room.

III Blankets : "C" Company will return all Blankets to CANDLE FACTORY properly rolled in bundles and labelled, + receipt obtained from a/CSM.
"D" Coy will draw their blankets.

4 Duties : Working parties, Carrying parties, Mess Orderlies, and GUARDS, with instructions will be handed over by Companies to each Other. Note the special Guard at NICHOLLS Redoubt.

Issued at
3pm

A.C.H. McDonald Capt
BANK. Adjt

OPERATION ORDER. 3R/25.

SECRET.
By O.C. BANK.
O.C.
A
D
B

App: 269

219

PATROLS.

Right and Left Front Line companies Sub-section J III will each send out a patrol into "No Mans Land" tonight 28/12/1916, not leaving their own front line before 1.a.m.

These patrols to report upon our own and the enemy's wire.

Strength of Patrol.
Right Front Company. 1 Officer and 2 men.
Left Front Company 1 N.C.O. and 2 men.

The patrols of "JUMP" leave from right of their sub-section at 2.a.m. Every precaution must be taken to notify units on flanks the time of departing and probably time of return of party.

The senior Company Commander will arrange a signal pass-word.

5.P.M. (Sd) A.W.H.McDonald.
Capt & Adjutant.

B A N K.

OPERATION ORDER.   3 R / 3 1.

S E C R E T.   26/12/1916.   267

By O.C. B A N K.   app 220

O.C. A Coy.
D "
B "

P A T R O L S.

Right and Left Front Line Comapnoes, sub-scetion J III will each send out a patrol into "NO Mans Land" 26/12/1916, not leaving their own front line before 1.a.m.
These patrols will report upon our own and the enemy's wire.

Strength of Patrol

Right Front Company. 1 Officer and 2 men.
Left -do- 1 N.C.O. and 2 men.

The patrols of "JUMP" leave from FACE OF CUTHBERT at 2.a.m. working SOUTH. Every precaution must be taken to notify units on flank the time od departing and probable time of returning.

Issued 4 .P.M.   Sgd A.W.H.McDonald.

Capt & Adjutant.

B A N K.

Operation Order 3R/27

Secret 31-12-16

O.C. C Coy BANK
B "

221

App 272

PATROLS

The O/C Right and LEFT FRONT LINE Coy's Sub Section J.III will each send out a Patrol into "NO MANS LAND" tonight 31/1/17. to move out at 1.30 AM. to examine our own and enemy's wire and Patrol NO MANS LAND.

Strength of PATROL R. Front Coy 1. N.C.O. 2 men
do — L " " 1 Officer 2 men

The PATROL of "Jump" leaves Sap 95 at 1 Am. working Right.

The PATROL Signal tonight will be one long and 2 Short blasts of the whistle or with the mouth.

Vyvyan's on Flanks to be notified the time of departure of Patrol and probable time of Return.

Issued 7/50 pm

A. O. Hall [illegible]
Capt
BANK
O.C.

OPERATION ORDER. 3R/22.

27/12/1916.

app 268

222

S E C R E T.
By O.C.
B A N K.

O.C. A Coy.
D "
B "

P A T R O L S.

Right and Left Front Line Companies sub-section J III will each send out a patrol into "NO Mans Land" tonight 27/12/1916 not leaving their own front line before 1.A.M.

These patrols to report upon our own and the enemy's wire.

Strength of Patrol

Right Front Company. 1 N.C.O. and 2 men.
Left -do- 1 Officer and 2 men.

The patrols of "JUMP" leave from Right of their sub-section at about 2.a.m. Every precaution must be taken to notify unit on flank the time of departure and the probably time of return of patrol.

5.30.P.M.

(Sd) A.W.H.McDonald.
Capt & Adjutant.
B A N K.

Operation ORDER 38/25

Secret 29.12.16 223

O/C "A" Coy
"B"

APP 270

PATROLS

Right and Left Front Line Coys Sub Section J.III. will each send out a Patrol into "No Mans Land" tonight 29/30th inst leaving their own Front Line before 1 AM. These patrols to report upon our own and the enemy's wire – Strength of Patrols –

Right Front Coy. 1 N.C.O and 2 men

Left Front Coy 1 Officer + 2 men. "Thump" Patrol leaves 2 [illegible] from Sap 95 working Right between CLARENCE and CUTHBERT.

Right Patrol of Bn to inspect fully our wire in front of Clarence Crater.

The Senior Coy. Cdr to arrange verbal signal word – Units on flank to be notified of patrol movements and time.

Issued 3.15 pm A.W. McDonald Capt Adjt

"C" Form (Original).

Army Form C. 2123

MESSAGES AND SIGNALS.

No. of Message ....

Prefix S. E. Code A.M. Words ....

Charges to collect £ s. d.

Received From 224 By ....

Sent, or sent out At .... m. To apD By ....

Office Stamp. 2y 3

Service Instructions. Priority S Z A

Handed in at .... Office .... m. Received .... m.

TO 3rd and 4th S A I

*Sender's Number	Day of Month	In reply to Number	AAA
B M 927	1st		

Warning	Orders	A A A	Brigade	moves
into	line	A A A	further	orders
later.				

FROM PLACE & TIME S A Bde.

7.15 A.M.

* This line should be erased if not required.

W 12250/4108. 37,500 Pads. 11/15. McC. & Co., Ltd. Forms C 2123.

Copy

Secret. Issued 3.30 p.m. APP. 260

3R/14

4.12.16

O.C. A Coy / D Coy BANK.

Patrols Wiring

Companies holding Right & Left Sub Section of Front Line will send out each a PATROL into No MANS' LAND after 10 p.m. for night 4.12.1916. to report upon the ground, our own and enemy wire.

3 RWK are sending out PATROL from 9.15 p.m. between CUTHBERT and CLARENCE CRATERS.

WIRING parties to be sent out where necessary.

A.W.H. McDONALD
Capt &
BANK Adjt

SECRET. J 7.

14/12/1916.

260 226

To O.C.

---

1. MOVE. Instructions in regard to MOVE 15/12/1916.
"W" and "Z" Companies to CONVENT, ARRAS. "Y" Coy. will occupy Redoubts in Reserve LINE, viz. 2 Platoons NICHOLS REDOUBT with Company Headquarters, 2 Platoons ~~xxxxxxxx~~ FORESTIER REDOUBT.
X Company to occupy billeting AREA behind CANDLE FACTORY, and be in RESERVE, with one platoon BOSKY REDOUBT.
Headquarters Company, less Canteen and Staff will move into ARRAS. Headquarters at Hotel UNIVERSE.

2. GUIDES. Company Commanders will arrange to send guides to [illegible] Company Headquarters to obtain all information concerning quarters, and for the purpose of guiding the Company to its ~~xxxxxxxx~~ new area of occupation.
These guides will report at 3 p.m. to-day with instructions from Company Commanders. The relief of the Line will be as follows:-
"W" Company by "D" of BROOK, commencing 1.45 p.m. 15/12/16
"Z" Company by "A" of BROOK, commencing 2.30 p.m. 15/12/16
"Y" Company by "C" of BROOK commencing 3.10 p.m. 15/12/16.
"X" Company by "B" of BROOK commencing 3.50 p.m. 15/12/16.
Lewis Gunners and Sentries will be relieved commencing 12 Noon. Headquarters at 2 p.m.
"W" Company will furnish 4 guides to be at JUNCTION AUGUST AVENUE and Headquarters Trench at 1.15 p.m. to guide relieving Company, BROOK, via NOVEMBER AVENUE to the LINE.
Companies when relieved will return as follows:- LEFT Companies via NOVEMBER AVENUE, and Right Companies via OCTOBER AVENUE. "X" Company will arrange for the relief of the platoon in Bosky Redoubt at 3 p.m.

3. TRENCH STORES. Great care must be taken that all Trench Stores are handed over, and duplicate receipts on yellow card, sent at once to this Office, this copy has to go to Brigade, and must explain all permanent Stores, and be signed by both the officer handing over & relieving.
4. LOG BOOKS. These must be handed over, made up to date, showing work performed and work in hand, work programme & schemes. R.E. Stores indented for and not received, also list of stores on hand at Company Dump. Receipts must be obtained for all Maps, Log Books etc.
5. GENERAL. Cleanliness of Trenches and Dug-outs. Latrines to be kept in good condition, SALVAGE completed.
The Relief will be reported by runner to Headquarters, Hotel Universe, ARRAS.
Cookhouses to be ready for handing over 1 p.m., 2 Company kitchens will remain at Candle Factory for "X" and "Y" Coys. The Company kitchens of "W" and "Z" Coy. will be brought to Candle Factory to-night, Companies will arrange to have all cooking utensils sent back to complete these vehicles, also for the cooking of meal for the men when relief effected.
6. TRANSPORT. The Transport Officer will arrange the necessary number of wagons for conveyance of blankets for "W" and "Z" Companies to Convent, ARRAS.

1E

No.________

ACQUITTANCE ROLL (ALL ARMS).

Army Form N. 1513.

________ {Squadron / Battery / Company} of the ________

Impress a/c No.________

Regl. No.	RANK AND NAME.	*Adapt if necessary.	Cash Payment. *Francs	Cash Payment. Centimes.	Sterling Equivalent (To be completed in Fixed-Centre Pay Office). s.	d.	Receipt of Soldier.
		Total					The undermentioned (1) and (2) to be completed by Paymaster i/c Clearing House—

To be inserted by Paying Officer. Total, in words—

Francs________

Centimes________

s. d.

(1) Rate of Exchange—5 =

(2) Total Sterling equivalent, in words—

________Pounds,

________Shgs., and ________Pence.

Signature of the Officer making the Payments________

Date of Payment________19 Officer Commanding________Company.

________Regiment.

Certified that the above amounts have been charged in the ledger accounts of the men concerned.

Date________19 . ________Paymaster________

(C6410) Wt. W. 3146/M542. 100,000 Pads. 6/16. J. P. & Co., Ltd. Books/6/4. (E. 152.)

[illegible] Company Dinners to GARDEN FACTORY.

Company Breakfasts to the [illegible] Battalion will also be delivered as above.

[illegible] Quartermasters, [illegible] wagon and [illegible] as early as possible after 4.30 p.m. [illegible] the order of [illegible].

[illegible] Companies are reminded that they are themselves responsible for ration states rendered correctly, to avoid any hitch in the delivery of the correct numbers.

[illegible] Company Commanders will hand over the details of all permanent [illegible] to the Relieving Company and include:-

1. Carrying parties 1 N.C.O. and 1 [illegible]
2. Permanent [illegible] November Avenue [illegible] Avenue, Headquarters Police Posts.

[illegible signature]

[illegible]

app 20

No. ____________ **ACQUITTANCE ROLL (ALL ARMS).** Army Form N. 1513.

______________________ Squadron / Battery / Company of the ______________________

Imprest a/c No. ______________________

Regl. No.	RANK AND NAME.	*Adapt if necessary.	Cash Payment. *Francs	Cash Payment. Cen-times.	Sterling Equivalent (To be completed in Fixed-Centre Pay Office). s.	d.	Receipt of Soldier.
	Total						The undermentioned (1) and (2) to be completed by Paymaster i/c Clearing House— s. d.

To be inserted by Paying Officer. Total, in words—

Francs ______________________

Centimes ______________________

(1) Rate of Exchange—5 =

(2) Total Sterling equivalent, in words—

______________________ Pounds,

__________ Shgs., and __________ Pence.

Signature of the Officer making the Payments ______________________

Date of Payment ______________ 19 Officer Commanding ______________ Company.

______________________ Regiment.

Certified that the above amounts have been charged in the ledger accounts of the men concerned.

Date ______________ 19 . ______________ Paymaster ______________

(C 6410) Wt. W. 3146/M542. 100,000 Pads. 6/16. J. P. & Co., Ltd. Books/6/4. (E. 152.)

1st SOUTH AFRICAN INFANTRY BRIGADE. Copy No 3.

app 262

228

Map Reference
51B,N.W.3.
1/10,000. SECRET. 21/12/1916.

O

OPERATION ORDER NO 79.

1. RELIEFS. The following reliefs will place on the 23rd inst.
(a) The 3rd S.A.I. will relieve the 4th S.A.I. in Sub-section J III.
(b) The 4th S.A.I. will relieve the 1st S.A.I. in sub-section J I. On relief the 1st S.A.I. will become the Battalion in Brigade Reserve, and will take over the position and duties at present occupied and carried by the 3rd S.A.I.

2. MOVEMENT AND TIME OF RELIEF. Reliefs will be carried by day as far as possible. Details will be arranged direct between Battalion Commanders but will be such as to prevent overcrowding of the trenches at any part or any portion of the line beinf vacated during the relief.
The Regulation regarding movement in ARRAS must be strictly adhered to.

3. WORKING PARTIES ETC. Battalions will take over the duties (including standing working parties, police, trench wardens, etc.) at present found by the units they are relieving.
Os.C Battalions will be careful to hane over particaulars of work on hand in the sub-section from which they are being relieved.

4. LOG BOOKS, etc. Log Books, Maps, etc will be handed over to the relieving Battalions.

5. TRENCH STORES. Trench stroes will be taken over and duplicate receipts therefore forwarded to Brigade H.Q. as usual.

6. TELEPHONES. In accordance with orders in force, regarding the use of telephone, etc, no message whatever will be sent onver the lines regarding this relief, except the cord word reporting the relief complete.

7. COMPLETION OF RELIEF. Completion of Relief will be reported to Brigade H.Q. by cord word "PRINCE".

Sgd. J. MITCHELL BAKER.
Major.
Brigade Major.
1st S.A. Infantry Brigade.

Issued through signals, at 2.45.p.m.

at CANDLE FACTORY.
The Company in REDOUBT LINE are permitted to retain their blankets.

8. RATIONS. Companies will render their state by 10 a.m. shewing total of Company Strength with attached, and Secondly No. attached to Headquarters for Rations. The Company Q.M. Sergeant or Storeman to take over rations at CANDLE FACTORY at 5.30 p.m.

9. TRANSPORT. The Transport Officer will arrange for conveyance of blankets to CANDLE FACTORY to-morrow night.
B Company)
C Company) at CONVENT.
H.Q.Company HOTEL UNIVERSE.
2 G.S.Limbered wagons for "B" and "C" Companies Kits &c to report at CONVENT 5 p.m.
1 G.S. Limbered wagon)
1 Officers' mess cart) To be at HOTEL UNIVERSE
1 Maltese cart) by 5 p.m. for conveyance H.Q. Officers kits, Orderly Room and Medical Officer's panniers etc.

10. DRESSING STATION. The Medical Officer will arrange to take over R.A.P. in LINE during the morning.

11. COMPLETION RELIEF. To be notified by runner immediately on completion of relief.

Capt & Adjt. B A N K.

<u>Completion of relief</u> (Continued)
Company Commanders will report when their Companies are in occupation of new billets.

15. Each company will mount a gas guard immediately on arrival, and no lights may be shown.

[illegible]

Capt. & Adjutant.
[illegible].

<u>Issued at 9.a.m. 4/4/16.</u>

Copies		
	1-4	"A-D" Coys.
	5	Carrying Coy.
	6	Blister
	7	Adjutant
	8	War Diary
	9	Q.M. & T.O.
	10	Headquarters.

12. COMPLETION OF RELIEF will be reported to Battalion Headquarters in the Line by Code Word "B E A R". Company Commanders will also report when their Companies are in at FINS to Battalion Headquarters there.

13. BATTALION HEADQUARTERS will close in the line on completion of relief, and will open at FINS Camp on arrival.

Capt. & Adjutant.
BLUST.

Issued at 8.a.m. 13/1/18.

Copy No. 1 to "A" Company
2 "B" "
3 "D" "
4 Carrying Coy.
5 BALK
6 Adjutant
7 Q.M.
8 Head Quarters
9 War Diary

SECRET. ORDER NO 3 R / 115 COPY NO. 8
by BLUSH.

~~4.1.18.~~ 232

Map reference.
GOUZEAUCOURT 1/20,000.

1. In accordance with BLOSSOM Order No. 161 dated 3/1/18, the following reliefs will be effected on night of 4th/5th January 1918.

2. BLOOM will relieve BLEACH in right Sub Section, relief to be complete by 8.30.p.m. On completion BLEACH will become Battalion in Support.

3. BLISTER will relieve BLUSH in left Sub-Section, commencing about 8.30.p.m. as follows :--
"D" "X" Coy. BLISTER will relieve "D" Coy. BLUSH LEFT FRONT LINE.
"A" "X" " " " " "C" " " CENTRE FRONT LINE.
"B" "X" " " " " "B" " " RIGHT FRONT LINE.
"C" " " " " "A" " " IN SUPPORT.
Carrying Coy. will move out on relief by BLISTER at about 6.30.p.m.
Headquarter details will move out in small parties as relieved after dark.

4. On relief Coys. will move out by platoons at five minute intervals to Hutments at FINS, where the Battalion will become Battalion in Reserve.

5. Lewis Guns. On completion of relief, Coys. will stack their Lewis Gun boxes by Coys at Headquarters ration dump in Yoke Lane, near present Battalion Headquarters, leaving one man per team in charge.
Guns and 16 magazines per gun will be carried out to Hutments, FINS.
T.O. to arrange for limbers to pick up Lewis Gun boxes at Headquarters ration dump at 15 minute intervals, starting at 9 p.m. in following order :-- "D", "C", "B" and "A".

6. Officers kits, Mess boxes and Canteen Stores. Must be at respective Company ration dumps at 7.p.m., with one man per company in charge.
T.O. to arrange two limbers for this.
Mess cart and one limber will call at Battalion Headquarters at 7.p.m. for Headquarter kits, Orderly Room Boxes and Mess kit.

7. Dixies, water and rations. All dixies, except Headquarters, will be handed over to BLISTER. As much water as possible to be ~~kept~~ left at QUARRY, and three full water carts near Battalion Headquarters.
BLISTER will arrange to send our dixies and water cart to FINS about 8. p.m.
Rations will be drawn in Billets.

8. Advance Parties. Each Company will detail one officer and 4 other ranks including a signaller to proceed immediately after lunch to take over Hutments, FINS, and act as Guides to their Companies. "A" Coy. officer to report to the Adjutant before proceeding, for instructions. Parties must move in twos only.
BLISTER will send small advance parties to take over during daylight.

9. Details. All available men at Detail Camp will report at Hutments, FINS, at 2.p.m. for duty.

10. Trench stores. Defence schemes, maps, works orders and patrol suits will be handed over to BLISTER, and receipts in duplicate rendered to Regimental Orderly Room not later than 9.a.m. 5th instant.

11. Blankets and hot tea. Q.M. to arrange for an extra blanket per man, and hot tea to be available on arrival of Companies at FINS.

12. Signalling apparatus will be left in Line, and taken over in Billets at FINS.

13. Sanitation. All trenches and shelters to be left in a thoroughly clean condition.

14. Completion of relief to be reported to Battalion Headquarters by Code Word C A T.

Company

SECRET. ORDER NO. 3 R / 1A8 COPY NO. [illegible]
by BLUSH.

War Diary

app. 4/10

233

Map references.
Gouche Wood Sheet 1/10,000
" " " 57 c 1/40,000.

1./. In accordance with BLOSSOM Order No. 163, and Addendum No. 1 to same, BALK will relieve BLUSH (less "C" Company) on night of 13th/14th instant, starting at 5.30.p.m. as follows :- Two platoons BALK will relieve "D" Company BLUSH in Left Front Line; two platoons BALK will relieve "A" Company BLUSH in Centre Front Line; one platoon BALK will relieve "A" and "D" Platoons in Immediate Support Line; two platoons BALK will relieve "B" Company as Counter Attack Company in Support Line.

Medical Officer BLUSH will be relieved in Quarry by M.O. and stretcher bearers of BALK.

Carrying Company will not be relieved, but will move out at 4.45.p.m. under 2/Lieut. W.A.COOK. Sergt. ALLEN and one man per Company will be left in charge of dixies, food containers, etc., and will be responsible for loading these on transport at 6.p.m. at the Quarry.

2. On completion of relief Companies of BLUSH will move out to Billets in FINS, five minute intervals between platoons will be observed, and Company Commanders must ensure that no block of troops occurs en route.

3. LEWIS GUNS. - On relief all Lewis Guns, boxes and magazines will be stacked by Companies at Battalion Headquarters ration dump in YORK LANE. One man per team will be left in charge, and will be responsible for loading.

Q.M. to arrange for Lewis Gun Limbers to report at this point as follows :- "B" Coy, 6.15.p.m. "A" Coy, 6.30.p.m. "D" Coy, 6.45.p.m.

4. OFFICERS KITS, COMPANY MESS BOXES, DIXIES, FOOD CONTAINERS AND CANTEEN STORES. - These must be dumped at Quarry by Companies ready for loading at 5.p.m. - no movement to take place before dark.

Q.M. will arrange for transport to call at that time and place.

"B" Coys. Officers kits and mess boxes, and Headquarters officers kits must be at Battalion Headquarters ration dump at 4.30.p.m., when a limber will call for same. Q.M. to arrange for mess cart to call at Battalion Headquarters for Hqrs mess boxes.

5. WATER CARTS. - Q.M. to arrange to send teams for three water carts at 5.p.m. These will be taken away empty. As many full tins of water to be left at Battalion Headquarters and Quarry as possible.

6. SIGNALLING APPARATUS will be brought out by BLUSH.

7. TRENCH STORES. - All trench stores, aerial photos, maps and trench name boards will be handed over, and receipts in duplicate will be rendered to Battalion Headquarters in line on moving out.

Defence Schemes and orders will not be handed over, but will be destroyed.

All gum boots, wiring gloves, food containers, Company axes and patrol suits will be brought out of line, and a list of these must be taken in FINS Camp on 14th instant and submitted to Regimental Orderly Room by 6.p.m.

8. RATIONS will be delivered to FINS Camp, together with one extra blanket per man, and officers kits. Q.M. to arrange.

9. ADVANCE PARTIES will proceed as already detailed, and will act as guides to their Companies.

10. DETAILS AT DETAIL CAMP. - All officers and O.R. at Detail Camp will rejoin their respective Companies at FINS on 13th instant.

11. SANITATION. - All trenches and shelters must be left clean. Company Commanders will render a certificate to this effect before moving out.

12. COMPLETION

Order No. 3 / R. 117
by BLUSH

COPY NO.......9.

234

479

Map references.
Gauche Wood 1/10,000
Sheet 57. c.1/40,000

1. The BLOSSOM BRIGADE is being withdrawn from the Line on nights of 12th/13th and 13th/14th January 1918 into rest in MOISLAINS area and FINS.

2. BEAK BRIGADE will take over Southern portion of BLOSSOM Sector on night of ~~xxxxxxxxxxxxxxx~~ 12th/13th instant.

3. SABBLE BRIGADE will take over the Northern portion of BLOSSOM Sector on night of 13th/14th instant.

4. Dividing line between Brigades holding Front Line on completion of relief will be :-- R.31.d.50.35, R.31.d.15.35, W.6.b.50.85.

5. In accordance with BLOSSOM Order No. 163 dated 11/1/18, BLEACH will take over from BLUSH portion of line up to sap at R.31.d.50.35 to-night, 12th instant, commencing at about 5.30.p.m.

6. After this relief BENCH will relieve BLEACH, starting at about 6.30.p.m. to-night.

7. On completion of relief in par. (5), "C" Company BLUSH will move out to Billets in FINS. Five minute intervals between platoons will be observed. Platoon on Quarry Road will evacuate via that road, and platoons on right of Quarry Road will evacuate via Right C.T. and across country.

8. "C" Company BLUSH will bring out all Company Lewis Guns, boxes and magazines on relief. Left Platoon will stack these at Battalion Headqrs ration dump YORK LANE, and Right Platoons will stack them at Old Support Battalion ration dump on FINS-GOUZEAUCOURT Road. One man per team to be left in charge, who will load up on transport.
One ration limber will report to O.C. Carrying Company at 5.p.m. to load up "C" Company dixies, food containers, officers kits and mess boxes for conveyance to FINS Camp. "C" Coy. cooks and carriers will proceed with this limber, and will prepare hot tea or soup for the Company on arrival in Billets.

9. O.C. "C" Coy. will ensure that all gum boots, ordinary boots, Lewis Gun magazines, and Company Signalling apparatus are brought out with the Company. Should any of these be missing, parties will be sent back from FINS to recover same.

10. O.C. "C" Coy. will make out trench store cards for portion of his line, to be handed over to BLEACH, and the remainder of trench stores will be handed over to O.C. "A" Coy. BLUSH. Receipt in duplicate to be handed to present Battalion Headquarters to-night.
All maps and trench name boards will be handed over. Defence Schemes will not be handed over, but will be destroyed.

11. Rations for "C" Coy. will be delivered to FINS, together with one extra blanket per man, and officers kits.

12. O.C. "C" Coy. to ensure that his trenches and shelters are left perfectly clean and tidy - he will render a certificate to this effect to Battalion Headquarters.

13. O.C. "C" Coy. will report completion of his relief to present Battalion Headquarters by Code Word " T E D D Y " He will also report by wire <u>if possible</u> arrival in billets in FINS.

14. The Battalion will be relieved by BALK on night of 13th/14th instant, orders for this relief will be issued later.

Capt. & Adjutant.
BLUSH.

Issued at 1.30.p.m. 12/1/18.

Copy No. 1 to "A" Company.
2 "B" "
3 "C" "
4 "D" "
5 "Carrying" Company.
6 BLEACH
7 Adjutant
8 Q.M.
9 War Diary

12. Sanitation.
The Camp and all Huts must be left in a clean and sanitary condition, and Company Commanders will render a certificate to this effect before moving off.

13. March/In and Out States. (ing)
Marching Out State will be rendered to the Adjutant before 9 a.m. and Marching In State will be submitted to Regimental Orderly Room half an hour after arrival of each Company in new billets.

14. As there is no furniture or beds in the new Camp at MOISK LAINS, everything that is useful should be taken to-morrow. Any R.E. Material should be collected together, and if sufficient Transport is available, this will be carried on transport.

15. The Orderly Officer (2/Lieut. A.K.PARROTT) will remain in Camp to assist the Q.M., until all stores, etc. have been moved.

16. DRESS for Parade. Full Marching Order, wearing Jerkins, One blanket in pack.

[signature]
Capt. & Adjutant.
3rd South African Infantry.

9. continued.
Headqrs.

10. LEWIS GUNS. -
On completion of relief, Companies will carry out all Lewis Guns, magazines and boxes, and will stack them at Ration Dumps as follows :-
"A" and "B" Companies - [illegible] LANE. Ration Dump.
"C" and "D" " - STATION " "
One man per team will be left in charge, and special instructions must be given to these men that they are responsible for the proper loading up, and that carriers are placed in boxes. Immediately the limbers are loaded they will proceed to the Transport Line and one man only per Company will accompany limber. The remaining three men will rejoin their Companies at entraining point. T.O. to arrange for Lewis Gun Limbers to call at dumps as above at [illegible].p.m.

11. OFFICERS' KITS, AND MESS BOXES -
These, if required the same night, or following morning must be loaded up with cooking utensils, para. 7. If required to go to Transport Line they should be loaded on Lewis Gun Limbers.

12. The Sergeant Cook and one Cook per Company will leave the Line at [illegible].p.m. and will report to Q.M. at entraining point to make arrangements for a supply of hot tea for men on arrival.

13. DETAILS AT DETAIL CAMP. -
All details will rejoin their Companies at entraining point on the night of 31st instant.

14. RUN-OUT PLATOON. -
This platoon will remain under command of O.C. "A" Coy. until the Battalion reaches Billets in New Area on 1st instant, when personnel will rejoin their respective Companies.

15. ENTRAINING POINT. -
Company Commanders are reminded that no lights will be allowed at the entraining point. This must be strictly enforced.
On entraining at 11.p.m., 31st instant the Battalion will be conveyed by rail to PERONNE, and will bivouac for the night, when each Company will detail a gas guard from details personnel. Breakfast will be at 7.30.a.m. on the 1st ~~instant~~ post, and the Battalion will entrain again at 9.a.m. for LE PLATEAU, which should be reached at 10.a.m.

16. SANITATION. -
Trenches, shelters, and dug-outs must be left scrupulously clean and a certificate will be rendered to this effect with trench store cards.

17. MARCHING IN STATE. -
This will be rendered by Companies and Headquarters one hour after reaching new billets in new area.

18. COMPLETION OF RELIEF
Completion of relief in the Line will be reported by Fullerphone to present Battalion Headquarters by Code Word "A B S L". In addition Company Commanders will personally report at Battalion Headquarters when their Companies have moved out.

Capt. & Adjutant.
2nd S. A. Infantry.

Issued at ~~[illegible]~~ 8 am 31/1/18

Copies. - 1/4 - "A/D" Companies.
5 - Q.M.
6 " Details.
7 Adjutant.
8 War Diary.

COPY NO.....2...   ORDER NO. 3 R/124   SECRET.
By BLUSH.

488

Map reference.
GAUCHE WOOD 1/10,000.

238

1. The following inter-company reliefs will be effected to-night.

2. "C" Coy. will relieve "D" Coy. in LEFT FRONT LINE, and on relief "D" Coy. will become "Counter Attack Company".

3. "B" Coy. will relieve "A" Coy. in RIGHT FRONT LINE, and on relief "A" Coy. will become "Garrison Company".

4. Reference para. 2, "C" Coy. will relieve "D" Coy. by platoons, (6 pm) starting at 6.00.p.m., and at least half hour intervals between platoons. Relief to be complete by 8.00.p.m. to-night.

5. "B" Coy. will commence to move out of GOUZEAUCOURT Village to the (8 pm) relief of "A" Coy. at 8.00.p.m. 200 yards interval between platoons will be observed.

6. Every precaution must be taken against enemy observation of any movement of advance parties by day, and O.C. "B" Coy. must so arrange that no bunching of his men takes place in the Village prior to moving out.

7. LEWIS GUNS. Each Company will take out its own Lewis Guns, and 16 magazines per gun. All L.G. boxes and balance of magazines will be left in present positions, and handed over to incoming Company.

8. RATIONS. "A" and "B" Coys. rations will both be dumped at "B" Coy. Ration dump to-night. O.C. "B" Coy. must arrange to distribute his Coy. rations before moving up.
"C" and "D" Coy. rations will be delivered as usual.

9. DUG OUT PLATOON. Dug Out Platoon will remain in its present position, and on completion of relief will come under command of O.C. "A" Coy.

10. COOKING UTENSILS. Each Company will retain its own cooking utensils, and will arrange to carry them where necessary.

11. BLANKETS. All blankets will be handed over by "B" and "C" Coys to Coys. they relieve.

12. All other details of relief will be arranged between Company Commanders concerned.

13. COMPLETION OF RELIEF will be reported to Battalion Headquarters by Code Word "D O N E".

Sgd S B Stokes
Capt. & Adjutant.
BLUSH.

Issued at 1.p.m. 29/1/18.

Copy No.		
	1/4	"A/D" Coys.
	5	Q.M.
	6	BLOSSOM
	7	Adjutant.
	8	War Diary.

27. 1. 18.

SECRET.

O.C.
....Coy.

239

Instruction No. 1.
Reference Order No. 3 R / 123 issued this morning.

1. COOKING ARRANGEMENTS. - "A" Coy. and Medical Personnel etc. will cook in the QUARRY. O.C. "A" Coy. to include all details in the QUARRY on his ration indent, to be shown separately.

"C" and "D" Coys. cooking will be done at the STATION under the supervision of O.C. "C" Coy, who will be responsible for carrying up all hot meals, water, and other necessaries to "D" Coy. O.C. "C" Coy. to detail a definite party for this work.

"B" Coy. O.C. "B" Coy will arrange his own cooking arrangements for his Company including his detached garrison platoon.

Every precaution must be taken against the smoke of fires being observed by the enemy. Company Commanders must give the necessary instructions to their cooks in this matter.

2. FOOD CONTAINERS. - Each Company will hand over two Food Containers to Advance Parties of BLISTER to-day. There are 14 food containers at the QUARRY and STATION belonging to another Unit, which will be taken over, but will have to be sent out of the line later. Instructions will be given in due course.

3. REPORTS. - Intelligence Reports and Works Reports will be sent to Battalion Headquarters in line not later than 9.a.m. It is important that these reports are punctual.

4. MOVEMENT BY DAY. - All ranks must be warned that as little movement as possible by day is allowed, as a considerable portion of the line to be taken over is under direct observation by the enemy.

5. FOOT TREATMENT. - R.S.M. will arrange to supply three bottles of whale oil to "A" and "D" Companies this morning. These bottles must be taken into the line by their respective platoons to-night, and must be refilled at the STATION as required.

"B" and "C" Companies will also be supplied with whale oil to-day.

6. ~~DRYING ROOM FOR SOCKS AND GUM BOOTS.~~
DRYING ROOM FOR SOCKS AND GUM BOOTS. - There are two Drying Rooms established in the Line, one at the QUARRY under Sergt. ALLEN, the other at the STATION under O.C. "C" Coy. Every opportunity must be taken to make use of these Drying Rooms.

7. STARTING POINT. - With reference to starting point Q.35.b.85.65, where guides will be met, Company Commanders will arrange to reconnoitre the most suitable route to this point in daylight to-day.

S A Stokes

Capt. & Adjutant.
BLUSH.

COPY NO..8.....

SECRET.

u87

ORDER NO. 3 R / 123.
by BLUSH.

Map reference.
GAUCHE WOOD 1/10,000
Sheet 57 C. 1/40,000.

1. The following inter-Battalion reliefs will be effected on the night of 27th/28th January 1918.

2. BLEACH will relieve BLOOM in the Left Sub Section, and on relief BLOOM will become the Battalion in Brigade Reserve in Hutments W.2.c.

3. BLUSH will relieve BLISTER in the Right Sub Section, and on relief BLISTER will become Battalion in Support.

4. BLUSH will relieve BLISTER as follows :-
   "D" Company BLUSH will relieve the Company of BLISTER in LEFT FRONT LINE.
   "A" " " " " " " " " in RIGHT FRONT LINE.
   "C" " " " " the Counter Attack Company of BLISTER.
   "B" " " " " " Garrison Company of BLISTER.
   The Companies of BLUSH will take over the positions as held by the Companies of BLISTER.
   Companies will parade under Company arrangements and will move off to pass the starting point at junction of road with QUEEN'S CROSS-GOUZEAUCOURT Road Q.33.b.25.65, where one guide per platoon will be met at following times :-
   "D" Coy. 8.30.p.m.
   "A" " 8.45.p.m.
   "C" " 9. 0.p.m.
   "B" " 9.15.p.m.
   Fifty yards interval will be observed between platoons.
   In the case of "D" and "A" Companies, the order of march of platoons will be left, right, and support.
   Each Company will carry four Lewis Guns and twenty magazines per gun, no tin boxes.
   "B" and "C" Companies will carry one blanket per man.

5. **ADVANCE PARTIES.** - Each Company and Headquarters will send a small Advance Party under an officer to take over Trench Stores during daylight. Every precaution must be taken against enemy observation of movement.

6. **LEWIS GUN AMMUNITION AND BOXES.** - These will be dumped at present Company Ration dumps ready for loading at 5.p.m. One man per team to be left in charge. These boxes will be conveyed by limbers to respective Company Ration dumps in Forward Area, and must be picked up and carried to Gun positions in the Line on the way in.

7. **COOKING UTENSILS, FOOD CONTAINERS, BLANKETS, MESS KIT AND BAGGAGE.**
   "A" and "D" Companies will roll their blankets in bundles of ten, and these, together with Company kit as above, will be stacked at present Company ration dumps ready for loading at 5.p.m. Cooks to remain in charge. This kit, with the exception of the blankets, will be loaded on Lewis Gun Limbers, and delivered to respective Company forward ration dumps.
   Blankets of "A" and "D" Companies will be loaded on a limber which will take them back to Q.M.Stores.
   One limber and the officers' mess cart will be at Battalion Headquarters at 5.p.m., and will load up Headqrs. Officers kits, Orderly Room boxes, Canteen stores, Cooking utensils, and Mess boxes for conveyance to Forward Battalion Headquarters.
   Q.M. to arrange for teams for Field Kitchens to take same back to Transport Lines, and for transport as detailed.

8. **WATER.** - Q.M. to arrange for two Water carts to fill all tins at Battalion Headquarters Water Point, YORK LANE, and to leave the carts filled

3RD S.A. INF
(TRANSVAAL REGT)

WAR DIARY

3 S A Infy

IN LIEU OF
A.F. C 2118

Vol 10

PLACE	DATE	HOUR	SUMMARY OF EVENTS & INFORMATION	REMARKS & references to APPENDICES
ARRAS J III SUB-SEC:	1/1/17.		Strength of Regiment IN TRENCHES 21 Officers & 459 O. Ranks.	
			Attached, 1st LINE Tpt etc. (NOT IN TRENCHES) 17 Officers & 322 O Ranks	
			TOTAL STRENGTH 38 Officers & 781 O. Ranks – D Coy Right FRONT LINE A Coy	
			LEFT FRONT LINE C Coy RIGHT & LEFT SUPPORTS with B Coy in RESERVES	APP 273
			Situation normal – nightly patrols sent out also wiring parties.	
	2/1/17.		Situation unchanged patrols wiring parties as usual	
	3/1/17.	7. a.m.	Operation Order No 81 dtd 2/1/17 received from BHQ detailing object and method of carrying out RAID	APP 274
		1. p.m.	Regtl Operation Orders issued (3R/29) to all Officers & units concerned	APP 275
		4. 15 p.m	All necessary preparations and instructions having been issued the raiding party of 2 Officers and 52 O.R moved up to Battle H.Qrs at JUNCTION of CANNON ST & SUPPORT LINE	
		5. 0 p.m	The RAID was successfully carried out. Enemy dug-outs bombed with STOKES TRENCH MORTAR BOMBS. MACHINE GUN emplacement demolished and numbers of enemy caught below in their dug-outs. Object of RAID achieved.	APP. 276
		5. 50 p.m	All RAIDING PARTY returned (including wounded) and reported to BATTLE H.Qrs – one prisoner brought in belonging to 107th SAXONS. Our casualties slight (3 O. Ranks slightly wounded) Success due to minute attention paid to every small detail and valuable and efficient co-operation of artillery and fighting qualities of the RAIDING PARTY During T.M. Bombardment of enemy lines prior to RAID a premature STOKES BOMB exploded in S.A.P. 101 killing one and wounding 6 other ranks.	
			[illegible] INTER [illegible]	APP. 277

242

3RD S.A.I (TRANSVAAL REGIMENT) WAR DIARY

IN LIEU OF A.F. C2118

PLACE	DATE	HOUR.	SUMMARY OF EVENTS & INFORMATION	REMARKS & REFERENCES TO APPCES
ARRAS JIII SUB. SEC	4/1/17	10.30 pm to MIDNIGHT	with GAS SHELLS. WIRING PARTIES & usual PATROLS sent out at night and usual working parties furnished with view to strengthening and consolidating JIII SUB SECTION throughout - Working party of 24 O. Ranks daily with R.E. Congratulatory wire from Div! Commdr & Bde Commdr on success of RAID. Draft of 3 O. Ranks arrived. Casualties 1 Killed 8 O.R wounded.	app. 778
	5/1/17	→	Capt H MONTGOMERY assumed duty as 2nd in Command of Regt. Nightly patrols wiring and working parties as usual. occasional T.M. activity. Situation generally quiet. Capt LANGDALE off Strength. Sick to ENGLAND	
	6/1/17	9.49 am	Brigadier General arrived and inspected TRENCHES. Enemy put over considerable number of T.M. doing damage to Support & FRONT LINE trenches. 1 O.R. slightly wounded. Usual patrols & wiring parties sent out, and working parties furnished	
		4/30 to 5 pm	C.O. and Adjutant inspected FRONT & SUPPORT LINES	
	7/1/17	1/5 pm	Regtl Operation Order issued re inter Company Relief	app 779
		3 pm	Capt TOMLINSON reported. C.O. and Adjt inspected FRONT & SUPPORT LINES & Cooking arrangements. LEFT FRONT rather badly knocked about by Enemy T.Ms - STRENGTH in TRENCHES 22 Officers & 524 O. Ranks NOT IN TRENCHES 16 Officers & 247 O.R Regtl strength 39 Officers 767 O. RANKS. PATROLS WIRING & WORKING PARTIES furnished as usual.	
	8/1/17	NOON	Brig General & C.O. inspected FRONT and SUPPORT LINES. Situation quiet. Usual PATROLS, WIRING & WORKING PARTIES sent out.	
	9/1/17	10 AM	Brigade Major inspected SAPS 100 & 101	
		1/5 pm	Accidental explosion of truck load of T.M Bombs OCT'S TRAMWAY killing 8 and wounding 5 O.Ranks of S.A. Bde.	
		2.30 pm	[illegible] of O.Cs. JII SUB SECTION - Usual patrols, wiring & working parties furnished - Situation generally quiet. Capt LANE struck off strength. sick to England.	

3RD S.A.I
(TRANSVAAL REGIMENT)

WAR DIARY

IN LIEU OF A.F. C2118.

PLACE	DATE	HOUR	SUMMARY OF EVENTS & INFORMATION	REMARKS & REFERENCES TO APPces
ARRAS J III SUB SECTION	10/1/17.	Noon	Enemy using Rifle Grenades rather freely, and occasional T.M. shells as usual. Retaliatory measures adopted.	
		2.30pm	Adjt visited FRONT & SUPPORT LINES. Min Command warned for Court of Enquiry re Explosion of T.M. shells. 4. O Ranks wounded.	
			Regtl Operation Order issued detailing inter-Coy RELIEFS. Nightly PATROLS, WIRING PARTIES & usual working parties as usual.	App 780
	11/1/17.	9. AM	G.O.C & C.O. visited FRONT & SUPPORT LINES and conducted a general inspection of the SUB SECTION. Usual Enemy activity with T.M. of a normal character. 1 OR Killed 1 wounded.	
		10.30 AM.	Court of Enquiry held re Explosion of T.M. Shell. Nightly patrols & wiring parties sent out. Working party with R.E. as usual. Casualties 1 Killed 1 wounded.	
	12/1/17.	Noon	STRENGTH – IN TRENCHES 21 Officers and 519 O Ranks total Regimental strength. 38 Officers 763. O Ranks.	
			Hon Lt & QM Carding rejoined unit. Situation unchanged, usual normal T.M. activity by Enemy, and retaliatory measures taken	
		3.45 pm	Usual patrols & wiring parties detailed for tonight	
	13/1/17	9. 0AM	Capt Montgomery warned as waiting C.O. in view of Lt Col THACKERAY CMG DSO proceeding for C.O's Conference.	
		Noon	Situation unchanged. 1 O Rank Killed.	
		3pm.	Regtl Operation order issued detailing inter Coy RELIEFS. Patrols, wiring parties, and usual working parties to RE as usual.	App 781
	14/1/17.	8.30 AM.	C.O. left for C.O's conference. Capt H Montgomery temporarily assumed Command of Regiment and visited FRONT & SUPPORT LINE TRENCHES and made a general inspection of the whole of J III Sub-SECTION together with Adjutant. Situation [illegible]. 1 O Rank Killed [illegible] WIRING & WORKING parties as usual.	

244

3RD S.A.I (TRANSVAAL REGIMENT) WAR DIARY

IN LIEU OF A.F. C2118 — 4

PLACE	DATE	HOUR	SUMMARY of EVENTS & INFORMATION	REMARKS and REFERENCES to APPDX
ARRAS J III SUB SECTION	15/1/17	10 A.M.	The Brigadier General inspected LINES & SUB SECTION. Operation Order No 83 received from B.H.Q detailing move on 16th and RELIEF by 4th (SCOTTISH) REGT. - Patrols as usual	app. 282
		9/11 pm	Wiring parties sent out also working party furnished for work under R.E.	
	16/1/17		STRENGTH IN TRENCHES 19 Officers & 499 o. ranks. Not in trenches 19 Officers 245 O.R. Total REGTL strength 38 Officers 744 O Ranks	
		9 a.m.	In accordance with Operation Order No 83 from B.H.Q the 4th Regiment commenced RELIEF at 9. a.m.	app. 283
ARRAS		12.35 pm	RELIEF completed and disposition of REGT is as follows:- Batt. H.Q. Hotel de UNIVERS B and C Coy to CONVENT D Coy to ST NICHOLAS and FORESTIER. A Coy to BARBED WIRE SQUARE. No casualties.	
	17/1/17	10 a.m.	Officer temporarily Commdg and Adjutant visited St NICHOLAS and FORESTIER and made tour of inspection of other Coys. Draft of 17 O Ranks arrived - Working parties of 1 Officer and 160 O. Ranks supplied to R.E.	
	18/1/17	8 A.M.	Various working parties consisting of 9 Officers and 242 O Ranks furnished for R.E.	
		3 pm.	Major D Young returned from Hospital and assumed Command of Regiment with Capt. H MONTGOMERY temporarily 2/in Command	
	19/1/17	8 A.M.	Various working parties of 3 Officers & 731 O Ranks furnished to R.E. A Coy moved to relieve D Coy. [illegible] ST NICHOLAS & FORESTIER.	
	20/1/17	8 a.m.	parties for work with R.E. as previously detailed.	app. 284

245

3RD S.A.I (TRANSVAAL REGIMENT) WAR DIARY

IN LIEU OF A.F. C 2118 — 5.

PLACE	DATE	HOUR	SUMMARY OF EVENTS & INFORMATION	REMARKS & REFERENCES TO APPENDICES
ARRAS.	21/1/17	8 AM	STRENGTH. in the field 18 officers 507 O Ranks } Detached 20 Officers 240 O Ranks	
		10 AM	Officer temporarily i/c Command together with Adjutant inspected REDOUBT LINE. Enemy shelling was occasional whilst.	
			Working parties of 3 officers & 216 o ranks furnished to R.E.	
	22/1/17	8 AM	Working parties as above detailed.	
		4. pm	Operation Order No 84 detailing relief of 4th Regt by 3rd S.A.I on 24/1/17 received. Officer temporarily i/c Command inspected TRANSPORT at 1st LINE. O.C. left AUXY Conference & proceeded on LEAVE	App 285
	23/1/17	8 AM	Working parties furnished as detailed above	
		10. AM	Officer temporarily Commdg inspected Coys & H.Qrs ARRAS.	
		11 AM	Adjutant inspected REDOUBT LINE	
		12 Noon	Adjutant conferred with 4th S.A.I re MOVE	
	24/1/17	8 AM.	In accordance with Operation Order No 84 received at 4pm 22/1/17 the 3rd S.A.I commenced relief of 4th S.A.I in J III Sub section	App. 286
J III SUB.SEC.		12 NOON	RELIEF Completed by 12 NOON	App 287
		3. pm.	Officer Tempy i/c Command visited RIGHT & LEFT FRONT LINES, SUPPORTS and RESERVES. 2/Lieut D.C Ellis struck off strength sick to Eng 21/1/17. 2/Lts. AE SHARPE & S PEARSON reported for duty, FROM NORMAN	
	25/1/17	8 AM	STRENGTH. IN TRENCHES 21 officers 523. O. Ranks NOT IN TRENCHES 18 Officers and 274 O. RANKS TOTAL REGTL STRENGTH 39. Officers 797. O. Ranks.	
			Enemy's T.M's very active some damage to FRONT & SUPPORT TRENCHES	
			Two Officers arrived from 62ND DIVN belonging to 7/6 W. YORKS.	
		9. 30AM	Officer Tempy i/c Command visited & inspected LINE	
		2. 0pm	Adjutant inspected LINE. Our Aerial activity was most marked during the day.	
		9/15 pm to 12 M/NIGHT	Officer Tempy i/c Command inspected RIGHT & LEFT FRONT LINE and preparations & arrangements for any probable offensive or deployment	

246

3RD S.A.I — WAR DIARY

TRANSVAAL REGIMENT.

IN LIEU OF A.F. C2118

PLACE	DATE	HOUR	SUMMARY OF EVENTS & INFORMATION	REMARKS & REFERENCES TO APPENDICES
J III SUB-SECTION	25/1/17	9/15 to 12 MIDNIGHT	measures at night time. Nightly patrols & wiring parties sent out.	
	26/1/17	10 AM	Officer Temp'y Commdg. inspected FRONT LINE and SUB-SECTION. Enemy T.M. activity some damage to trenches.	
		2 pm	Adjt. with 2 Officers of 76th Bde visited LINE. 1 O.Rank wounded. Patrols & wiring parties as usual	
	27/1/17	9 AM	Officer Temp'y 2/in Command inspected LINE. Enemy T.M. very active on LEFT FRONT & SUPPORT.	
		9/40 AM	Regtl Operation Order issued detailing inter-Coy RELIEFS. 1 O.Rank wounded.	app. 288
		2 pm	Adjutant inspected REDOUBT LINE. Patrols & usual wiring parties	
	28/1/17	10 AM	Adjutant inspected LINE	
		NOON	Divl General passed through J III Sub-SECTION. Brigadier General & Brigade Major visited J III Sub SEC during afternoon.	
	29/1/17	11 PM	Patrols & wiring parties sent out as usual. 2nd/Command visited Line.	
		9. 30 AM	Adjt visited left FRONT LINE & SUPPORTS	
		2. 30 pm	O.C. & 2/in Command visited & inspected LINE. Usual nightly patrols & wiring parties sent out.	
	30/1/17	9. 0 AM	Adjutant visited LINE, Enemy T.M. very active, trenches considerably damaged in AUGUST AVE, CLARENCE, HOLBORN and SAP 99. One LEWIS GUN destroyed, 1 man killed & 1 wounded. Two officers attached from 62nd Divn left. Usual patrols & wiring parties sent out	
	31/1/17	8 AM	STRENGTH. IN TRENCHES:- 23 Officers and 530 O.Ranks. Not in trenches (DETACHED):- 16 Officers and 222 O RANKS TOTAL REGIMENTAL STRENGTH 39 Officers 752 O Ranks. INTER Coy RELIEF as usual last evening	app. 289
		9. 30 AM	The Divisional General visited & inspected LINE together with O.C.	
		2. 30	The 2/in Command visited the LINE. Two Officers 62nd Division arrived. Usual patrols & wiring parties sent out.	

GENERAL:- The weather has been very cold, and snow has

247

3RD SA I WAR DIARY In lieu of A.F. C 2118.

TRANSVAAL REGIMENT.

PLACE	DATE	HOUR	SUMMARY of EVENTS & INFORMATION	REMARKS & REFERENCES & APPENDICES
III SUB-SECTION ARRAS.	31/1/17.		been laying about during the past 2 weeks. (Since 16th.) The enemy have lately been more active with their T. MORTARS and MINENWERFER SHELLS, and retaliatory measures have been taken at every opportunity. During the past month, during this Regiments occupation of I III SUB SECTION, no opportunity has been missed, in effecting repairs to Dug-outs SAPS TRENCHES and FRONT LINE, and the general condition of the SUB-SECTION and our WIRE may be considered to be in a very much improved condition generally. TOTAL CASUALTIES during the past month were as follows OTHER RANKS:- Killed 5, wounded & Shell-Shock 19, Died of wounds 1. Total O. Ranks admitted to hospital during month 65.	

B. [signature] Major
for Commander
Tempy. Comm'dg 3RD S.A.I.

248

ET101/4. (1)
1.1.17.

249

Brigade Major
1st S.A.I. Bgde

Re Yours O-16-3. 30-12-16
I attach Provisional Operation Order re Raid J-III. in accordance with instructions laid down.
The Date and Time of Zero I have left blank for final approval after reconnaissance of wire & No Mans Land – which is very bad owing to heavy rains.
I suggest 3rd Jan. in order to give more time for the mud to dry if no more rain – and to enable the O.C. Raid to make his final inspection And for the G.O.C. to have an inspection should he so desire which I suggest for tomorrow. If two or three trolleys could bring in the party [illegible] it would save their strength.

F. A. Thackeray Lt Col
Comdg 3rd S.A.I.

Operation Order 3R/38
1-1-17.

Secret

To O/6 - A Coy BANK
B " "
C " "
D " "
L.G.O. "

Received Copy

250

1 RELIEF The following relief will take place today under arrangements between Company O/c. In Compliance with instructions previously issued a number of men must be detailed to effect the Relief over the Top and a Certificate to this effect added to Companies Report of Relief completed.

MOVE

"B" Coy. from Right Front Line to Reserve
" 2 Platoons with Hd Qrs Nicholls
" 2 " Bosky Redoubt.
"C" " from Left Front Line to Support Line.
"D" " from Reserve Redoubt Line to Right Front Line.
"A" " from Support Line to Left Front Line.

THIRD SOUTH AFRICAN INFANTRY.

251

SECRET. Copy No...... 275

OPERATION ORDER NO.3 R/29.

275

Reference Map No. ARRAS 51.b.N.W.3.
Edition 4.A. 1-1-1917.
and Aerial Photos.

1. INTENTION. A raiding party of 3rd S.A.I. will raid the enemy's trenches at approximately G.6.c.5.0, and clear it NORTH and SOUTH for 50 yards and obtain identity prisoners - kill enemy - bomb dug-outs, and do as much harm to the enemy as possible.

2. The raid will be carried out on the night of 3rd/4th January 1917. ZERO will be at 5.p.m. 3/1/1917.

3. HOSTILE WIRE. The enemy wire has been cut by gun-fire and Mortars along the front of Section.
Two 2" Trench Mortars from J. Sector and one from K Sector will open fire on the point of attack at 2-45.p.m. 3/1/1917 and continue until a suitable gap has been cut.
Lieut EGAN, Observation Officer, to report on this at 3-50.p.m. 3/1/1917.

4. STRENGTH OF RAIDING PARTY.
2/Lieut GOODWIN. 2 Officers.
2/Lieut THOMAS . 52 Other Ranks.
divided as follows :-
RIGHT PARTY.
2/Lieut GOODWIN - 1 Officer. 2 groups each of 1 N.C.O. and 5 men to block and hold Front Line and Communication trenches in right Sector.
2 N.C.Os and 14 men to clear Front and Control trenches, bomb dug-outs, and escort prisoners to our lines.
LEFT PARTY.
2/Lieut THOMAS - 1 Officer.
2 groups of 1 N.C.O. and 5 men each to block and hold front line trench to NORTH and communication trench to EAST.
2 N.C.Os and 8 men to clear front trench.
GUIDES, 1 N.C.O. and 1 man to remain on parapet at point of entry.
(in addition to above 6 men will lay 2 tapes for direction and act as connecting files.)
Groups will attack as Fighting Sections.
Covering parties for enemy saps on outer flanks.
Covering parties will also be placed under Lieut HARRIS.
5 men and 1 Lewis Gun at Sap 98.
5 men and 1 Lewis Gun at Sap 99.
10 men and 1 Lewis Gun at CLAUDE CRATER.
Double Sentries will be posted by Front Line Company at all posts.
Remainder of Garrison Front and Support Line in dug-outs.
Guides will be placed at junction of communication trenches to indicate Battle Headquarters.

5. Battle Headquarters will be at ~~Left~~ Right Support Company Headquarters - junction CANNON STREET and SUPPORT LINE.

6. Battalion Commanders and R.A.Liaison Officers at Battle Headquarters - junction SUPPORT and CANNON STREET.

7. Advanced Aid Post at Dug-out head of OCTOBER AVENUE. No 43
M.O. to arrange Stretcher Bearers and evacuations via OCTOBER AVENUE.

5. REINFORCING. In the event of at attack Companies will reinforce as under:-
(a) The Company holding FORESTIER REDOUBT to be reinforced at once by its two platoons at CANDLE FACTORY.
(b) The Company occupying St NICHOLAS Village West of the Guard, will move forward and occupy BRITANNIA WORKS, on present Garrison -The 4th S.A.I.- going forward.
(c) The Company at BARBED WIRE SQUARE under such circumstances will move forward and occupy St NICHOLAS Village.

6. RATION STATES. These will be rendered to Regimental Orderly Room by 12 Noon to-morrow to prevent any discrepancy in the number of rations required.

7. KIT & EQUIPMENT. Company Commanders will arrange their own Dumps, and will issue the necessary instructions to their C.Q.M.S. to effect this.

8. TRANSPORT. Transport will be available for conveyance of baggage, and will be detailed as necessary on arrival of rations at about 5 p.m. Field Kitchens will be brought forward for Company use.

9. GUARDS AND DUTIES. All Sentry Posts are to be taken over, and Guards posted immediately on occupation.

10. SANITARY. The necessary handing over certificate of cleanliness of Lines and Dug-outs will be submitted with the certificate of Relief.

11. RELIEF. This will be notified at once by Runner. The code word "John" being used.

A. C. H. MacDonald
Captain & Adjutant,
B a n k.

Issued
11.30 p.m.

Operation Order

3R/30
21-1-17.

To O/C. A. Coy
B "
C "
D "

L.G.O. 277

SECRET

253

1. Relief The following Relief will take place today under arrangements between Company Commanders, a number of NCOs and men from each Coy to be detailed to move over the top.

MOVE

D. Coy. from R. Front to Support Line.
A " from L. " to Reserve (Redoubts)
B " from Redoubts to R. Front Line
C " from Support to L " "

II TRENCH STORES Will be handed over as usual and Cards initialled.

III Blankets "B" Coy will return all blankets to Candle Factory properly rolled and labelled.
"A" Company will draw their blankets from Candle Factory.

H. Work All work reports to be handed over, on Relief.

Guard at Nicholls Redoubt and Bosky to be properly relieved by Left Coy of the Line

A. McDonald Capt.

Operation Order 3/R36 dated 23/1/1917.

Page (2).

254

10. TRANSPORT. Transport Officer will arrange for the removal of all blankets, Stores, Baggage etc. from Headquarters and Company Billets to CANDLE FACTORY.

11. COMPLETION OF RELIEF. Companies will report to Battalion Headquarters JIII when relief is completed, and runners to obtain receipts for same. Code word BAB to be used.

Captain & adjutant,
B A N K.

Issued 3.30 p.m.
23/1/1917.

255

OPERATION ORDER 3R/90.

by 3/1/1917.

B A N K

S E C R E T.

TO War Diary 3rd S.A.I.

Map Reference.

MAB N.W. 3.
1/10,000.

1. **RAID.** In compliance with 1st.S.A.Infantry Brigade Operation Order No 82, the 3rd South African Infantry will carry out a small raid today, the 3rd. of January, 1917.

2. **OBJECT.** - To capture prisoners, obtain identifications, and do as much harm to the enemy as possible.

3. **OBJECTIVE.** The Enemy's Front Line Trench will be entered at G.6.c.5.0. and cleared NORTH and SOUTH for 50 yards.

4. **HOSTILE WIRE.** At 2.45.P.M. 3rd January, (today) two 2"Trench Mortars from J Section and one from K section will open fire on the wire and continue until they have cut a suitable gap.

5. **STRENGTH.** 2 Officers and 52 Other Ranks.

6. **METHOD OF CARRYING OUT THE RAID.**
(a) At ZERO our Artillery and Stokes Mortars will bombard the enemy's Front Line Trench for about 100 yards to the NORTH and 100 yards to the SOUTH of the point where the wire has been cut. During this bombardment the attacking party will advance as close to the enemy's trench as possible.
(b) At ZERO plus 2 minutes the Artillery and Stokes Mortars will lift to the flanks, Support Line and 3 Communication trenches leading to the Front Line. The attacking party will then enter the Trench.
(c) At ZERO plus 14 minutes a BLUE ROCKET will be fired from our Front Line Trench. The party will then return to our trenches.
(d) At ZERO plus 20 minutes our Artillery will cease fire.
(e) At ZERO plus 25 minutes our Artillery will re-open fire on their last targets at 3 rounds per gun per minute for 3 minutes.

7. **ZERO** - at 5.P.M. today, 3rd January.

8. **GARRISON.** With the exception of the double sentries, and Lewis Gun teams employed, the remainder of the Garrison of the Front and Support Lines will be in dug-outs during the operation.

9. **SUPPORT IN OTHER SUB-SECTIONS.** The Lewis and Machine Guns in J.I, J.II, and K.I, will fire on the enemy's trenches opposite these sub-sections during the operation.

10. **WATCHES.** Watches will be synchronised at 3.30.P.M. at Battalion Headquarters G.11.c.3½.2.

11. TRANSPORT. The Transport Officer will detail all available Transport for conveyance of baggage, stores, Iron Rations, Canteen, blankets, etc., to be at the CANDLE FACTORY at 5.P.m.
2 G.S. Wagons.
2 limbers per Company.
1 limber Headquarters.
Mess Cart. Headquarters.
Maltese Cart. Headquarters.
Field Kitchens to be takento Compant Billets.
"D" Company kitchen to remain, at CANDLE FACTORY, for use both in FORESTIER and ST.NICHOLAS .

12. MOVEMENT OF TROOPS. The instructions conveyed in Town Major Orders re Movement of troops in ARRAS to be strictly carried out.

13. SANITATION. The Medical Officer will inspect and report on the Sanitary Condition of the Sub-section by 10.30.a.m.

14. COMPLETION OF RELIEF. Companies will report by runner to Headquarters J III the completion of relief, on passing junction Reserve Line and NOVEMBER AVENUE.

A.C.O'H. McDonald
Capt & Adjutant.
B A N K.

Issued 6.15.P.m.
15/1/1917.

Sheet II.

11. **DETAIL.**

(a) Companies will Stand To at 4.30.P.M. in their Dug-outs properly equipped, ready to meet any counter attack.

(b) All sentries to be posted and left only at the posts by 4.30.P.M. Picked men should be placed on Sentry with full instructions re RAID.

(c) Lewis Gunners will move into position by 4.30.P.M.

(d) Observation Officer and Runners to be at their posts by 4.30.P.M. except Runners detailed to the Raid party.

An Officer of "B" Coy. Redoubt Line to be detailed to report to Battle Headquarters at 8.p.m. junction Support Line and CANNON STREET, to take charge of and fire rockets.

Companies Right and Left Front Line to detail two runners each as runners to Battle Headquarters, CANNON STREET.

Headquarters Runners to be detailed to accompany Raid Party to Assembly Point Phone. 2.
To accompany Observation Officer CLAUDE CRATER. 2.
For O.C. Battle Headquarters. 6.

(e) The evening meal to be completed by 4.30.P.M. No unauthorised movement is to take place in the trenches which must be kept clear.

(f) Signalling Sergt. to arrange all phones to be checked at 4.30.P.M.

(g) Battalion Headquarters will be in operation at Company Headquarters in Right Support Trench near junction of CANNON STREET.

(h) All men at CANDLE FACTORY will stand to at 4.30.P.M.

(j) All Company Commanders will report at Battalion Headquarters in Support Line at 3.P.M.

(k) NO parties will be dismissed till the order "Stand Down" is given.

(l) ON NO account are any Very Lights to be fired during the operations of the Raid. Company Commanders will issue necessary instructions and take precautions.

(m) Time of all Battalion watches will be synchronised at Battle Headquarters at 4.P.M.

(n) Medical Officer and 2 Stretcher Bearers will be at Dug-out 42, Right Support Line, at 4.30.P.M. Companies will have their stretcher bearers detailed ready for assistance if required.

Capt & Adjutant.

B A N K.

Form
MESSAGES AND SIGNALS.

Army Form C. 2123.
(In books of 100.)

No. of Message

Prefix ... Code ... Words 22	Received	Sent, or sent out	Office Stamp.
Charges to collect £ s. d.	From J S 3	258 At ... m.	J C I
Service Instructions. J S 3	By J. Richs	To	4.1.17
		By	

Handed in at ... Office ... m. Received 9.10 am

TO J C I 278

*Sender's Number	Day of Month	In reply to Number	AAA
BM 221	4		

Divisional Commander wishes to congratulate you on successful raid AAA Brigade Commander adds his congratulations

4/1/17

FROM J S 3

PLACE & TIME 9.0 am

* This line should be erased if not required.

Operation Order No 3R/31.
9. 1. 17.

To. O.C A
B
C
D

279 279 259

L.G.O

SECRET

I. RELIEF The following reliefs will take place today under arrangements between Company Commdrs a number of NCOS and men from each Coy to be detailed to move over the top but not before dusk.

II MOVE "D" Coy from SUPPORT LINE to R. FRONT LINE
"A" " " RESERVE (REDOUBTS) to LEFT. FRON LINE
B " " R. FRONT LINE to SUPPORTS
C " " L. FRONT LINE to RESERVES

III TRENCH Will be handed over and usual STORES and cards initialed

IV BLANKETS A Coy will return all blankets to Candle factory properly rolled and labelled. C Coy will draw their blankets from Candle Factory

V WORK All work reports to be handed over on Relief

VI GUARDS NICHOLLS & BOSKY REDOUBTS to be properly relieved by LEFT Coy of the RESERVE

1/5 pm

A. W. H. McDonald Capt
BANK

SECRET

Operation Order 3 R/32

To A RKH 260 10/1/17
B
C 280 280
D
LGO. WRM.

I Relief The following reliefs will take place today under arrangements between Company Commanders. A number of NCOs & men from each Coy to be detailed to move over the top but not before dusk.

II MOVE B Coy from Support to R FRONT LINE
C " " Reserve (Redoubts) L. FRONT LINE
A " " R.F LINE to SUPPORT.
D " " R.F LINE to Reserve (Redoubts)

III Trench will be handed over and usual stores and cards installed.

IV Blankets C Coy will return all blankets to Candle Factory properly rolled and labelled. D Coy will draw blankets from Candle Factory.

V Work All work reports to be handed over on relief.

VI GUARDS Nicholls & Bosky Redoubts to be properly relieved and instructions handed over.

1/15pm

A W McDonald
Capt & Adjt
BANK

(17 on W. diary)

Operation Order

SECRET. 3R/33.

13/1/17

TO. A

B

C

D.

LG.O

To be initialed & returned

781

(I) RELIEF. The following relief will take place today under Company arrangements. A number of N.C.O's and men from each Coy to be detailed to move over the top but not before dusk.

II MOVE TO

RIGHT FRONT LINE	D Coy x	Reserves
LEFT " "	A Coy x	Supports
SUPPORTS	C Coy x	L. FRONT
RESERVE	B Coy x	R. " "

III TRENCH will be handed over with usual stores, & cards initialed

IV BLANKETS D Coy will return all blankets to candle factory properly rolled and labelled. B Coy will draw blankets from CANDLE FACTORY

V WORK All work reports to be handed over on relief

VI GUARDS. Nicholls & BOSKY REDOUBTS to be properly relieved and instructions handed over

3. p.m. 13/1/17 781

[signature] Capt & ADJT.

BANK.

Commanding reported at 5.7pm
bombed Dug outs, Right flank
with P Bombs and Stokes.
one man of the left clearing
party wounded and returned
Lieut Thomas reported 5.37pm
enemy trench were
completely cut proceeded
up trench to T N found
the first Dug out on fire,
blazing.
a concrete M G emplacement
which he destroyed with
Stokes Bombs.
Corpl Maltman wounded
and returned
ARTILLERY barrage very
good -
L/Corp. Hawthorne & Left
clearing party returned 5.45pm
All party reported
returned at 5.59pm
3 GREEN lights fired up
enemy on our front at 5.48
4 Green lights at 5.52
6 do do at 6.4
appeared to define roughly
section attacked.
Lieut Goodwin and Thomas -

S E C R E T. War Diary 263 283

OPERATION ORDER. 3R/34.

By Captain H.MONTGOMERY.
Temporarily Commanding 3rd S.A.Infantry. IN THE FIELD.
(Transvaal Regiment.) 15/1/1917.

1. RELIEF. In accordance with Operation Order No 83 Bde. Headquarters of 14th January, the following move will take place on the 16th.inst.

The 2nd S.A.I. will relieve the 4th S.A.I. in J II Sub-Section. The 4th S.A.I. will relieve the 3rd S.A.I. in J III Sub-Section. On relief the 3rd S.A.I. will become the Battalion in Brigade Reserve, and will take over the positions and duties at present accupied and carried out by the 2nd S.A.Infantry.

2. MOVE. In accordance with the foregoing, Company reliefs will be affected as under :-

"A" Coy BY "D" Coy. 4th S.A.I. 10.a.m.
"D" Coy BY "A" Coy 4th S.A.I. 10.30.a.m.
"C" Coy BY "B" Coy 4th S.A.I. 10.45.a.m.
"B" Coy BY "C" Coy 4th S.A.I. 11.15.a.m.
The relief of Lewis Gunners will commence 9.15.a.m.
Snipers and Observers. 9.15.a.m.
"B" and "C" Companies will move to CONVENT, ARRAS. On relief
"A" Coy to Billets "BARBED WIRE SQUARE".
"D" Coy will occupy RESERVE LINE with 2 platoons in FORESTIER REDOUBT and 2 platoons ST.NICHOLAS with Company Headquarters.

3. ROUTE. The 4th S.A.I. will relieve from the Right via CANNON STREET.
The 3rd S.A.Infantry will move back via NOVEMBER AVENUE and on no account is there to be a stop or block in the trenches.
All parties relieved must be under the supervision of an officer and on no account is straggling to be permitted.
The 2 platoons in BOSKY REDOUBT will be relieved at 9.a.m. and will move back direct to CONVENT.

4. TRENCH STORES. Trench Stores to be carefully handed over and duplicate receipted Store handed into Regimental Orderly Room immediately, signed and completed.

5. WORKING PARTIES.etc. Companies will hand over particulars of all work inhand and weekly work diaries, and any working parties detailed.

6. LOG BOOKS. Log Books, Maps, etc., will be handed over by Companies and the Battalion on Relief.

7. BILLETS. Company Commanders will arrange to carefully take over all billets from the billeting officer and will send C.S.M. or Senior Sergt. to take over same, also any tools, stores, etc., by 9.a.m.
R.S.M. will take over billets at Hotel d L'Univers.

8. TELEPHONES. In acordance with orders in force regarding the use of telephone, etc., no messages whatever will be sent over the lines regarding this Relief.

9. BLANKETS, BAGGAGE, etc. Companies will arrange to have dump formed at CANDLE FACTORY under their own guard, for the safety of all stores, baggage etc., to be moved by Transport same evening.

10. RATIONS. States giving numbers and distribution to be rendered by 9.a.m. All Headquarters Details will rejoin Headquarters at Hotel D L'Univers tomorrow, 16th. unless otherwise instructed.

1st SOUTH AFRICAN INFANTRY BRIGADE.

SECRET.
Map Reference
Sheet 51B.N.W.
1/10.000.

28 3 ~~282~~

14th January 1917.

264

Diary

OPERATION ORDER No.87.

I. RELIEFS. The following reliefs will take place on the 16th instant.-
The 2nd S.A.I. will relieve the 4th S.A.I in JII Sub-Section. The 4th S.A.I. will relieve the 3rd S.A.I. in JIII Sub-Section. On relief the 3rd S.A.I. will become the Battalion in Brigade Reserve and will take over the positions and duties at present occupied and carried out by the 2nd S.A.I.

2. MOVEMENT AND TIME OF RELIEF.
The relief will be carried out by day as far as possible. Details will be arranged direct between Battalion Commanders, but will be such as will prevent overcrowding of the trenches at any part, or any portion of the line being vacated during the relief. The regulations regarding movement in ARRAS must be strictly adhered to.

3. WORKING PARTIES ETC.
The Battalions will take over the duties (including standing working parties, police, trench Wardens, etc.,) at present found by the Unit they are relieving. O.C., 3rd S.A.I. will be careful to hand over particulars of all work in hand in the Sub-Section in which his Unit is being relieved.

4. LOG BOOKS ETC. Log Books, Maps, etc., will be handed over to the relieving Battalion.

5. TRENCH STORES. Trench Stores will be taken over and duplicate receipts forwarded to Brigade Headquarters as usual.

6. BILLETS. The O.C., 2nd and 3rd S.A.I. will arrange for their billeting officers to report to the Town Major - ARRAS, at 4.pm 15th instant to arrange details of handing over billets.

7. TELEPHONES. In accordance with orders in force regarding the use of the Telephone, etc, no message whatever will be sent over the lines regarding this relief, excepting the codeword reporting relief complete.

8. COMPLETION OF RELIEF. Completion of relief will be reported to Brigade Headquarters by means of the codeword in the "B.A.B." trench code.

9. Please acknowledge.

A.P. Pepper
Captain.
Acting Brigade Major.

Issued by Orderly at 11 am.

Copies to	
1/4 to 1st to 4th S.A.I.	12 to 27th Inf. Brigade.
5 to 28th M.G. Company.	13 to 9th Division.
6 to SALTM. BATTERY.	14 to Brigadier-General.
7 to 64th Field Co. RE.	15 to Brigade Major.
8 to Brigade Sig/Officer	16 to Staff Captain.
9 to 107th Coy. ASC.	17 to Bde Transport Officer
10 to SAF. Ambulance.	18 to 20 WAR DIARY.
11 to 26th Inf Brigade.	21 to Post Corporal.
22 to Central Group RFA.	23 to 9th Div. T.M.s.
24 to Town Major - ARRAS.	

OPERATION ORDER

3R/35

265

19. 1. 17

SECRET

284

O.C. A Coy BANK
" D " BANK.

MOVE

A Coy will relieve 'D' Coy tomorrow afternoon (20/1/17) under Company arrangements

A Coy will move to St. NICHOLAS & FORESTIER

D Coy will move to BARBED WIRE SQUARE

TRENCH STORES The usual trench stores will be handed over after careful checking, and T S cards initialled

CLEANLINESS The usual certificate will be furnished

COMPLETION of RELIEF Coy Commdrs will report by runner to R.O.R 'HOTEL de UNIVERS" when relief is complete

Issued 7/pm.

A W H McDonald
Capt &
Adjutant
BANK.

War Diary

Operation Order by

B A N K.

No.3/R 36.

23/1/1917.

266

286

S E C R E T.

To O.C. "A" Coy.
"B" Coy.
"C" Coy.
"D" Coy.
"H.Q." Coy.
L.G.O.

Sig.Offr.
Int.Offr.
Med.Offr.
Q.Mr.
Transpt.Offr.

1. RELIEF. In accordance with Operation Order No.84 of 22/1/1917 (B.H.Q.) the 3rd S.A.I. will relieve the 4th S.A.I. in JIII sub-section to-morrow the 24th instant. The 4th S.A.I. are relieving the 1st S.A.I. in J I sub section, the latter unit becoming Battn. RESERVE and will take over St NICOLAS and Billets in ARRAS from 3rd S.A.I. The 4th S.A.I. will take over FORESTIER REDOUBT.

2. MOVEMENT & TIME OF RELIEF. "A"Coy . 3rd S.A.I. to relieve "D"Coy. 4th S.A.I. in REDOUBT LINE 2 Platoons BOSKY REDOUBT to move forward at 9 a.m. from St NICOLAS via NOVEMBER.
2 Platoons in FORESTIER REDOUBT to relieve NICHOLS REDOUBT at 9 a.m. and will move via BRITTANIA WORKS. Coy H.Q. in NICHOLS REDOUBT.
"D"Company relieves "A"Company 4th S.A.I. in SUPPORT LINE at 9.45 a.m., relief of LEFT SUPPORT to be completed first, moving via NOVEMBER AVENUE. 4th S.A.I. evacuate along SUPPORT LINE THROUGH AUGUST AVENUE.
"B"Company of the 3rd S.A.I. relieves "B"Company of the 4th S.A.I. holding RIGHT FRONT LINE at 10.15 a.m. The 3rd S.A.I. moves forward via NOVEMBER, SUPPORT LINE and CANNON STREET. The 4th S.A.I. via AUGUST AVENUE.
"C"Company of the 3rd S.A.I. relieves "C"Company of the 4th S.A.I. in LEFT FRONT LINE at 10.45 a.m., moving forward via NOVEMBER AVENUE. The 4th S.A.I. evacuating via CANNON STREET.
HEADQUARTERS. Lewis Gunners and Observers to relieve by 8.30 a.m. The RIGHT FRONT and its SUPPORT moving forward via AUGUST AVENUE, and LEFT FRONT and its support via NOVEMBER AVENUE.
HEADQUARTERS DETAILS. Observation Posts, Signallers and Candle Factory at 9 a.m., also Medical Officer and Staff. Movement carried out in compliance with ARRAS Standing Orders, and to be such as will prevent overcrowding of the trenches at any point.

3. WORKING PARTIES. All Duties, such as Guard, Standing Working Parties, Police to be taken over as furnished by the unit relieved.

4. LOG BOOKS, MAPS &c & WORK SCHEME. To be taken over.

5. TRENCH STORES. Trench Stores to be carefully taken over, and duplicate receipts given to unit relieved and one copy forwarded to Orderly Room.
Store Cards for FORESTIER REDOUBT and Billets where Stores are handed over to be rendered in duplicate at the same time as certificate of Relief.

6. BILLETS. Care to be taken that all Billets are handed over clean, and sanitation dealt with. Certificates from Officers taking over to be obtained and rendered to Regtl. Orderly Room.

7. TELEPHONES. On NO account may the telephone be used in connection with this relief.

8. BLANKETS & BAGGAGE. Companies will arrange to send forward and ~~obtain~~ form their own Dumps at Candle Factory, and at Billets, pending arrival of Transport.

9. RATIONS. Company to render Ration States by 11 a.m. accurately compiled for rations for the following day.

WAR DIARY ~~288~~ 288

Operation Order   SECRET 3R/37.

17. 1. 17.

267

To. O.C.
A
B
C
D
L.G.O

to be initialed + returned

I RELIEF The following relief will take place today under Company arrangements. A number of N.C.Os and men from each Coy to be detached to move over the top but not before dusk -

II MOVE D Coy to RIGHT FRONT LINE
A Coy to LEFT FRONT LINE
B Coy to RESERVE (BOSKY NICHOLLS)
C Coy to SUPPORTS

III TRENCH STORES will be handed over and T Store Cards initialed

IV BLANKETS
A Coy will return all blankets to Candle factory properly rolled and labelled B Coy will draw blankets from Candle factory.

V WORK All work reports to be handed over on Relief

VI GUARDS NICHOLLS & BOSKY REDOUBTS to be properly relieved and [illegible] handed over also OCTOBER TRAMWAY

VII SANITATION Coy Comm^drs to see that all Sub. sections are in a clean and sanitary condition

9/40 AM.

17/1/17.

[signature] Capt & Adjt

BANK.

1st SOUTH AFRIC[illegible] BRIGADE. Copy No. 3

Map Reference
51.B.NW.3.
1/10.000.

2nd January 1917.

274 268

OPERATION ORDER No.81.

1. The 3rd South African Infantry Regiment will carry out a small raid on the evening of the 3rd JANUARY 1917.

2. OBJECT. To capture prisoners, obtain identifications, and to do as much harm to the enemy as possible.

3. OBJECTIVE. The enemy's front line trench will be entered at G.6.C.5.6. and cleared NORTH and SOUTH for 50 yards.

4. HOSTILE WIRE. At 2.45 pm. on the 3rd JANUARY, 1917, two 2 inch Trench Mortars from J. Section and one from K. Section will open fire on the wire, and continue until they have cut a suitable gap.

5. STRENGTH. Two Officers and 52 Other Ranks.

6. METHOD OF CARRYING OUT THE RAID.
   (a) At ZERO our Artillery and Stokes Mortars will bombard the enemy's front line trench for about 100 yards to the NORTH, and 100 yards to the SOUTH of the point where the wire has been cut. During this bombardment the attacking party will advance as close to the enemy's trench as possible.
   (b) At ZERO plus 2' the Artillery and Stokes Mortars will lift to the flanks, Support line, and three communication trenches leading to the front line. The attacking party will then enter the trench.
   (c) At ZERO plus 14' a blue rocket will be fired from our front line trench. The party will then return to our trenches.
   (d) At ZERO plus 20' our Artillery will cease fire.
   (e) At ZERO plus 25' our Artillery will reopen fire on their last targets at three rounds per gun per minute for three minutes.

7. ZERO. At 5 pm. 3rd JANUARY.

8. GARRISON. With the exception of the sentries the remainder of the garrison of the front and support lines will be in dug-outs during the operation.

9. SUPPORT IN OTHER SUB-SECTIONS. The Lewis and Machine Guns in J.1, J.2, and K.1 will fire on the enemy's trenches opposite those sub-sections during the operation.

10. WATCHES. Watches will be synchronized at 3.30 pm. at BATTALION Headquarters G.11.c.3½.2.

11. Please acknowledge.

[signature]

Captain.
Acting Brigade Major.

Issued at 7 a.m. 3/1/17

Copies 1 to 4 1st to 4th S.A.I.
5 to 28th M.Gun Coy.
6. to S.A.L.T.M.Battery.
7. to 64th Field Co. R.E.
8. to Brigade Sig.Officer.
9. to 107th Coy. A.S.C.
10. to S.A.Field Ambulance.
11. to 26th Infantry Brigade.
12 to 27th Infantry Brigade.
13 to 9th. Division.
14 Brigadier-General.
15 Brigade Major.
16 Staff Captain.
17 Brigade Transport Officer.
18/20 War Diary.
21 Post Corporal.

****

Cm

269

(5396) Wt. W 2186/509 7/16 100,000 Pads. D. D. & L. E 111.

Army Form C 2121.
(In pads of 150).

"B" Form.

MESSAGES AND SIGNALS.

No. of Message ....

Prefix ...... Code ...... m.		Received	Sent	Office Stamp.
Office of Origin and Service Instructions.	Words.	At ...... m.	At ...... m.	app 287
		From	To	
		By	By	

TO CHASE 287

Sender's Number	Day of Month	In reply to Number	AAA
R10	24/1/17		

AAA 3423

From BANK

Place

Time 12 Noon

* This line should be erased if not required.

270

Capt. Glenn Thomas carried out the RAID
Full report follows.

[illegible signature]

Lieut Col
Commandg 3rd Regt IA Infy

To initial & return –

SECRET 271

OPERATION ORDER No 3R38 30/1/17.

289

O.C.
A Coy [initials] D [initials]
B . [initials] L.G.O [initials]
C . [initials]

(I) RELIEF The following relief will take place to-day under Coy arrangements, a number of N C O S and men from each Coy to be detailed to move over the top but not before dusk.

II MOVE B Coy to RIGHT FRONT LINE
C " " LEFT FRONT LINE
D " " RESERVE BOSKY & NICHOLLS
A " " SUPPORTS

III TRENCH STORES will be handed over and T.S. Cards initialed

IV BLANKETS B Coy will return all blankets to CANDLE FACTORY properly rolled and labelled D Coy will draw blankets from CANDLE FACTORY.

V WORK all work reports to be handed over on relief

VI GUARDS NICHOLLS & BOSKY REDOUBTS to be properly relieved and instructions handed over also Orders ...

IN LIEU of A.F. C2118

3RD S.A.I. WAR DIARY TRANSVAAL REGT

PLACE	DATE	HOUR	SUMMARY of EVENTS & INFORMATION	REMARKS + REFERENCES to APPENDICES
J III ARRAS.	1/7/17.	8 A.M.	STRENGTH of REGIMENT IN TRENCHES 23 Officers and 528 O RANKS. DETACHED (NOT IN TRENCHES) 16 Officers and 224 O. RANKS	
		10. A.M.	2/in Command together with C.O. visited + inspected LINE during morning	
		2. P.M.	Adjutant visited SUPPORTS. Our aerial activity most marked during day over Enemy lines and positions. SITUATION. generally quiet. SNOW still laying about.	
		6 P.M. to 8 p.m.	Heavy enemy artillery + T.M. strafe. 1 O.Rank Killed 1 wounded. Nightly PATROLS and wiring partys sent out.	
	2/7/17.	9.30 A.M.	2/in Command visited + inspected LINE	
		3 p.m.	Adj! visited + inspected LINE	
		11 p.m.	O.C. visited + inspected LINE. INTER Coy Reliefs effected during day and at dusk Coys allocated as follows:- "D" Coy RIGHT FRONT LINE "A" Coy LEFT FRONT LINE "B" Coy SUPPORTS "C" Coy RESERVES. ENEMY T.M. active during evening - 1 O.RANK Killed and 2 wounded - usual PATROLS and wiring parties sent out	APPDC 290
	3/7/17.	10. A.M.	Brigadier General inspected line together with 2/in Command.	
		3.p.m.	Adj! inspected RIGHT FRONT and SUPPORTS. Situation generally quiet. MILLS HAND GRENADE accident 3. O.RANKS wounded. Nightly patrols + wiring parties sent out as usual.	
		11 p.m.	O.C. inspected Line.	
	4/7/17.	9.30 A.M.	2/in Command visited line. Situation Quiet	
		10.0 P.M.	Adj! inspected FRONT LINE. patrols + wiring parties sent out as usual.	
	5/7/17.	9. AM	O.C. and 2/in Command inspected LINE	
		2 P.M. 4 P.M.	Adjutant inspected LINE - patrols + wiring as usual.	

272.

WAR DIARY

3RD S A I (TRANSVAAL REGIMENT).

IN LIEU OF A.F. C.2118.

PLACE	DATE	HOUR.	SUMMARY of EVENTS & INFORMATION	REMARKS & REFERENCES TO APPENDICES
JIII ARRAS	5/7/17.		INTER-COY reliefs during afternoon and at dusk - Disposition as follows:- "B" Coy R.F. LINE "C" Coy L.F. LINE "D" Coy SUPPORTS + "A" Coy RESERVES.	APP 291
		9.15 P.M. till 12 MID	2/in Command and Adjutant visited FRONT + SUPPORT LINES and conducted a general inspection of arrangements and dispositions of units. Situation generally quiet one O.R. wounded.	
	6/7/17	8. A.M.	STRENGTH IN TRENCHES 22. OFFICERS 513. O.R DETACHED (NOT IN TRENCHES) 17. OFFICERS and 227 O.R	
		9.30 AM.	2/in Command inspected line	
		11.0 AM	Brigadier General inspected REDOUBTS together with Officer Commanding. Situation unchanged. patrols wiring parties sent out as usual	
	7.7.17.	10. A.M.	Brigadier General and O.C visited line and inspected disposition of units and arrangements generally. Lt Col THACKERAY. C.M.G. D.S.O having returned from leave, assumed Command of the REGt. and JIII SUB SECTION. MAJOR B YOUNG relinquished Tempy Command & proceeded on leave. Capt H. MONTGOMERY remaining temporarily 2/in Command. Operation order No 86 d/d 7/7/17 received, detailing relief of 3rd S.A.I by 4th S.A.I. Situation unchanged. Nightly patrols, wiring parties as usual. one O.R. WOUNDED.	APP 292
	8.7.17	10. A.M	2/in Command inspected 1st Line Transport. Situation unchanged patrols wiring working parties furnished as usual. Inter Coy RELIEFS during afternoon and dusk, disposition of units as follows:- "A" Coy L.F. LINE. "D" Coy. R.F. LINE. "C" Coy SUPPORTS. "B" Coy RESERVES	APP 293.
	9.7.17.	9.0 AM.	2/in Command visited and inspected FRONT LINE returning at 2 p.m.	
		2.30 P.M	O/Commanding visited LINE for purpose of carrying out general inspection of units and dispositions, also cooking + sanitary conditions. Successful trial of daylight S.O.S in K1. SUB SECTION. Usual patrols wiring parties	
		10.15 pm	Adjutant visited LINE	
		1.0 AM	Commanding Officer visited Line.	

273

3rd S.A. INFANTRY. WAR DIARY. TRANSVAAL REGT.

PLACE.	DATE	HOUR.	SUMMARY OF EVENTS & INFORMATION.	REMARKS & REFERENCES TO APPENDICES.
JIII ARRAS.	10.7.17		Operation Order No 87 d/d 10/7/17 detailing relief of 3rd S.A.I by 4th S.A.I and 9th Scottish Rifles received and preliminary instructions issued accordingly. Enemy fairly active. Situation unchanged. 2 O RANKS wounded.	APP 294.
		11 p.m.	Regimental Operation Order issued No R43 d/d 10/7/17 detailing RELIEF for tomorrow. Patrols and wiring parties sent out as usual.	APP. 295.
	11.7.17	9.0 A.M.	In accordance with operation order No 87 d/d 10/7/17 relief of 3rd S.A.I by 4th S.A.I and 9th Scottish Rifles commenced at 9.0 A.M. and completed by NOON. DISPOSITION OF UNITS. A Coy BARBED WIRE SQUARE ARRAS. "B" Coy 2 PLATOONS in NICHOLLS REDOUBT with 2 platoons still holding BOSKY REDOUBT until relieved tomorrow by 9th SCOTTISH RIFLES. "C" Coy with Coy H.Qrs in FORESTIER REDOUBT and two platoons located at CANDLE FACTORY. "D" Coy at St NICHOLAS. 4th S.A.I now hold RIGHT HALF JIII SUB-SEC: & SUPPORTS and 9TH SCOTTISH RIFLES LEFT HALF JIII SUB. SECTION and SUPPORTS. RELIEF effected with no undue demonstration on part of enemy. No casualties.	APP. 296.
		2 p.m.	One of our aeroplanes fell (after an engagement with enemy planes) in JII SUB SECTION and burst into flames. DRAFT of 2 Officers and 93 O Ranks having arrived at RAILHEAD are taken on strength of REGt. Batt HQ still at JIII.	
	12/7/17	9.30 AM	Adjutant visited Coys and with a view to accommodation necessary for unit, under instructions from C.O.	
		11 AM.	C.O. made a general inspection of location of units and reports inadequate accommodation, and arrangements necessary made to facilitate matters with reference to Battn HQrs remaining "as you were" and occupation of CANDLE FACTORY until further notice. Working parties supplied 4 Officers & 240 men. During day relief effected of remaining 2 platoons of B Coy in BOSKY REDOUBT by 9th Sco. RIFLES. 27th INF BDE.	
	13/7/17.	9. A.M.	CO. 2nd in Command & Adjutant inspected all billets and details of arrangements for accommodation, cooking, sanitation etc. Working parties furnished as above mentioned.	
		8.15 pm	A meeting of C.Cs. called by O.C. to discuss programme of training while in rest area.	

In lieu of A.F. C2118 — 11.

3rd S.A. Infantry. War Diary. Transvaal Regt.

PLACE.	DATE	HOUR.	SUMMARY OF EVENTS & INFORMATION.	REMARKS & REFERENCES TO APPENDICES.
J III. Batt. HQrs – (Reserves)	14/2/17.	8 A.M.	4 Officers + 300 O Ranks furnished for working parties. STRENGTH. IN RESERVE 22 Officers 600 O RANKS DETACHED 18 Officers 229 O Ranks. The Commanding Adj. + Intelg. Officer visited No 1 SECTION. R. SECTOR. with view to taking over.	
	15/2/17.	8 A.M.	5 Offcrs + 280 O Ranks furnished for working parties.	
		2 pm.	C.O. attended conference at BHQ	
	16/2/17	8 A.M.	Working parties furnished as for yesterday. Adj. visited No 1 SECTION. RIGHT SECTOR. Capt Montgomery + Lt Sharpe slightly wounded.	
		12 Noon	Operation Order No 88 received from BHQ re detail of relief of 1st S.A.I	app 297.
	17/2/17.	8 AM	Working parties furnished as above stated. Situation NORMAL. one O.R. wounded.	
No 1 Section RIGHT SECTOR.	18.2.17	9 A.M.	In accordance with Operation Order No 88 the 3rd S.A.I relieved the 1st S.A.I in No 1 SECTION RIGHT SECTOR. Move was commenced at 9. A.M. and relief completed by 12 NOON. DISTRIBUTION OF UNITS:- A Coy. 3 platoons at OIL WORKS. 1 PLATOON at LAUNDRY POST. B Coy. RIGHT FRONT LINE C Coy LEFT FRONT LINE + CENTRE. D Coy. REDOUBT LINE. 2/Lts SCALLAN and MACKINTOSH reported from BASE.	app. 298.
		10 pm.	C.O. inspected line.	
	19.2.17	4 AM 6. AM.	Officers + NCOs patrols sent out into No MANS LAND.	
		8. A.M.	STRENGTH IN TRENCHES 29 Officers and 622 O Ranks. Detached: NOT IN TRENCHES 11 officers 208 O Ranks TOTAL REGt STRENGTH 40 Officers 830 O. RANKS. Trenches in very bad condition owing to thaw. Large working parties put on to remedy conditions generally. Especially MAIN COMMn. TRENCHES.	

275

In Lieu of AF C2118.

3rd S.A. INFANTRY. **WAR DIARY.** TRANSVAAL REGT. 17.

PLACE	DATE	HOUR	SUMMARY OF EVENTS & INFORMATION.	REMARKS & REFERENCES & APPENDICES.
No1 SECTION RIGHT SECTOR.	19/7/17.		Man of 1st Regt recovered from NO MANS LAND (PTE PHILLIPS)	
		9 AM	O/in Command inspected Line	
		3 pm	C.O. inspected Line	
		4 pm	Adjt inspected REDOUBT LINE	
		10 pm.	C.O. inspected Line.	
	20/7/17.	4 AM & 6 AMS.	Officers & N.C.Os patrols sent out into NO MANS LAND.	
			Condition of trenches getting worse despite of efforts of large working parties put on to remedy conditions.	
		9. 30 AM	O/in Command visited Line	
		10. 0 AM	Brigadier General and O.C. visited Line	
		7. 0 PM	Adjutant visited Laundry POST. No1	
		NOON	Enemy shelled OIL WORKS demolishing CHIMNEY STACK. O.P. 1 O.R. Killed 7 wounded. Draft of 24 O.Ranks arrived.	
	21/7/17.	3. AM. 5. AM	Officers & N.C.Os patrols sent out into NO MANS LAND	
		9. 30 AM	O/in Command inspected TRENCHES and general conditions of SECTION	
		6. p.m.	Officer Commanding with Adjutant visited and inspected Line	
	22/7/17.	3. AM 5. AM.	Patrols sent out as usual.	
		9. AM.	O/in Command inspected Trenches.	
		NOON.	Inter. Coy relief effected disposition now as follows:- 'A' Coy RIGHT FRONT LINE 'D' Coy LEFT FRONT & CENTRE. 'C' Coy REDOUBT LINE 'B' Coy 3 platoons at OIL WORKS and 1 platoon at LAUNDRY POST.	APP 299.
		3. pm.	Officer Commanding inspected TRENCHES. Major WEBBER reported	

276

3RD S.A. INFANTRY. **WAR DIARY.** In Lieu of A.F. C2118. TRANSVAAL REGT. 13.

PLACE	DATE	HOUR.	SUMMARY OF EVENTS & INFORMATION.	REMARKS & REFERENCES TO APPENDICES.
No 1 SECTION RIGHT SECTOR	22/7/17.		from BASE. 1 O Rank wounded.	
		11 p.m.	Div Commander visited line.	
	23/7/17.	8. A.M.	STRENGTH IN TRENCHES 29 Officers 646 O.Ranks NOT IN TRENCHES 17 Officers 214 O.RANKS (DETACHED) REGTL STRENGTH 41 Officers 850 O.RANKS	
		10 AM.	Divisional General, Brigadier General, and Officer Commanding inspected LINE	
		7 pm.	Div Commander visited LINE usual large working parties put on to clear and repair trenches etc. Patrols sent out at night as usual.	
	24/7/17		Brig General visited REDOUBT LINE during morning	
		9.30 AM	Operation order No 89 received from B.H.Q re move for FEBY 26.	APP 300
		3pm to 6/30 pm	Officer Commanding visited line with Div Commander on tour of inspection.	
		11 pm.	Report received enemy had evacuated LINE to the NORTH. Special patrols of Officers & O.Ranks sent out with view to ascertaining position of affairs and to gather information	APP 301.
	25/7/17.	3.45 A.M.	Special patrols returned reporting enemy still in occupation of trenches opposite this SECTION and apparently no evacuation had taken place in the direct vicinity of No 1 SECTION RIGHT SECTOR.	

277

In Lieu of A.F. C. 2118.

3rd S. A. INFANTRY. **WAR DIARY.** TRANSVAAL REGT. No. 14

PLACE	DATE	HOUR.	SUMMARY OF EVENTS & INFORMATION.	REMARKS & REFERENCES TO APPENDICES
No. 1 SECTION R. SECTOR.	25/2/17.	10 A.M.	Officer Commdg together with 2/in Command inspected Line. Enemy artillery more active than usual.	
		2 p.m.	One of our battle planes brought down in our lines	
			Warning order issued ref: move tomorrow	app. 302
		9. p.m.	Patrol sent out as usual.	
	26/2/17.	1 p.m.	In accordance with Bde Operation Order No. 89 d/d. 24/2/17 the 1st S.A.I commenced relief of 3rd S.A.I	app. 303.
ARRAS J III		3. 30 pm.	Relief completed. Distribution as follows:- A Coy. FORRESTIER REDOUBT "B" Coy BARBED WIRE SQUARE "C" Coy St NICHOLAS "D" Coy NICHOLLS REDOUBT with Batn. H.Qrs at old J III. SUB SECTION.	
	27/2/17.		Commanding Officer & 2/in Command visited and inspected Coys in billets etc during the day. Lieut S.B. STOKES arrived with 2/Lt N BUREN from BASE	
		6. 30 pm	Working parties of 2 Officers + 100 O.Ranks furnished. These parties sustained casualties of 1 O Rank killed and 2 O Ranks slightly wounded.	
	28/2/17.	8. A.M.	STRENGTH IN RESERVES 32 Officers and 668 O Ranks. Detached 10 Officers and 187 O Ranks TOTAL REGtl STRENGTH 43 Officers and 855 O. Ranks. Large working parties have been furnished owing to bad condition of trenches generally.	
		3.30 PM.	B Coy evacuated billets in BARBED WIRE SQUARE on representations by TOWN MAJOR under authority from and instructions from B.H.Q. and took up quarters by Gas WORKS with one platoon in DIVl WORKSHOPS.	

278

In lieu of A.F. C2118.

15

Vol XI

279

3rd S A. Infantry.

War Diary.

Transvaal Regt.

Place	Date	Hour	Summary of Events and Information.	Remarks & References to Appendices.
ARRAS old J III SUB SECTION	28/7/17.		Total working parties found by regiment today and this evening consisted of 6 officers and 310 o.Ranks. The total casualties for the month have not been excessive they are as follows KILLED 3 O Ranks DIED OF WOUNDS 1. O Rank WOUNDED 2 officers and 13 o.Ranks of which 1 officer and 5. o.Ranks were only slightly wounded and have returned to duty, while 5. o.Ranks were accidentally wounded of which two returned to duty. The general situation has been normal throughout except for increased artillery activity on one or two occasions, the enemy has relied principally on his T.M.s. but during last few days, has shewn more artillery activity. During the regiment's occupation of old J III Sub-section and No1 SECTION. R SECTOR no opportunity has been missed in reconnoitring enemy's line and positions, while nightly patrols and wiring parties have been sent out without a break. In addition continual work has been in operation on Trenches Saps Bomb. stores dug-outs etc and a considerable amount of wiring, and strengthening has been done with a view to improvement of SECTORS generally. Total number of NCOs and men sent to hospital during month not including dental cases (13) Ear cases (2) 53- Daily average o.Ranks reporting sick 10- general health of Regiment good. E F Thackeray Lieut Col Comdg 3rd S.A.I	

OPERATION ORDER. 3 R/43. 280

SECRET. 10/2/17.

296

O.C. "A" Company. Bank L.G.O. BANK
"B" Company. Bank S.O. BANK
"C" Company. Bank I.O. BANK
"D" Company. Bank Q.Mr. BANK
"H.Q" Company. Bank T.O. BANK

1. MOVE. In compliance with Brigade Operation Order No. 87 of even date the 3rd South African Infantry will be relieved by the 4th South African Infantry, in RIGHT HALF SUB SECTION of JIII to St PANCRAS inclusive, and in SUPPORT LINE to "D" Works inclusive.

The 9th Scottish Rifles will relieve the LEFT FRONT Company 3rd S.A.Infantry in LEFT FRONT of SUB SECTION JIII, from St PANCRAS exclusive to TRENCH 101.

Two Platoons 3rd S.A.Infantry holding LEFT SUPPORT" NOVEMBER AVENUE and Communication Trench inclusive, to be relieved By 9th Scottish Rifles to-morrow the 11th instant.

Two Platoons of "B" Company occupying BOSKY REDOUBT to be relieved by the same unit on the 12th instant. From this date NOVEMBER AVENUE will be exclusive to the South African Brigade.

2. RELIEF. "D" Company holding RIGHT FRONT SUB SECTION will be relieved by 4th South Africab Infantry, commencing 9 a.m. to-morrow the 11th instant. The 4th S.A.Infantry will move in ~~front~~ from the right - "D" Company 3rd S.A.Infantry evacuating via CANNON STREET, SUPPORT LINE and AUGUST AVENUE, and will take up billets in St NICHOLAS Village, West of the Guard.

Two platoons of "C" Company, Right Support will be relieved by Two Platoons of 4th S.A.I. moving in from Right. The 3rd S.A.I. to evacuate via SUPPORT and NOVEMBER AVENUE, and will move into and occupy FORESTIER REDOUBT, with Company Headquarters.

Two Platoons "C" Company LEFT SUPPORT will be relieved by the 9th Scottish Rifles at an hour to be notified later, via NOVEMBER AVENUE, and will occupy billets in dug-outs at CANDLE FACTORY.

"A" Company 3rd S.A.I. holding LEFT FRONT LINE will be relieved by 9th Scottish Rifles at an hour to be notified later, and will evacuate via NOVEMBER AVENUE, and will take over and occupy billets in "BARBED WIRE SQUARE".

"B" Company 3rd S.A.I. will occupy NICHOLLS REDOUBT, as at present. The two platoons now in occupation at Bosky Redoubt will be relieved by the 9th Scottish Rifles on the 12th instant, at a time to be notified later, and will reinforce their Company in NICHOLLS REDOUBT.

Battalion Headquarters will not move from their present position, also Regimental Aid Post, Headquarter Details.

The Regimental Canteen and other Headquarter Details will remain at CANDLE FACTORY, as at present.

Lewis Gunners will remain with their Companies.

Carriers will return to their Companies during the day.

3. TRENCH STORES. Trench Stores are to be properly handed over and signed for in duplicate. The receipts to be handed in to Regtl Orderly Room immediately this is done.

4. BILLETS. Company Commanders will each send an Officer or Senior N.C.O. to take over Billets reporting as follows:-

"D" Coy. 1 Officer to be at CANDLE FACTORY at 9 a.m.
"C" Coy. 1 Officer to be at FORESTIER REDOUBT at 9.45 a.m.
"A" Coy. 1 Officer or N.C.O. to report at CANDLE FACTORY at 10 a.m

SECRET.

Copy No. ......

Map Reference Sheet 51B.N.W.3

1st SOUTH AFRICAN INFANTRY BRIGADE. 7th February 1917.

ORDER No. 99.

1. RELIEF. The 4th S.A.Infantry will relieve the 2nd South Afric Infantry in JII Sub-Section on the 9th FEBRUARY. On relief the 2nd S.A.Infantry will become the Battalion in Brigade Reserve and will take over the positions and duties at present occupied and carried out by the 4th South African Infantry.

2. MOVEMENT AND TIME OF RELIEF. The relief will be carried out by day as far as possible. Details will be arranged direct between Battalion Commanders, but will be such as will prevent over-crowding of the trenches at any part, or any portion of the line being vacated during the relief. The regulations regarding movement in ARRAS will be strictly adhered to.

3. WORKING PARTIES ETC. The Battalions will take over the duties (including standing working parties, police, trench wardens etc.) at present found by the unit they are relieving. O.C., 2nd S.A.Infantry will be careful to hand over particulars of all work in hand in the Sub-Section in which his unit is being relieved.

4. LOG BOOKS ETC. Log books, Maps, etc, will be handed over to relieving Battalions.

5. TRENCH STORES. Trench Stores will be taken over and duplicate receipts forwarded to Brigade Headquarters as usual.

6. BILLETS. The Os.C 2nd S.A.I and 4th S.A.I will arrange for their billeting officers to report to the Town Major ARRAS at 4.pm 8th instant to arrange details of handing over billets.

7. TELEPHONES. In accordance with orders in force regarding the use of telephones etc., no message whatever will be sent over the lines regarding this relief, except the code-word reporting relief complete.

8. COMPLETION OF RELIEF. Completion of relief will be reported to Brigade Headquarters by the S.A.B.trench code.

9. Acknowledge.

A L Pepper
Captain.
Acting Brigade Major.

Issued by Orderly at 2.30 p.m.

Copies 1/4	to Ist to 4th SAI.	12	to 27th Infantry Brigade.
5	to 28th M.Gun Coy.	13	9th Division.
6	SALTM.Battery.	14	Staff Captain.
7	64th Field Coy.RE.	15	Brigade Transport Of.
8	Brigade Sig.Officer.	16/18.	War Diary.
9	107th Coy. A.S.C.	19	Brigade Post Office.
10	S.A.F.Ambulance.	20	Centre Group R.F.A.
11	26th Infantry Bde.	21	9th Div, T.M's.
22	Town Major -ARRAS.	23	37th Infantry Brigad

Operation Order SECRET. 3/R.I.R. 8/7/17

O.C. A D
B L.G.O.
C

293
282

I RELIEF. The following reliefs will take place today under Coy arrangements. A number of N.C.O.s and men from each Coy to be detailed to move over the top but not before dusk.

II MOVE
A Coy from RESERVES to LEFT FRONT LINE
D " " SUPPORTS to R FRONT LINE
C " " L FRONT LINE to SUPPORTS
B " " R " " to RESERVE

III TRENCH STORES will be handed over & T.S. cards initialled.

IV BLANKETS. 'A' Coy will return all BLANKETS to CANDLE FACTORY properly rolled up and labelled. B Coy will draw blankets from CANDLE FACTORY.

V WORK. All work reports to be handed over on relief.

VI GUARDS – NICHOLLS & BUSKY REDOUBTS and OCTOBER TRAMWAY to be properly relieved and instructions handed over.

VII SANITATION Coy Commdrs to see that all SUB-SECTIONS are in a clean & sanitary condition.

VIII WIRING. Details of wiring required to [illegible] gaps etc to be handed over.

[illegible signature]
BH [illegible]

Operation Order SECRET. 3R. 40.

OC [illegible] CC

A. [illegible] D

B. LGO

C. " 7/7/17

283

290

I. RELIEF The following reliefs will take place today under Coy arrangements. A number of NCOs and men from each Coy to be detailed to move over the [illegible] and before dusk.

MOVE D. Coy to RIGHT FRONT LINE

A. Coy to LEFT FRONT LINE

B Coy to SUPPORTS

C. " to RESERVES BOSKY & [illegible] REDOUBTS

III TRENCH STORES. Will be handed over and T.C. [illegible]

IV BLANKETS "A" Coy will return all blankets to CANDLE FACTORY properly rolled up and labelled. "C" Coy will draw blankets from CANDLE FACTORY.

V WORK. All work reports to be handed over on relief.

VI Guards [illegible] & BOSKY REDOUBTS to be properly relieved and instructions handed over also OCTOBER TRAMWAY

VII SANITATION Coy Commdrs to see that all [illegible] SECTIONS are in a clean and sanitary condition

VIII WIRING. Details of wiring req'd to fill gaps to be hand over.

7/7/17

[illegible] Capt & Adjt.

BANK.

Operation Order by B A N K. 3 R 45.

SECRET.

To O.C. "A" Company.
"B" Company.
"C" Company.
"D" Company.
Lewis Gun Officer.

299
284

21/2/1917.

1. INTER-COMPANY RELIEF. The following reliefs will take place to-morrow morning before midday, under Company arrangements. A number of N.C.O.S and men from each Company to be detailed to move over the top, but not till dusk.

2. MOVE. "A" Company to relieve "B" Company RIGHT FRONT.
"D" Company to relieve "C" Company LEFT FRONT, & CENTRE.
"C" Company to relieve "D" Company REDOUBT LINE.
"B" Company to relieve "A" Company OIL WORKS with one Platoon at LAUNDRY POST. This post is NOT to be relieved until DARK.

3. TRENCH STORES. To be taken over and T.S. cards initialled.

4. GUARDS & DUTIES. All sentry posts to be taken over immediately on relief.

5. BLANKETS. All blankets in possession of A and D Company to be handed in to Stores at OIL WORKS, rolled in bundles of 10 and properly labelled. C and B Companies will draw blankets from OIL WORKS.

6. SANITATION. Company Commanders will see that their respective sub sections are left in as clean and sanitary a condition as possible.

7. WIRING & WORK REPORTS. Details of wiring and work contemplated to be handed over.

8. PATROLS. Particulars and information relating to patrols etc. to be handed over.

9. GENERAL. All possible information likely to be of service to Companies holding RIGHT AND LEFT FRONT LINE to be handed over.

(sgd) A.W.H.McDONALD.

Capt. & Adjutant,
B a n k.

In the Field.

OPERATION ORDER by BANK. 3/B/44.

S E C R E T. 17/2/1917.

O.C.	"A" Company.	L.G.Officer.
	"B" Company.	Sig.Officer.
	"C" Company.	Int.Officer.
	"D" Company.	Qr.Mr.
	"H.Q." Company.	Transport Officer.

1. MOVE. In compliance with Brigade Operation Order No.88 dd. 16th February,1917, BANK will relieve DITCH in the LINE to-morrow February 18, 1917.

2. RELIEF. Reliefs to take place as follows:-
"B" Company of BANK will relieve "B" Company of DITCH,and will move off at 9 a.m. proceeding via REDOUBT LINE,FORESTIER REDOUBT into FEBRUARY AVENUE, and will take over RIGHT FRONT LINE of No.1 Section,Right SECTOR.
"C" Company BANK will relieve "B" and "C" Companies,DITCH, and will move at 9.30 a.m. from FORESTIER REDOUBT via MAY AVENUE, and will take over LEFT FRONT LINE. RELIEF will evacuate via MAY AVENUE.
"D" Company BANK will move into REDOUBT LINE, moving off at 9.30 a.m.via FEBRUARY and MARCH AVENUES. RELIEF will evacuate via REDOUBT LINE.
"A" Company BANK will relieve "A" Company DITCH in OIL WORKS, one platoon LAUNDRY POST moving off at 10.30 a.m. via FEBRUARY AVENUE. LAUNDRY POST RELIEF must not be effected before dark. L.G.Posts, Snipers and Observers,Signallers and Bombers will move forward to relieve at 8.30 a.m.
DITCH will take over all accommodation at present occupied by BANK.

3. MOVEMENT. The regulation regarding movement in ARRAS etc will be strictly adhered to.

4. TRENCH STORES. Trench Stores are to be properly handed over by outgoing units, and TRENCH STORE CARDS to be signed and rendered in duplicate to Regimental Orderly Room,No.1 Section RIGHT SECTOR, immediately on completion of relief.
Companies occupying new SUB SECTION will each obtain a store card for their SUB SECTION.

5. RATION STATES. These will be rendered to Regimental Orderly Room to-morrow by 12 noon to prevent any discrepancy in No. of rations required.

6. GUARDS and DUTIES. All sentry posts to be taken over immediately, and guards posted etc except as stated for LAUNDRY POST.

7. COOKS. Cooks will take over immediately after breakfast, and must be clear of REDOUBT LINE by 9 a.m.
HEADQUARTERS R.S.M.to take over all Headquarters accommodation and will hand over CANDLE FACTORY by 9 a.m. Carrying Party for Battalion Orderly Room to be detailed to report at 8 a.m. to Orderly Room Sergeant.

8. BILLETS. O.C. Commanding "A" Company will detail an Officer to hand over Company Billets to an Officer being detailed by O.C. DITCH.

9. SANITATION. Necessary handing over certificates of cleanliness of LINES and DUG-OUTS will be submitted with certificate of Relief.

10. TRANSPORT. Ration Limbers can be utilised on their arrival to-morrow night with rations for the conveyance of any heavy

15. COUNTERSIGNS. will be taken as enemy signals.

16. IDENTIFICATIONS. No badge of rank, badge, correspondence or name of man or regiment is to be worn or carried.
Should any man be captured only his rank and name is to be given.

The following phones will be established :-

1. Phone from Raid Party at Assembly Point to Battle H.Q.
2. Phone from Observation Officer at CLAUDE CRATER.
3. Phone from Right and Left Front Company H.Q. to Battle H.Q.
4. Phone from Battle H.Q. to Brigade H.Q.
5. Phone from Battle H.Q. to R.A. for R.A.Liaison Officer.

2. Runners will be at 1, 2, and 3, and six at Battle H.Q.

A reconnaissance will be made on the night of 2nd/3rd January by raiding party to report on ~~wire~~ ground and enemy wire.

The Assembly Base will be marked on the night of January 2nd/3rd.

The raiding party will be in position on the Base at 4-45.p.m. 3-1-17, and report when ready to start at ZERO - 5 mins - to Battle H.Q.

ROLL CALL. Men returning will report at Battle Headquarters, and then proceed to CANDLE FACTORY.

Commanding, 3rd S.A.I.

Copy to each c/c

297

.SECRET
Map Ref.
Sheet 51B
NW 3
1/10,000.

Copy No........

IST SOUTH AFRICAN INFANTRY BRIGADE

16th February 1917

ORDER NO. 86.

287

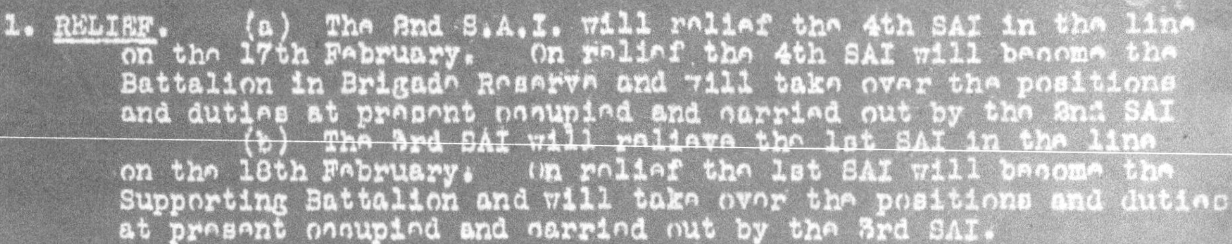

1. RELIEF. (a) The 2nd S.A.I. will relief the 4th SAI in the line on the 17th February. On relief the 4th SAI will become the Battalion in Brigade Reserve and will take over the positions and duties at present occupied and carried out by the 2nd SAI
(b) The 3rd SAI will relieve the 1st SAI in the line on the 18th February. On relief the 1st SAI will become the Supporting Battalion and will take over the positions and duties at present occupied and carried out by the 3rd SAI.

2. MOVEMENT AND TIME OF RELIEF. All details of relief will be arranged direct [illegible] between Battalion Commanders.
The regulations regarding movement in ARRAS etc., will be strictly adhered to.

3. LOG BOOKS ETC. Log books, maps etc., will be handed over to relieving battalions.

4. TRENCH STORES. Trench stores will be taken over and duplicate receipts forwarded to Brigade Headquarters as usual.

5. BILLETS. Officers Commanding Units will arrange for their billetting officers to report to the TOWN MAJORS concerned to arrange details of handing over billets.
The hour at which these officers are to report to the Town Majors should be arranged between C.Os concerned.

6. COMPLETION OF RELIEF. Completion of relief will be reported to Brigade Headquarters by code-word "CHARLEY".

7. ACKNOWLEDGE. Ack.

J. Mitchell Baker
Major
Brigade Major

Issued thro' Signals at 11 am.

Copies			
1/4 to	1st to 4th SAI	14 to	9th Division
5	28th M.G.Coy	15	Staff Captain
6	SALTMBattery	16	Bde Transport Officer
7	64th Field Co. RE	17/19	War Diary
8	Bde Sig. Officer	20	Bde Post Office
9	107th Co. ASC	21	Centre Group RFA
10	S.A.Field Amb.	22	9th Divl. T.Ms
11	26th Inf. Brigade	23	Town Major ARRAS
12	27th Infantry Bde.	24	Town Major ST NICHOLAS
13	36th Infantry Bde	25	

297

F.7.9 Copy No. 3..

294

288

1ST SOUTH AFRICAN INFANTRY BRIGADE

SECRET

10th February 1917

Map Reference ORDER NO. 87.
Sheet 51B
NW 3 . 1/10,000.

1. (a) On the 11th February The 27th Infantry Brigade will take over from the South African Infantry Brigade that portion of the ~~xxxx~~ front line system between the present right of the 27th Infantry Brigade and ST PANCRAS trench exclusive, and Machine Gun positions Nos. 9,10 and 11 at present in the South African Brigade Section.
(b) On the 12th February the 27th Infantry Brigade will take over BOSKY REDOUBT from the South African Infantry Brigade.
(c) The 9th Scottish Rifles will relieve the 3rd S.A.Infantry in these portions of the line.

2. The boundary between the 27th Inf. Brigade and the South African Inf. Brigade will then be ST PANCRAS trench (incl. to S.A.Bde) "D" WORK (incl. to S.A.Bde) November Avenue (incl. to 27th In.Bde).

3 On the 11th February the 1st S.A.Infantry will take over trench 89 from the 4th S.A.Infantry, and the 4th S.A.Infantry will take over trenches 96 and 97 from the 3rd S.A.Infantry.

4. All details re taking over portions of the line etc., will be arranged direct between Battalion Commanders and Machine Gun Company Commanders concerned.

5. Completion of each relief will be reported to Brigade H.Q.

6. On relief, the 3rd S.A.Infantry, less four platoons, will be accommodated in ST NICHOLAS and will become the supporting battalion. It will relieve the company of the 2nd S.A.Inafntry at present accommodated there and that company will then be accommodated in ARRAS.

7. The C.O., 3rd S.A.Infantry will detail two platoons as garrison for NICOLLS and two platoons as garrison for FORESTIER Redoubts from the 11th instant. These garrisons will be found from different companies.

ACKNOWLEDGE.

10 FEB.1917 NOON

[signature]
Major.
Brigade Major.

Issued by Orderly at 11 a.m.

Copies 1/4 to	1st to 4th SAI.	13 to	9th Division.
5 to	28th M.G.Coy	14	Staff Captain
6	SALTM Battery	15	Bde Transport Offr.
7	64th Field Co. R.E.	16/18	War Diary
8	Bde Sig. Officer	19	Bde Post Office
9	107th Co. ASC	20	Centre Group RFA
10	S.A.F.Ambulance	21	9th Div. T.Ms
11	26th Infantry Bde	22	Town Major ARRAS
12	27th Infantry Bde	23	38th Infantry Bde.

acR

OPERATION ORDER. 3 R 43.

SECRET. 10/2/17.

298

289

O.C. "A" Company. Bank — L.G.O. BANK
"B" Company. Bank — S.O. BANK
"C" Company. Bank — I.O. BANK
"D" Company. Bank — Q.Mr. BANK
"H.Q" Company. Bank — T.O. BANK

1. MOVE. In compliance with Brigade Operation Order No. 87 of even date the 3rd South African Infantry will be relieved by the 4th South African Infantry, in RIGHT HALF SUB SECTION of JIII to St PANCRAS inclusive, and in SUPPORT LINE to "D" Works inclusive.

The 9th Scottish Rifles will relieve the LEFT FRONT Company 3rd S.A.Infantry in LEFT FRONT of SUB SECTION JIII, from St PANCRAS exclusive to TRENCH 101.

Two Platoons 3rd S.A.Infantry holding LEFT SUPPORT" NOVEMBER AVENUE and Communication Trench inclusive, to be relieved By 9th Scottish Rifles to-morrow the 11th instant.

Two Platoons of "B" Company occupying BOSKY REDOUBT to be relieved by the same unit on the 12th instant. From this date NOVEMBER AVENUE will be exclusive to the South African Brigade.

2. RELIEF. "D" Company holding RIGHT FRONT SUB SECTION will be relieved by 4th South African Infantry, commencing 9 a.m. to-morrow the 11th instant. The 4th S.A.Infantry will move in front from the right - "D" Company 3rd S.A.Infantry evacuating via CANNON STREET, SUPPORT LINE and AUGUST AVENUE, and will take up billets in St NICHOLAS Village, West of the Guard.

Two platoons of "C" Company, Right Support will be relieved by Two Platoons of 4th S.A.I. moving in from Right. The 3rd S.A.I. to evacuate via SUPPORT and NOVEMBER AVENUE, and will move into and occupy FORESTIER REDOUBT, with Company Headquarters.

Two Platoons "C" Company LEFT SUPPORT will be relieved by the 9th Scottish Rifles at an hour to be notified later, via NOVEMBER AVENUE, and will occupy billets in dug-outs at CANDLE FACTORY.

"A" Company 3rd S.A.I. holding LEFT FRONT LINE will be relieved by 9th Scottish Rifles at an hour to be notified later, and will evacuate via NOVEMBER AVENUE, and will take over and occupy billets in "BARBED WIRE SQUARE".

"B" Company 3rd S.A.I. will occupy NICHOLLS REDOUBT, as at present. The two platoons now in occupation at Bosky Redoubt will be relieved by the 9th Scottish Rifles on the 12th instant, at a time to be notified later, and will reinforce their Company in NICHOLLS REDOUBT.

Battalion Headquarters will not move from their present position, also Regimental Aid Post, Headquarter Details.

The Regimental Canteen and other Headquarter Details will remain at CANDLE FACTORY, as at present.

Lewis Gunners will remain with their Companies.

Carriers will return to their Companies during the day.

3. TRENCH STORES. Trench Stores are to be properly handed over and signed for in duplicate. The receipts to be handed in to Regtl Orderly Room immediately this is done.

4. BILLETS. Company Commanders will each send an Officer or Senior N.C.O. to take over Billets reporting as follows:-

"D" Coy. 1 Officer to be at CANDLE FACTORY at 9 a.m.
"C" Coy. 1 Officer to be at FORESTIER REDOUBT at 9.45 a.m.
"A" Coy. 1 Officer or N.C.O. to report at CANDLE FACTORY at 10 a.m

290

22 JAN 1917
4 pm

Copy No. 3........

1ST SOUTH AFRICAN INFANTRY BRIGADE.

SECRET
Map Reference
Sheet 51B NW 3
1/10,000.

Jan
23rd ~~February~~ 1917.

285

OPERATION ORDER NO. 84.

1. **RELIEFS.** The following reliefs will take place on the 24th inst. The 3rd S.A.I. will relieve the 4th S.A.I. in J.III sub-section. The 4th S.A.I. will relieve the 1st S.A.I. in J.I sub-section. On relief the 1st S.A.I. will become the Battalion in Brigade Reserve/ and will take over the positions and duties at present occupied and carried out by the 3rd S.A.I.

2. **MOVEMENT AND TIME OF RELIEF.** The relief will be carried out by day as far as possible. Details will be arranged direct between Battn. Commanders, but will be such as will prevent overcrowding of the trenches at any part, or any portion of the line being vacated during the relief. The regulations regarding movement in ARRAS will be strictly adhered to.

3. **WORKING PARTIES ETC.** The battalions will take over the duties (including standing working parties, police, trench wardens, etc.,) at present found by the unit they are relieving. O.C. 1st S.A.I will be careful to hand over particulars of all work in hand in the sub-section in which his unit is being relieved, also instructions re clearing trenches when the HEAVY T.M. is firing.

4. **LOG BOOKS ETC.** Log books, maps etc., will be handed over to relieving battalion.

5. **TRENCH STORES.** Trench stores will be taken over and duplicate receipts forwarded to Brigade Headquarters as usual.

6. **BILLETS.** The Os C. 1st and 3rd S.A.I. will arrange for their billeting officers to report to the Town Major ARRAS, at 4 pm 23rd instant to arrange details of handing over billets.

7. **TELEPHONES.** In accordance with orders in force regarding the use of telephones etc., no message whatever will be sent over the lines regarding this relief, ~~excepting the code word reporting~~ relief complete.

8. **COMPLETION OF RELIEF.** Completion of relief will be reported to Brigade Headquarters by means of the code-word in the "S.A.B." trench code.

9. Please acknowledge.

Ack

A. L. Pepper
Captain.
A/ Brigade Major

Issued by orderly at 3-30 pm.

Copies to			
1/4 to	1st to 4th S.A.I.	12 to	27th Inf. Brigade
5 to	28th M.G.Coy	13	9th Division.
6.to	SALT Battery	14	Brigadier General
7	64th Field Company R.E.	15	Brigade Major
8	Bde Sig. Officer	16	Staff Captain
9	107th Co A.S.C.	17	Bde Transport Officer
10	S.A.F.Amb,	18 to 20	War Diary
11	26th Inf. Brigade	21	Post Corporal
22	Centre Group RFA	23	9th Div. T.Ms
24	Town Major ARRAS		

S E C R E T. 3R/47.

O P E R A T I O N O R D E R. 24/2/17.

301291

By
B A N K.

1. INFORMATION. It is reported the enemy have evacuated their FRONT LINE. This report received from Brigade on LEFT. Patrol from Battalion of left just returned, reports enemy lines still ~~xxxx~~ occupied and normal. They are sending out another patrol.

2. INTENTION. "D" Coy to send out Officer's Patrol immediately to verify above, and report if enemy line ~~xxxx~~ occupied or otherwise - should line be found to be unoccupied, a patrol of 20 men under an Officer to be pushed forward to re-open touch : report to Battalion Headquarters by runner result of patrol as soon as possible. All necessary precautions to be taken to cover this patrol, and Battalion on left and right to be warned of your patrols.
"A" and "D" Coys to forward Patrol Reports from their patrols who went out between 7.a.m. and 9.a.m. tonight, immediately. The 2nd patrol of 1 Officer and 20 men is not to proceed until the report to O.C. BANK has been received, and a direct order is sent by BANK for it to proceed.

Copies to "A" and "D" Coys.

(Sgd) A.W.H.McDonald.
Capt & Adjutant.
B A N K.

Issued 12.10.AM.

24/25/2/1917.

292

OPERATION ORDER BY BANK. S/R/44.

10. TRANSPORT (Continued). Company baggage from CANDLE FACTORY to NEW H.Q.DUMP.

11. BLANKETS. Blankets of "A" and "D" Company will be retained by them. "B" and "C" Companies will return their blankets to store at HEADQUARTERS under their C.Q.M.Sergeants.

12. Re STORES &c. Trench Store Cards to be made out for R.E. Stores, also DUG-OUT equipment, LOG BOOK, MAPS etc being handed over.

13. COMPLETION OF RELIEF. To be notified by code word "CHARLEY" immediately RELIEF is complete.

Time 4 p.m. Captain & Adjutant,

Date 17/9/1917. B a n k.

8. All guards with prisoners to report at Battle Headquarters, junction SUPPORT and CANNON STREET. Prisoners will be evacuated to CANDLE FACTORY via OCTOBER AVENUE for examination and disposal.

9. Support in other Sub-Sections Lewis and Machine Guns in J.1, J.11, and K.1 will fire on enemy's trenches opposite these sub-sections during these operations.

10. ASSEMBLY POINT. In front of our wire EAST of Sap 98, one hundred and twenty yards from enemy trench G.6.c.5.0.

11. FORMATION. Two lines of sections in Single file the front sections each consisting of the two right and left groups for blocking trenches. The clearing parties will form the rear sections.
The 6 Guides will be about 50 yards in advance in front of the right and left sections, and drop a connecting file at each 40 yards.
The first two - a N.C.O. and 1 man - to remain on parapet, and mark the exit from enemy trench.
The distance and interval between sections will each be about 50 yards.

12. METHOD OF CARRYING OUT RAID.
(a) At ZERO our Artillery and Stokes Mortars will bombard the enemy's front line trench for about 100 yards NORTH and about 100 yards SOUTH of the point where the wire has been cut.
During this bombardment the leading sections will advance as close to the enemy wire as possible. The Artillery and Mortars will also bombard the Support and Communication trenches.
(b) At ZERO plus 2' (two) minutes the Artillery and Stokes will lift from the front to the flanks, support line and 3 communication trenches, leading to the enemy front line.
The front sections will then enter the trench and each group make its way 50 yards up the trench assigned to it, and form a block. The rear sections will enter the trench and carry out the duties assigned to them.
The two leading guides will remain on parapet to mark the point of exit.
(c) At ZERO plus ~~15~~ 14 minutes a ~~golden~~ Blue rain RECALL rocket will be fired from the front line trench. The guard on parapet will sound a French Horn, which signal will be repeated by Officers and section leaders, and the party return to our trenches.
(d) At ZERO plus 20 minutes our Artillery will cease fire - reopening on Support and Communication trenches at ZERO plus 25 minutes for five minutes.

13. ARMS AND EQUIPMENT. Revolver and 12 rounds or rifle and 20 rounds - S.A.A. in breast pockets.
Knife or bayonet.
8 bombs per man
The guides and 2 men in front section to carry wire cutters.
One man in each section for clearing trenches will carry 2 Stokes bombs for use in dug-outs - if none, to destroy trench on leaving.
Torches to be carried by all ranks.

14. DRESS. Steel helmets - covered-jacket - bomb waistcoat, trousers tucked in socks, and body shields. Buttons and patch on back painted with phosphorus. Faces and hands blackened.

15. COUNTERSIGNS. These to be decided and issued at 2.p.m. 3-1917. No other signals but those laid down will be used, i.e. Rocket, French Horn and countersign. Whistles and the order to retire will

S E C R E T. to initial & return **BR/49.**

O P E R A T I O N   O R D E R.

by

B A N K.

294 303 **26/2/1917.**

O.C.

"A" Coy.	"D" Coy.	L.G.Officer.
"B" "	-Intell.Offr.	-Sig.Officer. S.O. [illegible]
"C" "	Q.Master.	Transport Officer.

1. **MOVE.** In compliance with Brigade Operation Order No [illegible] dd 24th.February, BANK will ~~relieve~~ be relieved by DITCH and go into RESERVE today, 26/2/1917.

2. **RELIEFS.** Reliefs will take place as follows :-
1.30.PM. "B" Coy will move from OIL WORKS to BARBED WIRE SQUARE via FEBRUARY AVENUE.
2.15.PM. "C" Coy will move from REDOUBT LINE to ST.NICHOLAS via FEBRUARY AVENUE.
3.0.PM. "D" Coy LEFT FRONT, via NEW CUT and AUGUST AVENUE to NICHOLAS REDOUBT.
3.45.PM. "A" Coy via FEBRUARY and REDOUBT LINE to FORRESTIER REDOUBT.
Headquarters will move as early as possible, but must be clear of REDOUBT LINE, (if evacuating via FORRESTIER) by 1.30.PM. otherwise MARCH AVENUE and CANDLE FACTORY route must be taken. Dinners must be up by 12 noon.

3. **MOVEMENT.** The regulations regarding movement in ARRAS etc., will be strictly adhered to.

4. **TRENCH STORES.** Trench Stores are to be properly handed over and duplicate receipted Store Cards obtained and forwarded to Battalion Headquarters old J III immediately on relief. On taking over new positions a signed store card must be obtained from the out-going units, and kept till called for.

5. **RATION STATES.** These will be rendered to Regimental Orderly Room tomorrow by 12 noon to prevent any misunderstanding in distribution of rations required.

6. **GUARDS AND DUTIES.** All Sentry Posts to be taken over immediately and Guards posted etc.

7. **BILLETS.** Signalling Officer will assume duties of Billeting Officer, and will take over Headquarter and Company Billets. An Officer of each Company to be detailed to take over from the 1st Regiment at 1.PM.

8. **BLANKETS.** Company Commanders will see that Blankets are issued for the use of all ranks when relief is affected.

9. **SANITATION.** Necessary handing over certificates of cleanliness of lines, dug-outs, etc., will be submitted with certificate of relief.

10. **LOG-BOOKS.** Maps, Small Plans, etc., property of No 1 Section, Right Sector, to be handed over on Trench Store Cards and receipt obtained thereon.

11. **COMPLETION OF RELIEF.** Immediately on Completion of Relief notification will be sent to Battalion Headquarters, No 1 Section, Right Sector, by code word " HARRY".

(Signed) A.V.H.McDonald.
Capt & Adjutant.
B A N K.

5. REINFORCING. In the event of at attack Companies will reinforce as under:-
(a) The Company holding FORESTIER REDOUBT to be reinforced at once by its two platoons at CANDLE FACTORY.
(b) The Company occupying St NICHOLAS Village West of the Guard, will move forward and occupy BRITANNIA WORKS, on present Garrison -The 4th S.A.I.- going forward.
(c) The Company at BARBED WIRE SQUARE under such circumstances will move forward and occupy St NICHOLAS Village.

6. RATION STATES. These will be rendered to Regimental Orderly Room by 12 Noon to-morrow to prevent any discrepancy in the number of rations required.

7. KIT & EQUIPMENT. Company Commanders will arrange their own Dumps, and will issue the necessary instructions to their C.Q.M.S. to effect this.

8. TRANSPORT. Transport will be available for conveyance of baggage, and will be detailed as necessary on arrival of rations at about 5 p.m. Field Kitchens will be brought forward for Company use.

9. GUARDS AND DUTIES. All Sentry Posts are to be taken over, and Guards posted immediately on occupation.

10. SANITARY. The necessary handing over certificate of cleanliness of Lines and Dug-outs will be submitted with the certificate of Relief.

11. RELIEF. This will be notified at once by Runner. The code word "John" being used.

(sgd) A.W.H.McDONALD.

Issued Captain & Adjutant,

11.30 p.m. B a n k.

"A" Form.

MESSAGES AND SIGNALS.

Army Form C.2121
(in pads of 100).
No. of Message

Prefix .... Code .... m. | Words | Charge

Office of Origin and Service Instructions.

This message is on a/c of: 296 Service.

(Signature of "Franking Officer.")

Sent
At .... m.
To ....
By ....

Recd. at .... m.
Date ....
From ....
By 30V

TO ②

Sender's Number.	Day of Month.	In reply to Number.	AAA
* W 7	25th.	—	

of	the	raid	on	our
right	at	8.30 am	aaa	The
necessary	precautions	must	be	taken
aaa	O's	C	Coy	E
initial	below			

A Coy. [illegible]
B .. [illegible]
C .. [illegible]
D [illegible]
Hqs. ..

From OC BANK
Place
Time 9.15 pm

The above may be forwarded as now corrected. (Z) [signature illegible]

Censor. | Signature of Addressor or person authorised to telegraph in his name.

* This line should be erased if not required.

750,000. W 2186—M309. H. W. & V., Ld. 6/16.

Operation Order SECRET 3R 41. 9/7/17

OC A · OC D 297

B · L.G.O 291

C.

(I) RELIEF The following reliefs will take place today under Coy arrangements. A number of NCOs & men from each Coy to be detailed to move over the top but not before dusk.

II MOVE B Coy to RIGHT FRONT LINE

C " to LEFT FRONT LINE

D " " Support LINE [illegible].

A " " Reserves. BOSKY & NICHOLLS

III TRENCH STORES Will be handed over and Trench Storeboards initialed

IV BLANKETS C Coy will return all blankets to CANDLE FACTORY properly rolled up and labelled A Coy will draw blankets from Candle Factory

V WORK All work reports to be handed over on relief.

VI GUARDS NICHOLLS & BOSKY REDOUBTS and OCTOBER TRAMWAY to be properly relieved and instructions handed over.

VII SANITATION Coy Commdrs to see that all their sections are in a clean & sanitary condition.

VIII WIRING. Details of wiring required to fill gaps etc to be handed over

A.C.S.H. McDonald Capt & Adj
BANK

4

Troops returned to Candle Factory
at 6 pm.
Enemy Retaliation with Field
Guns, Mortars and Machine
Gun feeble. 298
No Casualties
Regret to report that at 4 pm
O/C 'A' Coy LEFT Front Half
Sub Section informed
me that about 8 pm a
STOKES Gun on our RIGHT
fired in our SAPS, the
MORTAR Bomb falling in
SAP 101. Killing one man
(Private MARTIN) and slightly
wounding six others, all
the men of that Post.
Lieut EGAN the Trench Mortar
Officer at once and warning
of this misdirected Fire.
Returned from BATTLE HEAD
QUARTERS to BATTALION
H.Qrs. 7 pm
Informed ALL wounded are
Slight
Wish express our appreciation
of splendid Artillery barrage,
and the manner in which
Lieut GOODWINS dealt with

Barrage Ceased 5. 2[illegible] pm
Barrage Re-opened 5. 25 pm
for 5 minutes.
Private ATKINS, Right Clearing
party reported his party
returned without casualty
at — 5. 27. Hole bombed
enemy of the DUG OUT.
Reached SOUTHERN SAP
Private GORDON, i/c Right
Covering party reported
5 men all present his party
5 – 30 pm.
One Prisoner. Corporal [illegible]
[illegible] of the 7th Saxon brought
in [illegible]
Sergeant WARD i/c Centre
Communication Trench party
reported all returned [illegible]
at — 5. 36 pm. Bombed
occupied Dug Outs with
STOKES. Bombs (mortar)
Sergeant HUGHES i/c LEFT
Clearing party reported
bombed 3 Dug Outs the
[illegible] occupied bombed
with STOKES and Mills
GRENADES.
Lieut GOODWIN Commanding

SECRET

Map Reference
Sheet 51B
NW 3 1/10,000.

1ST SOUTH AFRICAN INFANTRY BRIGADE

Copy No. 3

300

ORDER NO. 89.

24th February 1917.

1 RELIEF. (a) The 4th SAI will relieve the 2nd SAI in the line on the 25th February. On relief the 2nd SAI will become the Battalion in Brigade Reserve and will take over the positions and duties at present occupied and carried out by the 4th SAI.
(b) The 1st SAI will relieve the 3rd SAI in the line on the 26th February. On relief the 3rd SAI will become the Supporting Battalion and will take over the positions and duties at present occupied and carried out by the 1st SAI.

2. MOVEMENT AND TIME OF RELIEF. All details of relief will be arranged direct between Battalion Commanders.
The regulations regarding movement in ARRAS etc., will be strictly adhered to.

3. LOG BOOKS ETC. Log Books, maps etc., will be handed over to relieving battalions.

4. TRENCH STORES. Trench stores will be taken over and duplicate receipts forwarded to Brigade Headquarters as usual.

5. BILLETS. Officers Commanding Units will arrange for their billeting officers to report to the TOWN MAJORS concerned to arrange details of handing over billets.
The hour at which these officers are to report to the Town Majors should be arranged between Commanding Officers concerned.

6. COMPLETION OF RELIEF. Completion of relief will be reported to Brigade Headquarters by code-word "HARRY".

7. ACKNOWLEDGE.

Pepper
Captain
A/ Brigade Major.

Issued thro' signals at 7 a.m.

Copies			
1/4 to	1st to 4th SAI	14 to	9th Division
5	28th M.G.Coy	15	Staff Captain
6	SALTH BATTERY	16	Bde Transport Officer
7	64th Field Co. R.E.	17/19	War Diary
8	Bde Sig Officer	20	Bde Post Office
9	107th Co ASC	21	Centre Group RFA
10	S.A.Field Amb,	22	9th Divl. T.M,
11	48th Inf. Bde	23	Town Major ARRAS
12	102nd Inf Bde	24	Town Major ST NICHOLAS
13	56th Infantry Bde	25	

4th S. A. Inf. TRANSVAAL REGT. 9/30 AM 24 FEB. 1917

301

CONFIDENTIAL.

0.14/7.

1st S.A.I.
2nd "
3rd "
4th "

Further to my 0.14/7 of the 14th instant, it has now been dedided that reliefs will take place as stated below and my minute of the 14th is accordingly cancelled.

The 2nd S.A.I. will relieve the 4th S.A.I. on the 17th February. The 4th S.A.I. taking over the accommodation vacated by the 2nd.

The 3rd S.A.I. will relieve the 1st S.A.I. on the 18th February. The 1st S.A.I. will be accommodated in the billets and posts vacated by the 3rd S.A.I.

16 FEB. 1917

Major.

Brigade Major.

17/.

"A" Form.
MESSAGES AND SIGNALS.

Army Form C.2121
(in pads of 100).
No. of Message

Prefix ... Code ... m. | Words | Charge
Office of Origin and Service Instructions.

Sent
At ... m.
To
By

This message is on a/c of:
302 *Service.*
(Signature of "Franking Officer.")

Recd. at ... m.
Date 307
From
By

TO OC A, B, C, D, Hqrs.

Sender's Number.	Day of Month.	In reply to Number.	AAA
* W 7	25th.	—	

Reliefs	tomorrow	will	be	begun
as	follows	aaa	B	Coy
1.30pm	via	FEBRUARY	to	BARBED
WIRE	SQUARE	aaa	C	Coy
2.15pm	via	FEBRUARY	to	ST.
NICHOLAS	aaa	D	Coy	3pm
via	NEW	CUT	and	AUGUST
to	NICHOLLS	REDOUBT	aaa	A
Coy	3.45pm	via	FEBRUARY	and
REDOUBT	LINE	to	FORESTIER	REDOUBT
aaa	Hqrs.	will	move	as
early	as	possible	but	must
be	clear	of	REDOUBT	LINE
before	1.30pm	aaa	Dinners	must
be	up	by	12 noon	aaa
Operation	order	will	follow	aaa
O's	C	Coys	are	reminded

From
Place
Time

The above may be forwarded as now corrected. (Z)

Censor. Signature of Addressor or person authorised to telegraph in his name.

* This line should be erased if not required.

750,000. W 2186—M509. H. W. & V., Ld. 6/16.

"C" Form.

Army Form C. 2123.
(In books of 100).

MESSAGES AND SIGNALS.

No. of Message

Prefix SM Code Words 56
Charges to collect
Service Instructions.

Received. From By

Sent, or sent out. At 8.03 m. To By

Office Stamp. JMS 29/3/17

Handed in at J 1 3 Office 10.30 p.m. Received 10.40 p.m.

TO JMS

*Sender's Number	Day of Month	In reply to Number	AAA
BM789	29		

Please cancel my verbal instructions re relief AAA orders just received from HUNT that para 2 of Bde order no 97 must be adhered to AAA acknowledge /

Ack
[illegible]

Recd [illegible] 29/11/16
29/[illegible]

FROM CHASE
PLACE & TIME 10·20 pm

* This line should be erased if not required.

(4). Wt. W7403/M857. 500,000 Pads. 10/16. D. D. & L. (E 189). Forms C/2123/3.

Place.	Date.	Hour.	Summary of Events and Information.	Remarks and References to Appendices.
RESERVES. OLD J III H QRS. ARRAS	1/3/17.	8. A.M.	REGIMENTAL STRENGTH 43. OFFICERS 852 OTHER RANKS DISTRIBUTED as follows:- IN RESERVES 34 OFFICERS & 662 O. RANKS – DETACHED 9 OFFICERS 194 O. RANKS "A" COY. FORRESTIER REDOUBT "B" COY 3 PLATOONS at GAS WORKS and 1 platoon at DIVL WORKSHOPS. "C" COY ST NICHOLAS. "D" COY NICHOLLS REDOUBT and BATTN H QRS at old J III SUB SECTION	
"			Working parties furnished 6 Officers & approx 300. O Ranks. Considerable Enemy artillery & T.M. activity 2. O. RANKS wounded. Our own and Enemy aeroplanes very active.	
		10. AM.	C.O. & 2nd in Command inspected RESERVES	
"		10 PM 11.30 PM	Very heavy enemy bombardment of FRONT & SUPPORT LINES by ENEMY lasting for one & half hours.	
"	2/3/17	5 AM to 6.30 AM	Very heavy bombardment of line by enemy, who afterwards attempted a raid but was repulsed with severe loss, one only succeeded in getting through and was killed. Considerable sniping of enemy during day who were hung up in barbed wire and endeavouring to get back.	
"		9.30	C.O. & 2nd in Command inspected RESERVES Working parties furnished as for yesterday.	
"		6.0 PM	Operation Order No 91. dated 2/3/17. re move to "Y" HUTMENTS & PENIN received from B H qrs.	APP 303
"	3/3/17	9.30 AM	In accordance with O.O No 91 the 3RD S A INF was relieved by the 10th ARGYLL & SUTHERLAND HIGHLANDERS relief commenced at 9.30 AM and effected by 1.0 P.M. Companies as relieved marched out and occupied Y HUTMENTS ETRUN where good accommodation was secured. 1. OTHER RANK wounded. Advised MAJOR YOUNG in hospital and struck off strength	APP 304

304

3rd S.A. Infy. **War Diary.** Transvaal Regt. 17

Place	Date	Hour	Summary of Events and Information	Remarks and References to Appendices
ETRUN. Y HUTS PENIN	4/3/17	8.45 A.M.	REGIMENT moved out from "Y" HUTMENTS en route for PENIN for training	
		12.0 NOON	Skirting AUBIGNY the REGt. halted for mid-day meal.	
PENIN		2.40 P.M.	REGIMENT arrived PENIN and occupied BILLETS. accommodation good.	
	5/3/17.	8 AM	REGIMENTAL STRENGTH 42 OFFICERS 850 O.RANKS INCLUDING DETACHED Commanding Officer & 2nd in Command spent the whole of the day inspecting Coys: Kit & Equipment, and holding conference with Company Commanders with a view to re-organisation compatible with organisation and training instructions received from B.H.Qrs. programme of Training drawn up and issued to Coy. Commdrs. for coming week.	
	6/3/17	9 AM	REGIMENTAL STRENGTH 42 OFFICERS 850 O.RANKS AVAILABLE FOR TRAINING 32 OFFICERS and 627 O.RANKS DETACHED - NOT AVAILABLE for TRAINING 10 OFFICERS and 223. O.RANKS these are on Divl. & Brigade Employ Hospital Courses & various duties - The whole of Regt went into training special attention being given to "NEW FORM OF ATTACK" BOMBING, DUMMY and RIFLE GRENADES	
			Notification received striking 2/Lt WILLIAMS G.W. off strength - unfit Working party of 1 Officer and 60 O.R. furnished yesterday & today with T.M. School to be continued until further notice.	APP 305
	7.3.17	9 AM	REGT in training as per programme - O.C. Regt inspected billets and accommodation - Usual working party of 1 Officer & 60 o.ranks furnished	
	8.3.17.	9 AM	Training as per programme during fore-noon - The whole of Regiment put through baths and supplied with clean clothes during afternoon - Lectures and instructions given.	

305

3rd S.A. Infy. **War Diary.** Transvaal Regt. 18

Place	Date	Hour	Summary of Events and Information	Remarks and References to Appendices
PENIN	MAR 9	9 A.M. 1 P.M. 2/30. 4/30	REGIMENT in training as per programme. MUSKETRY. also LEWIS GUNS. working party furnished as usual (1 officer 60. O. RANKS).	
"	10	9. A.M.	Regiment in Training + Musketry - Operation Order No. 92 d/d 9/3/17 detailing move to MONCHY BRETON TRAINING AREA.	APP 306
"	11	1. A.M.	Wire received from BHQ postponing move for 24 hours and Regt continued training in consequence.	APP. 307
"		9.10 A.M.	Wire received from BHQ ordering Regt to parade at 3.30 pm at HERMAVILLE for inspection by Secretary for Colonies x and Regiment brought in from Training Ground accordingly. (x Div. Commdr)	APP 308
"		12.30 p.m.	Regt marched to HERMAVILLE by Colonial Secretary unable to inspect the Regt owing to break-down of Motor car	APP 309
"	12	9. A.M.	In accordance with Brigade Operation Order No 93 d/d 9.3.17 the Regiment moved to MONCHY BRETON training area via AVERDOINGT and LIGNY ST FLOCHEL	APP. 310
MARQUAY		11.30 A.M.	Regiment arrived and went into Billets accommodation not very good. Disposition as follows:- A.D.C + Batt. H.Qrs at MARQUAY with B Coy at OSTREVILLE O.C + 2nd in Command inspected Billets and accommodation and TRAINING facilities generally.	
"	13	9. A.M.	Battalion went into training at O.27.d due N.E ROCOURT	
		8/9 p.m	The O.C. gave a lecture to all Officers of the Regiment on NEW SCHEME and Generalities - Major YOUNG Struck off Strength -	
"	14	8 A.M.	TOTAL REGIMENTAL STRENGTH 42 Officers and 850 O.Ranks of which 4 Officers and 114 O.Ranks are detached on various duties + in Hospital leaving a total of 38 Officers and 736 O.Ranks at training.	
"		9 A.M. 4 P.M.	Batt. in training and Musketry - at approx U.3 a 1/40.000. Working party, 1 Officer and 60 O.Ranks returned from LIGNY ST. FLOCHEL	

306

Place.	Date.	Hour.	Summary of Events and Information.	Remarks and References to Appendices.
MARQUAY	MAR 14	8/9 pm	Lecture given by Officer Commanding to all Officers of the Regiment on NEW SCHEME and Tactics	
"	MAR 15	9 AM to 4 pm	Battalion at training and MUSKETRY.	
"	MAR 16	7 pm 4 30 / 6/9 pm	Battalion in training as per instructions laid down in circular of instructions received from B.H.Q. under this date specialising in NIGHT WORK which particular training was carried out by the 4 Batts of S.A.1 Bde from 6 to 9 pm. 2/Lieut INGARFIELD reported for duty.	APP. 311
"	MAR 17	2 pm 5 pm / 6.30 to 8/30 pm	Battalion training as usual / 3rd & 4th Regiments S.A.I. carried out NIGHT ATTACK	
"	" 18		Resting with Concerts & amusements for all ranks. C.O. inspected Billets. etc.	
"	" 19	9 AM to 12 30 pm	Battn. practised Scheme of Offense.	
"	"	1/30 to 4 pm	Battn. practised Scheme of Offense & Musketry. Concert & amusements in Evening. The day very wet & cold.	
"	MAR 20	9.15 AM	In accordance with Brigade circular d/d 16/3/17 the Regiment marched out to training area to participate in Brigade attack. Weather bitterly cold and sleet & snow fell intermittently.	(APP. 311)
"	"	11 AM	Offensive operations commenced, and various phases of form of attack carried out by S.A. 1 Brigade.	
"	"	2 pm	[illegible] returned to Billets.	

307

3rd S.A. Infy. **War Diary.** Transvaal Regt. 20

Place.	Date.	Hour.	Summary of Events and Information.	Remarks and References to Appendices.
MARQUAY	20/3/17	8 pm	Warning received of probable move early 21/3/17. M.O. (Capt Manning) returned to duty off leave (attached).	App 311 A
"	21/3/17	1 AM	Operation Order No 93 d/d 20/3/17 received from B.H.Q detailing move to HAUTE AVESNES	App 312
		10 AM	In accordance with Bde Hq O.O No 93 the 3rd SAI evacuated billets at MARQUAY and OSTREVILLE and proceeded via MAIN ARRAS-ST POL ROAD to HAUTE AVESNES	App 313
HAUTE AVESNES		3.30 pm	Regiment arrived at HAUTE AVESNES and occupied Huts. Capt H Montgomery reported sick at MARQUAY and admitted to hospital. Bitterly cold day, windy, with snow & sleet. REGIMENTAL STRENGTH 43 Officers 840 O RANKS. including hospital, Courses & detached on various duties (6 Officers and 116 O. Ranks.)	
"	22/3/17	8 AM	Battalion at rest. Working parties detailed for work with 17th Corps heavy ARTILLERY at ANZIN consisting of 4 Officers 4 Sgts and 200 O Ranks.	
"	23/3/17	9 AM	Move order No 94 received from B.H.Q re move to Y HUTMENTS tomorrow. Cold, Snow & sleet intermittently. 2/Lt DAVIS detailed for duty at TINCQUES 1 O.R. acc. wounded. (RSM LAWSON)	App 314
	"	9 Am to 4 pm	Training from 9 am. Offensive instruction & Firing on Range	
"	24/3/17	9 Am	Training from 9 am to 12 Noon	
	24/3/17	3. 0 pm	In accordance with Bde Operation Order No 94 d/d 23/3/17 the 3rd SAI Evacuated HUTMENTS at HAUTE AVESNES and moved to Y HUTMENTS move being completed by 4. 30 p.m.	
Y Huts ETRUN	"	4. 30 pm	Arrived in billets	

308

In lieu of A.F. C 2118.

3rd S.A. INFANTRY. WAR DIARY. TRANSVAAL REGT.

PLACE	DATE	HOUR	SUMMARY OF EVENTS & INFORMATION.	REMARKS & REFERENCES TO APPENDICES.
Y. HUTMENTS ETRUN	25/3/17	8. A.M.	REGIMENTAL STRENGTH. 43. OFFICERS. 837 O. RANKS this includes 11 Officers and 340. O. RANKS detached on courses hospital & various duties including 4 Officers and 204 O. Ranks as permanent working party, detached with 17 Corps HEAVY ARTILLERY	
"		10. A.M.	Inspection carried out by C Commdrs of all Specialists Equipt clothing &c.	
"		pm.	G.O.C. Div Command carried out a general inspection of Battalion special attention being paid to clothing & equipment with view to making up any deficiencies.	
"		6. 30	Draft of 2 Officers (2/Lts C.F. COXEN & H KIRKBY) and 81 O.RANKS arrived and posted to COYS. – Working party of 4 Officers and 204 O Ranks returned from 17 Corps HEAVY ARTILLERY.	
"	26/3/17	8. A.M.	2 Officers and 100. OTHER RANKS furnished for working party with Canadian Heavy Artillery, other Officers & remaining portion of Regt at training as per programme. REGTL STRENGTH 45 Officers 913. O. RANKS WITH UNIT. 37. Offrs 754 O. RANKS. DETACHED on various duties 8 Officers. 159. O. RANKS.	~~APP~~
"		2. 45 pm	Warning telegram received from BHQ re move to ARRAS on 28th.	APP. 315.
	27. 3. 17	8. AM.	Working party furnished as for yesterday. Regiment at training musketry. Baths. amusements in evening.	
"		3. p.m.	Billeting party sent forward to ARRAS. re move	
		10 p.m.	Operation Order No 96 d/d 27/3/17 received from B.H.Q re move to ARRAS	APP. 316
	28/3/17.	8. AM	Usual working party furnished (2 Offs 100 O.Ranks) Regiment at training, Bombing & Baths.	
"	"	6 PM	In accordance with Brigade Operation Order No 96 d/d 27/3/17 the 3rd SAI evacuated Y HUTMENTS and moved to ARRAS for relief of 5th CAMERON HdRS 26 INFY BRIGADE – VIA MAIN ST POL – ARRAS Road.	
ARRAS	"	11 PM	RELIEF completed – Disposition of Battn. A.B.C Coys at CONVENT	

309

Place	Date	Hour	Summary of Events and Information	Remarks and references to Appendices
ARRAS	28/3/17	11 PM	"D" Coy at ST NICHOLAS with Batt. HQ at HOTEL DE L'UNIVERS	
"	"		CAPT. H MONTGOMERY returned to duty.	
"	29/3/17		STRENGTH 45 O and 912 OR – with unit 36 Officers and 714 O Ranks DETACHED 9 Officers and 178 O Ranks.	
"	"		14 Officers and 349 O Ranks furnished for various working parties and duties during day. Casualties 1 Killed 1 Died of wounds 1 Wounded. (other ranks) Casualties sustained while on working parties.	
"	"		G.O.C. in Command inspected Quarters & Billets and arrangements for accommodation & cooking during day. Operation order No 97 received from BHQ re relief of 2nd Regt in FRONT LINE tomorrow	App. 317
"	30/3/17		Numerous working parties furnished during the day	
		7/15 pm	In accordance with Bde O.O. No 97 d/a 29/3/17 the 3rd S.A.I commenced relief of 2nd S.A.I in front line and supports of CENTRE BATTn J.II. TRENCHES 86 F to JUNCTION 91/92	
ARRAS CENTRE BATTN		10 pm	Relief of 2nd S.A.I completed. Disposition: B & C Coys in FRONT LINE and SUPPORTS with D Coy at CANDLE FACTORY and A Coy at BRITANNIA WORK with Battn HQs at Brigade BATTLE H.Q. DUGOUTS. BEHIND FORRESTIER REDOUBT.	
IN TRENCHES	31/3/17		Working party of 2 Officers & 100 O Ranks D Coy working on Artillery TRENCH and small parties furnished for general clearing of trenches. SITUATION NORMAL. 1 O.R Killed & 4 wounded.	
"				

Instructions regarding War Diaries and Intelligence Summaries are contained in F. S. Regs., Part II. and the Staff Manual respectively. Title pages will be prepared in manuscript.

WAR DIARY
or
INTELLIGENCE SUMMARY.
(*Erase heading not required.*)

Army Form C. 2118.

23

Place	Date	Hour	Summary of Events and Information	Remarks and references to Appendices
ARRAS CENTRE BATTⁿ	31/3/17	10pm	O.C. + 2/in Command visited LINE. TRENCHES in a bad state and every endeavour being made to clean and repair them in view of forthcoming operations.	
			GENERAL	
"	"	"	The casualties for the past month have been slight, only twelve (12) having occurred in all ranks. 1 OR Killed 2 OR died of wounds and 9 OR wounded one of which was accidental.	
"	"	"	AVERAGE DAILY STRENGTH OF REGT 850 O Ranks, of which the average daily number reporting sick was 23. while the actual number of admissions to hospital for the whole month was only 70 O Ranks inclusive of 8 O Ranks DENTAL TREATMENT 6 EAR CASES and 1 EYE CASE.	
"	"	"	During the Regiment's occupation of trenches particular attention has been paid to cleaning and strengthening them and altho very little time has been put in by the Regiment in occupation of trenches during the month, the most has been made of the time.	
"	"	"	TRAINING The Regiment has been thoroughly trained in various methods of attack, new formation, and N.C.Os and men have been selected and trained in the various methods of fighting they are most adaptable to. SPECIALISTS have been fully equipped and instructed in their various duties, and the whole Regiment has been reorganised for tactical purposes under NEW SCHEME as laid down by Brigadier General S.A. 1 Bde – while full advantage has been taken of the opportunities and facilities of carrying	311

Instructions regarding War Diaries and Intelligence Summaries are contained in F. S. Regs., Part II. and the Staff Manual respectively. Title pages will be prepared in manuscript.

WAR DIARY
or
~~INTELLIGENCE~~ SUMMARY.
(Erase heading not required.)

Army Form C. 2118.

24

Place	Date	Hour	Summary of Events and Information	Remarks and references to Appendices
ARRAS CENTRE BATTN	31/3/17		out preliminary operations, on the training area allotted on a similar scale to actual scheme laid down for forthcoming operations. All ranks have been given facilities for bathing and changes of clean clothes, while amusements have been arranged in the ~~shape~~ form of Smoking Concerts, Cinemas etc toning up the spirits of the men whose morale is excellent.	
"	"			

E. F. Thackeray. Lieut. Col.
Commanding 3rd S A INFANTRY

312

A5834 Wt. W4973/M687 750,000 8/16 D. D. & L. Ltd. Forms/C.2118/13.

Secret

Copy 3 303

313

1ST SOUTH AFRICAN INFANTRY BRIGADE.

Map Reference
Sheet 51C
1/40,000

ORDER NO. 91. 2rd March 1917.

1 MOVE. The 1st South African Infantry Brigade will be relieved by the 26th Infantry Brigade on 3rd and 4th instant as per March table attached.

2. MOVEMENT. Each unit will proceed to new area by march route and will move from ARRAS to Y Hutments by parties not larger than platoons at intervals of 400 yards. In ARRAS and ST NICHOLAS troops must move in single file on one side of street or road and every precaution taken to conceal movement. Beyond Y Hutments Units will march by companies at intervals of 400 yards.

3. ADVANCE PARTIES. Each unit will sendusual advance parties under an officer 24 hours prior to times of marching off.

4. LOG BOOKS & MAPS. These will be handed over to relieving battalions.

5. TRENCH STORES. Receipts in duplicate (A.F.W. 3405) will be forwarded to Brigade Headquarters by noon 5th instant.

6. TRANSPORT. All first line transport will accompany units to new area. If any used for removal of stores from ARRAS, it must not enter the Town before dark.
Lorries will be provided for conveyance of stores for which no wheeled transport is allowed.

7. MEDICAL. One ambulance wagon will be detailed by A.D.M.S. 9th Division to accompany the 3rd Regiment on the march to PENIN.

8. BILLETS. Where billets are handed over by Units the usual certificates regarding their cleanliness will be sent in to Brigade H.Q. on following days.

9. BRIGADE HEADQUARTERS. Brigade Headquarters will open at PENIN at 5 pm, 4th instant.

10. REPORTS. Completion of reliefs will be reported to Brigade H.Qrs by code word "PELELE".
Arrival in new area will be reported to Brigade Headqrs within one hour of such. The time of arrival and numbers of men falling out will be given in this report.

11. ACKNOWLEDGE

A L Pepper
Captain.
A/Brigade Major.
1st S.African Infantry Brigade.

Issued thro' Signals
at 2-30 pm.

Copies			
1/4 to	1st to 4th SAI	14 to	9th Division.
5	28th M.G.Coy.	15	Staff Captain
6	SALTMBattery	16	Bde. Transport Offr.
7	64th Field Co RE	17/19	War Diary
8	Bde. Sig. Officer	20	Bde Post Office.
9.	107th Co ASC	21	Centre Group RFA
10	S.A.Field Amb.	22	9th Divl T.Ms
11	26th Inf. Bde	23	Town Major ARRAS
12	46th Inf. Bde	24	Town Major ST NICHOLAS
13	36th Inf Bde	25	102nd Inf. Bde
27	A.D.M.S. 9 Division	26	Int. Officer.

ack

SECRET. OPERATION ORDER. SE/48. 304

By B N K. 2/3/17 314

O.C. "A" Coy. "D" Coy.
"B" " H4. "
"C" "

Companies will each detail 1 Senior N.C.O. and 4 men (1 per platoon) as advance party for move of Battn on the 3rd March, 1917.

Each Company party will move off independently and report to 2/Lt W.J. DAVIS at Y HUTMENTS before 4.pm. today 2/3/17 to take over Company billets.

They must be instructed to meet their Companies at a suitable point outside the billeting area. The same advance party will proceed the following day to PENIN to take over the billets in that village, reporting under the Billeting Officer to the Town Major.

The kits of these N.C.O s and men should be returned to 1st Line Transport tonight under Company arrangements.

Rations will be deducted from tonight's issue and arranged for by the Quartermaster at the 1st Line Transport.

These billeting parties should be held in readiness to be called up to move at short notice from Y HUTMENTS to PENIN.

(sgd) A.W.H. McDonald.
Capt & Adjutant.
B A N K.

IN THE FIELD.
2/3/17. 10.0.AM.

MARCH TABLE to accompany S.African Infantry Brigade Order 91 dated 2/5/17.

DATE	UNIT	FROM	TO	REMARKS.
3/5/17	2nd S.A.Inf.	ARRAS	"Y" Huts.	On relief by 8th Black Watch, who move off from Y Huts at 8 am. Guides 2nd Regt. to be at PORTE BAUDIMONT at 9-30 am.
	3rd S.A.Inf.	ARRAS ST NICHOLAS REDOUBT LINE	"Y" Huts	On relief by 10th Argyll & Sutherland Hrs who move from Y huts at 8.5 am. Guides 3rd Regt to be at OCTROI, ST NICHOLAS (G.21.B.5.7) at ~~2-30 pm.~~ 9-30 am.✓
	26th M.G.Coy & SALT Battery	ARRAS & Right Sector.	"Y" Huts	On relief by corresponding Units of 26th Inf.Bde. who moved off from Y huts at 1 pm. Guides to be at OCTROI, ST NICHOLAS (G.21.b.5.7) at 2-30 pm.
4/5/17	S.A.Bde H.Q.	ARRAS	PENIN	
	1st S.A.I.	No.1 Section Right Sector.	"Y" Huts	On relief by 7th Seaforth Hrs., who move off from Y huts at 8 am. Guides 1st Regt to be at OCTROI ST NICHOLAS (G.21.b.5.7) at 9-30 am.
	2nd S.A.I. (less 2 Coys)	"Y" Huts	HERMAVILLE	Hour of starting to be fixed by Battalion Commander.
	2 Coys 2nd SAI	"Y" Huts	Tilloy les HERMAVILLE	Hour of starting to be fixed by Battalion Commander.
	3rd S.A.I.	"Y" Huts	PENIN	Hour of starting to be fixed by Battalion Commander.
	4th S.A.I.	No.2. Section Right Sector	"Y" Huts	On relief by 10th Argyll & Sutherland Hrs. Time of relief to be arranged between Commanding Officers concerned.

315

ECRET.

0.13.

316

~~2nd~~ Regiment.
3rd "
~~[illegible]~~
~~[illegible]~~

In connection with the forthcoming move please arrange to send your usual advance parties under an officer to take over the billets to be occupied by you at "Y" Hutments. The advance parties should report at "Y" Hutments before 4 pm today, 2nd March.

The same advance parties should proceed the following day to PENIN. to take over the billets in that village, reporting to the Town Major

A L Pepper Captain.
A/ Brigade Major.

2/3/17.

S E C R E T. O.13 317

3rd Regiment.

In connection with the forthcoming move, please arrange to send your usual advance parties under an officer to take over the billets to be occupied by you at "Y" hutments. The advance parties should report at "Y"hutments before 4 p.m. to-day 2nd March.

The same advance parties should proceed the following day to PENIN, to take over the billets in that village, reporting to the Town Major.

(sgd)------ Captain

2/3/17. A/Brigade Major.

Copies Sent - to

Assy 2/3/17
T/O
B/O

Ist SOUTH AFRICAN INFANTRY BRIGADE.

3/8

2nd Regiment.
3rd Regiment.

With reference to para.6 of Operation Order, which you will receive today.

I have to inform you that a Motor lorrie will be in the Theatre Square ARRAS at 6.p.m.3rd.instant for the purpose of moving such kits etc as you are unable to pack on Ist Line Transport. You should arrange for a guide to meet the lorrie and take it to the place where your Surplus kits etc are dumped. This will have to be at a spot of easy access to Motor Transport.

You will make your own arrangements regarding your Horsed Transport, as to time, place etc, bearing in mind that no Transport can come into ARRAS in daylight.

A Motor lorrie will be at the "Y" Hutments at 9.a.m 4th.instant to assist you in your move to (PENIN).

2.3.1917.

Captain,
Actg/Staff Captain.
Ist S.A.Infantry Brigade.

S E C R E T. 3.R.48.

OPERATION ORDER BY B A N K.

2.3.17.

319

To ____________

Companies will each detail 1 Senior N.C.O.& 4 men(1 per platoon) as advance party, for move of Battalion on the 3rd March,1917.

Each Company Party will move off independently, and report to 2/Lt W.F.DAVIS at "Y" Hutments before 4 p.m. to-day 2/3/17 to take over Company billets.

They must be instructed to meet their Companies at a suitable point outside the Billeting Area. The same Advance Party will proceed the following day to FENIN to take over the billets in that village, reporting under Billeting Officer to Town Major.

The kits of these N.C.O.s and men should be returned to 1st Line Transport to-night under Coy.arrangements.

Rations will be deducted from to-night's issue, and arranged for by Quartermaster at 1st Line Transport.

These billeting parties will be held in readiness to be called up to move at short notice from "Y" Hutments to FENIN.

Captain & Adjutant,
B a n k.

In the Field,
2/3/1917.
10.0 a.m.

3rd Regiment.

With reference to para 6 of Operation Order which you will receive to-day, I have to inform you that a motor lorry will be in the Theatre Square ARRAS at 6 p.m. 3rd instant, for the purpose of removing such kits etc. as you are unable to pack on 1st Line Transport. You should arrange for a guide to meet the lorry and take it to the place where your surplus kits etc are dumped. This will have to be at a spot of easy access to Motor Transport.

You will make your own arrangements regarding your own horsed transport, as to time place etc.,bearing in mind that no Transport can come into ARRAS in daylight.

A motor lorry will be at the "Y" Hutments at 9 a.m. 4th instant to assist you in your move to (FENIN).

2/3/1917. (sgd) ----- Staff Captain

Copies each to Cmd.
T/O
Billeting Officer } 11am 2/3/17

Copy No 320

Operation Order. 3R/49

Secret

2-3-17

By BANK

1 Move. The 1st South African Infty Bgde will be relieved by 26th Infty Bgde on the 3rd/4th inst as per march table.
The 3rd S.A. Infty will be relieved by 10th ARGYLE and SUTHERLAND HIGHLANDERS who move off from "Y" Huts ETRUN at 8.15 Am, 3/3/17.
The 3rd S.A Infty as relieved will march to ETRUN and occupy "Y" Huts.

2 Relief. Companies will be relieved by Corresponding Companies of 10th A. and Sutherland Highlanders, and will be effected in following order
B Coy
A "
D "
C " LAST
Companies will move off independently as soon as relieved.

to initial & Return 321

SECRET 3 R 48.

OPERATION ORDER
BY BANK.

Copies to
O.C.
A
B
C
D

2. 3. 17.

H.Q.

Coys will each detail 1 Senior N.C.O and 4 men (1 per platoon) as advance party for move of Battn. on the 3rd March

Each Coy party will move off independently & report to 2/Lt W.F. DAVIS at Y HUTMENTS before 4 pm today 2/3/17 to take over Coy. billets.

They must be instructed to meet their Coys at a suitable point outside the billeting area. The same advance party will proceed the following day to PENIN to take over the billets in that village, reporting under billeting officer to Town Mayor

II.

The Kits of these NCOs and men should be returned to 1st Line Transport tonight under Coy arrangements.

Rations will be deducted from tonights issue, and arranged for by QrMr at 1st Line Transport.

These billeting parties will be held in readiness to be called up to move at short notice from Y hutments to PENIN

[illegible]
Capt & Adjt.
BANK.

To the Field
7/2/17.
10. 0. AM.

323

"C" Form.

MESSAGES AND SIGNALS.

Army Form C. 2123
(In books of 100).

No. of Message 271

Prefix SM Code DGM Words 26	Received. From SZA By B.H. [illegible]	Sent, or sent out. At ... m. To ... By ...	Office Stamp. SIAE [illegible]
£ s. d. Charges to collect			
Service Instructions.			

Handed in at SZA Office 4.35 P.m. Received 4.47 P.

TO 3rd REGT

*Sender's Number	Day of Month	In reply to Number	AAA
BM630	20th		

Warning order aaa Brigade will move into PENIN HERMAVILLE TILLOY HAUTE-AVESNES area tomorrow aaa Further orders follow

Sergt [illegible]

Received 4.57 P.m. @ [illegible]

Qm [illegible]

FROM S A Bde
PLACE & TIME 4.30 PM

* This line should be erased if not required.

(6344). Wt. W7496/M857. 500,000 Pads. 10/16. D. D. & L. (E 489). Forms C/2123/3.

RD 271

305

324

Ist SOUTH AFRICAN INFANTRY BRIGADE.

3rd.Regiment.

-----------   W.P.3/5.

Will you please detail a permanent working party 60 strong under an Officer with proportion of N.C.Os, to relieve a similar party of the 27th.Brigade working at the Third Army Trench Mortar School, LINGNY St FLOCHEL. The relief is to take place on the 5th.instant.

Rations for day should be carried.

3.3.17.

[signature] Pepper
Captain,
Actg/Brigade Major.
Ist S. A. Infantry Brigade.

325

V

relieving. Observing strict interval of 400 yards between platoons when on the march between ETRUN in ARRAS and St NICHOLAS. Troops must move in single file on one side of the street or road and every precaution taken to conceal movement.
B Coy. to move by Platoons as relieved.
A Coy. when relieved will evacuate via APRIL AVENUE. The relief will move forward via MAY AVENUE.

'D' Coy. on relief will evacuate via OCTOBER. The relief will move forward via NOVEMBER AVENUE.

"C" To move by Platoons as soon as relieved. through St NICHOLAS VILLAGE.

HQrs Coy. Will move as soon as relieved. and move to ETRUN in 2 parties under the Intelligence Officer and Signalling Officer.
Companies will report relief

326

3

Relief by runner by Code as "PELELE"

O/C A.B.C.D. and HQ Companies will each furnish an NCO and 4 men (1 per platoon) as guides to the relieving Battalion. They must report to R.S.M. MEREDITH at the OCTROI ST NICHOLAS G.21.B 5.7. at 9.30 AM tomorrow 3-2-17

3. Advance parties - as detailed.

(4.) LOG BOOKS & Maps these will be handed over to relieving Battalions

(5) TRENCH STORES Receipts in duplicate (AFW 3405) will be furnished to Battalion O Room on arrival at ETRUN

(6) Transport. The T/O will detail the following transport to report as soon as possible after dusk tomorrow evening. 9th to H.Q. and Companies baggage Dumps

To 9th	1	Officers Mess Cart	CANDLE FACTORY
	1	MALTESE "	do
	2	G.S. Limbered Wagons	do
	2	do for Lewis Guns	do
	1	do - do	B Company

328

"C" Form.

Army Form C. 2123.
(In books of 100).

MESSAGES AND SIGNALS.

No. of Message

Prefix S B Code M D Words 11	Received.	Sent, or sent out.	Office Stamp.
£ s. d. Charges to collect	From S Z N By C Huttempton	At m. To By	20/5/17
Service Instructions. S Z A Priority			

Handed in at Office m. Received m.

TO 3rd Regt

*Sender's Number	Day of Month	In reply to Number	AAA
BM 613	20th	—	

Gas alert

FROM S Z A Bde
PLACE & TIME 12.40 pm

* This line should be erased if not required.

(6346). Wt. W7495/M857. 500,000 Pads. 10/16. D. D. & L. (E 489). Forms C/2123/3.

3rd South African Infty   329

BR/53   MARCH 29th 17.

1. MOVE. The 3rd South African Infty will relieve the 2nd South African Infty in the LINE tomorrow the 30th Inst. Companies will each detail an Officer and N.C.O. to report to the O/C 2nd S.A.I. at OB J 111 Head Quarters at 2/30 pm today for the purpose of taking over disposition of the Line.
Companies will take over from their opposite numeral Coy of the 2nd S.A.I.
The above Officers with Lieut HARRIS for Bn Head Qtrs will furnish by 8pm tonight a report of how their Company Line is held, and disposition of Lewis Guns.

A.W.H. McDonald Captn
Adj
3rd S.A.I.

Issd 11/40 pm

Adjt Embody & adjust for R.O.
X Dress full marching order.

3

1st SOUTH AFRICAN INFANTRY BRIGADE

SECRET. ORDER No. 92. Copy No.,....

Map Ref. Sheet ~~51B~~ 51C
Scale 1/40.000. 9th March 1917.

1. MOVE. The Brigade will move, Regt at 9 AM, to the MONCHY BRETON Training Area on March 11th ~~as per attached March Table.~~
B Co to OSTREVILLE. H.Q. A C D A Co at MARQUAY. Starting point C Co. Bn.

2. MOVEMENT. Movement will be by Companies with 400 yards interval and usual precautions will be taken regarding enemy aircraft.
In the following order - B. C. D. A. - Band & H.Q. with C Co. - A Co. to find 1 Platoon Rear Guard. M.G. with A Co.

3. BILLETING PARTIES. The usual billeting parties will proceed at 2 PM 11-3-17 ~~twenty four hours~~ in advance. under Lt. Egan - to consist of 1 N.C.O. per Co. 1 man per platoon & H.Q. Band 1. M.O. 1 Sig. 1.

4. INSPECTIONS. Immediately the Unit has marched off, the vacated huts and billets will be inspected by the 2nd in Command (and ~~in Infantry Units~~ the Medical Officer) ~~of each Unit.~~
A written report of such inspection will be sent in to Brigade Headquarters by 6.p.m.11th instant. (Regt 4 PM)

5. TRANSPORT. Transport will accompany Units to New Area. Lorries will be provided for special stores. Transport in following order:
4. L.G. Limbers. Medical Cart - 2 W Carts - Cooking Carts - SAA

6. WORKING PARTIES. (a) The 2nd and 4th Regiments will furnish the usual working parties of 200 and 50 men at BOIS D'HARBARCQ and LARESSET respectively on March 11th. On completion of work these parties will be conveyed by lorries to Training area.
(b) On March 12th. The 27th. Infantry Brigade will relieve the working party of 8 Officers and 250 Other Ranks furnished by 1st and 4th Regiments for work at ANZIN under XVII Corps Heavy Artillery.
(c) On March 14th. the 26th Infantry Brigade will relieve the permanent party of 1 Officer and 60 men of the 3rd. Regiment at the Third Army Trench Mortar School, LIGNY St FLOCHEL.

7. MACHINE GUNS. On March 12th. the 26th. M.G.Coy. will relieve one Section (4 guns) of 28th. M.Gun Coy. employed on anti-aircraft defence of LARESSET and BOIS D'HABARCQ.

8. REPORTS. Marching in States will be sent to Brigade Headquarters (Regt) within one hour of time of units' arrival. On this state will be given Map Reference of Units Headquarters and also the number of men who fell out on the march.

9. BRIGADE HEADQUARTERS. Close at PENIN 10.a.m. and open at ORLENCOURT at same hour.
Batt. H.Q. MARQUAY.

10. Acknowledge.

[stamp: 1 MAR 1917]

A. G. Pepper
Captain,
Acting Brigade Major.
1st S. A. Infantry Brigade.

Issued at 8.15.p.m. through Signals
as per Brigade Distribution List.

All Buglers at (?) Qm by 8 am
L.G.O.
T.O.
M.O.
Q.M.
S.O.

MARCH TABLE.

TO ACCOMPANY BRIGADE ORDER No.92.

Unit.	From.	To.	Route.	Approximate Distance:Miles.	Remarks.
BRIGADE H.Qrs.	PENIN.	ORLENCOURT.	Via la NEUVILLE PLANQUETTE and BAILLEUL - AUX - CORNAILLES.	6¼.	
1st REGIMENT H.Qrs & 2.Coys.	Y.HUTS.	MONCHY BRETON	Via HERMAVILLE - TILLOY - BERLES - CHELERS.	15½.	Head of Column to pass X Roads at C.4.d.9.3 at 2.50.p.m.
2.Coys.	-do-	ORLENCOURT.	TINQUES.	16¼.	
2nd.REGIMENT.	HERMAVILLE & TILLOY les HERMAVILLE.	MONCHY BRETON.	Via VILLERS BRULIN - GUESTREVILLE AND HERLIN le VERT.	9¾.	
3rd.REGIMENT less 1 Coy.	PENIN.	MARQUAY.	Via AVERDOINGT LIGNY St FLOCHEL.	5¼.	
1.Company.	-do-	SOUTHERN PART OF OSTREVILLE.			
4th.REGIMENT.	'Y' HUTS.	OSTREVILLE.	Via HERMAVILLE - TILLOY - BERLES - TINQUES - Along ARRAS St POL MAIN ROAD MARQUAY.	16.	Head of Column to pass X Roads at C.4.d.9.3. at 3.30.p.m.
20th.Coy.M.G.Corps.	-do-	ORLENCOURT.	As for Ist.Regiment.	16¼.	-do- at 3.10.p.m.
S.A.L.T.M.BATTERY.	-do-	-do-	As for Ist.Regiment.	16¼.	-do- at 3.15.p.m.

All Units to be clear of billets by 10.a.m. Hours of starting left to Unit Commanders. Mid-day halt for Units from 'Y' Huts will be made off road between TILLOY - BERLES. Transport will not halt on Main ARRAS - St POL ROAD except at authorized hourly halts.

331

332

"C" Form

Army Form C. 2123.

MESSAGES AND SIGNALS. No. of Message

Prefix ... Code ... Words ...	Received	Sent, or sent out	Office Stamp.
£ s. d.	From	At	
Charges to collect	By	To	
Service Instructions.		By	

Handed in at ... Office ... m. Received ... m.

TO

*Sender's Number	Day of Month	In reply to Number	AAA
	10		

transport is to move with you to new training area.

*This line should be erased if not required.

333

1st S.A.I.
2nd "
3rd "
4th "

Wire 9 am See C 23

6.13.

A horsed ambulance wagon from the South African Field Ambulance will accompany each battalion on the march tomorrow.

Please wire this office time of starting so that S.A.Field Ambulance may be notified of time to send Ambulance wagon.

W.

A. L. Pepper

Captain.

A/ Brigade Major.

10/3/17. 1st S.AfricannInfantry Brigade.

333

334

"C" Form

Army Form C. 2123.
(In books of 100.)

MESSAGES AND SIGNALS.

No. of Message ....

Prefix .... Code .... Words	Received	Sent, or sent out.	Office Stamp.
£ s. d.	From	At .... m.	
Charges to collect	By	To	
Service Instructions.		By	

Handed in at [illegible] Office [illegible] Received [illegible]

TO [illegible]

Sender's Number	Day of Month	In reply to Number	AAA
[illegible]	[illegible]		

[illegible]

A [illegible]
B
C [illegible]
D [illegible]
HQ [illegible]
QM [illegible]
TO [illegible]
RSM [illegible]

Acknowledged

FROM [illegible]

PLACE & TIME [illegible]

* This line should be erased if not required.

(B 5/79) Wt. W. 7490—M857 250,000 Pads. 10/16 H & S (E436.) Forms/C.2123/3.

335

"C" Form
MESSAGES AND SIGNALS.

Army Form C. 2128.
(In books of 100.)

No. of Message

Prefix BM Code 016 Words 43

Received From Copied By Fraser

Sent, or sent out — At — To — By

Office Stamp: ARMY ... 17 ... TELEGRAPHS

Charges to collect

Service Instructions.

Handed in at S.A. Office 8.15 a.m. Received

TO 3rd Regt. S.A.I. 308

*Sender's Number	Day of Month	In reply to Number	AAA
BM 560	11th		

Reference visit of Secretary for Colonies Divisional Commander desires Battalions to parade as follows aaa 1st and 4th Regts by Huts 2.20 pm aaa 2nd and 3rd Regts at HERMAVILLE 3.15 pm aaa Further instructions later

9/10/1917

FROM S.A. Bde

PLACE & TIME 8.5 am

* This line should be erased if not required.

(B 9070) Wt. w. 7496—M257 250,000 Pads. 10/16 H & S (E436.) Forms/C.2123/3.

3

336

ADDENDUM No.1 TO OPERATION ORDER 92.

Please make the following correction to South African Infantry Brigade Order No. 92 dated 9th March.

PARA 6. WORKING PARTIES.

(b) For "27th Infantry Brigade" read "26th Inf. Brigade"

10/3/17.

[signature]

Captain.
A/ Brigade Major.
1st South African Infantry Brigade.

336

THIRD SOUTH AFRICAN INFANTRY.

3R/82. 9th March, 1917

336A

Map reference sheet 51c, 1/40,000
and
Sheet 51 B NW 3

Preliminary Instruction.

1. MOVE. The 3rd South African Infantry will relieve the 2nd South African Infantry in the Line to-morrow the 10th instant.
Companies will each detail one officer and N.C.O. to report to the O.C., 2nd S.A.I., at old [illegible] Headquarters at 8.30 p.m. to-day for the purpose of taking over disposition of the Line.
Companies will take over from their opposite numeral Company of the 2nd S.A.I..
The above officers with 2nd Lieut. HARRIS for Battn Headqrs. will furnish by 6 p.m. to-night a report of how their Company Line is held,, and disposition of Lewis Guns.

(sgd) A.W.H.McDONALD

Captain & Adjutant,

Issued 12.40 p.m. 3rd South African Infantry.

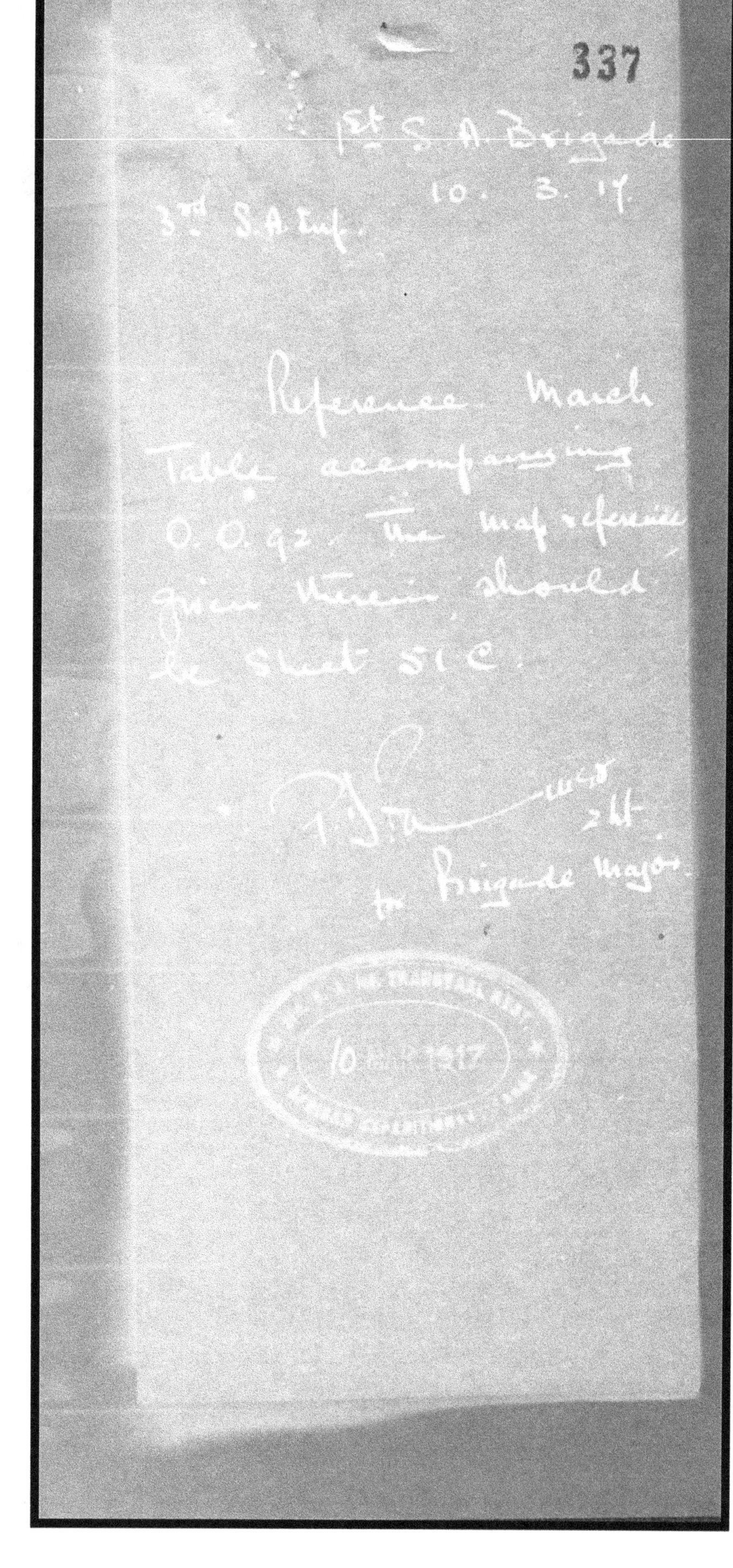
337

1st S. A. Brigade
10. 3. 17.

3rd S. A. Inf.

Reference March Table accompanying O. O. 92. The map reference given therein should be Sheet 51 C.

P. J. [illegible] 2 Lt.
for Brigade Major.

338

"C" Form

MESSAGES AND SIGNALS.

Army Form C. 2[illegible] (In books of 100)

No. of Message ....

Prefix .... Code .... Words ....

£ s. d.

Charges to collect

Service Instructions.

Received From [illegible] 4/30 pm By ....

Sent, or sent out At .... To .... By ....

Office Stamp. ARMY TELEGRAPHS 11.III.17

Handed in at [illegible] Office 4.05 p.m. Received .... m.

TO Brank.

*Sender's Number	Day of Month	In reply to Number	AAA
BM 369	11		

Moves	of	reliefs	as	per
Bde	Order	no	92	will
take	place	tomorrow	aaa	Please
arrange	time	of	starting	and
C =	Os.	conference	at	PENIN
at	11 am	tomorrow	aaa	Acknowledge

Recd 4.40 p.m. [illegible]

Ack [illegible]

FROM S.R. Bde.

TIME 7.15 pm

* This line should be erased if not required.

M.S.7 250,000 Pads. 10/16 H & S (E436.) Forms/C.2123/3.

Urgent

309

B.M. 20

339

1st S.A.I.
2nd "
3rd "
4th "
SALTMBattery

With reference to the visit of the Secretary for the Colonies, the following parades will take place.

(1) 1st and 4th Regiments with Trench Mortar Battery will be formed up by 2.10 p.m., on the same ground as that occupied on the recent inspection by the Field Marshall, Commander-in-Chief, and in the same formation.

Should it not be possible for the Staff Captain to place Base Markers, the Adjutant of the 4th battalion will carry out this duty.

(2) 2nd and 3rd battalions will be formed up by 3-5 p.m., on the football ground at HERMAVILLE.

The Adjutant of the 2nd Battalion will place Brigade Markers.

These battalions will be formed up in close column of companies at 12 paces distance.

Companies will be equalised in size.

Officers will take posts in review order.

The Divisional Commander will be received with the "General Salute".

[signature] Pepper
Captain.
A/Brigade Major
1st S. African Infantry Brigade.

11/3/17.

310

3rd SOUTH AFRICAN INFANTRY.

SECRET ORDER No. 3 R/50. Copy No. ______

Map ref. Sheet ~~36-B.~~ 51a
Scale. 1/40,000. 10th March, 1917.

340

1. MOVE. The Regiment will move at 9 a.m. via AVERDOINGT and LIGNY St FLOCHEL (5½ miles) to the MONCHY BRETON Training Area on 11th March. "B" Company to OSTERVILLE. Headquarters, "C", "D" and "A" Companies at MARQUAY.
Starting Point "C" Company Quarters AVERDOINGT Road.

2. MOVEMENT. Movement will be by Companies with 400 yards interval in the following order "B", "C", "D", and "A" - Band and Headquarters with "C" Company. "A" Company to find 1 Platoon Rearguard - M.O. with "A" Company.
The usual precautions will be taken regarding enemy aircraft.

3. BILLETING PARTIES. The usual Billeting Parties will proceed at 2 p.m. 10.3.1917, in advance, under 2/Lt.C.M.EGAN - to consist of 1 N.C.O. per Company, 1 man per Platoon, and Headquarters: Band 1, M.O. 1, Signallers 1, Quartermaster 1, Orderly Room 1.

4. DRESS. Full Mraching Order.

5. INSPECTIONS. Immediately the Unit has marched off, the vacated huts and billets will be inspected by the 2nd in command and the Medical Officer. A written report of such inspection will be sent in to Regimental Headquarters by 4 p.m. 11th instant.

6. TRANSPORT. Transport will accompany Units to New Area, Lorries will be provided for special stores.
Transport in following order:- 4 Lewis Gun Limbers, Medical Cart 2 Water Carts, Officers' Mess cart, 4 Company Cookers, S.A.A. and G.S. wagons.

7. KITS. All baggage to be at Company Headquarters by 8 a.m.

8. WORKING PARTIES. On March 14th the 26th Infantry Brigade will relieve the permanent party of 1 Officer and 60 men of the 3rd Regiment at the Third Army Trench Mortar School, LIGNY ST FLOCHEL.

9. REPORTS. Marching in States will be sent to Regimental Headquarter within one hour of time of Company's arrival. On this State will be given Map Reference of Company's Headquarters, and also the number of men who fell out on the march.

10. BATTALION HEADQUARTERS : MARQUAY.

Issued at 11.30 a.m.
per Runner.

J Estill
2/Lieutenant,
for Captain & Adjutant,
3rd South African Infantry.

Issued to "A" Coy. L.G.O.
"B" Coy. T.O.
"C" Coy. M.O.
"D" Coy. I.O.
"H.Q."Coy. S.O.
Q.Mr.

341

SECRET.

3rd South African Infantry.

Order No 3R.50.

MAP REFERENCE 10 March 1917.

Sheet 51E Scale 1/40.000.

(1) MOVE. The regiment will move at 9 am. via AVERDOINGT and LIGNY ST. FOCHEL (5½ MILES) to the MONCHY BRETON training area on 11th March. B Coy to OSTREVILLE. Hqrs "C" + "D" and "A" Coys at MARQUAY Starting Point "C" Coy Qrs AVERDOINGT Road.

(2) MOVEMENT: Movement will be by companies with 400yards interval in the following order "B" "C" "D" and "A" - Band and Head Qrs with "C" Coy "A" Coy to find 1 platoon Rearguard - M.O. with "A" Coy

The usual precautions will be taken regarding enemy air-craft.

3. BILLETING PARTIES The usual billeting parties will proceed at 2 p.m. 10.3.1917 in advance under 2/Lt. C.M.EGAN to consist of 1 N.C.O. per Coy 1 man per platoon, and Headquarters, Band 1 MO 1 Signallers 1

II

Quarter Master 1 Orderly room 1

342

4 Dress Full marching Order

5 INSPECTIONS Immediately the unit has marched off, the vacated huts and billets will be inspected by the Offr commanding and the M.O. A written report of such inspection will be sent in to Reg HQrs by 4 pm. 11th inst.

6 TRANSPORT. Transport will accompany Units to New Area. Lorries will be provided for special stores. Transport in the following order:- 4 Lewis Gun Limbers Medical Cart, 2 water carts, Officer's mess cart 4 Coy Cookers S.A.A & G.S. wagons.

7 KITS. All baggage to be at Coy headquarters by 8 A.M.

8 WORKING PARTIES On March 11th the 76th Infantry Bde will relieve the permanent working party of 1 Officer and 60 men of the 3rd Regt at the 3rd Army T.M. School, LINGY ST FLOCHEL

III.

(9) REPORTS Marching in STATES will be sent to Regimental Headquarters within one hour of time of Coy's arrival. On this State will be given map reference of Coy. Head Quarters and also the number of men who fell out on the march.

(10) BATTALION HEADQUARTERS :: MARQUAY

(Signed) J. Eskill

Lieut. for
Capt. & Adjutant
3rd South African
Infantry

Issued 11.30 AM
per runner

Issued to A Coy | L.G.O.
B Coy | T.O.
C Coy | M.O.
D Coy | I.O.
HQ Coy | S.O.
Q.M.

Ist SOUTH AFRICAN INFANTRY BRIGADE.

Ist Regiment.
2nd Regiment.
3rd Regiment.
4th Regiment.
28th.M.G.Coy.
S.A.L.T.M.Battery.

Please note that my Minute T.8 of the 14th.instant is cancelled, and Training will be carried out as detailed hereunder :-

NIGHT WORK:

FRIDAY	16th inst.	...	all 4 Battalions.
SATURDAY	17th inst.	...	3rd and 4th Regts.
MONDAY	19th inst.	...	1st and 2nd Regts.

On the days units are doing NIGHT work no morning work will be done - Units are to be on the ground ready to commence work at 2.p.m.

Battalions will carry out the attack over the Taped-out trenches on the following days :-

SATURDAY	17th inst.	...	Ist Regiment, morning.
"	" "	...	2nd Regiment, afternoon.
MONDAY	19th "	...	3rd Regiment, morning.
"	" "	...	4th Regiment, afternoon.

The Brigade will carry out attack on the 20th instant.

There will be no training on the 18th instant.

The Range will be allotted as follows :-

SATURDAY	17th inst.	...	Morning 2nd Regiment.
"	" "	...	Afternoon 1st "
MONDAY	19th "	...	Morning 4th "
"	" "	...	Afternoon 3rd " -

16.3.17.

Captain,
Brigade Major.
Ist S.A.Infantry Brigade.

SECRET.

Ist SOUTH AFRICAN INFANTRY BRIGADE.

Copy No......

Map. Reference
Sheet 51.C
1-40,000

ORDER No.93.

30th March, 1917.

1. MOVE. The Brigade will move tomorrow 31st. instant to the PENIN - HERMAVILLE AREA in accordance with March table attached.

2. MOVEMENT.

Time of starting is left to Battalion Commanders. The following distances will be maintained between Units on the March.-

Between Companies 200 yards.
" Battalions 400 yards.
" Transport of individual Units 100 yards.

3. TRANSPORT.

Transport will accompany Units. If possible one lorry per unit will assist in conveying Stores.

4. BILLETTING PARTIES.

The usual billetting parties will proceed to New Area as early as possible.

5. WORKING PARTIES.

Working parties will be furnished by Units as per attached working table.

6. MEDICAL.

A horsed Ambulance wagon will accompany each Infantry Unit.

7. BRIGADE HEADQUARTERS.

Brigade Headquarters will close at ORLENCOURT at 10.a.m. and open at PENIN noon tomorrow.

8. REPORTS.

Marching in States showing numbers falling out will be sent in to Brigade Headquarters within one hour of arrival in new billets.

Please ack

A. T. Pepper
Captain,
Brigade Major.
Ist S.A. Infantry Brigade.

Ack

Issued to Orderly at 10.p.m.,
as per Brigade Distribution List.

Recd 1 AM 21/3/17

346

1st SOUTH AFRICAN INFANTRY BRIGADE.

MARCH TABLE ISSUED WITH BRIGADE ORDER No. 95, 20/3/1917.

Unit.	From.	To.	Route.	Remarks.
Brigade Headquarters.	Orlencourt	Penin	Via Bailleul - La Neuville - Planquette	Not to arrive at destination before 11.a.m.
1st. Regiment S. A. Infantry.	Monchy - Breton and Orlencourt.	Haute Avesnes.	Via Chelers, Tinques and Main Arras - St Pol Rd.	-do-
2nd. Regiment S.A. Infantry.	Monchy - Breton.	Hermaville Tilloy	Via Chelers - Tinques.	=do=
3rd. Regiment S.A. Infantry.	Marquay.	Haute - Avesnes.	Via Main Arras - St Pol Rd.	Road from C.12.B.9.7 to D.19.B.4.7. and from D.13 Central through Berles to D.9.c.10.2 is closed. Not to arrive at destination before 11.a.m.
4th. Regiment S.A. Infantry.	Ostreville	Penin.	Via Marquay - Averdoingt.	=do=
28th. Coy. M.G. Corps.	Orlencourt.	Penin	= As for Brigade Headquarters.	=do=
S.A.L.T.M. Battery.	Orlencourt.	Penin	= As for Brigade Headquarters.	=do=

No halts other than the authorised halts every hour must be made on the main St. Pol - Arras Road.

Captain,
Brigade Major.
1st S.A. Infantry Brigade

1st SOUTH AFRICAN INFANTRY BRIGADE.

WORKING PARTY TABLES.

Brigade Order
No.93.

Item.	Work.	Under.	Strength of Party.	At present found by.	To be furnished by. 22nd.	To be furnished by. Until further orders	Remarks.
1.	Savy Stn.	O/C.i/c Roads 18th Cheshire Regiment	50.	26th.I.B.	2nd S.A.I.	2nd S. A. I.	(a) Daily:party to report at 8.am (b) Haversack,rations to be taken. (c) No tools required.
2.	Haute Avesnes.	Road Construction. Officer - Town Majors Office.	50.	26th.I.B.	Ist. S.A.I.	Ist S. A. I.	(a) Daily party to report at 8.am (b) Haversack rations to be taken. (c) No tools required.
3.	Habarcq Dump.	R.A.Officer i/c Dump.	15.	26th.I.B.	2nd S.A.I.	2nd. S. A. I.	Lives with R.A.at Bois d'Habarcq.
4.	Habarcq Dump.	R.A.officer i/c Dump.	15.	26th.I.B.	2nd S.A.I.	2nd. S. A. I.	Guard. on Dump.
5.	Anzin.	Corps Heavy Artillery.	200.	26th.I.B.	3rd S.A.I.	3rd S.A.I.	(a) Permanent party live and work at Anzin. (b) Relief to take place after work on March 22nd. Party of 26th.Bde rejoins Battalion on completion relief.
6.	Marœuil.	Corps Heavy Artillery.	50.	26th.I.B.	Ist S.A.I.	Ist S.A.I.	(a) Permanent party as above but at Marœuil. (b) As for (5).

The numbers shown are of men required for work, Officers and N.C.O.s should be detailed in addition. One Officer to be detailed for every 50 men.

All reliefs of permanent Working parties will be carried out so as not to interfere with continuity of work.

Officers and N.C.O.s i/c parties will ascertain all details of relief on 21st.instant from Units to be relieved.

To O.C. A Coy. B Coy. C Coy. D Coy. H.Q.Coy. I.O. L.G.O. T.O. Q.Mr.

348

1. MOVE. The Battalion will move at 9 a.m. to-morrow the 12th March, 1917 in accordance with operation order 3 R/50 dated 10th March, 1917.

Issued at 8.15 p.m.
by Runner

Captain & Adjutant,

11/3/1917. 3rd Regiment, S.A. Infantry.

9.7.9

3RD SOUTH AFRICAN INFANTRY 313

SECRET. 3R.51 MARCH 23/17.

1 MOVE. AS PER MOVE ORDER. 349

The Battalion will move from HAUTE AVESNES to Y huts tomorrow (24/3/17) commencing 9.30 AM. by PLATOONS with 50 YARDS interval in the following order–
HEAD QRS. D. A. B + C Coys

2 ROUTE
VIA ST POL - ARRAS MAIN RD

3 TRANSPORT Transport will accompany Battn. as far as Y huts and will remain there until further orders.

4 CARRYING PARTY. Carrying party for BRIGADE will be detailed and will be held in readiness to report to Brigade Head Qrs tomorrow–

5 SANITATION Coy Commdrs will see that the HUTMENTS + VACINITY are left in a clean and sanitary condition.

A Coy H.Q. M.O
B " QM I.O
C " L.G.O S.O.
D " T.O.

A. W. H. McDonald
Capt + Adjt
3rd S.A.I.

O.C.
A
B
C
D
~~HQ~~

1350

Company Commanders ~~and~~ O.C. ~~HQ~~rs will each detail a N.C.O ~~and 4 men~~ to report ~~~~ tomorrow at Y HUTMENTS for purpose of taking over.

They will leave here at 7.30 A.m. in charge of 2/Lt EGHAN

O.C. H.Qrs will detail 1 N.C.O + 2 men also for this purpose.

Parties will parade outside R.O. Room. 7.30 AM 24/3/17. Equipped and ready to march off.

23/3/17.

[illegible]
Capt + Adjt
3rd S.A. Inf.

SECRET.
Map References
Sheet 51C - 1/40.000
and
Sheet 51B. N.W.3.

1st SOUTH AFRICAN INFANTRY BRIGADE.

Order No. 94.

Copy No........

351 314

22nd March, 1917.

1. MOVES. (a) The 2nd Regiment S.A.Infantry, 28th Coy. M.G. Corps and S.A.L.T.M.Battery will move to 'Y' HUTS tomorrow at hours to be arranged by Unit Commanders.

Units are to be clear of billets by 10.a.m.

(b) On 24th.instant 2nd Regiment S.A.Infantry, part of 28th Coy.M.G.Corps and part of S.A.L.T.M.Btty. will move from 'Y' Huts to front line trenches.

These Units will take over from 26th and 27th Infantry Brigades that portion of the Divisional Front as shown in Appendix 'A'.

Each Unit will send forward two Officers to make the necessary arrangements for taking over.

(c) On 24th instant the 3rd Regiment S.A.Infantry will move from HAUTE AVESNES to 'Y' HUTS - To be clear of billets by 10.a.m.

Start 9.30 by platoon 50 yds int

2. ROUTES. (a) For 23rd inst. for 2nd Regiment S.A.Infantry via road running S of BOIS d'HABARCQ to main St POL - ARRAS ROAD; for 28th Coy.M.G.Corps and S.A.L.T.M.Battery via VILLERS SUR SIMON, IZEL les - HAMEAU - HERMAVILLE and road running S. of BOIS d'HABARCQ.

(b) On 24th instant for 3rd Regiment via main St POL - ARRAS ROAD.

3. INTERVALS. The usual intervals between Units and Companies will be kept.

4. TRANSPORT. Transport will accompany Units as far as 'Y' HUTS, and will remain there until further orders.

5. RELIEFS. Reliefs, with the exception of the part of the M.G.Coy. and T.M.Battery will be carried out in daylight, all moves being made along the road 'Y' HUTS, ETRUN - LOUEZ - St VAAST BRIDGE St CATHERINE - OCTROI. Platoons will move at 400 yards interval, which must be strictly maintained. The usual precautions will be taken when moving through ARRAS .

Details of relief will be arranged between the Commanding Officers concerned.

6. REPORTS. Arrival at 'Y' HUTS and completion of relief in trenches will be reported to Brigade Headquarters which remains at PENIN.

Acknowledge.

Captain,
Brigade Major,
1st S.A.Infantry Brigade.

Issued by Orderly at 11. 50p.m
as per Brigade Distribution List.

4

1. G.S. Limbered Wagon for Coy
2. Do for Spare Kits Equipt 1 per A.B. 1.
for C.P.

6. A Motor Lorry will pick up all spare Kits etc including blankets and will be met at THEATRE Sq. ARRAS at 6 pm 3/3/17
O/C Hd Qrs Details to detail a reliable NCO guide to guide Lorrie to where Kits are dumped for Transport at CANDLE FACTORY and "B" and "C" Company Dumps (baggage)

7. Medical [illegible]
ALL Sick will report at RAP at 7.30 am with [illegible]

8. BILLETS All Billets to be handed over and the usual Certificate regarding cleanliness will be sent to Battalion H.Qrs with Relief Certificate, this is required by Brigade.

9. BAGGAGE Dumps Companies will

5

will arrange for an baggage dumps and will detail an NCO and 2 men to guard and load up same on arrival of Transport
D Company will detail a Subaltern to remain until all baggage is loaded and will take charge of all details with baggage and will march the party to ETRUN

10. Cooking The Sergeant Cook with 2 cooks per Company will move off at 5 Am and proceed to ETRUN.
Companies will arrange to have all Rations for meals after breakfast to be packed ready for loading under the charge of Coy Cooks at 4/30 AM 3/3/17
2 G.S. Limbered Wagons have been detailed to report at 4/30 am at Candle factory at this hour.
B Coy Rations & Cooks will be picked up en route. All available Cooking utensils which can be spared to be sent forward so that Meal can be prepared for the arrival of Battalion at [illegible] Huts.

6

XI MARCH DISCIPLINE Strict
March discipline will be enforced
XII The Battn 2nd in Command will move with R^r Party
The O/Command with Adjutant & M/O with Main party.

A.W.H. McDonald
Capt
for
Adj^t 3rd Reg^t A Inf^ty

Copies to
O/C A Coy
B
C
D
Q.M.
R.S.M.
I/O
S/O
M/O
2 Copies Diary

to initial

353

3rd Regiment
S. A. I.

I am directed to inform you that Mr. Walter Long asked the Brigadier General Commdg. to convey to you his disappointment at not being able to see your Regiment today and his regret that it was kept so long on parade.

Owing to an accident to his car he was delayed for upwards of two hours.

11/3/17.

A L Pepper
Capt.
Brigade Major

To O/C A Coy H.Q.
B " [illegible]
C " [illegible]
D " [illegible]
HQ [illegible]

Please cause to be conveyed to your men.

A W H McDonald
Capt.
Adj.
3rd S.A. Infy

12/3/17

ORDER NO. 60.

Copy No.. ..4.. .

354

Map Reference
Trench Map ARRAS
1/10000.

30/3/1917.

No. 1.
RELIEF.

The Battalion will be relieved in the line by the 3rd S.A.Infantry to-night, the 30th inst.
"D" Coy. 3rd S.A.I. will relieve "D" Company in the Candle Factory by platoons at 5 minutes interval, commencing at 7.15 p.m.
"A" Coy. 3rd SAI. will relieve "A" Company in BRITTANNIA WORKS by platoons at 5 minutes interval commencing at 7.35 p.m.
"C" Company 3rd SAI will relieve "C" Company in Front Line commencing at ~~XXXX~~ 7.55 p.m. by Platoons at 5 mins interval
"B" Company 3rd SAI. will relieve "B" Company in Front Line commencing at 8.15 p.m. by Platoons at 5 mins interval
Headquarters - 7.15 p.m.
Signallers on all stations will be relieved at 7.15 p.m.
Lewis Gunners will be relieved with their Companies.
Companies on relief will be in billets at ARRAS.
On relief Battalion will be in Brigade Reserve.

No. 2.
ROUTES.

"A" Company will withdraw from BRITTANNIA WORKS down AUGUST AVENUE.
"C" Company. - Platoon in Support will withdraw along SUPPORT LINE and down JULY AVENUE. Front Line platoons will withdraw down JULY. The whole will enter AUGUST AVENUE by Trench leading past the Regimental Aid post, and continue withdrawal along AUGUST AVENUE.
"B" Company will withdraw via NEW CUT, JULY and AUGUST AVENUE passing the Regimental Aid post en route.

Company Commanders must pay special attention to the movement of platoons to avoid congestion.
JULY AVENUE and NEW CUT are to be as near as possible left clear for the passage of the 3rd S.A.I.

No. 3.
MOVEMENT.

The movement as far as the CANDLE FACTORY will be in platoons at five minutes interval.
From the Candle Factory to the billets in ARRAS in parties of EIGHT, at one minutes interval.
Orders as regards movement in ARRAS must be strictly adhered to.
Lieut. KING will control movement from the Candle Factory.

No. 4.
TRENCH STORES.

Trench Stores will be handed over and duplicate receipts obtained and forwarded to Battalion Headquarters by 9.a.m. to-morrow.

No. 5.
LOG BOOKS.

Log Books, Maps. etc. will be handed over complete.

No. 6.
COMPLETION OF RELIEF.

Completion of relief will be reported to Battalion Headquarters in ARRAS by memo.

Captain & A/Adjutant.
2nd S.A.I.

Copies 1 - 4 - Retained.
Copies 5 - 8 - "A" - "D" Companies.

Issued by orderly at.... a.m. 30/3/17.

SECRET. Copy No.....

317 355

1st SOUTH AFRICAN INFANTRY BRIGADE.

Order No. 97.

Reference
1/100000 - Lens Sheet.11.
1/10,000 - Trench Map -
ARRAS - 51B. N.W.3.

29th March 1917.

1. The following move and relief will take place tomorrow 30th.instant.

(a) The 1st Regiment S.A.Infantry will move from PENIN to 'Y' HUTS, at an hour to be fixed by Battalion Commander.

Advance parties will proceed today.

(b) The 3rd Regiment S.A.Infantry will relieve the 2nd Regiment S.A.Infantry in the Front line.

On relief the 2nd Regiment will become the Battalion in Brigade Reserve in ARRAS.

2. Relief will be carried out during evening . No movement involving entering or leaving ARRAS will take place before 7.15.p.m.
Details will be arranged direct between Battalion Commanders. It will be such as will prevent overcrowding of the trenches at any part or any portion of the line being vacated during relief.

3. The 3rd Regiment S.A.Infantry will continue to provide the working party of 100 men with 184 Tunnelling Company R.E.

4. Duplicate copies of receipts for Trench Stores taken over will be sent in to Brigade Headquarters.

5. No message, except the Code Word UMTATA, regarding the relief, will be sent over the telephone line.
1st.Regiment S.A.Infantry will report by wire their arrival at 'Y' HUTS.

6. Completion of relief will be reported by Code Word UMTATA.

7. Please acknowledge.

Ack

Captain,
Brigade Major.
1st S.A.Infantry Brigade.

Issued thro' Signals
at 2.30 p.m.

Copies			
1/4 to	1st to 4th Regts.	13 to	9th.Division.
5	28th M.Gun Coy.	14	Staff Captain.
6	S.A.L.T.M.Battery.	15	Bde Transport Off.
7	64th Field Coy.R.E.	16/19	War Diary.
8	Brigade Sig/Officer.	20	Bde Post Office.
9	107th Coy.A.S.C.	21	Centre Group R.F.A.
10	S.A.F.Ambulance.	22	9th.Divsl.T.M's.
11	26th Inf. Brigade.	23	Town Major, Arras.
12	27th Inf. Brigade.	24	Intelligence Officer.
25	A.D.M.S.9th.Divsn.		
	45th Infantry Bde.	27	46th Infantry Bde.
	7th Seaforths Hrs.	29	12th Royal Scots.

Recd 4/50 pm 29/3/17

THIRD SOUTH AFRICAN INFANTRY.

6. REPORTS. Companies will report completion of relief immediately completed by Code word 'KLAAR.'

356

Captain & Adjutant,

3rd Regiment, S.A.Infantry.

Issued 1 p.m.

26/3/1917.

1st SOUTH AFRICAN INFANTRY BRIGADE.

No. X.7/2347/14. 13th March, 1917.

The following instructions will be observed with regards working parties employed with 184th Tunnelling Company:-

1. Parties will report every 8 hours at ST.NICHOLAS in time to relieve each other at the various works they are employed on at 8 a.m., 4 p.m. and 12 midnight.
2. These parties pick up at St NICHOLAS material on their way up to relieve the parties at work.
3. Regimental Officers should not give their men instructions to leave work before time or at any definite hour - parties relieve each other on the work.

(sgd) H.HENDERSON, Major.
General Staff, 9th(Scottish) Div.

Certified true copy.

(sgd) A.L.PEPPER
Captain,
Brigade Major, 1st S.A.Infantry Brigade.

3rd Regiment.

357

THIRD SOUTH AFRICAN INFANTRY.

GR/52. March 28th, 1917.
Map reference
Sheet 51c 1/40,000 and Sheet 51 B N.W.3

1. MOVES. In compliance with Brigade Operation Order No.96 of 27th March, the 3rd South African Infantry will move to ARRAS, and will relieve the 5th Cameron Highlanders 26th Infantry Brigade, and will become the Battalion in Brigade Reserve. 28.3.17
The Battalion will march via Main St POL-ARRAS Road, but not move into ARRAS before 7.15 p.m. Movement will ~~be by Platoons at 200 yards interval.~~
The Battalion will parade at 6 p.m., and will move off in the following order "A","B","C","D",
Headquarters will be accommodated at HOTEL de L'UNIVERS
"A","B","C" Companies at CONVENT, ARRAS.
"D" Company at St CATHERINE, ARRAS.

2. DRESS. Full marching Order.

3. TRANSPORT. 1 Lorry (3 tons) will be at "Y" Huts at 5 p.m. for conveyance of blankets and stores, to return at 9 p.m. from CONVENT, ARRAS, with Stores of 5th Camerons.
The following Transport to be detailed by T.O. as under
Headquarters: 1 Limber G.S., 1 Officers' Mess Cart, Maltese Cart for medical stores, 2 water carts,
1 G.S. wagon for blankets and Officers' kits "A" Coy.
1 G.S. wagon for blankets "D" Coy.
1 G.S. wagon per Company for Lewis Guns.
Field kitchens to accompany the Battalion, and will remain in ARRAS, and surplus limbers are for use in conveying rations and Canteen Stores.

4. BLANKETS AND STORES. Company blankets to be rolled in bundles of 10, and properly labelled, and stacked in Company Dump with Stores, to be picked up at 5 p.m.

5. WORKING PARTIES. A daily working party of 6 Officers, 6 sergeants and 130 Other Ranks will be furnished by the Regiment to report to 184th Tunnelling Coy., R.E. St NICHOLAS, the above detail to work in three reliefs, commencing to-night 12 midnight, 28/29 as under.
"A" Company from 12 midnight to 8 a.m. (29th)
"B" Company from 8 a.m. to 4 p.m. (29th)
"C" Company from 4 p.m. to 12 midnight (29/30th)
"D" Company from 12 m.n. 29/30th to 8 a.m. 30th.
The above parties to report as per special instructions issued to Companies, the detail to be 4 Platoons of 32 men each, under its own Platoon Officer and Sergeant.
"A" Company to send forward one Officer and an N.C.O. per platoon to take over details of work from 5th Camerons immediately on arrival in ARRAS.

6. GUARDS. Guards will be mounted as follows:-

Headquarters	1 N.C.O. and 4 men.
CONVENT	1 N.C.O. and 4 men.
St CATHERINE	1 N.C.O. and 3 men.

Brigade Headquarters 1 N.C.O. and 4 men, detail as per instructions issued.

7. SANITATION. Company Commanders will see that the Hutments and vicinity are left in clean and sanitary condition for immediate occupation by ~~[illegible]~~. A and S.H.

8. LINES. The 2nd in Command accompanied by M.O. will inspect the Lines, and render the necessary certificate for Bde. H.Q.

9. REPORTS. Companies will report completion of relief immediately completed by Code word "KLAAR".

Issued 1pm

A. W. McDonald Capt. adj.
3rd S.A.I.

358

Y Huts ETRUN

To O/C A Coy ~~B.V.V.~~
B " T.A.S.
C " ~~D.M.C.~~
D " D.W.T.
H.Q. " ~~W.R.A.A.~~
T/O " R.C.B. Sgt

Re Move

a Billeting party of 1 Officer (2/Lieut Harris) one Senior N.C.O. of H.Q. A. B. C & D Coy, also 1 man from each Platoon [and H.Q. Coy] will parade to-day at 3 pm at Battalion O. Room and proceed to ARRAS, to take over Billets of Battalion in ARRAS as per attached Copy of wire from Bgde HQrs. S/C 364.

Companies to arrange detail in accordance with the above. The Transport Officer to arrange Transport of Blankets and Rations. The Rations for tomorrow to be taken.

Issued 1/50 pm
27-3-17

A.D.H. McDonald Capt Adjt
20 S.A.I.

359

Prefix .... Code .... m.	Words	Charge	This message is on a/c of:	Recd. at .... m.
Office of Origin and Service Instructions.	Sent		.... Service.	Date ....
D.R.L.S.	At .... m.			From ....
	To			
	By		(Signature of "Franking Officer.")	By ....

TO { 3rd S.A. Infantry

Sender's Number.	Day of Month.	In reply to Number.	AAA
* SC 364	26th ~~27th~~		

Please arrange to send on necessary Billeting party to ARRAS on 27th inst

The Billeting Officer should report to TOWN MAJOR ARRAS to obtain Billets in accordance with Standing Orders.

The Battalion will be Billeted in CONVENT ARRAS and HQ will be situated at HOTEL DE L'UNIVERS as the Brig Genl Commanding intends to take up this position in old Bde HQ ARRAS.

From
Place 26/3/17
Time

[Signature]

The above may be forwarded as now corrected. (Z)

Censor. Signature of Addressor or person authorised to telegraph in his name.

* This line should be erased if not required.

750,000. W 2186–M509. H. W. & V., Ld. 6/16.

360

Ist SOUTH AFRICAN INFANTRY BRIGADE.

AMENDMENT TO BRIGADE ORDER No.96.

27th.March 1917.

1. MOVES. Para (c) first paragraph is cancelled and the following substituted :-

"Working parties for ARRAS, furnished by 1st. Regiment South African Infantry will proceed to ARRAS tomorrow under Regimental arrangements but will not enter the town before 7.15.p.m.

9/40pm
29/3/1917

R. Pepper
Captain,
Brigade Major.
Ist S.A.Infantry Brigade.

Issued to all recipients
of Brigade Order No.96.

SECRET. Copy No........

1st SOUTH AFRICAN INFANTRY BRIGADE.

Map.References
Sheet 51C.1/40,000
and
Sheet 51B.N.W.3.

ORDER No.96.

27th March 1917.

1. MOVES. (a) On March 28th.1st S.A.Infantry Brigade Headquarters and 3rd Regiment S.A.Infantry will move to ARRAS. The 3rd Regiment S.A.Infantry will relieve the 5th Cameron Hrs:26th.Infantry Brigade and will become the Battalion in Brigade Reserve.

Details of relief will be arranged direct by Battalion Commanders concerned.

(b) On March 29th.the 4th.Regiment S.A.Infantry (less Working parties) will move from HERMAVILLE to 'Y' HUTS. To be clear of billets by 10.a.m.

(c) Working parties for ARRAS, furnished by 1st.Regt., S.A.Infantry will proceed to 'Y' HUTS on 28th.instant and will be accommodated there for the night 28th/29th.

Working parties for ARRAS furnished by 4th.Regt. will proceed to ARRAS tomorrow - under Regimental arrangement but will not enter the Town before 7.15.p.m.

2. MOVEMENTS. (a) The 3rd Regiment S.A.Infantry will march via main St POL - ARRAS road but not move into ARRAS before 7.15.p.m.

Guides from 5th.Cameron Hrs: will be at PORTE DE BAUDIMONT at 7.45.p.m.on 28th.

Movement will be by platoons at 200 yds.interval.

(b) The 4th.Regiment S.A.Infantry will march, via road running South of BOIS D'HABARCQ, by Companies at [illegible] 200 yards interval.

3. ADVANCE PARTIES. Usual advance parties will proceed 24 hours in advance of Units moving.

4. TRANSPORT. Transport of Brigade Headquarters, 3rd Regiment and 4th.Regiment will move to ETRUN.

5. COMMAND.

The G.O.C., 1st S.A.Infantry Brigade will take over Command of the RIGHT SECTOR from the G.O.C., 26th.Infantry Brigade at 12 noon on 28th.instant.

6. BRIGADE HEADQUARTERS. 1st S.A.Infantry Brigade Headquarters will close at PENIN at 10.a.m.and will be established at PLACE St CROIX, ARRAS at 12 noon 28th.instant.

7. WORKING PARTIES. Working parties will be furnished as per attached table. Parties will not enter ARRAS before 7.15pm.

8. REPORTS. Completion of reliefs and moves will be reported by wire to Brigade Headquarters by Code Word KLAAR.

9. Please acknowledge.

Captain,
Brigade Major.

Issued through Signals at 8.30pm.
as per Brigade Distribution List.

362
END

"C" Form.
MESSAGES AND SIGNALS.

Army Form C. 2123.
(In books of 100).
No. of Message

Prefix / Code Words
Charges to collect
Service Instructions.

Received.
From
By TC

Sent, or sent out
At m.
To 3/15
By

Office Stamp.

Handed in at SZA Office 12.12 m. Received 1.15 m.

TO 3rd Regt SAI

*Sender's Number | Day of Month | In reply to Number | AAA

Warning order aaa First regt will move to Y huts and 3rd regt to ARRAS on 28th aaa Further orders later.

For attachment warn order

2/45 pm
26

FROM S A Bde
PLACE & TIME 12.15 pm

* This line should be erased if not required.

(6354). Wt. W7493/M637. 500,000 Pads. 10/16. D. D. & L. (E 469). Forms C/2123/3.

www.ingramcontent.com/pod-product-compliance
Lightning Source LLC
Chambersburg PA
CBHW080808010526
44113CB00013B/2347
* 9 7 8 1 4 7 4 5 0 7 7 9 0 *